MAKING BELIEVE

MAKING BELIEVE

Questions About Mennonites and Art

MAGDALENE REDEKOP

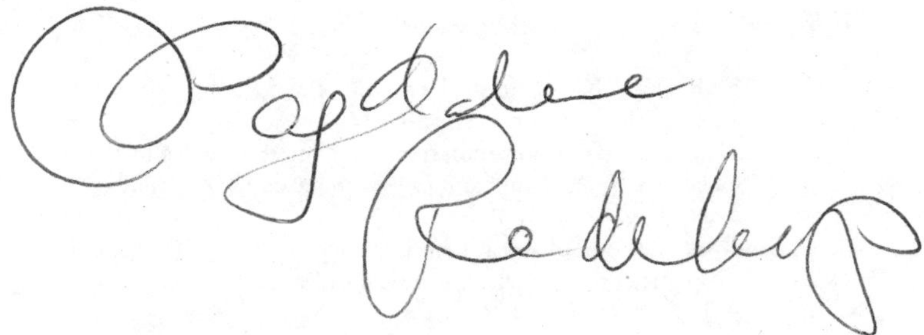

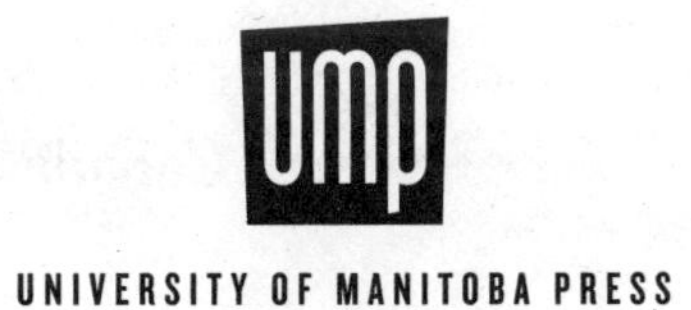

UNIVERSITY OF MANITOBA PRESS

Making Believe: Questions About Mennonites and Art
© Magdalene Redekop 2020

24 23 22 21 20   1 2 3 4 5

University of Manitoba Press
Winnipeg, Manitoba, Canada
Treaty 1 Territory
uofmpress.ca

Cataloguing data available from Library and Archives Canada
ISBN 978-0-88755-857-3 (PAPER)
ISBN 978-0-88755-859-7 (PDF)
ISBN 978-0-88755-858-0 (EPUB)
ISBN 978-0-88755-881-8 (BOUND)

Cover design by David Drummond
Interior design by Jess Koroscil

Printed in Canada

This book has been published with the help of a grant from the
Federation for the Humanities and Social Sciences, through the Awards
to Scholarly Publications Program, using funds provided by the
Social Sciences and Humanities Research Council of Canada.

Publication of this book has also been made possible with the generous
support of the D.F. Plett Historical Research Foundation.

The University of Manitoba Press acknowledges the financial support for
its publication program provided by the Government of Canada through
the Canada Book Fund, the Canada Council for the Arts, the Manitoba
Department of Sport, Culture, and Heritage, the Manitoba Arts Council,
and the Manitoba Book Publishing Tax Credit.

Funded by the Government of Canada | Canada

*To all my former students
with gratitude*

CONTENTS

LIST OF ILLUSTRATIONS

Plates (*following page 164*)

Plate 1. Magdalene Redekop, *Pochinko Masks* (2008), papier-mâché.
Clockwise from top left: *Fesh*/Fish; *Naze*/Nose; *Kjniepa*/Bug; *Loch*/
Hole; *Boum*/Tree; Foss/Fox. Photograph by Peter Legris, 2018.
Courtesy of the artist.

Plate 2. Wanda Koop, *Untitled* 2010, from *Hybrid Human.* Copyright
Visual Arts CARCC, 2019. Courtesy of the artist.

Plate 3. Rembrandt van Rijn, *Artist in His Studio,* c. 1628, oil on panel.
Photograph, 2019, Museum of Fine Arts, Boston.

Plate 4. Wanda Koop, *Tear,* 1996 (*See Everything/See Nothing*).
Copyright Visual Arts CARCC, 2019. Courtesy of the artist.

Plate 5. Wanda Koop, *Untitled (Native Fires),* 1996 (*See Everything/See
Nothing*). Copyright Visual Arts CARCC, 2019. Courtesy of the artist.

Plate 6. Wanda Koop, *Sightline – Green Crosshair,* 1999. From the
collection of Jeff Neufeld and Katrina Lee Kwen. Courtesy of the artist.

Plate 7. Norman Schmidt, *ssockaboom typoem,* 2012. Hand-printed
paper, cut and pieced. Courtesy of the artist.

Plate 8. Gathie Falk, *Development of the Plot III #1 The Stage is Set,* 1992,
oil on canvas, 228.6 x 160.0 cm. Photo by Teresa Healy, Vancouver Art
Gallery. Collection National Gallery of Canada, Ottawa. Courtesy
of the artist.

Plate 9. Gathie Falk, *Development of the Plot III #8 Conclusion,* 1992, oil
on canvas. Photo by Teresa Healy, Vancouver Art Gallery. Collection
National Gallery of Canada, Ottawa. Courtesy of the artist.

Plate 10a. Susan Shantz, *Creatures in Translation, AGGV Website 3D:
Frog Print Paper Tolle,* 2011–12, mixed media on paper (mounted on
gatorboard), 167 x 112 x 13 cm. Collection of the Regina Public Library.
Courtesy of the artist.

Plate 10b. Susan Shantz, *Creatures in Translation, AGGV Website 3D
Print Fragment (Frog Crown),* 2011–12, thermoplastic, 18 x 35 x 35 cm.
Collection of the Saskatchewan Arts Board. Courtesy of the artist.

APOLOGIA

Vann aul, dann aul.

If already, then already.

This book is the product of "slow scholarship," a term coined in resistance to the "publish or perish" slogan that has long ruled in the academy. Often I have said to myself: *Vann aul, dann aul*—a Low German expression meaning: "What's worth doing at all is worth doing well" (Friesen 1988, 101). The saying also echoes maxims such as the English: Might as well hang for a sheep as for a lamb. It was retirement that allowed me the luxury of taking risks and the time for in-depth exploration of ideas that had long fascinated me. Gradually this scholarly project became part of a retrospective effort to bridge the gap between where I come from (a small farm in Manitoba) and where I ended up (a large university in Toronto). One thing is certain: I did not travel that cultural distance without breaking a few rules. That might explain why my book evolved into something that is part criticism, part memoir. Something about the challenge of that duality made it hard to know when I should stop writing and rewriting. I became aware of the need to wrap it up in 2014 when my seventieth birthday brought to mind a line from a favourite poem by A.E. Housman: "of my threescore years and ten, / twenty will not come again." The word *score* is from the Old English *scoru*, which means twenty. Luckily for me, life expectancy has gone up since 1879, when Housman wrote "loveliest of trees the cherry now. . . . (1965, 11). It would take several more years and the help of more than one excellent editor before I could package my exploration in a form suitable for publication.

Team-based research grants were already becoming the norm when I retired, but my research has been of the old-fashioned single-scholar kind. Even for a scholar working alone, however, the benefits of slowing down are collective as well as individual. Time to ruminate about ideas is a good thing, to be sure, but equally important is time to talk about those ideas with others and to listen for questions that help to define the audience for a book. In different social settings over the years, the first question is almost always "What is your book about?" Usually I answer by saying that it is my response to a particular phenomenon—the remarkable recent increase in art made by Mennonites in Canada since about 1980. Depending on the person asking, I sometimes add that I am considering that phenomenon within historical contexts going back to the Protestant Reformation. If the inquiry comes from an academic with shared interests, then I might go on to say that I am particularly interested in how the phenomenon can be viewed as a response to the crisis of representation. In most social situations, however, any reference to a Mennonite phenomenon leads instantly (even in academic contexts) to personal questions. Who are the Mennonites? Are you a Mennonite? Although I stubbornly persist in thinking of this as a crossover book, the reality is that if the word *Mennonite* is in the title, then the majority of my readers will be Mennonite. This does not make the personal questions any less insistent or any easier to answer. It only means that they become charged with interethnic differences. What *kind* of a Mennonite am I? Do I go to church? Am I a believer?

As a result of experiencing these conversational loops, I have decided to break the unwritten rule that an author should deal with *what* questions before going on to *why* questions. It would be misleading, in any case, to say simply that this book is about the flowering of Mennonite art in Canada. It is true that I will focus on that phenomenon, and my introduction will begin with a brief description of it, followed by a short history of Mennonites. There is a contradiction, however, at the core of this book: while engaging with art by Mennonites, I will argue that there is no such thing as Mennonite art. This contradiction is inevitable in all studies of art by people from minority groups in Canada, and I will engage closely with individual works of art (by both Mennonites and non-Mennonites) to show how art escapes the net of identity. In *Mothers and Other Clowns: The Stories of Alice Munro* (Redekop 1992a), I argued against essentialized views of maternity; many of the "mothers" in that book are men. In this book, similarly, many of the Mennonites are not Mennonites. I view all artists as tricksters located on a borderline between identities.

My argument is twofold: first that the Mennonite phenomenon stages a crisis of representation and second that cultural identity is dialogical. I begin here by dealing with questions about intention because I see the need to defend the rather peculiar form that this book has taken over time. My answers will not be short because I have found that I could not do this without reflecting at the same time on the particular cultural circumstances that necessitate this kind of prefatory statement in the first place. I have opted to call this an "apologia," a term that goes back to classical rhetoric and refers to a formal defence. That seldom-used word should not be confused, however, with the commonly used word *apology*. I have no regrets about writing the book in this way, and I make no apologies for my bias. I seek only to be clear about it so as to make it possible for readers to define their own responses to the same phenomenon. Whether it is an earthquake or the birth of a baby, any phenomenon looks and sounds different depending on the vantage point of the witness.

A literary phenomenon inevitably evokes subjective responses, as John Keats shows in "On First Looking into Chapman's Homer" with the lines "Then felt I like some watcher of the skies / When a new planet swims into his ken" (1959, 18). There is no question, however, that this particular phenomenon exists. Multiple observers, both Mennonite and non-Mennonite, have observed this new literary planet and have commented on it. Readers might be surprised, therefore, to hear that there has never been a time, during the years of writing, when I have not felt as if my topic could vanish into thin air at any moment. A central dilemma remains persistent and inescapable, and I will return to it again and again. I concede at the outset that the qualities of the art that I will discuss can be found in any number of works of art by non-Mennonites. It might well be the *least* important thing to note about their art, for example, that novelist David

Bergen or visual artist Wanda Koop or composer Randolph Peters are Mennonite. These three, like all the artists who are part of the phenomenon, make their art within multiple overlapping communities. For many of the artists I write about, a Mennonite community might not exist at all except as a floating imaginary construct. I will take such constructs seriously, but I am nonetheless aware that separating out artists who happen to have Mennonite names is an arbitrary act that should not be performed lightly. We live in a dangerous time when it behooves us all to be careful about encouraging divisions based on ethnicity or religion. Many times I was tempted to abandon the category "Mennonite" and along with it my work on this book. Inevitably I was lured back to both. My apologia began as a list of five reasons that I came up with to explain to myself why I began writing and why I continued to do so. I will itemize them here in order of increasing complexity.

First, and most obvious, is the burgeoning of art made by Mennonites in Canada. I was first drawn in by individual works of art and then kept moving forward because of curiosity about what was causing this flowering and why it was taking such diverse forms.

Second is the fact that the roots of this cultural renaissance are tangled up with the roots of my own cultural identity. The flowering began in southern Manitoba, where I lived for the first two decades of my life. Perhaps it was inevitable that I would be fascinated by the art made there after I left. What I did not predict was the degree of difficulty that I would have in maintaining the distance necessary to do my job as a critic. A constant danger while writing has presented itself as an undertow pulling me back into my own past, a danger complicated by the fact that the Manitoba of my memory no longer exists. My need to deal with the resulting undertow is part of the reason why I interrogate the concept of nostalgia in Chapter 3.

A third reason for persisting was my need to formulate a response to the perpetual provocation of stereotypes about Mennonites in North American culture. It's not as if I have not always known that the stereotypes were out there. During my first session with a psychiatrist after I fell suddenly into a profound depression in 1993, I happened to mention my Mennonite childhood. Her face lit up, and she asked "How did you escape?" What I felt in that moment could be called "double-consciousness." That is the influential term coined by W.E.B. Du Bois in *The Souls of Black Folk* to describe the "peculiar sensation . . . this sense of always looking at one's self through the eyes of others" (1961, 16–17). I experienced another version of it during my year living in Japan as a white *gaijin* or foreigner. Because of that experience, and because my children are adopted and mixed race, I share the view that it is a mistake to write "as if the differences of religious or cultural background are equivalent to those of 'race'" (Coleman and Goellnicht 2002, quoted in Zacharias 2013, 44). I nevertheless find that the term coined by Du Bois helps me to understand my response when Mennonites are represented as a stand-in for the very *idea* of difference.

As many of us discover when we are "outed" during conversations, there is no problem if you answer the question that my psychiatrist asked me in a way that shows you accept the definition of yourself as "the one that got away." That phrase was the headline for an article about Miriam Toews that appeared in *The Guardian* not long after she published her first novel about Mennonites (Williams 2004). As long as both author and interviewer accept the implied stereotype, they can play the part of us in the game of us against them. The trouble begins in the swampy territory where the writer concedes that she or he is, after all, still one of them. The stereotypes can mostly be shrugged off in everyday life if you are a secular Mennonite who does not dress oddly and can pass. The fact that I was taking time to write this book meant that my assimilation was thrown into question in various social settings. Chapter 2 deals explicitly with ways of reimagining us and them, but in a sense this entire book is the product of my efforts to do that.

A fourth reason for persisting is that I was lured into dialogue because I received invitations to write and talk about Mennonite subjects for various audiences. The first such invitation came in 1981, when my colleague W.J. Keith asked me to write an essay on Rudy Wiebe's *The Blue Mountains of China* for the collection *A Voice in the Land: Essays by and about Rudy Wiebe*. The next came in 1988, when Harry Loewen invited me to contribute to a collection entitled *Why I Am a Mennonite*, the result of which was a wrenching essay: "Through the Mennonite Looking Glass." The reception of that essay, to which I will return in later chapters, had a profound influence on all my subsequent writing. Other invitations followed, and they tended to reinforce the pattern of those first two essays, setting up a movement back and forth between criticism and autobiography. In November 1992, again at the invitation of Harry Loewen, then chair of Mennonite studies at the University of Winnipeg, I gave a series of three lectures there under the heading "Mennonite Makers." My focus on the *making* of stories, songs, and pictures marked the first time that I began to give serious consideration to cross media questions about representation. In the years that followed I was lured deeper into interdisciplinary territory by invitations from Carol Ann Weaver, who urged me to present papers at a series of conferences on Mennonites and music that she hosted in Kitchener at Conrad Grebel University College (see Epp and Weaver 2005; Epp et al. 2011; Weaver et al. 2015).

This book is not a compilation of previously published essays and should not be seen as replacing them. I have used fragments from them here and there, but my ideas have changed over time. Although I have had occasional opportunities for dialogue with Mennonite scholars at conferences, my primary scholarly activity has not been in Mennonite studies. An important turning point for me came when I received an invitation to participate in a symposium organized by Robert Zacharias and Julia Spicher Kasdorf and hosted by Kasdorf at Pennsylvania State University in May 2013. There I found myself sitting at a table surrounded by nine scholars, all wrestling with questions about Mennonites and literature. Although I had retired from teaching by that time, the symposium was a reminder of how the practical challenges of pedagogy help to bring questions into focus. I was intrigued when Margaret Steffler reflected on her classroom experience in her review of *After Identity: Mennonite Writing in North America* (2015), the book of essays that resulted from the symposium. As a non-Mennonite who teaches Mennonite literature at Trent University, Steffler commented: "In my teaching, I am all too aware that readers not only want 'the Mennonite thing,' but crave it as if it will somehow satisfy vague expectations and even longings" (Steffler 2017). I have sensed similar longings on those few occasions when I have taught a text by a Mennonite at the University of Toronto. As a Mennonite, my response to them is complicated by my personal experience with the stereotypes built into student presuppositions. At the Pennsylvania symposium, there were as many approaches to such questions as there were people at the table, and this helped me to define what kind of contribution I might make to the conversation (see Redekop 2015).

As a result of my dialogue with other literary scholars, my fifth and most complex reason for writing became a feeling that I should do my part, however belatedly, in the shared effort to correct a longstanding imbalance in Mennonite studies. Scholarship dealing with Mennonites and art is minuscule compared to the amount done in the areas of history and theology. However, because of the pioneering work of critics such as Hildi Froese Tiessen, Al Reimer, Ervin Beck, and Ann Hostetler, this entrenched dominance is now questioned even by scholars from those disciplines. Philip Stoltzfus, an American Mennonite theologian, offers a forceful account of the gap. "Is it possible," he wonders, "for Mennonite thought to find a way out of its own 475-year 'drift' into self-induced aesthetic masochism?" (1998, 77). As Stoltzfus notes, the absence of scholarship about art has not stopped Mennonites from making art, and the North American phenomenon illustrates his point. He observes, however, that "Mennonites have to date produced little in the way of second-order thinking concerning the . . . interaction of our forms of material culture with larger cultural and artistic styles . . ." (76).

Making this list of five reasons was an exercise that brought home to me the peculiar nature of the challenge confronting me. The kind of scholarship called for by Stoltzfus describes, to some extent, what I was trying to do. As long as I was dealing with fiction and poetry, my knowledge of Canadian literature offered useful contexts. It was when I stepped outside of the box of my own discipline that the gap described by Stoltzfus began to feel like a vacuum. No scholar claiming to deal with Mennonite attitudes to representation can avoid coming to terms with what Priscilla Reimer has described as a "veritable explosion of productivity in the visual arts" among Mennonites in Canada (1990, 5). After curating an exhibition in 1990, however, Reimer concluded: "Artists of Mennonite extraction contributed to the 'Golden Age' of Dutch art in the 17th and 18th centuries but there is no recognizable, historic continuity which links contemporary Mennonite artists to their Dutch ancestors" (Reimer 1990, 5). Scholars have begun to look for hidden continuities that are obscured by the different narratives of assimilation to which I will turn my attention in the next chapter (see Hamilton, Voolstra, and Visser 1994). As my account of Mennonite history will show, however, I only gradually became aware of the possible explanations for why there is no cultural map available to scholars asking questions about Mennonites and art. It was a relief to read an essay by Piet Visser that helped me define the limits of my contribution. "Until this still young multidisciplinary interest results in a comprehensive cultural history of Dutch Anabaptism and Mennonitism in which new frameworks can be created," Visser writes, "we must content ourselves with soundings in different areas, with case studies. . . . On this microlevel there is room for a great deal more research before a detailed survey can be given of the entire social and cultural history of this religious group" (Visser 1994, ix).

This situation amounts to a crisis for scholars and responses to it vary depending to a large extent on choice of discipline. As a theologian, for example, Philip Stoltzfus, has found a way of countering the "475-year 'drift'" he described by developing a theology based on performance (1998, 2006). Although his arguments are in tune with my own thinking, I am a practical critic. What I offer in this book are examples of the "soundings" that Visser describes and I am most comfortable working from the inside out, from case studies of particular texts outwards to the larger historical contexts. To some extent, however, I am also putting forward representation studies as a possible framework for other scholars. This is because the questions that keep coming up for me when I engage closely with art almost invariably have to do with representation. Although little "second-order thinking" about aesthetics makes explicit reference to Mennonites, there is plenty that offers transferable ideas and tools. Given the scarcity of studies focused on Mennonites and art, my close engagement with the art drew me outward into increasingly capacious historical and theoretical contexts. Although I was greatly helped by recent work on representation studies, in the end the only antidote to vertigo was to come back to myself and reflect on my own responses. Although I am a critic, I am also a Mennonite writing from inside the muddy middle of this particular cultural phenomenon. There is simply no way that I can do this job and set aside questions about my own identity. After trying and failing to do that, I came around to the reluctant concession that, whatever the reasons for writing it, this book is an "autoethnographic text." My predicament felt like a private frustration, but in fact it is familiar to all scholars from minority groups who choose to write about their own group. Although autoethnography is a contested term, there is consensus on the basic definition offered by Carolyn Ellis, who describes it as "research, writing, story, and method that connect the autobiographical and personal to the cultural, social, and political" (2004, xix).

In a helpful essay on how Mennonite writers deal with the frustration that I have described, American poet Julia Spicher Kasdorf pays particular attention to books, such as this one, that attract "audiences from within and outside Mennonite contexts." She notes that "autoethnographic texts" suffer "'highly indeterminate' receptions, for what satisfies outsiders might not please insiders and vice versa" (2015, 23). Kasdorf observes how often Mennonite writers compose "autoethnographic announcements . . . in response to outsider ignorance or insider expectations," and she notes that these "enable writers to negotiate among various audiences" (25). As one example of such an announcement, she puts forward an often-quoted passage from a novel by Miriam Toews. Nomi, the teenaged narrator in *A Complicated Kindness*, imagines Menno Simons as a fellow classmate, "the least well-adjusted kid" who starts a "breakaway clique" that forbids "media, dancing, smoking, temperate climates, movies, drinking, rock 'n' roll, having sex for fun, swimming, make-up, jewellery, playing pool, going to cities, or staying up past nine o'clock. That was Menno all over. Thanks a lot, Menno" (Toews 2004, 5).

The notion of ubiquitous "autoethnographic pressure" fits with my own experiences. For example, when I joined a panel on the CBC Radio show *Talking Books*, convened to discuss *A Complicated Kindness*, I assumed that I had been invited as a specialist in Canadian comic fiction. The first question that I was asked by host Ian Brown was whether or not the account in the novel matched my own experience as a Mennonite. I believe I answered with some version of both yes and no. As an "autoethnographic announcement," it left something to be desired. Why was I so flummoxed by such an understandable question? In my review of that novel for the *Literary Review of Canada*, I tried again with a facetious complaint about how I would now have to explain at dinner parties not only that I do not quilt but also that I do not shun. "Thanks a lot, Miriam!" I wrote (Redekop 2004, 19). When I tacked on an exclamation mark to the laconic voice in the original, I was thinking it would add an extra ironic spin. Some Mennonites who read this, however, heard it as a taunt and expressed to me the concern that I must have a quarrel with Toews, a writer whom I had not even met at that time.

Linda Hutcheon (1994) has argued persuasively that irony is not something inherent in a text but something that happens (or does not happen) between text and reader, depending on numerous cultural variables. By the time Rhoda Janzen (2009) wrote *Mennonite in a Little Black Dress: A Memoir of Going Home,* five years had passed since the publication of *A Complicated Kindness.* It was in part the reception of Toews's breakthrough novel that prepared readers for the possibility that irony might happen to some Mennonites. Janzen ends her mock memoir by tacking on a hilarious "Mennonite History Primer" and claiming that it "is probably much more to the point than whatever's on Wikipedia" (241). I myself am inclined to resort to similar evasive strategies, and often I reveal in order to conceal. Since my desire here is to communicate, however, I still need to make clear what *kind* of a book I have written. Where should readers draw the line between autobiography and cultural criticism? Unlike the slyly embedded "autoethnographic announcement" in *A Complicated Kindness,* the ones in academic books often detach themselves from the body of the book, regardless of the specific label—preface, prologue, foreword, et cetera. The frequency of such prologues in scholarly writing creates an expectation that subjectivity can be stated once and for all and then set aside. I therefore need to make clear that it has not been possible in my case to set aside the personal. As a critic, I aim for objectivity, to be sure, but I find that when writing about my own ethnic group I can best achieve it, paradoxically, by not attempting to conceal my subjective bias. I tend to thicken the autobiographical threads when they surface, hoping in this way to prevent them from being dissolved into some essentialized stereotype of *Mennonitism,* a word for which I confess I have an aversion.

The form that this book has taken, then, is a result of the fact that I am deeply implicated in the problems that come with what Charles Taylor, a pre-eminent Canadian philosopher, has called "the politics of recognition" (1994, 25–73). Do I or do I not recognize myself in *A Complicated Kindness*? The question is political, but it is important to note that Brown asked it in a dialogical context and that my response was one voice in a radio panel discussion. This illustrates a point that Taylor makes: "The crucial feature of human life is its fundamentally *dialogical* character" (32). Identity is interactive, as numerous scholars following Mikhail Bakhtin have argued. Taylor describes it as something constructed collectively, using many different kinds of language, which include the various languages of different art forms. As he acknowledges, however, the common views of identity still cling to a "monological ideal" (33). Although scholars in all disciplines are confronting and dealing with unequal distributions of power, this task becomes difficult when the debates are framed as tribal wars between competing monological identities.

Given the charged nature of all the questions I explore in this book, I should make clear that I do not intend my own choices to be prescriptive for other literary critics who also happen to be Mennonite. Of all the differences that shape responses to the recent flowering, perhaps none is as important as generational difference. I sometimes amuse myself by thinking of the Mennonite literary scene as a family romance. The most identifiable character in this romance is Rudy Wiebe, who plays the role of a mostly benign literary father for any number of younger writers. Although a focus on absent mothers recurs in texts written by Mennonites, supportive mothers have a strong presence in the lives of many writers. Take, for example, Elvira Toews, the mother of Miriam Toews, who steals the show whenever her daughter is interviewed. Sometimes I think of Hildi Froese Tiessen as a kind of sister, and I have even joked that Robert Zacharias is the baby brother I never had. If I were inclined to have fun with the pious rhetoric of some churches, I might say that God sent Brother Zacharias to us because He knew that we urgently needed someone to fill the shoes of Sister Froese Tiessen after her retirement.

The fact is that I am the youngest of twelve. I have six sisters (three of them still living) and five brothers (one still living). I also had a baby brother, Menno, who was stillborn, about whose funeral I have written in "Still Life with Menno" (Redekop 1990b). Zacharias, in any case, is probably young enough to be my grandson. I have not done all the arithmetic, but joking aside, these age differences do matter to our different ways of responding to the Mennonite renaissance. Since age is invisible in print and people tend to be coy about it in public, I need to spell out at least one way in which my age is related to the kind of book that I have written. When I began my studies, there was not even a Canadian literature, let alone a Mennonite literature. There is now emerging a younger generation of scholars, some of whom are devoting their careers to Mennonite literary studies. I am grateful for the work of those scholars and encouraged to see that some of them are not Mennonite. The kind of contribution that I can make, however, is necessarily more personal and highly selective.

Confronted with the enormity of my subject matter and the intensity of my response to the art, I was on the lookout for models to follow when I happened upon one in an airport bookstore. As an antidote to boredom I bought a copy of *The Gene: An Intimate History* (2016) and found it engrossing. Siddhartha Mukherjee hooked me in with his own family story, after which I found it possible to read a history of science that would otherwise have seemed too daunting. I hasten to say that I do not know as much about my subject as Mukherjee knows about his, but his way of moving back and forth between the intimate close-up and the panoramic resembled what I was already doing. I found the model appealing because it meant that I did not have to choose between my tendency to be a "lumper" (somebody who enjoys large ideas) and a "splitter" (somebody who tends to read closely for details). These contrasting tendencies, usually attributed to Charles Darwin, seem like a false dichotomy to me. Working consciously as both a lumper and a splitter has been a tricky balancing act, but it is consistent with my view that the critic is a clown, an approach grounded in my teaching practice. The writing felt less like a high-wire act once I established a back-and-forth rhythm between close-up and panoramic, but the two clown interludes act a little like the poles held by tightrope walkers.

If I had waited until I no longer felt ambivalent about being Mennonite, this book would never have been published. In my daily life, I seldom identify myself as a Mennonite, nor have I brought up my children to do so. I have lived almost all my life in Toronto, a city about which the most important thing to be said in this context is that it is not Winnipeg or Waterloo. The idea of living in any kind of separate community fills me, quite frankly, with horror. I take comfort from the fact that my ambivalence resonates not only with artists from Mennonite groups but also with artists from many other minority groups. Zacharias has noted that "the exploration of Mennonite literary identity has become an ambivalent project for many critics" (2015a, 6). In this it is part of what Homi Bhabha calls "the ambivalence of colonial discourse" (1994, 85).

The premise of this book is that identity is always in process, something that we create while interacting with others. Since I have been previously misunderstood on this subject, I need to make clear at the outset that acknowledging the potency of Mennonite collective ideals does *not* mean that I see art of any kind as "offering a set of perspectives on a single 'true' or 'essential' Mennonite identity" (Zacharias 2013, 167). In 1988, I walked "through the Mennonite looking glass" to show that such a thing does not exist. I have been picking up the shards of that broken mirror ever since, and I have been a constructivist for as long as I can remember. After many years of making futile arguments against essentialist thinking among feminists, however, I came to the conclusion that the tendency is an inescapable part of being human. What is often said about icons is true of stereotypes—the more you try to destroy them, the more they bounce back, like a Bozo the Clown punching bag. The result, amplified by digital technology, is that they appear to have lives of their own. It is therefore difficult to define questions about agency, but I consider it the job of a critic to try to do just that. At various points in this book, I will insist on my own agency and, indeed, on my very existence when my responses do not fit expectations based on stereotypes.

When I have had email exchanges with artists about this book, they have been unanimous in their gratitude when I explain that I do not write about them as Mennonite artists. They are artists who happen to be Mennonite. Because of the ubiquity of something called "the Mennonite game," however, I need to state my policy on the question of family relations. When two or three Mennonites get together, so the game goes, they will always find out that they are related to each other. I have little interest in genealogy, but a friend once fed a few of my family facts into GRANDMA (a Genealogical Registry and Database of Mennonite Ancestry) and came back with the information that I am related to novelist Sandra Birdsell—a writer I have never met. Apparently we are connected via a distant ancestor called Schroeder. I confess that I experienced a small thrill at the thought of being related to an author I admire. I have also learned, as an adoptive mother, not to discount the importance of biological identity. My preference, however, is for cultural models that are not based on blood and my goal will therefore be to minimize the distraction of the "Mennonite game." When I think it contributes to my bias I will be open about my relation to an artist so that readers do not have to guess. As would be the case with any ethnic group, however, readers should not assume that people with the same surname are necessarily related to each other. The surname Friesen, for example, is usually assumed to refer to somebody from Friesland and most of the Friesens mentioned in this book are not related to each other. My father's name was Falk, but as far as I know I am not related to the well-known artist Gathie Falk, whose art will feature prominently in this book.

When I finally met Miriam Toews after she moved to Toronto, we had lunch in my favourite Mexican restaurant, Maizal, in Liberty Village, near where she now lives. Toews expressed gratitude to me and other literary critics and seemed to see our activity as a form of translation. Her novel *Irma Voth* (2011), about translation, became a kind of touchstone text for me while writing. I immersed myself in it while writing Chapter 2, after which Irma and Aggie—surely among the most lovable children ever imagined by a novelist—kept wandering into my book in chapters that had nothing to do with them. Often they were laughing at me, as my grandchildren often do. I deleted many of the references to them in later drafts, but I am still grateful for their laughter, which kept me moving forward.

Such deep levels of dialogue are more important to me than whatever claims can be made for this as an "autoethnographic text." For all of us, the dialogues that matter the most are the ones we have on a daily basis with those who are nearest and dearest. While writing drafts of this apologia, I wondered aloud to my husband why I so hated the term "autoethnographic text" when there was no question that it described what I had written. He said my comment reminded him of a line in a Peter DeVries novel, *The Vale of Laughter* (1967), in which autoeroticism is defined as two people necking in a car. My husband is not a Mennonite, but he has lived with one long enough to know that anything to do with automobiles has the potential to become a Mennonite joke. His comment made me realize that I was bracing myself for the "auto" in the term "autoethnography" to collide head on with the argument about dialogue that I keep nudging along throughout this book. When I read *The Vale of Laughter,* I was intrigued to discover that, despite the radical difference in style, the comic vision in it resembles the one that informs the fiction of Toews. My husband refers to such discoveries as "bright, shiny objects" that send me off on yet another round of revisions. As the years of revising have passed, he has cautioned me with increasing urgency against picking up bright, shiny objects. That does not stop him from scattering them in my path during every conversation.

It is true what John Lennon said, that life is what happens while you are making other plans. I was planning, for many years, to write a book on comedy and fiction in Canada. In the end, I abandoned that topic because this one chose me. It is important, however, for readers to know the limits of the contribution that I can make. Needed now is an inclusive survey to document the various forms of art that are part of the Mennonite cultural phenomenon. This is not that book. Indeed, such a survey could not be done by any single scholar. It would need to be a coordinated effort by scholars from various disciplines. Although this study is partial, it is my hope that my response as a witness who also happens to be both a Mennonite and a critic will be a resource for scholars of the future who will embark on more comprehensive studies. The false starts and stops have often led me to think of this as a foolhardy enterprise, but then I remind myself that my mistakes might well be more important than my successes. It is my hope that my errors, along with such insights as I can offer, will provoke or inspire other scholars to pursue work in one of the many under-studied areas over which I linger briefly. A critic's job, on one level, is an expression of gratitude. Faced with a cornucopia of art by Mennonites, I found that gratitude in itself became a reason to write this book. There is no better way to give thanks for art than to pay close attention to it.

MAKING BELIEVE

ON BEGINNINGS

Kommt, wir wollen wandern,
Von einer Stadt zur andern,
Und wenn wir nicht mehr weiter kann
Dann fangen wir von vorne an
Liesche, Liesche, drei dee.

Come, we want to wander
From one town to another
When we no more wander can
Then we'll start where we began:
Lizzie, Lizzie, turn ye roon.
(translation by Jay Macpherson)

Taking in "a Mennonite Miracle"

Looking back in 2005, Andris Taskans (founding editor of *Prairie Fire*) predicted that "what people will remember about writing in Manitoba during the final quarter of the 20th century" is the "blossoming of largely secular Mennonite writers" (quoted in Walker 2005). His description of the phenomenon as "a Mennonite miracle" has been often quoted. It conveys the sense of wonder that comes with distance, perhaps reflecting his sense of himself as an outsider—not a Mennonite. A miracle is revealed, not made by human hands, but this phenomenon did not come out of nothing, *ex nihilo*. Indeed, informed observers would agree that Taskans himself is one of those who helped make it happen. Setting aside the possibility that the hand of God was involved, I will identify, in this introductory chapter, a few of the root causes of the phenomenon. All of them can be seen as related in some way to a crisis of representation. Although my argument will be multilayered, my focus will be on Mennonite ways of dealing with that crisis. A crisis is not inherent in events but a way of constructing them. In a sense, this crisis has been kept alive because scholars keep writing about it. Since the "crisis" is perpetual, *malaise* might be a more accurate word. Indeed, the problems related to that crisis are inseparable from those related to identity, about which Charles Taylor writes in *The Malaise of Modernity* (1991). After some reflection, however, I have decided that the word *crisis* is apt for the art now being made by Mennonites. The "Mennonite miracle," as I see it, was a dramatic restaging, at the end of the twentieth century, of a crisis about art that was created by radical reformers in the sixteenth century. Artists are simultaneously confronting the crisis of representation and the crisis of identity that is endemic to our time.

The "Mennonite miracle" has not happened in some Mennonite ghetto. At their best, the artists are generating cross-cultural dialogues in ways that vary according to the choice of medium and genre. The resulting art resonates with centuries of religious history. In a fascinating book about Puritan allegory, Thomas Luxon observes that "the crisis over representation endemic to Protestantism has roots in Christianity's earliest formulations" (1995, x). He describes literalism as "the rallying cry of advanced Puritanism" and notes that "Quakers, in some ways the most radical of Puritans, epitomized this broad commitment to literalism" (ix). Although Luxon does not mention them, Mennonites are located on this spectrum of Protestant groups. Mennonite and Amish insistence on "plain style" is not just a marker of identity but also a stance that goes to the heart of what we human beings do when we make art.

The restaging that I have described is visible in Wanda Koop's *Hybrid Human* series, which contains repeated representations of a single human figure with a shadow, standing in front of an abstract rectangle (Plate 2).

These look to me like visual allusions to Rembrandt's *Artist in His Studio* (Plate 3). About that painting Julian Barnes writes "so we are to understand: it is the art which illuminates, which gives the artist both his being and his significance, rather than the other way round" (2015, 237). These paintings by Koop ask a basic question: what is art? That is not to say that they can be reduced to some statement about art or even that they illustrate the crisis of representation. Far more important than any message that can be verbalized is the visual rhetoric; for example, how the colours change from one painting to the next in the series. These hybrid humans seem to be urging the viewer to pay attention to visual languages and to perform what E.H. Gombrich called "the beholder's share" (1960, 30). Given centuries of collective efforts by Mennonites to evade that responsibility, it is indeed a miracle that so many have now chosen to confront the double crisis of representation and identity.

Taskans implicitly gestures toward a place and time: Manitoba at the end of the twentieth century. Why did the "Mennonite miracle" begin in that particular place and at that particular time? Why were those developments followed by Mennonite flowerings elsewhere on the continent? Unlike the multiplying loaves and fishes in the Bible (Matthew 14:17), the goods that make up the "Mennonite miracle" have travelled as the result of marketing. The first major novel to be marketed as Mennonite in Canada was Rudy Wiebe's *Peace Shall Destroy Many*, published by McClelland and Stewart in 1962. The high point of the "blossoming," however, happened in the 1980s. A partial list of the Mennonite novelists and poets who emerged during that decade includes Sandra Birdsell, Di Brandt, Patrick Friesen, Sarah Klassen, David Waltner-Toews, and Armin Wiebe. Those who choose a non-literary art are not as often marketed as Mennonite, identity being most tightly attached to narrative in our culture. This makes it harder to identify a parallel blossoming in the other arts, but Aganetha Dyck, Gathie Falk, and Wanda Koop are only three of the many visual artists who have emerged. Changes in the Mennonite music scene are even more difficult to identify, Mennonites having been active in music performance in Canada long before the literary ferment began. Observable as a new development is the emergence of composers such as Leonard Enns, Stephanie Martin, Randolph Peters, and Carol Ann Weaver. Not all these artists are from Manitoba, but the majority are from western Canada and are Russian Mennonite. The exceptions tend to be in music, where Swiss Mennonites in Ontario have made notable contributions. The problems of a regional focus are familiar, and I will address them, but geography matters. Northrop Frye sometimes observed that there is something vegetable and local about art, which works in tandem with cosmopolitan influences. Readers will find me returning, again and again, to the soil of Manitoba. Geographic concentration has become less apparent with the passage of time, but I view the ongoing literary flowerings across the continent as indebted to the collective efforts of Manitoba writers who worked hard during the 1980s to establish the category "secular Mennonite." This was no small achievement, particularly since much of the writing, like the visual art and music, is deeply spiritual. What does it mean to believe? How does that relate to what we do when we make art? Such questions, as my title signals, are at the heart of this book.

Taskans was referring to a literary phenomenon when he pointed to "a Mennonite miracle." I have broadened my study to include the other arts, but literature is my primary guide even when I move out of my own discipline. Such is the embarrassment of riches that the first challenge for any critic taking it in is to find a word for it. A sudden increase of any kind, for example, could be called an explosion. *Boom: Manufacturing Memoir for the Popular Market* is the title of Julie Rak's (2013) account of a different literary phenomenon, the recent increase in the number of published memoirs. While describing the larger Canadian literary phenomenon of which the Mennonite one is a small part, Nick Mount refers to a "CanLit boom" and describes how it "echoed across the country" (2017, 11). My preference is for quieter alternatives. I grew up on a farm and prefer images such as the one that Taskans used: "blossoming." Some critics use the fancier word *efflorescence*, but the metaphor is the same and reflects the legacy of the Romantic Revolution, a preference for words that invite us to envision an act of creation as an organic process.

How did this miracle happen? "How do you grow a poet?" The latter question echoes repeatedly in Robert Kroetsch's long poem *Seed Catalogue* (1977). I have already referred to roots, and that organic metaphor is no less powerful if you are, as I am, a constructivist convinced that we are all making things up as we go along. When used by critics as labels for a literary phenomenon, however, the metaphors are all conspicuously inadequate. I eventually decided to refer to this as a Mennonite renaissance. This was in part a pragmatic decision and happened because I grew tired of trying to find awkward synonyms for the word *phenomenon*. I found, however, that I could not use the word *renaissance* without qualifying it. French for rebirth, the word is still commonly understood to refer to *the* Renaissance—a period in art and intellectual history that began in Italy during the fourteenth century and spread across Europe over the next three centuries. When I began (and abandoned) a doctoral dissertation on Herman Melville in 1973, I was working in a literary period known as the American Renaissance. Among literary critics in Canada, however, there has always been an unspoken consensus that *renaissance* is too grand a word for the literary phenomenon that began around the time of Canadian centenary celebrations in 1967. There appears to be less resistance to the word when critics refer to the literatures of marginalized groups who are part of CanLit. Stephanie McKenzie (2007) has referred to the flowering of Indigenous writing as a "Native Renaissance." Government policies promoting multiculturalism are responsible in large part for many smaller renaissances in Canada. The Jewish renaissance was one of the first to be definably separate within the "CanLit boom," but other renaissances have happened within other groups. In Manitoba, they have included flowerings of Francophone, Icelandic, Indigenous, Jewish, Métis, Scottish, and Ukrainian literatures. In Canada there is a consensus that we have many literatures, a pluralism assumed in the title of a book by George Elliott Clarke: *Odysseys Home: Mapping African-Canadian Literature* (2002). I locate the Mennonite renaissance among these others and I see all of them—to continue the organic metaphor—as cross fertilizing each other constantly.

Taskans suggested a temporal demarcation with his reference to "the final quarter of the 20th century," as did historian Royden Loewen (2015) when he described it as a *fin de siècle* event. My own definition refers to a similar period of time. I focus primarily on the 1980s and 1990s because hindsight offers some clarity. The picture becomes more blurred for me when I look at recent events, but it seems to me likely that the fate of the Mennonite renaissance will be similar to those of other groups. At the height of the Jewish Canadian renaissance in the 1970s, I remember marvelling (while teaching Leonard Cohen, A.M. Klein, Irving Layton,

Mordecai Richler, Miriam Waddington, Adele Wiseman, and others) at how many different ways there are of being Jewish. New Jewish writers have kept appearing since then but not with that same thrill of being part of an emerging group. Something similar seems to be happening with the "Native Renaissance," surely not surprising since the many different Indigenous tribal identities and languages resist being dissolved into one homogenized literature. As a Mennonite, I am hopeful that one result of this renaissance will be to make it harder to generalize about Mennonite cultural identity.

This book, as I have already said, is not a survey, and I will not provide coverage of the phenomenon. What I can do from my position as both participant and spectator is to identify recurring patterns. One pattern is worth foregrounding at the outset because it is at the core of my understanding of any renaissance. I think of it as an experience of time warp, but it could also be called culture shock. My first effort to define it was in an essay on Wiebe's *The Blue Mountains of China*. The rhythm of Mennonite history in that novel involves recurring culture shock in response to geographic dislocation, followed by reflection. Since then I have become increasingly aware of radical temporal dislocations and thus now refer to time warp. My mental picture of Mennonite time travel back and forth across centuries is the Low German word *shtuckrich*, which means bumpy. When somebody who has lived in a separated community enters a modern urban world, it is a bumpy ride. Suddenly the values defined in the sixteenth century cannot be taken for granted because they jar with the surrounding environment. To be clear, I am not suggesting that all Mennonites who make art deal with time warp as a theme or that people make an entry into modernity as a group. I have sensed it often enough in the art made by Mennonites, however, that I have come to see it as a distinguishing feature of this particular renaissance. Hans-Jürgen Goertz seemed to be responding to time warp when he attributed "the crisis of the Mennonites" to anachronism. Mennonites, he wrote, are "children of a past social order, since dissolved by so-called 'bourgeois society.'" Their "way of life patterned on gestures of resistance against a past age" has not only produced an ongoing crisis but also led to an "anachronistic position" (1988, 5).

Goertz's description of this crisis came to mind when I read *Anachronic Renaissance*, a book in which art historians Alexander Nagel and

Christopher Wood challenge existing views of chronology and art history. The work of art, as they see it, comes out of a particular time and place, but it points away from the moment of its creation and "backward to a remote ancestral origin, perhaps, or to an origin outside time, in divinity" (2010, 9). They offer the word *anachronic* as "an alternative to 'anachronistic,' a judgmental term that carries with it the historicist assumption that every event and every object has its proper location within objective and linear time" (13). Nagel and Wood provide a description of the kind of art made as part of an "anachronic renaissance": "The work of art when it is late, when it repeats, when it hesitates, when it remembers, but also when it projects a future or an ideal, is 'anachronic'" (13). This approach to renaissance is the antithesis of the Enlightenment assumption that we are all moving together toward increasing secularization and freedom from old ways. Instead, there is a move to regenerate by moving into the past, as Karina Vernon does, for example, in *The Black Prairie Archives: An Anthology* (2019). This movement backward in time to recover deeply buried treasures is at the same time a movement forward into an ideal vision of the future. Such movements can easily become nostalgic, but they are also intrinsic to positive revolutions. I think, for example, of Adrienne Rich's poem "Diving into the Wreck," which had a transformative impact on me and innumerable other readers. It enacts a movement back, or rather down, into the wreckage of the past and it helped many of us to move forward with our lives (Rich 1975, 65–68).

There is no question that this kind of digging and diving requires courage. The closer my engagement with individual works of art, the more I am in awe of the bravery involved in taking on the challenge of making art out of this process. My book will pay tribute to the artistry and courage of those who take on the challenges peculiar to the Mennonite situation. Doing this has drawn me back repeatedly to the early modern times of my ancestors and to earlier versions of the problems that we still confront. Edward Said observes that "beginning is basically an activity which ultimately implies return and repetition rather than simple linear accomplishment" (1975, xiii). The act of beginning again and again comes through as something insistent and recurrent in Mennonite history and fiction. With relation to the "primordial asceticism" of beginning, Said writes that "we all like to believe we can always begin again, that a clean start will always be possible" (1975, 41). The American version of this belief tends to be highly individualized and is expressed in a phrase adapted from the ending of *Huckleberry Finn*: "lighting out for the territory" (Twain 1977, 229). In a seminal essay, "Melodramas of Beset Manhood," Nina Baym (1981) exposed theories that exclude women writers from American literary history. The story itself, however, has an older history, going back to Homer's *The Odyssey*. Against such individualism is the value of community, which remains, when all is said and done, perhaps the most enduring of Mennonite values. If a community is not to become a ghetto, however, then there must be dialogue between communities. The result is a constant and urgent need for translation. With a few comparative case studies in this book, I will attempt to show the various forms taken by cross-cultural dialogue. The larger comparative study so badly needed is outside the scope of this book, but all artists, including Mennonites, are working on a common ground that is a space *in between* identities (Said 1975, 3).

As individuals, then, Mennonites are crossing borders and entering modernity at different times, dealing with time warp and translating as they go. Those Mennonites who make art in this liminal space reach for different mediums and genres, depending on the contingencies of their lives. Their makings are interwoven into the larger global reality as people from other groups create answering dialogical art. What then, you might well ask, is to be gained by separating Mennonites from this global phenomenon? As I conceded at the outset, that question will keep coming up, and I will not be able to answer it once and for all. This perpetual deferral is inherent in any study of a minority group that begins, as mine does, with a rejection of the idea that identity is monological. I can do no more than confront the question every time it surfaces and suggest a possible response. At this introductory point in my book, I take it not only as an invitation to listen for dialogue but also as an urgent call to respect different histories. If time warp resonates widely in postcolonial art around the world, then the crucial thing to remember is that it takes different forms depending on different histories. Lazy pieties that affirm unity by erasing differences among groups do not result in productive dialogues of the kind that might ameliorate conflicts. Only a respectful awareness of different histories can do that.

Dealing with Mennonite History

When Fredric Jameson coined his now famous slogan "Always historicize!," he referred to it as "the one absolute and one may even say 'transhistorical' imperative of all dialectical thought" (1981, ix). He pointed out, however, that historicizing can take two paths: "the path of the object and the path of the subject." My choice, like his, is the latter, a foregrounding of the "interpretive strategies or codes" used by subjects (ix). I consider this to be a logical consequence of my focus on art. In the days before his death, Tony Judt argued eloquently (in conversation with Timothy Snyder) that "mythological narratives" are sometimes so powerful that "getting the actual history right becomes almost impossible." He concluded, based on his experience with Zionist myths, that "to allow memory to replace history is dangerous" (2012, 277). This passage was brought to my attention by anthropologist James Urry, who is well known for his many fine books on Russian Mennonite history. Like Urry, I have found that the collective memory of Russian Mennonites can act as an obstruction, especially when it takes the form of a martyr myth. I notice, however, that the two historians, Judt and Snyder, said nothing about where art fits into the picture. In between the unreliability of memory and the facts of history are the stories and songs and pictures and, yes, myths, without which human beings cannot survive.

When Mennonite novelists deal with the complexities of history, they often end up clowning and deliberately refusing the job of "getting the actual history right." In *Truth Is Naked All Others Pay Cash: An Autobiographical Exaggeration*, Byron Rempel opts for a genre reminiscent of *1066 and All That: A Memorable History of England* (Sellar and Yeatman 1930). "While most people tend to think of history as a linear chain," writes Rempel, "in reality it is more like pudding. This is most clearly shown when Mennonites talk about themselves, which is like watching someone try to massage a squid" (2005, 37). Of course, Mennonites are not alone in looking absurd when they try to deal with their own history. As Wallace Stevens wrote in a poem entitled "Connoisseur of Chaos," "the squirming facts exceed the squamous mind" (1990, 215). My interest is not in history itself but in how the artists who are part of the Mennonite renaissance deal with "the squirming facts" of history, Rempel's hilarious book being one example.

Encyclopedia entries might or might not be consulted by a particular artist who happens to come from a group in which shunning is still performed and who decides to write or create something in response. It might well seem that the artist is making a mountain out of a molehill. The scholar who then turns her attention to that mountain, however, has a responsibility to be as accurate as possible about facts. In conversation with Snyder, Judt prescribed a solution to the problem that he identified: "Without history, memory is open to abuse. But if history comes first, then memory has a template and guide against which it can work and be assessed" (2012, 278). This may sound like good advice but it is deceptively tidy when it comes to art. It is a mistake to see written history as a template against which a work of art is held and judged. In *Art and Illusion: A Study in the Psychology of Pictorial Representation*, E.H. Gombrich (1960) made a crucial distinction between matching and making. The most important questions about art have to do with what an artist *makes* of the facts, but the way these facts squirm is a constant reminder that matching remains important. The recent spectacle of an American president who is a compulsive liar shows how dangerous it is to ignore facts. The relation between fact and fiction is not susceptible to neat answers, but Snyder, in his response to Judt, usefully qualified the memory/history binary in a way that sheds some light on this problematic area. He made the cogent observation that *"memory exists in the first person. . . . Whereas history exists above all in the second and third person"* (2012, 278). The clarity of this distinction points to a rhetorical tool central to all fiction: point of view. I am, as I have acknowledged, in the story about which I write—all the more reason to push myself back from that story and write a short history using a third-person point of view.

Mennonite History in the Third Person

In her account of capsule histories written by Mennonites, Julia Spicher Kasdorf (2015) observes that they invariably contain errors. Mine will doubtless be no exception, but I will aim for clarity. Let me begin by suggesting that one way to simplify the bewildering complexity of Mennonite history is to keep in mind that the term "Anabaptist" covers all the groups. There are Anabaptists (e.g., Hutterites) who are not Mennonite, but there are no Mennonites who are not Anabaptist, a word coined as a derisive way to designate those who rejected infant baptism. On 24 February 1527, a group of Swiss Anabaptist leaders, including Conrad Grebel, met and endorsed the Schleitheim Confession, a document setting out principles such as the belief in adult baptism, pacifism, the need to shun the world, and a refusal to swear oaths. In the sixteenth-century context, these were highly charged political statements. Historians have long debated how this revolutionary stance relates to the separation of church and state and to the development of the idea of a nation. The immediate effect, in any event, was to make Anabaptists targets of persecution. Women and men were interrogated and tortured. An estimated 5,000 were killed by various methods designed to maximize suffering: drowning (as a mockery of adult baptism), burning at the stake, beheading, and burial alive. What began among urban intellectuals was driven underground by this persecution and became a rural movement.

The job of tracing the Anabaptist roots of Mennonite culture is made challenging by what historians have termed the "polygenesis" of the movement and further complicated by the subsequent diaspora. In an essay entitled "Making Menno: The Historical Images of a Religious Leader," Royden Loewen (1999) challenges the "great man" approach to Mennonite history. Recent scholarship has also paid attention to the large number of women whose martyrdoms are recorded in the *Martyrs Mirror* and who presumably exercised some kind of influence (Van Braght 1660). This has not stopped a regular appeal to male historical figures when Mennonite history is summed up. Mennonites, in any case, are named after Menno Simons, a Dutch Catholic priest who, in 1536, belatedly left the security of his position (almost a decade after the Schleitheim Confession) to take up leadership. In doing so, he put his life at risk. He was motivated by the events at Münster in northern Germany, where fanatical Anabaptists used violence during their attempt to create a theocracy. The pacifist vision that came to dominate was forged in opposition to that event, and the most compelling argument for shunning at the time was the need to keep the church free from the violent Münsterites.

Religious persecution in the Low Countries led large groups of Mennonites to take refuge in the Vistula Delta, a region that was once in Prussia and is now in Poland. At that time it was called a "Jewish paradise" because of its reputation for religious tolerance, a painful irony given the later history of anti-Semitism and mass killings of Jews. Dirk Philips founded the first Mennonite church in Danzig (Gdansk) in 1569 and Mennonites lived there for 400 years. Dutch was the primary language for Mennonites when they arrived in the Vistula Delta and it remained so for 200 years. There were protests when the first High German sermon was preached in Danzig in 1762 and Dutch was briefly reinstated, but by 1768 most hymn books in the area were High German. Plautdietsch, the distinctive Mennonite version of Low German that developed during that time, is a mixture of Dutch and a Low Prussian dialect. It is tempting to speculate, given the sizeable Jewish population in Danzig at the time, whether Yiddish may also have influenced the development of the Mennonite version of Plautdietsch. Against all odds Plautdietsch has survived to this day, in part because those Mennonites who immigrated to Russia took it with them—along with the class conflicts it contained. When Catherine the Great issued an invitation to Europeans to settle in New Russia in 1763, Mennonites in Prussia responded in large numbers. The first Mennonite colony on the Dnieper River was Chortitza, settled in 1789; the second wave of immigrants founded the Molotschna colony in 1803.

Centuries of living in the Vistula Delta have had a continuing influence on Russian Mennonite culture, as Rudy Wiebe shows in his novel *Sweeter Than All the World* (2001). Historical accounts, however, often fail to mention that not all Mennonites in any particular group resettled and that those who stayed behind were usually the most "liberal" and least fearful of assimilation. Piet Visser observes that for the Anabaptists who remained in the Netherlands after the Reformation, "the question of an ethnic identity" quickly became "altogether irrelevant" as they rapidly assimilated into the fabric of the culture around them. In stark contrast, ethnicity and separation became central to the lives of "Mennonites who settled outside the Dutch borders." Visser notes that "almost three centuries later," those Mennonites are experiencing "a somewhat comparable process of assimilation" (Visser 1994, vii–viii). His analysis suggests that it would be useful to do comparative study but I have found that this is a nearly impossible task because of the absence of supporting scholarship. I see the art of Wanda Koop and Gathie Falk, for example, as resonating with a Dutch Mennonite sensibility and am sometimes tempted to make connections with the art of the many Mennonites who were prominent in Amsterdam during the Dutch Golden Age. Usually I refrain because of my fear of encouraging the reductive interpretations of art that are the product of contemporary assumptions about ethnicity.

The majority of the artists who are part of the Canadian renaissance, in any case, are from that portion of the Dutch/German/Polish ethnic branch that immigrated to Russia and then, almost a century later, to North America. The first Mennonites to arrive in North America, however, came directly from Switzerland to the United States in 1683 at the invitation of William Penn. Between 1786 and 1825, many of them, along with Amish groups, migrated to Ontario. Since they did not settle in the Canadian west, they are not part of the Manitoba renaissance. Swiss Mennonites in the United States, however, are experiencing a literary renaissance that is interwoven with the Russian Mennonite one in complex ways. Readers might find it helpful, given these tangled threads, to keep in mind that the primary "actors" in this book are the two main groups of Russian Mennonites in Manitoba: the *Kanadier*, who came as immigrants in the 1870s, and the *Russländer*, who came as refugees in the 1920s. These groups, in turn, split into a multitude of subgroups that resist generalization. At about the time that the Russländer were arriving, some Kanadier subgroups began leaving Canada to seek greater religious freedom in Mexico, Paraguay, and other countries. These Mennonites make a dramatic appearance in two novels by Miriam Toews: *Irma Voth* (2011) and *Women Talking* (2018).

To avoid confusion I will follow scholarly custom and refer to Russian Mennonites, though much of the land where Mennonites lived prior to arriving in Canada is now Ukraine. A third wave of Russian Mennonite refugees arrived in Canada after the Second World War, following a "Great Trek" from Russia to Germany. This group has never been given a catchy label, perhaps because there is still shame about the fact that Canadians disparagingly called them DPs, short for displaced persons. When I consulted Vern Thiessen, a playwright from this group, he suggested that they could be called the *Deutschländer*. A fourth group are the Mennonites who never left for Russia in the first place but stayed behind in Prussia. Some of them eventually made their way to North America. I consulted Andreas Schroeder, a writer from this group, and he suggested that they could be called the *Reichsländer*. Later I heard from Thiessen that his mother remembers that group being called *Danzigers*. Most important to note is that none of these terms matches up neatly with a particular spot on a map of the world. The terms contain inevitable distortions because of the complexities of Mennonite immigration patterns.

Complicating the global scene now are Mennonite churches in Africa, Asia, and Latin America, formed as the result of Christian evangelism. These converts, though vastly outnumbering North American Mennonites, have not, for the most part, engaged with the cultural and ethnic conflicts that are part of the flowering of art on this continent. They exist, however, as a potent challenge to ethnicity-based definitions of Mennonite identity. Their impact on culture can be felt (particularly in music) as a result of their participation in Mennonite World Conferences, which happen every six or seven years. Of equal importance, albeit far smaller in number, are North Americans who have no connection with the ethnic heritage but are drawn to the "Anabaptist vision." They are sometimes referred to as "intentional Mennonites." In "The Scope of This Project," Sofia Samatar (an American writer who is of Somali and Swiss Mennonite descent) has argued that the phrase "postcolonial Mennonite literature" ought to encompass the writing of all these non-ethnic Mennonites (2017). Although I am not familiar with Mennonite literature on a global scale, I find the suggestion intriguing. It is important, in any case, to remember that Christianity, like other world religions, is multiethnic, and that this is reflected in Mennonite churches. When church membership is taken into account, the two main Mennonite ethnic groups—the Swiss and the Dutch—are outnumbered by global multiplication. During the time period that the cultural renaissance has happened in Canada, immigration has also changed the ethnic makeup here. Across Canada, Mennonites now worship in at least fifteen different languages, including French, Hindi, Farsi, Punjabi, Korean, and Eritrean.

Mennonite History in the First Person: "Are You Not History Knowing?"

One important thing to say as I switch to a first-person point of view, is that the history I have just put together, not without some effort, is not what I learned in school. To some extent, I can match the bits of history that I have acquired belatedly with the fragments of unreliable memories of my own life. My continuing confusion makes me think that it is futile to rail against artists for not knowing the history of their people. A poem by David Waltner-Toews in a series about "Tante Tina," Aunt Tina, captures the bewilderment experienced by many. Tante Tina expresses her exasperation with Haenschen (little John) while revealing her own ignorance:

> Listen, bursch. I am about Russia talking.
> Are you not history knowing?
> Then Trotsky is to Mexico
> going, because there are so many Mennonites
> and he is the soup so much liking and at home
> to be feeling (2004, 77).

"Are you not history knowing?" The question can be heard in between the lines when historians write about Mennonite fiction. Royden Loewen, for example, writes that "Miriam Toews seems to conflate Menno Simons and Claas Epp in *A Complicated Kindness* . . . not caring that the historical Menno was patently anti-apocalyptic" (2015, 43). He might as well have asked "Are you not history knowing?" A novelist would respond "Who's asking?" The person doing the conflating in this case is not Toews but the adolescent narrator whom she has constructed as a filter. The speaker in the "Tante Tina" poem is not Waltner-Toews but an elderly Russländer refugee. Obviously neither of them has read much Mennonite history.

Based on my own experience, I conclude that written history is far less important as an influence on Mennonites who make art than the mythologies that they construct from the particular contingencies of their individual lives. As Northrop Frye wrote, "our cultural heritage is our real and repressed social past, not the past of historical record but the great dreams of the arts, which keep recurring to haunt us with a sense of how little we know of the real dimensions of our own experience" (1980, 13). Miriam Toews once spoke to me about the state of "unknowingness" out of which her stories emerge and I heard the echo: "Are you not history knowing?" The model of memory that works for artists is not the one used by historians. It is defined by anthropologist Michael Lambek. Memory, in this model, "has no unmediated essence, either as subjective experience or as objective fact, but is always in the act of being made" (1996, 242).

It is not the recorded history that I have just transcribed, but the untold oral culture of my childhood that puts me in touch with the "real and repressed" past that haunts "the great dreams of the arts." My memory of this culture, however, is "always in the act of being made." When I set out to tell my own story in the first person, I quickly come up against my limits as I deal with a moving target. The challenge of getting those "squirming facts" to hold still and not to multiply exponentially is familiar to every writer of memoir. What came to mind when I tried was the title of a story by Alice Munro: "Hold Me Fast, Don't Let Me Pass" (1990, 74). Munro is one of the greatest storytellers of all time, and she has spoken of how hard it is to hold stories still so that they can be set down in print. Frequently she writes about poetry recitation, as if to stabilize the story with reference to a text that holds still (see Redekop 1999).

I found that I could not hold fast to "the squirming facts" of my own history without constructing it as an analogy to the stable text of a poem. The one that came instantly to mind once I had decided to do this was Robert Frost's late poem "Directive," a reflection on perennial questions about the relationship between art and life (1963, 251–53). The speaker in the poem wanders through a wood, moving back in time. He finds or creates a "children's house of make-believe" that is like the *Spielraum* or play space that I will introduce in the next chapter. Like Frost, I envision all art as taking place in such a "house of make-believe," a space between fact and imagination. In my story, as in that poem, "There is a house that is no more a house / Upon a farm that is no more a farm" (251).

I grew up on a small farm in southern Manitoba, halfway between the towns of Altona and Rosenfeld. As far as I could see and hear on that small patch of earth, almost everybody was Mennonite and white. There was one major exception: once in a while the *Indiauna* would drive onto our yard in some battered vehicle to ask for food and sometimes to sell their wares. In my condensed third-person account of Mennonite history I made no mention of Indigenous people. In first-person accounts of where I come from, by contrast, they sometimes loom large. I have written elsewhere, for example, about how my father would invite the *Indiauna* to sleep in the *scheen,* the hay barn, and how he organized his daughters to provide them with food and blankets (Redekop 2019, 63). I do not know to what extent my father was aware of the dispossession those people had suffered as a result of Mennonite settlements. Perhaps he was simply responding to their extreme poverty. I remain grateful to this day that he insisted we offer hospitality, but the sad fact is that I am now only slightly less ignorant than I was then about the history of those people. My childhood "house of make-believe" would be a claustrophobic tomb if I did not admit to my own "not knowing" of history. Keeping that house open to new information leads to constant change in how I see the past—my own and that of others. The "house of make-believe" falls apart constantly and then is rebuilt, only to fall apart again.

As a child I thought we were rich and felt proud, if slightly guilty, living in a two-storey house that my grandfather had designed and the community had built. I had no idea then that I was one of the Kanadier and perceived as backward by other Mennonites called Russländer. My father preached in High German, and we spoke only English in the one-room school that I attended. At home we spoke only Low German by strict decree of our father. I later realized that his fierce insistence must have been a response to the arrival of the Russländer, who apparently made no secret of their efforts to wipe out Plautdietsch. At the time, Low German was simply the language in which we lived our daily lives. That early time is a blur of family quarrels punctuated by happy times of playing with my sisters. I remember that we braided the long stems of dandelions and made crowns and necklaces with them. Sometimes we wore this forbidden jewellery while playing house in a private space created by flattening a section of long grass in the pasture. Frost imagines the shattered dishes in the children's playhouse: "Weep for what little things could make them glad" (1963, 253). Without television or a daily newspaper, I was insulated from major world events. About the after-effects of the Second World War, I remember only that my father did not like us to say hi to our friends because it sounded like *Heil* to him and that he refused to shop in a menswear store in Altona because the owner was said to be a Nazi.

Before I was born, my father, Wilhelm Falk, had led a split from the Sommerfelder Church and co-founded the Rudnerweider Church with several other preachers. They included Peter Zacharias, the grandfather of poet Di Brandt and the great-grandfather of literary critic Robert Zacharias. My father's formal schooling had stopped at grade eight, but when he was elected as *Ältester* or Bishop and thrust into a leadership role he educated himself by reading. His onerous job, however, came without any remuneration, and my parents supported their family of twelve on a small mixed farm barely above subsistence level. There was no time left over for Bishop Falk to share with his children what he had learned. Although he served on the board of a nearby private high school where Mennonite history was part of the curriculum, he could not afford to send his own children to that school.

My father was outspoken in his scorn for fiction. "*Ütjedochte jeschichte!*" he would sometimes exclaim when he caught me reading a novel. Thought-up stories. My mother was twenty years younger than my father and fluent in English. Like me, she was a voracious, if somewhat furtive, reader of fiction. When the latest issue of the *Rundschau* arrived, she would read to us from a series called *Lieschen's Streiche*—Lizzie's Pranks. Rather, she would do a simultaneous translation from the High German into Low German. We would dissolve into giggles each time she came to the end and translated *fortsetzung folgt*—"to be continued"—as *fortzateck folgt*. The High German sound *fortz* happens to be the Low German word for fart. I hesitate to tell the joke because it could reinforce the stereotype of Low German speaking Mennonites as *prost*—coarse or vulgar. I must therefore add that I have no memory of any other Kanadier women making such off-colour jokes. My mother was a storyteller and her irrepressible high spirits often inspired her to play the part of *ueleshpael*. I always assumed the literal translation of that word was owl play, which was puzzling since owls are not playful birds. With her Grade 8 education my mother could not have known, any more than I did at the time, that it meant mirror and that it alluded to a sixteenth century Low German legend about Till Eulenspiegel. I will return to tricksters in the next chapter. For now let me point out the obvious, that fart jokes are popular with children everywhere, as are singing games that end in collapse or reversal. The children's game that goes with the folk song in the epigraph to this chapter had a special meaning in our family because it contained my mother's name, Elizabeth in English but Liesche in Low German. There are many versions of that folk song. We always chanted it in High German but then switched to Low German in the last line: "*Liesche, Liesche, drei dee.*" When Jay Macpherson translated it for me, she captured the spirit of that collapse while evoking the Scottish oral culture that I have come to love. "Lizzie, Lizzie, turn ye roon" (Redekop 1993a, 216–17).

Unlike my father, my mother (born Schellenberg) had little interest in Mennonite history. My maternal grandmother died when I was a teenager, but she was my link to an unusual family past. The story went that my Hiebert great-grandparents were both gypsies. As babies they were left on the doorsteps of different Mennonite homes in Russia and brought up in those families. When they grew up, they fell in love and married. The photograph in the family album showed them as having a strong resemblance to each other—two long, dark faces with high cheekbones, warm eyes, and gentle smiles. When I was younger, I imagined the gypsies making mournful music on the Russian steppe as they lamented the loss of the babies they had to give away. Later I was horrified when I learned about the genocide of the Roma during the war. Now that I myself am an adoptive mother, I have been made aware of the complex ways that fact and fiction interweave when we tell stories about where we come from. I have sometimes wondered if our "gypsy" heritage might explain why so many of my Schellenberg relatives write poetry and make music. Scientific discoveries now lend support for such a view, but I remain convinced that the myths we construct about our past are as potent as any gene.

In comparison with the oral richness around me, it would be difficult to exaggerate the gaps in my knowledge of written history. I heard stories about the past of our people, the Kanadier, stories about early pioneering and dangerous weather. About the Russländer I knew next to nothing. My father spoke with admiration about the educated Russländer preachers whom he met at conferences, and I knew that many of them lived in the town of Winkler. I heard no horror stories about Stalin or about fathers and brothers vanishing in Siberia. Education in literature transformed the world for me, but it was not academic study that advanced my knowledge of Mennonite history. My first glimpse of the history of the Russländer happened during my first year of university in Winnipeg, when I boarded in the home of the man who would become my husband. His father, as it turned out, was one of those educated preachers from Winkler. Abruptly history was present and painful, consumed along with supper while my future mother-in-law read out loud a German letter from a sister who had been left behind in what was then the Soviet Union. I can see it still, that thin blue aerogram that she held as she wept and trembled with fear. It was my first encounter with a person like those described by Lambek: "*They do not possess memories, rather they are possessed by them*" (1996, 246). I could not have put it into such helpful words, and I did not then have the benefit of Anne Konrad's moving compilation of stories from such letters in *Red Quarter Moon: A Search for Family in the Shadow of Stalin* (2012). All I could tell was that there had been suffering of such intensity that it was impossible to extract a narrative of what it was that had happened to make Mrs. Redekop cry.

I read very little about Mennonites in those years, but some things had a bigger impact than I realized at the time. Harold Bender's influential essay on the "recovery of the Anabaptist vision" had been published in 1944, the year of my birth, and I read it sometime during the 1960s. Its liberating impact came from his appeal to the power of a collective Mennonite imagination that had deep roots in history. It offered an alternative not only to the fundamentalist version of Christianity for which I felt a growing revulsion but also to a German-based ethnic identity, which I found equally repellent. I never considered pursuing Anabaptist studies, and I have not followed the debates among theologians about Bender's essay (see Hershberger 2001). Like any other collective ideal, the Anabaptist vision is not inherently good. It is open to abuse and this is especially so when it is used to rationalize separatism. In *Chosen Nation: Mennonites and Germany in a Global Era,* Benjamin Goossen has written about how Anabaptist ideals were twisted by Mennonite leaders in Germany to support fascism (2017). I feel revulsion when I read about Mennonites who fell into step with the Nazis. At the same time, I note that the Mennonites who repudiated those leaders and who found ways to escape to North America were motivated at least in part by a different version of an Anabaptist vision.

An Anabaptist vision of some sort still clings to my ways of making believe and living. I have other idealizations, of course, resulting from my experiences and reading since then. I take my Anabaptist vision so much for granted that I found myself having to coax it out to make it visible here. It is made up of a mixture of beliefs about community—mutual aid, pacifism, simple living, plain speaking, and other ingredients so familiar that I cannot even identify them. It is a pudding, really, but it is my pudding.

These are the values that I live by. They nourish me. Even when I cannot nail them down, I sometimes feel an urge to speak up for them, but mostly it is not about words at all. It never occurred to me to teach my children to identify as Mennonites or Christians, but you might say that the proof is in the pudding. My children are adults, and both of them live by community values that Mennonites call mutual aid.

I married Clarence Redekop in 1966. The tensions between Russländer and Kanadier about which I write in this book were never a source of conflict during our marriage. As a political scientist he did not turn a blind eye to class differences among Mennonites and he often expressed envy of my Low German heritage. Over the years, his family story, when told to new friends, came to resemble the story told by Barbara Smucker (1981) in her children's novel *Days of Terror*. When stories have been processed often, they acquire a rounded shape—a beginning, a middle, and an end. From her somewhat distanced perspective as a Swiss Mennonite, Smucker saw this clearly. The three parts of her version of the story are entitled "Peace," "Terror," and "Deliverance." Life goes on, however, and when capsule histories are broken up the taste can be bitter. Like many other Russländer Mennonites, my mother-in-law was able to travel to Ukraine during the 1990s after the fall of the Soviet Union. There she briefly reunited with the sister who had written those blue aerogram letters that had made her cry. She returned with stories that she mostly found too painful to tell. The stories now emerging are the accounts of those Mennonites—neither Kanadier nor Russländer—who did not escape to Canada or the United States and were left to find their way through the rubble of war-torn Europe. Some of these eventually found their way to Canada, not as a group but individually. Their stories illustrate the truth of what Cathy Caruth and others have written about how long it takes to "claim" the experience of trauma (Caruth ed. 1996). In a pioneering book called *Going by the Moon and the Stars: Stories of Two Russian Mennonite Women* (1994a), Pamela Klassen helped two survivors tell their stories. More recently descendants from that immigrant group are bearing witness in texts such as Hans Werner's *The Constructed Mennonite: History, Memory, and the Second World War* (2013; see M. Redekop 2013b) and Elsie K. Neufeld's *"Ort und Vertreibung: My Mother of the 1920s"* (2018).

Chronology has a way of seeming to speed up in the rear-view mirror in those places where loved ones die and where in fact time is experienced as slowing down or maybe even stopping. Clarence died suddenly on 15 August 2000 from cardiac arrhythmia. Not long after that, his mother died as well. Fast-forward to the year 2006, when I married Dennis Duffy, whose wife had died in 2001 and who had been my colleague for decades. Dennis was born in Kentucky, a "cradle Catholic," and is of Irish and German descent. The influence of "mixed marriages" is a subtext in this book and comes to the surface in Chapter 5 because of the part played by Ben Horch's marriage in the composition of *The Mennonite Piano Concerto*. My own two marriages, mixed in different ways, might also explain why, in Chapter 2, I imagine the us/them split as a lovers' quarrel.

When we tell or write parts of our own stories, there is often an uncanny sense that it is a story about somebody else and that the first person has become a third person. The speaker in Frost's "Directive," reflecting on his journey back in time, writes "And there's a story in a book about it" (1963, 252). Storytelling is something that we all do every day, a fact that is the egalitarian bedrock of Alice Munro's brilliant fictions. Her stories have absorbed me for much of my life, to the point where I sometimes see events in my life as happening in one of them. Once, on a flight back from Winnipeg with Dennis, something happened that felt like there must be "a story in a book about it." Out of the blue, the stranger sitting next to me volunteered the information that for a moment they had mistaken my partner for Rudy Wiebe. Now that would have been understandable if it had been my first husband, who had black hair and a black beard. When Mavis Gallant met Clarence, she was probably thinking of Rudy Wiebe when she admired his "Russian cheekbones." Dennis also has a beard, but there the resemblance ends. The situation was not so much clarified as deepened when we learned that our travel companion was none other than Ivan Coyote, a gender-bending storyteller whose trickster ways are reflected in their name. This fleeting exchange conveys the ambiguities that surround what Charles Taylor (1994) calls "the politics of recognition." In all our various travels, we do not arrive at a place where finally, echoing Saint Paul, we know as we are known. If we are lucky, however, then sometimes we come to a crossing where we meet with a trickster who offers the simple gift of common humanity. At such moments, there might be a feeling that goes with the epiphany that Frost creates at the end of "Directive." The speaker steals a broken goblet from the "children's house of make-believe," and, having discovered "a brook that was the water of the house," he hands the reader a gift: "Here are your waters and your watering place. / Drink and be whole again beyond confusion" (1963, 253).

Myths of Origin: Martyrs and Tricksters

On the vast panorama of history that I sketched out in the third person, the groups responsible for the "Mennonite miracle" constitute a mere pinprick. The story of my own life in the first person, to echo the title of Rempel's mock history (2005), is an "autobiographical exaggeration." If, however, you imagine that close-up with relation to the Mennonite renaissance, then it recapitulates the questions that are my focus in this chapter. Where did this blossoming come from? Why did it happen in this place? In responding to those questions, I find it useful to compare my Kanadier story with my late husband's Russländer story. Both of them show why origin myths have a perennial appeal. People ask "Where do you come from?" My answer begins with "I grew up on a small farm." My late husband's answer might have begun "I grew up in Winkler, Manitoba." Origin myths come into play when people push further back into the past to the mostly unknown lives of their ancestors. It was my second husband, Dennis Duffy, who reminded me that different origin myths result in different genres. To the question "Where do you come from?" he would answer "Louisville, Kentucky." Push the question into the dimmer reaches of his ancestry and you come up against Irish versions of the same origin myth that has attached itself to the Russländer experience. As Dennis pointed out, this myth goes with the genre of tragic nationalist narrative. It begins with the formulaic "Once we lived in a golden age." The genre that fits the Kanadier myth is different. It is pioneer pastoral, parodied by Paul Hiebert in *Sarah Binks* (1947) and again by Miriam Toews in *A Complicated Kindness* (2004).

Questions about master narratives are endlessly tangled on personal levels, but the recurrence of generic conventions offers welcome stability in swampy literary territory. How should a literary critic deal with the complex intertwining of myth and history when trying to make sense of the Mennonite renaissance? There is no single answer to this question, but there is now useful debate among Mennonite literary critics in response to it. Although our responses differ, we all have in common the need to deal with the extraordinary dominance of history and theology in Mennonite scholarship. The bias of historians is reflected in the conversation between Tony Judt and Timothy Snyder, which expresses the shared assumption that something is inherently wrong with "mythological narratives." The bias of theologians is more likely to be sympathetic to mythology. Karen Armstrong, for example, laments the "death of mythology" in the last chapter of *A Short History of Myth* (2005). In contrast to the five periods that she outlines, from the Paleolithic to the Post-Axial, the period that began in the sixteenth century appears as a radical turn indeed. She calls it "The Great Western Transformation" (2005, 119). Although Armstrong does not mention them, Anabaptist reformers helped to ensure the "death of mythology" during that period. The basic human need for myths has continued, however, alongside scientific advances, Newton's dabbling in the occult being one conspicuous example. I do not share Armstrong's nostalgia for the earlier periods, but her lucid account is invaluable.

Ambiguity now surrounds the word *myth*; it can be used as a synonym for fiction or to accuse somebody of telling an untruth. In Mennonite contexts, in which honesty is highly valued, this is of no small consequence. I am sometimes startled by the ferocity of Mennonite responses to factual errors in fiction. I had them in mind when I reviewed *A Complicated Kindness* and suggested that the distortions should be seen in the light of Oscar Wilde's essay "The Decay of Lying" (Wilde 1950). In his reflections on that essay, Northrop Frye noted that Wilde saw creative artists as liars, "people whose lives got smashed up in various ways, but rescued fragments from the smash of an intensity that the steady-state people seldom get to hear about. Their vision is penetrating and distorted: it is truthful because it is falsified" (Frye 1980, 9, quoted in Redekop 2004, 19). Mennonites who write fiction are liars in the sense that they recreate the world in disturbing ways. Far from imposing inherited narratives, they unleash powerful forces that have been repressed. To check such a fiction for accuracy of detail is to miss the power of the art completely. When Barbara Smucker wrote *Days of Terror* (1981), she was clearly aware that we tell such stories to our children because, on some deep level, we are all bewildered children. Labelling the story a myth does nothing to take away from the comfort that it can give, and certainly it does not make the story morally wrong. It is important to remember that the same myth can be put to different uses. To use a myth as novelists do or as people do in their everyday lives is different from how a literary critic uses it in the writing of literary history.

Almost all the origin myths that have been constructed by critics in response to the Mennonite renaissance involve martyrdom. It did not occur to me to mention martyrs when I told my own story of growing up, yet I have been often told that the *Martyrs Mirror* (Van Braght 1660) is a book that has a status next to that of the Bible in many Mennonite homes. Where are these homes? I never saw that book in my home or in anyone else's home while growing up. Indeed, I did not know it existed until I was in graduate school. I have read that in some Amish and Swiss Mennonite communities it is traditional to give a bridal couple that book as a wedding present. My wedding present from my parents was a copy *of The Mennonite Treasury of Recipes* (Steinbach Committee, 1961). Despite my personal distance from the martyrdom stories, however, I do not find it surprising, given the facts of Anabaptist history, that the origin stories told by Mennonites from all the subgroups are often martyr myths. Martyrdom is a powerful idealization of suffering, and it is shared by many other religious groups. It is not a big step from the celebration of martyrs to a view of the artist as a suffering hero or heroine and art as the reward for that suffering. When the suffering is not only of an individual but also of a people, and when the theology of "the suffering church" is mythologized in a secular context, the questions become inescapably political. This is true not only for Mennonites, and the political implications of this process are many, a topic that Alan Davies explores in *The Crucified Nation: A Motif in Modern Nationalism* (2010).

I have an aversion to martyr myths because of how they tend to conceal nationalist narratives while slipping into identity politics, where they become part of what historian Margaret Macmillan has called an "unseemly competition for victimhood" (2008, 59). For these reasons, I have struggled for many years to understand the part played by martyrdom in the fiction and poetry of Mennonites. I came at the question sideways in 1985 when I did a close reading of a long poem by E.J. Pratt about Jesuit martyrs. The title of that paper was "Authority and the Margins of Escape in *Brébeuf and His Brethren*" (Redekop 1985). My first experience with the *Martyrs Mirror* took place after that while preparing a talk published in 1993 as "Escape from the Bloody Theatre: The Making of Mennonite Stories." At that time, I actually bought a copy of the book and found it riveting even as I looked for ways to distance myself from it. This distancing effort is most apparent in how "Bloody Theatre," an implied curse lifted from the subtitle of the *Martyrs Mirror*, implicitly blasphemes against this sacred text (Van Braght 1660).

Martyrdom recurs in the fiction and poetry of Mennonites. In "Escape from the Bloody Theatre," I wrote that "books like *Saint Joan* and *Murder in the Cathedral* still are very important for us to read as an aid to understanding books like *The Temptations of Big Bear*, in which Rudy Wiebe tells the story of Big Bear and turns him (in my view) into a Mennonite martyr" (1993b, 15).* Wiebe comes at martyrdom from another angle in *The Scorched-Wood People* (1977), where it combines with apocalyptic thinking in the life of Louis Riel. Noon Park (2011) argues that Miriam Toews does so in *A Complicated Kindness*. I have argued elsewhere that Patrick Friesen does so in *The Shunning*. The suicide of Peter in that long poem is "a new kind of martyr's mirror. The story of Peter reflects back to us, in reverse, the very heart of our theology of martyrdom and challenges it" (1993b, 19). Grace Kehler (2011) explores the theme more broadly in "Representations of Melancholic Martyrdom in Canadian Mennonite Literature." Some idea of the variety of ways that writers have found to deal with a history of martyrdom can be seen in a collection entitled *Tongue Screws and Testimonies: Poems, Stories, and Essays Inspired by the Martyrs Mirror* (Beachy 2010).

---

* Since that sentence has been often misunderstood, I need to make clear that it was never my intention to suggest that Rudy Wiebe's fictions about Indigenous Peoples are acts of cultural appropriation. They are cultural translations, rather, in the sense described by Homi Bhabha (2004, 226). In a recent email to me, Wiebe reminded me that "the Anabaptist martyr of the *Martyrs Mirror* dies because she/he witnesses to their faith by refusing to renounce what they hold as their religious commitment. Big Bear is more like the Jews who died under the Nazis. He cannot renounce his being Cree any more than the Jews could renounce being Jews. I wouldn't draw a parallel between him and the Anabaptists" (Wiebe 2017; quoted by permission). Although this lucid distinction rightly names the colonial racism that caused Big Bear's death, I still see the man whom Wiebe recreated as dying for his belief in pacifism. Not all Cree people, after all, were non-resistant, and the title of the novel invites readers to remember the last "temptations" of Jesus Christ.

The connections between martyr myths and the writing of Mennonite literary history are complex and have exposed the fault lines between the two major Mennonite ethnic groups—the Swiss Mennonites and the Dutch/Prussian/Russian Mennonites. Theology is supposed to trump this troublesome split, but it has resisted erasure despite a centuries-long joint effort to construct a transnational identity and despite the mutual assimilation of these groups into mainstream North American cultures (see Osborne 2014). In 1713, Pieter Langendijk, a popular Dutch poet and playwright, published a comic poem the lengthy title of which translates as follows: "Swiss Simplicity, Lamenting the Corrupt Manners of Many Dutch Mennonites, or Nonresistant Christians" (Visser 1994, 67). Almost three centuries later Jeff Gundy, an American Swiss Mennonite poet, echoed this reproach in his tongue-in-cheek response to Hildi Froese Tiessen's account of the many prizes and public successes of "Canadian Mennonite writers and artists": "Simply the tone of this litany of worldly accomplishment was enough to make this Swiss Mennonite boy hang my head when I first heard it" (2005, 50). Julia Spicher Kasdorf, also an American Swiss Mennonite poet, has written about her baffled response to Di Brandt's frequent expressions of terror that "Mennonites from her farm village [Reinland, Manitoba] would kill her if she published her first book of poetry" (2001, 180). Brandt's fear, Kasdorf concludes, "contains the truth of myth. Because she seized the authority of literature and persecuted her community by telling its secrets and exposing its shame, it must punish her in turn—as happened after Rudy Wiebe's first novel, as happened to the martyrs of old" (182). Gundy has dissociated himself forcefully from what he describes as "the Ur-myth of the modern Mennonite writer, the agonistic story of how the most visible and prominent cried out against communal repression and endured the costs" (2005, 25). He notes that this "seems a variation of the Mennonite martyr myth" (25). This "myth of origins," he concludes, "is not *my* story" (26).

In a 2015 essay, American folklorist Ervin Beck (also Swiss Mennonite) returns to this territory, lamenting the "dominant role of the 'transgressive myth of origins' in Mennonite literary discourse'" (66). Beck associates this myth with Robert Kroetsch's comments after the 1990 conference on Mennonite/s Writing in Canada. Kroetsch, there as an observer, concluded that "the writer—in this culture—is, as I listen, a transgressor" (Tiessen

and Hinchcliffe 1992, 238, quoted in Beck 2015, 53). Although Beck does
not quote Di Brandt, she echoed Kroetsch when she wrote that "the new
Mennonite writing exists as transgression, a violation of the authority of
God and the Bible and the father" (1996, 36). She made that comment in
relation to a particular moment when many Kanadier writers in Manitoba
were insisting on the right to call themselves secular Mennonites in the
sense of that adjective as defined by Homi Bhabha. According to this definition, "secular" writing is blasphemy because it violates "the asserted
authenticity or continuity of tradition" and is "a transgressive act of cultural
translation" (Bhabha 1994, 225).

When I wrote "Escape from the Bloody Theatre" (Redekop 1993b),
more than a decade before these debates began, I did not anticipate that the
martyr stories I was writing about would infect the writing of Mennonite
literary history. I still believe, as I did when I wrote that essay, that the
figure of Menno as a trickster offers an alternative to literary martyrdom.
Twenty years later, in a "Sunday Morning Confession" at a conference on
Mennonite writing, Julia Spicher Kasdorf echoed my hope. After acknowledging her role in the construction of a martyr myth, Kasdorf concluded by
wondering whether, "instead of writer as transgressor . . . a more sustainable Mennonite archetype might be the trickster" (Kasdorf 2013, 8). I will
be returning to the figure of the trickster in the next chapter with relation
to the aesthetic of play that informs my argument. My concern at this stage
is with how martyr myths tend to homogenize very different histories.

As a Kanadier, I experience the "transgressive myth" with relation to
the particular history of my group. I identify with other Kanadier writers
like Di Brandt, Patrick Friesen, Miriam Toews, and Armin Wiebe, all of
whom have raged creatively against an experience of fundamentalism that
is familiar to me. Quite a different variety of martyr myth is the focus in
Rewriting the Break Event: Mennonites and Migration in Canadian Literature,
in which Robert Zacharias (2013) considers an "originary myth" that has
been constructed by literary critics on the basis of the Russländer immigration narrative. The claims made for this myth, according to Zacharias,
go beyond the identification of it as one of the causes of the Mennonite
renaissance. According to some critics, the destruction of the Mennonite
Commonwealth in Russia in the 1920s was a "break event" that "transcended the particularities of its history" and "has come to function as

an originary myth for the community as a whole" (14). Zacharias cites as evidence Al Reimer's essay "Coming in out of the Cold," an account of a Kanadier who rejected his own different history as "'utterly devoid of drama or glamour.'" After a trip to Ukraine, Reimer "adopted the history of the 1920s collapse of the Commonwealth as his own on the logic that 'the tragic curve of Russian-Mennonite experience . . . is, after all, the tragic curve of all Mennonites'" (Reimer 1988, 257, 263; Zacharias 2013, 13). In his introduction, Zacharias writes that Reimer "might well be right" that this single story has "transcended the particularities of its history" (14). In the body of his book, however, Zacharias offers close readings of four novels that are rewritings of the "break event." The cumulative impact of these readings supports a point made by Edward Said, who noted that "ideas about origins, because of their passivity," are problematic (1975, 6). "Beginning and beginning-again are historical whereas origins are divine. . . . In short, beginning is *making* or *producing difference*" (xiii). Like Zacharias, I see a need for scholarship that will keep in mind "divergent national contexts," "differing socio-political histories, [and] divergent migration histories" (2013, 32). *Rewriting the Break Event* is a breakthrough book on one of the most influential Mennonite migration stories, and it has cleared the ground so that critics can move on to explore those wider "divergent" contexts.

My intention in "Escape from the Bloody Theatre" (Redekop 1993b) was to question how martyr myths erase the differences between immigrant groups, not to argue for a myth that transcends those differences. I still believe that the friction *between* the Kanadier and the Russländer immigrants in Manitoba is in part why the renaissance began among Russian Mennonites. This is more likely because the two groups do not share a myth than because they do. David Perkins observes in *Is Literary History Possible?* that "the discipline of literary history, as it was practiced in the nineteenth century, could not narrate its own history without locating an origin" (1992, 1). Not all efforts to write literary history fall into the temptation to write a *Geistesgeschichte* (literally a story of the spirit). The premature writing of Mennonite literary history, however, has been infected with this nineteenth-century habit of thought because the genre that goes with the Russländer myths, tragic nationalist narrative, can be used to support that kind of literary history. As Zacharias shows in his readings of particular novels, all of them resist that master narrative, even Al Reimer's *My Harp Is Turned to Mourning*. I cannot speak for any other Kanadier, but I do not share Reimer's sense that the Russländer story has become my own myth. Exotic they are, those Russländer, and I continue to have deep admiration and respect for their remarkable endurance. Reader, I married one. That story became a part of my identity when I joined the Redekop family, but this was something forged through a living dialogue with my late husband and not the result of a belief in a shared myth.

Keeping an Eye out for Roots! "Know Where Your Feet Are!"

As a literary critic, I aim for distance from myths and generic structures. As the first person in my own story, however, I am repeatedly brought back to "the squirming facts" of my own life. There is no point, after all, in denying that to some extent I am bound to see the Mennonite renaissance in my own image. One way of making yourself aware of inevitable bias is to imagine yourself as seeing with only one eye. This is suggested by the title of Julian Barnes's book *Keeping an Eye Open: Essays on Art* (2015) and by the photograph that accompanies Patrick Friesen's contribution to *Why I Am a Mennonite* (1988). It pictures Friesen with one hand held over one eye. I look at the renaissance that way, with one eye closed, and imagine myself walking back into the woods of Frost's "Directive" (1963). Since I am elderly now, I am concerned with preventing falls. While on the lookout for root causes of the Mennonite renaissance, I also follow my doctor's advice: "Know where your feet are!" The roots are often gnarly on the surface of the earth, where "the squirming facts" can trip you up when they exceed "the squamous mind."

From where I am in time, I can orient myself by pointing to root causes that have been identified by other people. Even with one eye closed, I can see that Harry Loewen, Al Reimer, Hildi Froese Tiessen, and Robert Zacharias were right to identify the Russländer story as one of the causes of the renaissance in Manitoba. When I see how that root intertwines with the roots of the Kanadier story, however, I am also convinced that I am right to insist that the differences between those stories form a double root. On the surface are the facts and numbers that make this major root system visible, the primary one being the concentration of Mennonites from both groups in Manitoba. Another important root is one previously identified by Hildi Froese Tiessen (2000), namely the influence of postmodernism on the writers who emerged in Manitoba during the 1980s. Like Tiessen, I have taken some time to engage with visual art by Mennonites, and in the last chapter I will put a spotlight on that root.

My personal story, however, also leads me to give prominence to a root that I have not seen previously identified by literary critics as a cause of the renaissance, namely the revival movement of the late 1950s. I caution readers to watch out for this root in the chapters that lie ahead. It was while writing a chapter on music that it became most insistent. I found myself drawn back in time to a "children's house of make-believe" that was a house of horror—or, to be specific, a tent of horror. In 1957, when I was thirteen years old, a large tent was erected on a field not far from our farm. This was the setting for revival meetings conducted by George R. Brunk and his sons. Many have written about the terrifying sermons of Jonathan Edwards during the Great American Awakening, but the sermons were not what I remember as being the most frightening part of the Brunk campaign. More terrifying by far were the hypnotic refrains of the hymns used in altar calls to get people to move to the front to be saved. In "Charms and Riddles," Northrop Frye uses the example of medieval charms against rats. Words can "compel by the force of rhythm and sound alone, by getting the right words in the right order at the right speed, and so setting up a kind of movement that the thing being charmed will be forced to imitate" (1976, 124–25). Like the Pied Piper of Hamelin, these exotic American preachers were asked to come to our community to get rid of sinful rats. The children were the potential victims.

This is without question an "autobiographical exaggeration," but I note that others in my generation have constructed similar personal origin myths. Several essays in the 1988 collection *Why I Am a Mennonite* are by people who were teenagers in 1957. They write in different ways about the terror of that time. Most eloquent among these accounts is that of Patrick Friesen:

> Revival meetings were my blast furnaces. Here I learned to conceal emotions. I learned to play tough. I remember the choreography. The frightening sermon, the tear-jerking hymns, altar call, the men watching from the back of the church, or from the platform in front,

watching for signs of personal turmoil, watching, then moving
toward some troubled person, arm around his or her shoulder,
whispering into that torment, cajoling, pushing. . . . I think most
gave in out of fear. Some grew hard. Or, you became sly; skipping,
stumbling, lying, cursing, laughing toward a distant day of freedom.
Those voodoo evenings of spiritual violence. No matter what
choices were made, how many survived with their spirits full and
rejoicing? (1988, 100–101)

Whenever I read this description, I see it as a vivid picture of the beginnings of the Mennonite renaissance. What happened in the 1980s in Manitoba was, from my perspective, a belated recreation of the crisis of the
revival movement that happened there in the 1950s. Although I am conscious of going out on a limb with one eye closed, at least one scholar has
taken note of the revival movement as a possible explanation for the literary phenomenon. At the 1990 conference on Mennonite/s Writing in
Canada, David Arnason told a story about an earlier conference in Winnipeg during which, he said, James Urry "made a fascinating statement out
of the audience": "He spoke of the destruction—he called it 'the awful and
tragic destruction'—of the Kanadier community by the tent-revival movement in the 1950s, a movement that replaced the traditions of conservative Mennonitism with the fundamentalism of American Baptists and in a
sense destroyed a community. He said he was not surprised that a whole
batch of writing had come from the children of a generation who had had
their religious lives destroyed and overtaken and colonized by an *other* kind
of religious experience" (Arnason 1992, 214). When I reread that startling
passage in August 2019, I found myself wondering what James Urry might
have to say on the topic almost three decades later. When I emailed him, he
replied that he remembered making the comment and that the background
for it came from conversations he had with Mennonite academics, particularly David Schroeder, then a professor at Canadian Mennonite Bible College. Far from retracting his analysis, Urry sent me supporting evidence for
it, including a scanned copy of the pamphlet that was published in conjunction with the revival meetings, entitled *Revival Fires in Manitoba: The
Whole Gospel for the Whole World* (F. Epp 1957).

This brochure must have been in our house at the time, but I have no memory of it. I experienced a sort of pleasurable shock when I saw the fiery red cover, but it was the cool tone of the contents that was most disconcerting. That the brochure was edited by historian Frank H. Epp was a "squirming fact" that I could not easily fit into the "squamous" origin myth I had constructed. Frank Epp was a highly respected historian who lived in our hometown of Altona. During my adolescence he was an important influence because I heard him as a reliable voice of reason. That is the voice I heard when I began reading the brochure—a quiet voice calmly listing the reasons why revival was necessary. Central among these was a perceived imbalance between faith and "tradition." Too many people were of the opinion that "the mission of the church was cultural, rather than spiritual." Others were claiming that "the practices of the past were authority enough for the individual. . . . In all of the campaigns these falsehoods were exposed. The exposure struck deep into the heart of a formalistic and traditionalistic community life" (Epp, ed. 1957, n.p.). This is persuasive rhetoric, perhaps especially today when we are being confronted by evidence of calcification in Kanadier Mennonite communities in South America, the "ghost rapes" in Bolivia being only the most sensational example. It may be tempting to wonder if those Mennonites, stuck in their "traditional" ways, might not benefit from a revival campaign. However, although Epp lists the "fruits" of "ongoing revival" in positive terms, he leaves unasked any questions about whether the methods used to strike so deep might have had harmful side effects, particularly in the case of children, who are identified as targets of the campaign. I like to think that the Frank Epp I admired so much would, if he were alive today, agree with me that what those Mennonite children in Bolivia need is not revival. What they need is education.

I have heard many stories from Mennonites who lived through the 1950s revival movement and who remember the fear they felt. I find that usually it surfaces in the form of fragments that are etched in memory when all else is erased and I notice that people often remember precisely how old they were. James Urry told me about a friend of his who remembers being nine when he attended a tent meeting in Steinbach with his mother. The only detail that stayed with him was a single recurring phrase from a presentation for children: "and one little cheeldren stayed behind." His explanation for why he remembered those words was the odd grammatical error and the man's strange accent. Such hearsay evidence tends to be dismissed by historians, but ecclesiastical histories are profoundly inadequate when it comes to raising painful questions about religion. These kinds of sharp-edged fragments are well-known responses to trauma. They are also the stuff of poetry and fiction. If I were to make something out of this particular fragment, I would be tempted to construct a hybrid of the story of the Pied Piper and the parable of the lost sheep. Mixed in with those there would have to be a deep awareness that we are "not history knowing." I try and fail to imagine all the other children on that night, listening to the storyteller. I wonder if perhaps he was some hapless Low German–speaking farmer who, persuaded by the visiting evangelist to play his lowly part by telling the children's story, took it as his assignment to stir up fear. Perhaps he had a rebellious son who he feared was going to hell, some such motivation that made him blind to the faces of the children in front of him when he kept repeating: "And one little cheeldren stayed behind." As every mother knows, being left behind or abandoned is a common terror for children. Confronted by the enormity of the stories that will never be told, I celebrate the art created by the children who got away. They "became sly; skipping, stumbling, lying, cursing, laughing toward a distant day of freedom" (Friesen 1988, 101).

My account of the time is lopsided and short on facts, but some facts are worth noting with relation to the literary renaissance that will be my focus in Chapter 4. I do not think it a coincidence that poet Patrick Friesen and novelist Miriam Toews, major writers in Canada now, are both Kanadier Mennonites from Steinbach and that both grew up in the Kleingemeinde community. The repercussions of the revival meetings are dispersed and not unique to Kanadier churches, but my own observations support Urry's view that the evangelistic meetings were more traumatic for young people in conservative churches than for those in more liberal churches. I was surprised and envious, for example, when I read Hildi Froese Tiessen's account of how her father responded when the Brunk campaign came to Winnipeg. She asked him why he was not taking the family there, to which he replied: "Some preachers make it their business to scare people into heaven" (2019, 93). In contrast to Tiessen's memory, I now see that time through the filter of conflicts in my father's life. The church he helped found was called the Rudnerweider Kirchengemeinde, but after he was ousted from his leadership role it became the Evangelical Mennonite Mission Conference (EMMC)—a laboured renaming that marked a painful moment in our family history. The story is told by my sister in a chapter of her biography entitled: "'They Wanted Him Out': 1951–1955" (Neufeld 2008, 323–54). Since the Brunk meetings happened in the aftermath of these events, the hosting Ältester of the EMMC church was Jacob Friesen. Having always supported missionary endeavours, however, my father could not very well oppose efforts to evangelize in English. This left him with a dilemma, given his lifelong commitment to the preservation of Low German.

It is important to note that the visiting evangelists were not, as Arnason said, American Baptists. They were Swiss Mennonites. It was clearly Frank Epp's hope that the evangelists, as "outsiders," would purify the religious faith of Mennonites and eliminate ethnic contaminants. The fly in the ointment was the fact that the evangelists had a different ethnic identity despite being Mennonite. I try to imagine what mixed feelings they must have stirred in my father. In our family, Swiss Mennonites were perceived as the very model of true Mennonites—humble and devoted to plain living. This was a stereotype, of course, but no less powerful for that. In our church, my father was the only preacher who never wore a tie in an effort to avoid the sin of pride. He envied the Swiss Mennonite men their plain jackets with stand-up collars. Like the mother in Di Brandt's "shades of sin," my mother considered carefully before she ordered a hat from the Eaton's catalogue, worrying that the brim might be too wide (Brandt 1987, 9). The Swiss Mennonite women were enviable in their uniform humility, always wearing neat little white caps.

Since my father was no longer Ältester at the time, he was not acting in an official capacity when he invited the entire Brunk family to our farm house for *medach* (midday meal) one day. He was just extending hospitality. My sister Mary, who was seventeen at the time, remembers that we peeled quantities of potatoes. The only thing I remember clearly is a moment when the most handsome of the Brunk brothers pulled me onto his lap and admired my shoes. In 1957 all the girls my age were wearing navy saddle oxfords but my mother had ordered for me, from the Eaton's catalogue, a pair with red saddles. I was thirteen and I remember the guilty pleasure mixed with embarrassment when I saw how my legs dangled down almost to the floor. My father was notorious in the community for how fiercely he guarded his daughters. When local boys went in search of girls on Saturday nights, they did not dare turn onto the driveway leading to Bishop Falk's house. Why did he allow this egregious crossing of boundaries? I have puzzled over that question and wondered if perhaps he was not even in the room when it happened. Maybe he was in his little *schtäf-che,* or study, showing Reverend Brunk his collection of German books about Mennonites. Or perhaps it was just that he had his work cut out for him trying hard to speak a few words of English without embarrassment.

When I make an effort to look with both eyes open, I can see that there are larger historical contexts available and I urge readers to make use of those as a corrective to the distortions in my story. Earlier revivals among Mennonites, for example, had prepared some of the adults for the Brunk campaign and this may have been especially so for those in the Mennonite Brethren (MB) church, which was formed as the result of a revival movement in Russia. Perhaps the MB emphasis on pietism also offered a practical approach. One MB friend told me that getting saved at a revival meeting changed her life. After that she did not have to be reminded to wash the dishes. Another MB friend, who grew up in Ontario, told me that when the Brunk campaign came to Kitchener-Waterloo, he and his friends "treated it fairly lightly, and light-heartedly." I was taken aback by this comment and it made me wonder if perhaps the Swiss Mennonite presence in Ontario served to moderate collective response during the revival movement, as it did during the Second World War. After all, Swiss Mennonites have had a long history of dealing with the emotional excesses of American revivalism, going back to the Great Awakening in the eighteenth century. Each wave of intensified evangelical fervour resulted in pulling many out of the Mennonite church. Those who stayed and reframed their identity as Mennonites must surely have developed a collective resistance and a moderation that was unavailable to the newly arrived Russian Mennonites. Like my father, I believe that we have a lot to learn from Swiss Mennonites. I was grateful to Julia Spicher Kasdorf for pointing out to me that the revival meetings could also have been a cause of cultural renaissance in a positive sense because they encouraged individual identity. She made the cogent comment that you have to believe you have an individual voice in order to tell the story of how you were saved.

I can understand such positive interpretations on an intellectual level but at a deeper level I never seem to take them in. The words that best describe how I feel about those tent meetings now are the ones that Patrick Friesen used: "Those voodoo evenings of spiritual violence" (1988, 101). At least one therapist has expressed the view that what I experienced could be described as spiritual abuse. If that is the case, then it must be said that I was complicit in my own abuse. I sat willingly on that man's lap. And, after that, I sang happily when my mother insisted that my sisters and I perform for the Brunk family. One of my sisters tells me that the brothers joked that we should "go on the road" with them. When the Falk Sisters were invited to sing at a tent meeting, we chose a dramatic hymn based on the parable of the lost sheep: "There were ninety and nine that safely lay. . . ." Performing in front of that mass audience was a thrill, but was I gratified to see how many people responded to the altar call that night? Was I manipulating even as I was being manipulated? Once again, I draw a blank. My memory is unreliable, but what has endured over time is pride that I did not capitulate. I never walked down that aisle in my red saddle oxfords to be saved.

I will always be too conflicted to offer clarity on this subject, but I nevertheless insist on the crucial importance of this root. Like Urry, I believe it offers an explanation for why Kanadier writers took leadership in Manitoba during the 1980s. The tent revival meetings provoked a fierce swerve away from fundamentalism, and in my view this contributed to the creation of the "Mennonite miracle" two decades later. The lasting repercussions of revival movements are the subject of scholarly research, and this one invites more study. Fear of the Second Coming and the Last Judgement lent an eschatological edge to our adolescent lives, amplified by the Cold War. Belated ways of dealing with that gave the literature of the 1980s an edge. In the meantime, fundamentalist thinking has spread across the continent in toxic ways. These political developments have kept alive the counter-awakening that began in Manitoba and in the 1990s created an audience for novels such as *A Complicated Kindness* that confront the danger.

I have been stumbling over the surface of fragmentary memories, but there is one deeply buried root that I have come to see as supporting, more than any of the other roots, the notion of anachronic renaissance. This root helps to explain the kind of art that both "points backward to a remote ancestral origin" and "projects a future or an ideal" (Nagel and Wood 2010, 13). Oddly enough, given the depth of this root, my subconscious was alerted to it by an irritant on the surface: the multiplication of stories about Mennonite shunning in the mass media. Depending on your experience with stereotyping, these stories are a potential embarrassment among Mennonites. Shunning rituals are archaic and now extremely rare among Mennonites. The impact of these stories is amplified, however, within the culture of shame into which we have all been thrust by technology. I concluded that something about this constant irritation led to a eureka moment that I experienced during a night of insomnia in a hotel on Pembina Highway in Winnipeg. *Eureka* is an Ancient Greek word meaning "I have found it!" attributed to Archimedes, who made a major discovery when he stepped into a bathtub and saw the water level rise. Legend has it that he jumped out of the bathtub and ran naked through the streets of Syracuse shouting "Eureka!" I contented myself with stumbling around in the dark (in an effort not to wake my husband) in search of a scrap of paper and a pen. With my reading light as a guide, I wrote down the words that came to me. The next morning I found this question scrawled on the paper: "What would happen if we stopped looking for foundational narratives and instead took the act of shunning as our foundational gesture?"

When I returned to Toronto, I pondered this question and was struck by the historical resonance of the shunning gesture. Separation from "the world" was listed, after all, as a defining rule in the sixteenth-century Schleitheim Confession. Anabaptists were forced by persecution to scatter, but even if they had not been, economic realities would have made total separation impossible. It was a failed ideal from the start. What could be more charged for Mennonites than a gesture supporting this failed ideal for which our ancestors died? Contemporary shunning dramas are focused intensely on individual suffering, not surprising given the libertarian ethos of our time. The other aspect of the ancient root is still alive, however. Shunning the world to maintain a community is a gesture prerequisite to one version of that most potent of Mennonite idealizations, the Anabaptist vision of a community. Here, as in all areas of Mennonite studies, however, the historical roots intertwine with those of other religious groups. Shunning did not start during the Reformation. To keep his claustrophobic ideal republic in existence, Plato had to shun the troublesome poets. How does the ancient history of radical Anabaptism relate to the art being made now? That is a question that I have kept in mind as I engage closely with particular works of art. Doing so has persuaded me that the art by Mennonites now resonates with something anarchic that is a legacy of Anabaptism. Perhaps, if we could stop making up origin myths about martyrdom, we would be better able to see the evidence of growth nourished by the brook that runs near "the children's house of make-believe."

Listening for Mennonite Accents

As I come to the end of my introductory exploration of historical contexts, I am confronted with an overarching question that hovers over this book. It is the same as the one that Priscilla Reimer asked while curating an exhibition of visual art by Mennonites in Winnipeg in 1990: "Does art by Mennonites leave traces of what might be considered a Mennonite sensibility?" (6). My answer to that question is yes. From a comparative study of the film *Stellet Licht* and the novel *Irma Voth*, for example, I learned that doing justice to both works involved awareness of what happens when a Mexican Catholic sensibility interacts with a Canadian Mennonite sensibility. I am not saying that it is possible to put forward core beliefs that have caused a flowering of art by Mennonites. It would be presumptuous of me to suggest, for example, that the art about which I write in this book is made by artists all nourished by the pudding that I have described as my Anabaptist vision. Yet I did not concoct that pudding on my own. It is the product of centuries of dialogue by my Mennonite ancestors—a contested vision that is the result of a long tradition of dissent. I can no more disown my part in constructing the collective ideals that are part of an Anabaptist vision than I can fly to the moon.

In the case studies in this book, I show how a Mennonite sensibility is sometimes apparent as a part of cross-cultural dialogue. The back-and-forth rhythm, between the close-up and the panoptic, is the result of my constant effort to pay attention to the contexts of any particular work of art. I was therefore startled to read, in an essay by Hildi Froese Tiessen, that Brian T. Edwards has urged critics to abandon the notion that works of art are "in deep conversation with their historical contexts and the social worlds or publics they engage" (Edwards 2013, 232, quoted in Tiessen 2015, 210). The question for me is not whether or not that "deep conversation" with history exists but what form it takes and whether or not critics are listening in such a way that they can hear it. Tiessen points to a useful response to this dilemma when she refers to the fluidity of contexts and cites Wai Chee Dimock's essay "A Theory of Resonance" (1997). In her brilliant and influential essay, Dimock puts resonance forward as a "primarily aural and primarily interactive concept" "modeled on the traveling frequencies of sound" (1061). Works of art resonate in varying ways as part of a process that Dimock (whose theory is grounded in the writing of Mikhail Bakhtin) sees as happening in social contexts. A text is not insulated from change, and "every language resembles an echo chamber, the tones and accents of former users interacting with those of subsequent ones" (1062).

Tiessen reframes old questions by asking what if questions: "If the new 'Mennonite' literary text were to prove to be, simply, utterly *everyone's* text—the normative 'universal' text—what might remain to allow the Mennonite reader to say that *this text is particular*; in fact, it 'identifies me to myself?'" (2012, 14). To define what we are left with when a text does not identify us to ourselves, Tiessen adapts the term "trace," quoting Kroetsch's answer to the question "what remains of what does not remain?" (Kroetsch 2001, 8, quoted in Tiessen 2012, 14). Tiessen's question echoes the one asked by James Clifford in *The Predicament of Culture: Twentieth-Century Ethnography, Literature, and Art*: "Who has the authority to speak for a group's identity or authenticity?" (1988, 8). It is unhelpful, he observes, to "see the world as populated by endangered authenticities" and more useful to study how a particular text or a particular painting makes "a space for specific paths through modernity" (9). When it comes to "ethnic literature," the critical response, sadly, is still often to try to fix or pin down the identity of a writer. The 2012 special issue of *Rhubarb* about Manitoba Mennonite Writing contains responses from various novelists and poets to this persistent pressure. Novelist David Elias makes the telling observation that "there are times (at book clubs, conferences, readings) when I've felt as though Id [*sic*] been 'collected.'" He speculates that perhaps he is part of a species, *"Mennonitus Authorica Secularum"* (2012, 8). Such a response should act as an important corrective to the temptation to pester artists about whether they are or are not Mennonite.

To ask the artist such questions is a very different thing from questioning a work of art and listening to it, which is what I will do in this book. The "trace" that Tiessen is listening for is what I would call the trace of a Mennonite aesthetic accent. I note that Priscilla Reimer also refers to "traces" of a Mennonite sensibility (1990, 6). I have found it helpful to listen *for* Mennonite aesthetic accents. I do so not to confirm an "aestheticized understanding of ethnic difference" (Zacharias 2013, 43) but for the opposite reason. Listening for accents as part of dialogue undermines the forces that seek to fix some version of ethnic identity. Accents of one culture can never be separated from those of other cultures. In each case study, I will listen and look for Mennonite accents within a larger process of cultural poiesis. I have found some evidence that others are listening for Mennonite accents and that comparative discussion of them would be useful. Elias, for example, follows his comment about *Mennonitus Authorica Secularum* with this gloss: "*Individual members display a wide variety of calls that often rise in pitch near the end, as though asking a question*" (2012, 8).

The most compelling argument that I have read in support of listening for Mennonite accents is an essay by Jesse Nathan entitled "Question, Answer." Nathan shows that persistent questioning is a recurring feature of art by Mennonites, and he explores this by means of a close reading of the poetry of Jean Janzen. "Secrecy of meaning," he suggests, "is planted within the openness of simplicity and plainspoken diction," and goes on to conclude: "If there is a Mennonite *inflection* or *accent* to their handling, it is in the way that these poets rewrite the answers and transfigure the inherited forms. They keep asking questions. There is no closure, and there is the embrace of this lack of closure" (2015, 188, 190). Nathan's argument invites wider transnational applications beyond the scope of this book. I hear the kind of dialogue that he describes as coming from the deepest roots of the anarchic dissenting tradition that is the Mennonite legacy. This question-and-answer rhythm, this invoking of the conventions in order to challenge them, this cracking open of old answers to ask new questions and begin again—these are the parts of my tradition that I continue to honour.

Aesthetic accents are not static, like themes. They come alive only when they are heard or seen and shared in dialogue across borders. Elias asks if it is possible "for one piece of writing to be more Mennonite than another" and adds that this would mean that one Mennonite can *be* more Mennonite than another (2012, 8). I would substitute for the word *be* the words *sound* and *look*. It is possible, in my view, yes, for one work to sound or look more Mennonite than another. It is even possible for art by non-Mennonite writers to sound or look Mennonite, as I will show in relation to Glenn Gould in Chapter 2. Aesthetic accents can sometimes be noticed in art when a linguistic accent draws attention to itself. A mixed-media example of such a mingling of aesthetic and linguistic accents can be observed if you follow the fate of the Manitoba Mennonite accent of the people interviewed by Gould for his radio program *The Quiet in the Land*.

Although languages do not stay inside the neat lines of a map, different aesthetic accents are as locally based as our everyday ways of talking, and this is further complicated by national borders. The Canada goose might not change how it honks when it flies across the forty-ninth parallel, but aesthetic languages are another story. Having taught American literature for many years, I myself am deeply influenced by American poetry. In my approach to Mennonite culture, furthermore, I am indebted to the poetry and criticism of American writers, including Ervin Beck, Jeff Gundy, Ann Hostetler, and Julia Spicher Kasdorf. I am also aware, however, of how different histories inform literature in multiple ways. Since Americans are notoriously ignorant about Canada, it is usually easier to point to what our history does not have—a civil war, for example. Having done comparative study of British, German, and American Romanticism, I also have a heightened awareness of the fact that Canadian literature has had no period of Transcendentalism—the American version of Romanticism. If close comparative studies were done between American and Canadian Mennonite literatures, they would reveal aesthetic differences that reflect such historical differences. I note, for example, that the kind of nostalgia that Royden Loewen (2015) finds in the fiction of Dallas Wiebe, an American novelist, is nowhere to be found in the fiction of Rudy Wiebe, despite the fact that the two novelists are from the same subgroup of Mennonites. The influence of Transcendentalism on Dallas Wiebe is as important as the influence on Rudy Wiebe of Canadian government policies on multiculturalism. There is no doubt that the deepest shared Anabaptist roots result in strong affinities in the literatures of the two countries. At various points, I will suggest directions for possible comparative study, but for the most part American Mennonite literature is outside the scope of this book.

On the Use of Case Studies

My central argument, as I began by saying, is that the Mennonite renaissance consists of repeated confrontations with a crisis of representation that has roots going back to the sixteenth century. I make this argument by means of close engagements with individual works of art because doing so makes possible a dialogue deeper and more productive than what is now evident in public discourse. Since my case studies are few and highly selective, readers will wonder why I have chosen these particular works of art for close attention. To some extent, I have chosen works that make my points for me, as I did when I chose a painting by Wanda Koop to dramatize the central argument of this book. There are not always such clear reasons, however, for my choices in this book. In some ways, it feels as if particular works of art have chosen me, but to say that sounds like an evasion. I must also concede that we literary critics are notoriously squeamish about evaluation. There is in this book almost no mention of the various awards won by different artists. I learned from Northrop Frye that, when evaluation is done hastily, it can become an exercise in debunking: "It is often said that choosing one poet to talk about rather than another implies a value judgment; this is true and indicates where value judgments belong: in the area of tentative working assumptions, where they can be subject to revision" (1982, xvi). I cannot resist pointing out that my track record in this regard is not bad. I chose to write my doctoral dissertation about an almost unknown writer, James Hogg, now the subject of international study. When I began writing my book on Alice Munro, I had no idea that Hogg was her ancestor, and I confess that I am still puzzled about that strange coincidence. I do not pretend to understand all my own choices, and I am not suggesting that awards have no value at all. My husband claims that, on the morning that it was announced that Alice Munro won the Nobel Prize for Literature, my shriek was loud enough to be heard in Clinton, Ontario.

I also confess to feeling Mennonite pride when David Bergen won the coveted Giller Award for *The Time in Between* (2005). An entire book could be written about Bergen's highly crafted plain style, and his sensibility, in my view, is definably Mennonite. Indeed, now that I think of it, I cannot understand at the moment why I did not write a chapter on *The Time in Between*, since it embodies much of what I have just written about time warp and representation. I cannot emphasize strongly enough that readers should keep in mind that my choices are personal and that the texts I spend time discussing should not be considered as in some way representative.

The Low German rhymes that appear at the start of each chapter are a special kind of elliptical case study. A few of these were translated for me by Jay Macpherson, a poet known for her subtle use of rhyme. Her translations reflect her awareness of how the collective memory of oral culture will do almost anything to create a rhyme. This is evident in her response to a grammatical error in the rhyme at the beginning of this chapter: "Und wenn wir nicht mehr weiter kann." The correct end word would be *können* and Macpherson's translation draws attention to this error: "When we no more wander can." The resulting dissonance is at the same time a brief harmonizing of two languages as the English word can almost rhymes with the German *kann*. The final words complete the circular structure that is common to oral poetry: "Then we'll start where we began."

In "Charms and Riddles," Frye (1976) suggests that aphorisms are like kernels from which hybrid genres are created. I think of these sayings as seeds sprinkled in the furrows between chapters. I am aware, at the same time, that they are sites of conflict related to class differences about which Mennonites seldom speak. Some readers will take them as representing an authentic or *echt* Mennonite identity, which is not my intention. Others will assume that they are jokes intended as diversions, also not my intention. I spell them out, however awkwardly, in an effort to resist reduction to some transparent meaning. In relation to the debates now going on among translation theorists, my preference tends to be for "thick translation" (Appiah 2000). Although there have been concerted efforts to regularize the spelling of Low German, my decision on that matter is based on my hope that readers will be able to hear how the words actually sound to me. I have made some attempt at orthographic consistency, using two dictionaries in common use (see H. Rempel 1995; J. Thiessen 2003), but my spellings are phonetic approximations. The inevitable mistakes should be taken as a sign that the language is alive and constantly changing. Each saying has a rich microhistory. It is my hope that the white spaces around the words will invite participation from readers who might wish to translate them differently or list similar aphorisms from other cultures.

In those deep in-between places where art touches us, where the artists are going about their work, where trickster spirits are active, at these border crossings there are no Mennonites or Jews or Muslims or Buddhists. I don't think that any critic arrives at that deep place if she is not honest about where she comes from, but *Mennonite* is not an adjective modifying art. It is more like a floating place marker, so porous that it welcomes occupation. We are all part of many overlapping communities that make believe together.

PART I

REFRAMING OLD QUESTIONS

1

MAKING BELIEVE
SPARKS FLYING IN THE SPIELRAUM

Sposz mutt zenne.

Play there must be.

On Believing, Not Believing, and Making Believe

Mary Louise Pratt coined the influential term "contact zone" to describe a place "where cultures meet, clash, and grapple with each other" (1991, 34). When a group constructs a collective identity in that zone, a line is drawn between insiders and outsiders, but that line is always up for grabs. This is a contested space of potential violence but also a place for potentially positive social interaction. In *Sapiens: A Brief History of Humankind*, Yuval Noah Harari argues that the main reason for the survival of the human species is the ability to cooperate as a result of believing in things that do not exist (2011; 2014). The book has been dismissed as reductive by some scholars, but the positive public response to it has been global, suggesting that Harari struck a chord. A similar emphasis on the power of making believe appears in Kwame Anthony Appiah's *The Lies that Bind: Rethinking Identity, Creed, Country, Color, Class, Culture* (2018). As I write these words, it is by no means certain that our species will continue to survive. It follows from the arguments made by Harari and Appiah that, if we are to do so, then we must learn to imagine together in more cooperative ways. I begin with the presupposition that the art made in contact zones provides an opportunity to study collective acts of making believe and learn from them. In saying this I am going back to the lessons I learned from Northrop Frye's 1963 Massey Lectures, published as *The Educated Imagination.*

A major question to address is how the act of *making* art, which involves different materials and conventions, relates to the act of *making* believe, a more nebulous concept. My answer to that question develops out of the Low German proverb *Sposz mutt zenne.* Play there must be. In 1990, during his comments at the end of the first conference on Mennonite/s Writing in Canada, Robert Kroetsch said that he had observed anxieties about "the question of art as play" that seemed to "work against certain kinds of high seriousness" (Tiessen and Hinchcliffe 1992, 224). This tension remains within Mennonite culture, but the renaissance has happened because of how many Mennonites have been willing to play and be serious at the same time. Unlike the "high seriousness" of English theory and High German theology, the culture of Low German is intensely playful. Although play can be and is used for sinister purposes, it is a potentially liberating and humanizing force at the heart of culture.

Where the act of making and the act of believing come together is where I locate the concept of cultural poiesis. My use of the word goes back to the definitions adopted by both Plato and Aristotle that name poiesis as "any activity of making, as opposed to *theoria* (observing, theorizing) or *praxis* (acting, doing)" (Eldridge 1996, 7). As Richard Eldridge observes, "engaging in the activity of *poiesis* . . . is arguably central to the life of any human subject" (7). I would add that it is also central to how human subjects relate to each other. The questions laid out so clearly by Harari and Appiah are important for any person who sets out to make art. My reframing of the concept of belief here, however, is done in the hope of shedding light on the renaissance of art among Mennonites. My aim throughout this book is to show how art provides an alternative to the often circular and futile debates among scholars and in public discourse. I share the view expressed by Barbara Kingsolver (quoted in Neary 2009) that "the most interesting parts of human experience might be the sparks that come from that sort of chipping flint of cultures rubbing against each other." The flowering of

Mennonite art has happened not because of the imposition of a static set of beliefs or values and not because of a shared master narrative, but rather because of the dynamic forces liberated by artists daring to walk among the sparks. Mennonites are not set apart from other groups when they participate in cultural poiesis in contact zones. The so-called Mennonite miracle, in a sense, is not even Mennonite. It is rather the result of Mennonites interacting with other groups and individuals and with each other in the contact zone. As I have tried to show, however, Mennonites bring into this zone a particular history that results in confrontation with an acute form of the crisis of representation. A central achievement of the artists active in Manitoba during the 1980s was the creation of the category "secular Mennonite." It would be foolish to conclude, however, that acts of making believe within Mennonite culture can therefore be separated from questions about religious belief.

I envision the contact zone where sparks fly as secular in the sense that it is not bound by any set of religious beliefs, but in doing so I do not set aside the relationship between art and religious experience. "Religious trance is trance," as William James put it in *The Varieties of Religious Experience: A Study in Human Nature* (1916, 20). Although James noted the human tendency to intellectualize religious experience (458), his interest was in how belief works, not where it originates (19–20). A similar pragmatic emphasis is evident in the "Introduction" to the second volume of *The Norton Anthology of World Religions*. Series editor Jack Miles spells out the view that guided editorial decisions: "In common usage, religious and unreligious peoples are divided into 'believers' and 'unbelievers.' The editors have departed from this common usage, proceeding instead on the silent and admittedly modest premise that religion is as religion *does*" (Miles 2015, 7). After contemplating the questions posed in "stark and tragic terms" by so many of the religious texts, Miles concludes with an image of boys playing make believe and writes: "I confess that I experience a certain relief in thinking of play rather than explanation as quite plausibly the evolutionary taproot of religion" (49).

While reflecting on "what we do when we believe," Michel de Certeau similarly moves the discussion away from ideas about dogma to ideas about play (1985, 192–202). All of these writers are, in varying ways, following the example of Johan Huizinga, a Dutch historian who long ago observed, in his seminal book *Homo Ludens: A Study of the Play Element in Culture*, that "the distinction between belief and make believe breaks down" in the play of art (1970, 44). Since Huizinga is now seen as a founder of cultural history, I find it interesting to note that he was "a member of the Mennonite church until his death" (Van der Lem 1994, 210). Huizinga never identified as Mennonite in his writings, however, and he was not talking about ethnic identity when he expressed the view that the "quite simple question of what play really is . . . leads us deep into the problem of the nature and origin of religious concepts" (1970, 44).

By no means is *Spiel* or play an inherently benign concept. We know this intimately from living in what game designer Eric Zimmerman (2013) has termed a "ludic century." Theorists who write about play nonetheless return repeatedly to the possibility that play can be redemptive in some way. De Certeau argues that belief "makes openings; it 'permits' play within a system of defined sites. It 'authorizes' a playing-space (*Spielraum*) to be produced. . . . It makes habitable" (1985, 141). I have already invoked this playing space in the previous chapter in the form of the "children's house of make-believe" in Robert Frost's "Directive" (1963). With the interpolated High German word *Spielraum*, de Certeau points implicitly to how import-ant translation becomes when we play in this space in our pluralistic world. In Low German, the word would be *shpälrüm*, with *rüm* pronounced the way that Peter Sellers says it in *The Return of the Pink Panther* when Inspector Clouseau asks "Do you have a room?" De Certeau describes the "designated sites" of "making believe" as "makeshift" and as "made of fragments of world," and he sees our many "ways of making" as part of "the very ancient art of making do" (1985, 142).

If there is one quality that connects all the art that I engage with in this book, then it might be a vision of community accompanied by a confron-tation with the problems arising from the fact that any collective identity is achieved by means of exclusion of those who are not part of the group. This is the fly in the ointment. It is the trouble with *Gemeinschaft* (commu-nity) and with basing an aesthetic on it. That being the case, how then do we affirm and experience the joy of community in art without acting out an erasure of others? As a result of my study of how different artists deal with this dilemma, I have chosen to focus on the search for a "habitable" *Spielraum*—not a "true community" but one with porous boundaries. I see this as an alternative to a search for *Lebensraum* (living space or habitat), a word now primarily associated with Nazi Germany. The relation of German terms such as *Volk* and *Gemeinschaft* to Mennonite history is of a complexity far beyond the limits of this study. Even the brief history that I provided in the introduction, however, shows that these terms are related to the search for land, an organizing image for the histories of many groups. As is the case for many Christian groups, moreover, the facts of geography often blur into the metaphors of religious quest when Mennonite immigration stories are told. This tendency is reflected in the title of E.K. Francis's 1955 book *In Search of Utopia: The Mennonites of Manitoba*, echoed in the title of Samuel Steiner's 2015 book *In Search of Promised Lands: A Religious History of Mennonites in Ontario*.

Art authorizes a *Spielraum*, a playing space that makes possible the creation of communities that are interactive and open, multiple, and over-lapping. Different kinds of art do this in different ways, but all are defined sites where we make believe together. As Harari (2011) points out, there is an obvious advantage in our ability to hold shared beliefs about things, some-times large entities, and to act together "as if" they exist. *Sapiens* can band together in large numbers to achieve a common goal when they agree on a common myth or fiction. In *As If: Idealization and Ideals*, Appiah (2017) terms such collective beliefs "potent idealizations." Both scholars view these as potentially dangerous. It is one thing to delight in the ability to believe "as many as six impossible things before breakfast," as the queen does in *Through the Looking Glass* (Carroll 1960, 251). It is quite another for a group of *sapiens* to band together to agree on a Final Solution. Technology has compounded the problem. The temptation is to huddle inside digital bubbles of shared belief and call everything else fake news. The tendency is now so rampant that there is widespread consensus that questions about belief are urgent, which may account for the appeal of Harari's book, which has been translated and published in over forty countries.

My thinking on these matters has changed over the years. During my time as an undergraduate, I read Eric Hoffer's influential book *The True Believer: Thoughts on the Nature of Mass Movements* (1951). The after-effects of the 1957 tent revival campaign had left me with a horror of being at the mercy of fanatics and Hoffer's critique of "true believers" offered resistance to fundamentalist thinking. Sadly, it has turned out to be ineffectual against the delusional thinking that is now rampant on the continent. Motivated by his fear of communism, Hoffer championed a version of the libertarian-ism that now occupies the toxic heart of the American dream of individual liberty. Although many of Hoffer's insights remain useful, I found more enduring ways of resisting fundamentalism in the literary texts I was study-ing. I was still working through those questions when I wrote my doctoral dissertation on James Hogg, the author of a novel about fanaticism entitled *The Private Memoirs and Confessions of a Justified Sinner* (1824).

I remember learning about arguments for and against the existence of God when I was an undergraduate and feeling that they had nothing to do with me. I was already too deeply immersed in imaginary worlds. By contrast, my cousin John Schellenberg (who grew up in Altona) was drawn to philosophy and is widely known for the argument in support of atheism that he made in his first book, *Divine Hiddenness and Human Reason* (1993). According to the logic of that book, I am an atheist. I think of myself as having rejected Deism, which is not quite the same thing. I suppose some would call me agnostic, but I prefer the simple term open-minded. What matters most to me is the emphasis I hear in the title of another of Schellenberg's books: *The Will to Imagine: A Justification of Skeptical Religion* (2009). I value the freedom to be skeptical, to persist in asking questions—something that was discouraged in our community when my cousin and I were growing up.

Questioning is affirmed by the title of Paul Veyne's book: *Did the Greeks Believe in Their Myths? An Essay on the Constitutive Imagination* (1988). That title reflects my preferred focus, which is on a consideration and testing of the powers and limits of the human imagination. In *Sapiens,* Harari writes about the astonishing power of myth without following through to an awareness of the process that Northrop Frye wrote about in *The Educated Imagination* (1963). To say that believing is about imagining is to begin by acknowledging that human beings like to play. It is in the play of art that there appears a wealth of opportunity not only to exercise and educate the imagination but also to strengthen resistance to dangerous fanaticisms. Sad to say, Northrop Frye has had very little impact on curriculum, even in Canada. Courses in world religions should be required in public schools, since ignorance of this subject is obviously dangerous. In January 2015, a terrorist attack in Paris happened as a result of the publication of a hostile cartoon drawing of Muhammad. A single line drawing made visible how the powers of the imagination are hemmed in and dialogue made impossible by conflicts over belief that result from the crisis of representation that we all confront every day. The Paris events also illustrate what W.J.T. Mitchell refers to as "the first law of iconoclasm," "that the idolater is always someone else." Added to this law is "the law of 'secondary belief,' or beliefs about the beliefs of other people," which "depends upon stereotype and caricature" (2005, 19–20). The events in Paris and the coverage of them show how poorly we are equipped to deal with questions about representation and belief.

Hildi Froese Tiessen has asked two questions that bring these questions into focus with relation to identity: "Can you call yourself a Mennonite if you are not a believer? Is a novel about a Mennonite community, composed by a Mennonite unbeliever, a Mennonite novel?" (2004, 244). Her tone is calm because she is asking the questions as a scholar. The same questions, when asked in an evangelical contact zone, stir strong feelings—and not only among Mennonites. I once watched an African American man interviewed on television about religion. He told the interviewer that he had found it harder to tell his parents that he was an atheist than that he was gay. The resistance to fundamentalism that I defined in the previous chapter as a root cause of the Mennonite renaissance is felt across the continent. What, then, is the answer to the question "Can you call yourself a Mennonite if you are not a believer?" Just how loaded that question remains for some Mennonites was brought home to me at a conference on Mennonites and music. While giving a paper on poetry, I observed, almost as an aside, that I am not a believer. During the break, one musician told me in hushed tones how she admired my courage. She described herself as an atheist and said that, while performing in Mennonite settings, she was pained by her own hypocrisy. I tried to reassure her and qualified my statement by saying that I am not so much an atheist as an anti-Deist, which means that I do not believe in the God up in the sky that William Blake called a Nobodaddy (1979, 183). We lacked the common vocabulary of a shared discipline.

At that conference, I heard composer Stephanie Martin give a lecture during which she came up with a helpful analogy. "You don't have to believe in Santa Claus," she said, "to get the gifts." The ease with which any particular person can accept that analogy, however, depends on the context. In response to my comment about not being a believer, for example, another musician asked me if I would be so bold about saying such things if my parents were still alive. The answer to that question, in my case, is almost certainly no. Both my parents died in the late 1970s. When I wrote "Through the Mennonite Looking Glass" (1988), I was dealing with grief, but also, sad as it is to say this, liberated to speak my mind more freely. Every one of us comes to such questions with different life experiences and a different set of contingencies.

Did the Greeks believe in their myths? Ted Chamberlin repeats the question and sums up Veyne's answer to it: "Yes and no, he answers. 'Believe it and not'—rather than 'believe it or not'—is the challenge of every metaphor, of every myth, of every religion, of every community. When we forget that challenge, myth degenerates into ideology, religion into dogma, and communities into conflict" (2003, 34). The goal, as Chamberlin emphasizes, is not to achieve peace but to embrace contradiction (25). Hope lies not in any particular set of beliefs but in the shared *acts* of making believe that happen on the common ground that I envision as a *Spielraum*. E.H. Gombrich concluded *Art and Illusion* with the comment that "we may have made quite a good bargain when we exchanged the archaic magic of image making for the more subtle magic we call 'art.'" Separating art from a defined religious function, as he noted, means that it is no longer "hedged in by taboos." Gombrich admitted, however, that there were problems left over, namely the "devitalizing of the image" and the denial of magical thinking (1960, 115). George Steiner long ago commented that "the lapse from ceremony and ritual in much of public and private behaviour has left a vacuum. At the same time, there is a thirst for magical and 'transrational' forms" (1974, 93). What is taboo now is the subject of religious belief itself, and it comes just when virulent fundamentalisms threaten world peace.

In her introduction to a special issue of *Prairie Fire* on Canadian Mennonite writing published in the summer of 1990, Hildi Froese Tiessen wrote that, "if belief thrives in a world in which the code remains (at least to some degree) intact, and superstition consists of the disconnected elements of a once-coherent culture whose code has been lost, then many Mennonite writers . . . could be seen as occupying the discomforting gap between belief and superstition, between the coherence of an ethos where vision and purpose and faith sustain meaning and the fragmentation of a world where social and religious dogmas loom merely as abandoned monuments in a landscape of forgotten ceremonies" (1990, 10). What Tiessen described as the "discomforting gap between belief and superstition" is what I here designate as a place of making believe. To quote de Certeau once more, I choose to think of belief as something that "makes openings; it 'permits' play within a system of defined sites. It 'authorizes' a playing-space (*Spielraum*) to be produced. . . . It makes habitable" (1985, 141).

Mennonites and the Crisis of Representation

My focus is not on identity per se, whether religious or ethnic, but on how art reflects identity. I have therefore chosen for my primary theoretical context the capacious concept of representation. No key concept is without limitations, as Mitchell concedes, but representation "has the virtue of simultaneously linking the visual and verbal disciplines" (1994, 6). In relation to art by Mennonites, this offers, for example, ways to compare how versions of plain style work in literature, music, and visual art. In an article entitled "The Rhetoric of Plain Style in Mennonite Writing," E.F. Dyck put forward a bold claim: "The ethnicity that is called Mennonite is figured by a paradox called *plain style* . . . [that] reveals itself to be a topos which pretends it is the figureless figure of the truth" (1990, 36, 37). I take this bit of fancy prose as his way of insisting that plain style *is* a style. The problem, as Dyck shrewdly pointed out, is not plain style itself; "it is rather the insistence that the plain style is the right style, which is to say that it is not a style at all but a moral imperative" (41–42). The Reformation context of this problem is laid out by Thomas Luxon in relation to Puritan literalism. Luxon notes that "plain style was a homiletic credo" for Puritans (1995, ix). Dyck's essay, focused on the Mennonite version of this, shows that, when a critic within such a culture tries to look at art *as* art, he ends up exposing conflicts over belief. In ordinary discourse, the term "representation" is often used loosely as if it is unproblematic. The ironies that saturate memoirs, however, reveal the complexities of self-representation. They were explored by sociologist Erving Goffman in 1959 in a brilliant and seminal book entitled *The Presentation of Self in Everyday Life*. Goffman used the analogy of theatrical performance—not *representation* but *presentation*. He prefaced his study by noting that though "the stage presents things that are make believe . . . presumably life presents things that are real and sometimes not well rehearsed" (xi). Presumably. Today most scholars would question Goffman's use of the word *real*.

As Mitchell notes, "representation has been the foundational concept in aesthetics (the general theory of the arts) and semiotics (the general theory of signs)" since antiquity (1990, 11). Central to any study of ethnic representation, however, is awareness of the fact that "in the modern era (i.e., in the last three hundred years) [representation] has also become a crucial concept in political theory," as reflected in terms such as "'representational government'" (11). Mitchell extrapolates an "obvious question" from these multiple contexts. What is "the relationship between aesthetic or semiotic representation (things that 'stand for' other things) and political representation (persons who 'act for' other persons)"? (11). The vexed forms that question can take in the Canadian multicultural context were visible in 2017 as a result of the controversy that swirled around novelist Joseph Boyden, accused of having misrepresented himself as Indigenous. As it happened, Eden Robinson's *Son of a Trickster* was launched during the time of this controversy. When questioned about it by Marsha Lederman, Robinson gave an answer that implicitly recognized the distinction between the two different kinds of representation: "What I took away from it was that we really don't want a singular spokesperson for 600 different nations. That's what we don't want" (quoted in Lederman 2017). As Boyden himself conceded, he should not claim to be *representing* Indigenous people (in the sense of speaking for them in public) just because he is *representing* them (in the sense of writing about their lives). The controversy is one example among many of the complex issues raised about representation in the place where the aesthetic and the political intersect. Many commentators focus, as Lederman did during her interview with Robinson, on the problem of positive and negative stereotypes, failing to realize that representation *always* fails. As Stephen Greenblatt notes, representation has always been "built upon its own undoing" (1981, viii).

The word *crisis* comes from the Greek *krisis*, used by both Hippocrates and Galen to designate the turning point in an illness. The non-medical use of the word continues to convey the sense of a decisive moment after which things change, either for better or for worse. By definition, then, a problem never resolved is not a crisis. As I have already noted, however, a crisis is not inherent in events but a way of constructing a response to events. A more accurate word would be *malaise*, the one used by Charles Taylor for the title of his 1991 Massey Lectures: *The Malaise of Modernity*. Awareness of ambiguity has not prevented scholars, however, from reconstructing the crisis repeatedly and adapting the phrase "crisis of representation" in various contexts, as I am doing here (see, e.g., Ebert 1986; Quayson 2007). Anxieties about representation can be intensified for Mennonites because of the futility of a centuries-long attempt to resist new technology and because of "a paradox called *plain style*." Hans-Jürgen Goertz describes the situation now as "the crisis of the Mennonites": "The 'great refusal' of the Anabaptists and Mennonites was directed against the Christian-feudal order," but "a way of life patterned on gestures of resistance against a past age" led to an "anachronistic position" (1988, 3, 5). In my Introduction, I described the response of artists to this experience of time warp, amplified by the current crisis of representation, as anachronic renaissance.

Although heightened by technology, the ancient roots of this crisis are tangled up with the equally ancient roots of conflicts over religious belief. W.J.T. Mitchell refers to a "long tradition of discomfort" with the act of representation that precedes the Reformation (1990, 14). John Ruth cites Saint Augustine's agonized efforts to repudiate his love of music as part of this tradition and concludes that such an intense conflict "inheres in the basic dialectic of Western culture" and "can not be blamed on our Anabaptist heritage" (1978, 29–30). His point is supported by the writing of Alain Besançon (2000), who has traced the intellectual history of ambivalence about art back to the contradictions inherent in Platonic philosophy. Human beings are urged to look toward the divine, but at the same time representations of the divine are decreed to be foolish and even sacrilegious. Plato's banning of artists from his ideal republic is well known, but as Mitchell notes "some prohibitions or restrictions on representations have been practiced by every society that has produced them" (1990, 15).

How, then, is "the crisis of the Mennonites," about identity, related to the crisis of representation? Mennonite uneasiness about such questions cannot be separated from the history of how Mennonites have been represented by others, the subject of the next chapter. In 1594, Thomas Nashe caricatured Anabaptists in his picaresque novel *The Unfortunate Traveller: Or, The Life of Jack Wilton* (1594). Robert Weimann describes this as a time when "awareness of difference and the recognition of otherness" went hand in hand with "a heightened perception of a crisis in representation" (1996, 196). The difficult question to address, then, is how the Anabaptist vision of community relates, if indeed it does, to the art being produced by individual Mennonites now and how contemporary Mennonites who make art are dealing with the peculiar double pressure set up when "the crisis of the Mennonites" combines with the crisis of representation.

Mavis Reimer (1997) has suggested that some answers to these questions might be found if aesthetic choices are considered with relation to the Mennonite value of community. "A writer might be moulded by a community and its institutions into the person he or she has become," writes Reimer, "but, unlike the musicians, he does not produce his art within the discipline of the community" (118). Reimer points out that musical or dramatic performances present voice as an "embodied presence," that there is "an attachment of a producer to the message produced." Writing, in contrast, "is an event that can be radically split from the context of its production, split and circulated, its meanings taken up in new ways and recirculated." Reimer observes that "the fracture of sender from message can be terrifying" (120) and illustrates this by quoting Rudy Wiebe: "Anyone can pick it up [the book], read any line here or there, the worst or the best sentence, anything. . . . A thousand different people can take it home . . . and you can do nothing about what it creates in their mind. The book is there, you can change nothing" (Wiebe 1987, 8–9, quoted in Reimer 1997, 120–21).

There is no shortage of evidence from the writing of Mennonites to indicate that many share Reimer's suspicion "that it might be the very nature of writing itself, its susceptibility to being split from its context, that makes writing at once a challenge to the notion of a Mennonite community and a logical extension of Mennonite theology" (1997, 120). Early in his career, Patrick Friesen described publication as a "wrenching act," as "the biggest act of violence I've encountered," and compared it to taking your clothes off in public (Tiessen and Hinchcliffe 1991, 238). Reimer's essay raises more questions than it answers, and I will suggest in Chapter 5 that her distinction between writing and music needs to be qualified. Edward Said argues that "the transgressive element in music is its nomadic ability to attach itself to, and become a part of, social formations," changing its rhetoric in response to different occasions (1991, 70). Music is therefore a particular challenge for the scholar who seeks to study the relation of art to community, and musicians are certainly not exempt from the anxieties that Reimer describes so vividly. Her questions, however, are the ones that we need to start asking.

Tricksters, Fools, and Clowns: Alternatives to Martyr Myths

Sixteenth-century stories about how Menno Simons escaped martyrdom are arresting because they go against the grain of recorded Mennonite history. I have long been fascinated by the stories that accompany a collection of Dutch playing cards. These were recounted in 1868 by J.G. de Hoop Scheffer in *Doopsgezinde Bijdragen* (an annual publication of Mennonites in the Netherlands) in an essay entitled "Mennisten-Streken" or "Mennonite Tricks" (see Beck 1987, 68). I first learned about them from an essay by folklorist Ervin Beck. He introduces this Dutch tradition with stories about American Swiss Mennonite preachers, who, because of their plain coats with stand-up collars, are often mistaken for Catholic priests. There is a story about a preacher called J.C. Wenger speeding on the Ohio Turnpike: "And he got pulled over by a policeman and the policeman walked up to the window and said, 'Oh Father, I'm sorry to have stopped you.' And J.C. Wenger said, 'That's OK. You're forgiven,' and drove on" (83). Beck traces these modern Menno tricks to their origins in sixteenth-century oral culture. One central story about such a trick is attached to a card called *MennisteLeugen* or Mennonite Lies (Figure 1) and is told by Wenger himself, who claims that "we have pretty good evidence that it did happen": "Menno was riding on a stagecoach one time and instead of being in the coach he was riding up front, up high, with the driver. And the authorities dashed up on horses to arrest Menno if they could find him. And they said, 'Is Menno Simons in that coach?' And Menno turned around and yelled into the coach, 'Is Menno Simons in there?' And they said, 'No, he's not in here.' So Menno told the authorities, 'They say Menno's not in the coach.' So he lived to die in bed" (Beck 1987, 67–68).

In this incident the trickster appears to do nothing at all. De Hoop Scheffer, who provides additional examples, ties a sentence in knots as he tries to explain how this kind of lying works: "To say a truth and to withhold a truth, and then especially to say a half truth and appear that the truth has been told completely; to evade the answer on a question and yet give the person who asks the impression that nothing is lacking in the answer—that is what non-Mennonites label with the term 'Mennonite tricks'" (de Hoop Scheffer 1868, 28, quoted in Beck 1987, 91). As Beck puts it more simply, using a trope supplied by Erving Goffman, the Menno trickster simply observes the "opponent placing the wrong 'frame' on his experience" and

B. Doopsgezinde zegswijzen

B. Doopsgezinde zegswijzen

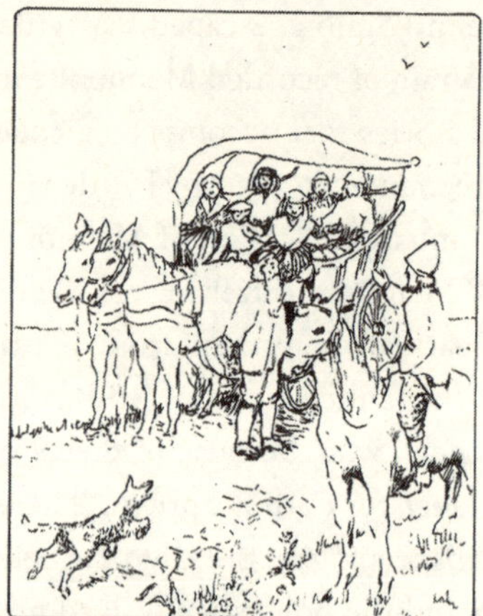

1. **Menniste leugen**
2. Menniste zoet
3. Menniste zusje
4. Menniste hemel

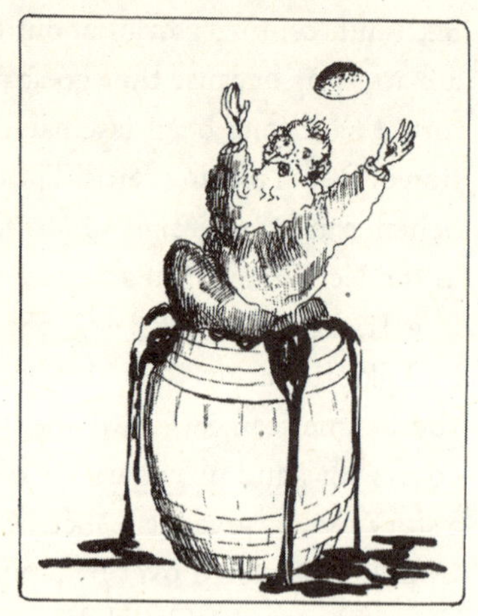

1. Menniste leugen
2. **Menniste zoet**
3. Menniste zusje
4. Menniste hemel

Figure 1. Mennisten-Streken: MennisteLeugen (Mennonite Tricks: Mennonite Lies).

Figure 2. Mennisten-Streken: MennisteZoet (Mennonite Tricks: Mennonite Sweetness).

Drawings by T. Schaap-Stuurman from *Doopsgezind-kwartetspel* (Mennonite Quartet Game) sixteenth-century card game printed by Firma J. Roggeband. Courtesy of the Landelijke Federatie van Doopsgezinde.

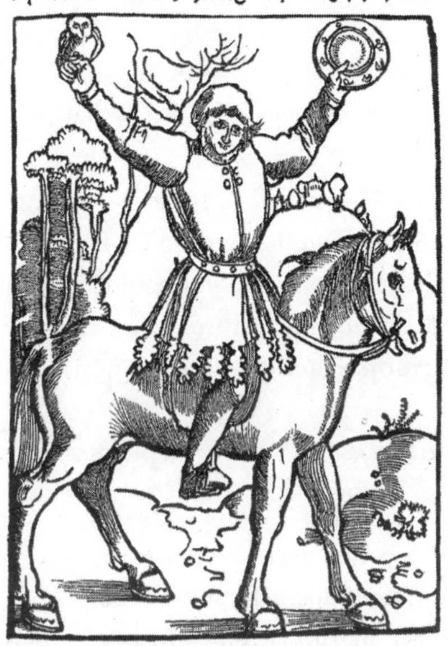

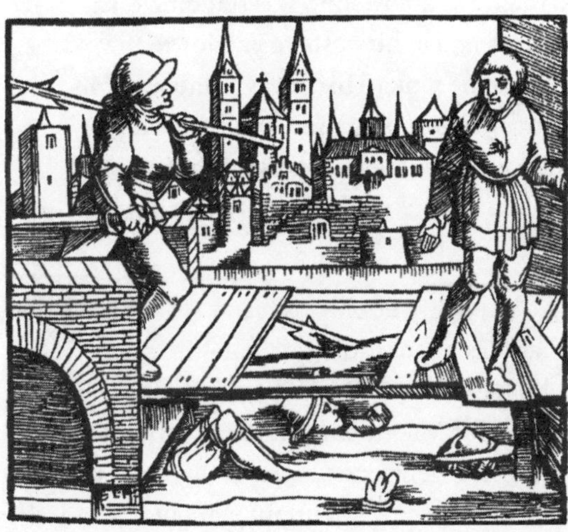

Figure 3. Till Eulenspiegel holding an owl and a mirror. Sixteenth-century woodcut. Source: https://en.wikipedia.org/wiki/Till_Eulenspiegel.

Figure 4. Till Eulenspiegel luring the watchmen of Nürnberg over a moat. Sixteenth-century woodcut. Historical image collection by Bildagentur-online, Alamy stock photo.

then "does not volunteer to correct it" (67). According to de Hoop Scheffer, Mennonites in the sixteenth century were perceived as tricksters "in the same way that 'pigheaded' was used to characterize Lutherans . . . [and] 'bigoted' was used for Calvinists" (de Hoop Scheffer 1868, 23 quoted in Beck 1987, 90). In defence of Mennonites, however, he notes that they were new to the idea of not swearing an oath. The goal was to obey Jesus and "let your communication be, Yea, yea; Nay, nay: for whatsoever is more than these cometh of evil" (Matthew 5:37). Dutch Mennonites hesitated to do this "since they could not honestly be certain that they could be faithful to their word." They opted for indirection and gestures interpreted by others as "sneaky equivocation" (de Hoop Scheffer 1868, 29, quoted in Beck 1987, 91).

Beck (1987, 70) retells the story that goes with a second playing card, *MennisteZoet* or Mennonite Sweetness (Figure 2):

> Menno was preaching in a barn. And as was the custom, the women
> sat in the center and the men around the outside to protect them. . . .
> And there was a shout outside that the sheriff had come to arrest
> him. So the men barred the way. And Menno was standing on a
> molasses barrel for his pulpit, and in his haste to get down, the
> end of the barrel caved in and he sank to his knees in molasses and
> would have laid a gooey track in escaping. And so all the women
> in the front row took one long lick of molasses off his hosen. And
> that explains why Mennonite children in Holland to this day have
> a sweet tooth.

Beck describes this story as "explicitly etiological" and sees this Menno both as a "foolish buffoon" and as a "quasi-divine figure near the creative origins of Mennonitism" who has given us the ability to survive (76–78). Far from being a saintly martyr, this Menno is a *picaro* or rogue and makes his escape with impunity. Beck's cogent conclusion is that "the trickster stories validate Mennonite culture—not Mennonite theology but the compromised *culture* that has emerged in applying ideal to reality" (94). Piet Visser notes that the current appeal in the United States of "bonnet rippers," a term for Amish romances, goes back to the Early Modern figure of the *het menniste susje,* a sweet Mennonite Sister who is prudish and often sanctimonious but easily seduced by a deceitful lover. As Visser points out, she is a literary relative of the seductive nuns in Boccaccios's *Decameron* (Visser 1994, 78).

These playful stereotypes show that scholars interested in Mennonite writing would do well to pay attention to the afterlives of Early Modern tricksters. Consider, for example, the trickster who is hidden inside the Low German word I have already mentioned: *ueleshpael*. In my family it was not only my mother but also my brother David who often played the part of *ueleshpael*, cleverly mocking various human failings, his own included. It never occurred to me to see his role as related to that of a Rabelaisian trickster called Till Eulenspiegel, whose pranks are recorded in a German chapbook published in 1515. The author of the chapbook has not been firmly identified but the legend has roots in Middle Low German folklore. The High German name *Eulenspiegel* means "owl mirror," and the character is often represented as holding an owl and a mirror (Figure 3). In Middle Low German, however, the name was read as a veiled pun and translated as "wipe-arse," which fits with the scatological humour in the text (Oppenheimer 1991, lxiii). Eulenspiegel acts like the fool in Shakespeare's plays. While he exposes his rear end, his words expose ordinary vices such as greed, pride, and hypocrisy, often by taking figurative language literally. The story ends with the death of Eulenspiegel as a result of the plague.

Of particular interest with relation to Mennonite tricksters is an 1867 adaptation of the story by the Belgian author Charles de Coster: *The Legend of the Glorious Adventures of Tyl Ulenspiegel in the Land of Flanders and Elsewhere*. In this version the Low German folk hero becomes a Flemish prankster moved forward in time from the medieval period to the Protestant Reformation. This text resonates with accounts of Anabaptists who escaped martyrdom. Indeed, I cannot help wondering if perhaps de Hoop Scheffer's 1868 essay about Mennonite tricks was influenced by de Coster's novel, which had been published in the preceding year. Intriguing also is the possibility that it influenced Richard Strauss in the composition of *Till Eulenspiegel's Lustige Streiche* (1894). Despite the seeming harmlessness of the "merry pranks" when translated into music, that tone poem ends with Eulenspiegel's execution for his misdeeds. Not everybody hears the death as a musical joke, but as the clarinet wails the death scream of Eulenspiegel and the pizzicato of strings mimics the sound of his neck snapping, I found myself thinking of the mock martyrdom of Sarah Binks, which will be my focus in a later chapter. Such shputting or mocking is considered blasphemous by many, but what if Jan Luyken was influenced by the legend of Eulenspiegel when he did the illustrations for the 1660 edition of the *Martyrs Mirror?* One woodcut illustration now brings to mind the popular Luyken etching of the martyrdom of Dirk Willems (Figure 9). Whereas Eulenspiegel leads his pursuers across a broken bridge and they fall into a moat (Figure 4), Willems rescues a pursuer who falls through ice. Is it possible that Luyken was superimposing an Anabaptist ideal onto an earlier trickster tale?

These tricksters come to life for me in the *Spielraum* that I imagine all art to be. A full account of their histories is beyond the limits of this study, but even these few details, have changed how I now look at pictures of Menno Simons. I was astonished the first time I looked at *MennisteZoet*, by the image of a helpless Menno, hands thrown up in the air. That was primarily because it contrasted so vividly with the way hands and eyes work together in the portrait of Menno Simons with which I am most familiar. It is an etching done by Arend Hendriks in 1948 (Visser and Sprunger 1996, 98) (Figure 5). A fascinating book entitled *Menno Simons: Places, Portraits, and Progeny* contains a collection of what the compilers, Piet Visser and Mary Sprunger, call "the many faces of Menno" (1996, 62–105). Daniel Horst, one of the many contributors to the volume, observes that "the portrayal of someone whose appearance is not known had been a centuries-long problem for artists" (Visser and Sprunger 1996, 65). In the earliest likeness of Menno, done forty-six years after his death in 1561, he appears with a crutch and Horst writes that "it was widely known that [Menno] walked with a limp" (62). He is also wearing what look like donkey ears (Figure 6). Over the years, in later portraits, the crutch has vanished and Menno is portrayed sitting with a Bible. "Menno was thus 'promoted' to the type-portrait of the learned which had come to flourish in the fifteenth century, with the portraits of Jerome and Erasmus acting as famous examples" (63). The final results are distilled into the Hendriks portrait that is now most familiar. Horst argues that "small variations" such as a physical disability are irrelevant because what is important is recognition: "Thus the image of Menno's head is engraved in our memory and we can say every time, without hesitation, 'yes, this is Menno Simons'" (Visser and Sprunger 1996, 63). Despite this certainty, Horst is clearly troubled by that first portrait. Could the donkey ears and the crutch have been intended by the Catholic Van Sichem, he wonders, as a "caricature of a foolish and spiritually crippled Menno"? He concludes that such a "fancied subtle derision is completely imagined" (62).

It is possible that Horst protests too much. When I put the images of Till Eulenspiegel alongside the ones of Menno on the Dutch playing cards, they tell me that the oral culture around both figures has more chance than the proper portraits of putting us in touch with what Northrop Frye referred to as "our real and repressed social past" (1980, 13). The fact that we have almost no idea what Menno Simons looked like goes to show once more how little "the past of historical record" has to do with the "great dreams of the arts" (Frye 1980, 13). I own a copy of *The Complete Writings of Menno Simons c. 1496–1561* (1956), and reading parts of this massive volume convinces me that Menno was a learned man who deserved to be represented with a book rather than with a crutch. In spite of that, I have found these trickster figures more helpful than any recorded history or theology when I try to account for the art made by Mennonites today. Those images and stories are like dreams that recur "to haunt us with a sense of how little we know of the real dimensions of our own experience" (Frye 1980, 13).

Ervin Beck raises the possibility that the trickster stories could be the basis of a Mennonite origin myth that would act as an alternative to the martyr myths that now dominate in Mennonite culture. Tricksters do figure in the origin myths of many cultures. My own sense, however, is that in the Mennonite context a focus on tricksters might help to counter the habit of looking for origin myths. Trickster stories have the power to subvert foundational narratives because, as Beck points out, "the classic trickster figure is so amorphous, so paradoxical as to render almost useless the single term—'trickster'—to cover all the behaviours" (1987, 87). This "amorphous" figure can play a vital role in multicultural societies, and in Canada it is Indigenous writers such as Tomson Highway who have shown how this can work. Identity politics has made authenticity a commodity, but it is not easy to brand a slippery trickster. Writers from different backgrounds play with trickster myths in different ways on a common ground, as Lewis Hyde shows in *Trickster Makes This World: Mischief, Myth, and Art* (1998). The name Menno might seem like a strange addition to any list of tricksters: Anansi, Coyote, Hermes, Mercury, Loki, Raven, Eshu, Eulenspiegel, Menno. The advantage of putting it there is that it shows art made by Mennonites as being in the same in-between places where trickster spirits are active. It

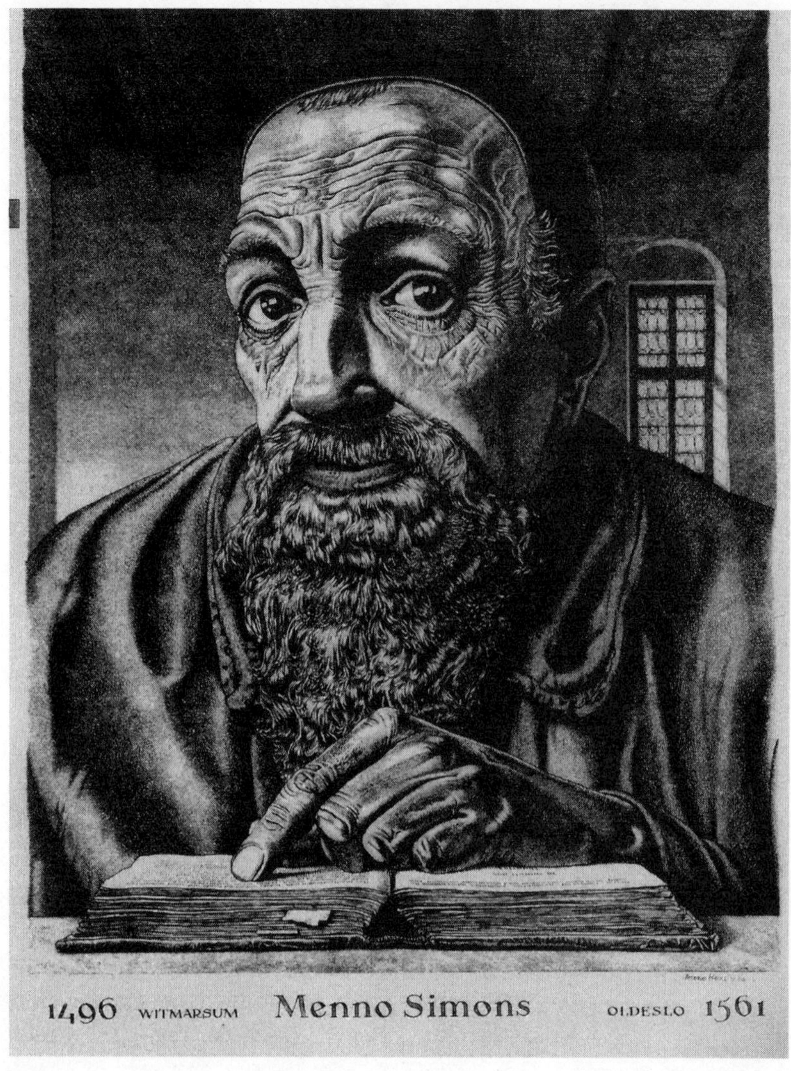

Figure 5. Arend Hendriks, *Menno Simons,* 1948. Etching. Commissioned by the Publicity Committee of the Dutch Mennonite Conference.

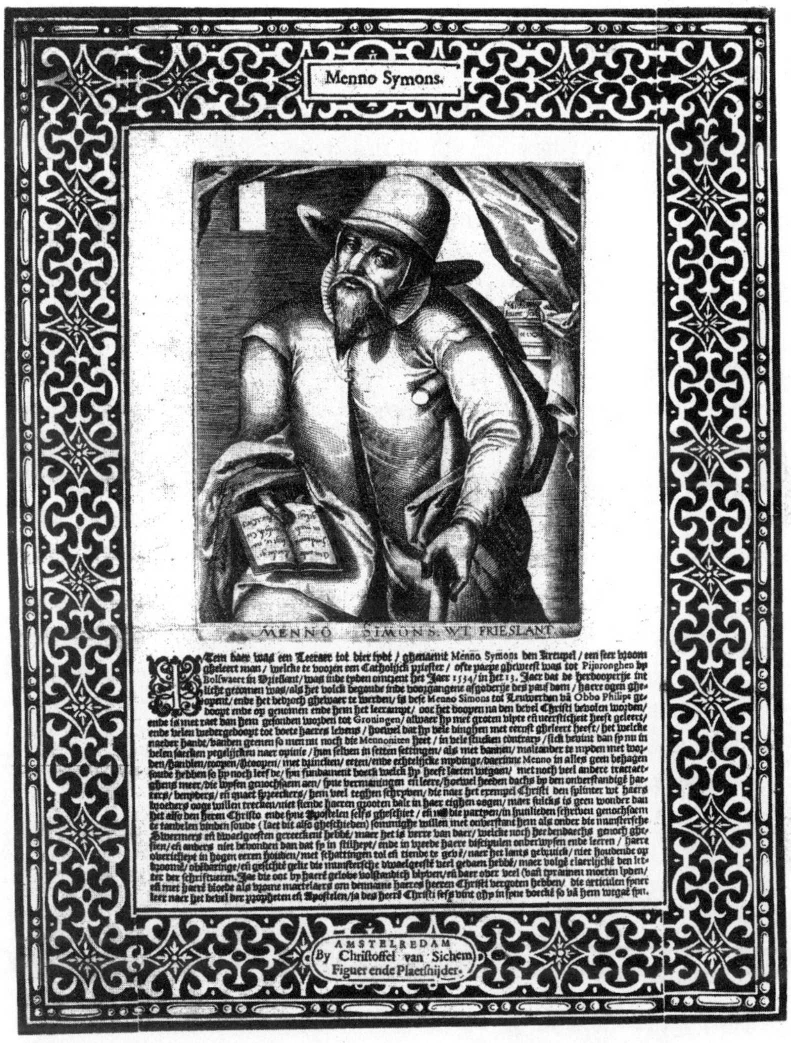

Figure 6. Christoffel Van Sichem, *Menno Simons*, c. 1607. Engraving. Reproduced in Visser and Sprunger, *Menno Simons: Places, Portraits and Progeny*, 62.

accepts that art affirms something deeper than anything that can be bounded by ethnic or religious identity.

The shape-shifting quality of the trickster makes it impossible for any one culture to own any of the images or stories. It is impossible to fix a story and make it static. The only option is dynamic dialogue between the representations. This cross-cultural reality already existed during the Reformation. The stereotype of sly liar might have stuck to Anabaptists more than to other groups, but all groups had their escape artists. Carlos Eire writes, for example, about the difficulties of John Calvin in dealing with a common response to persecution called Nicodemism: "Nicodemites were Protestants or sympathizers who pretended to be good Catholics to escape persecution, and who argued that their outward behaviour was not a sin or betrayal of their principles as long as their inner faith was pure" (2016, 303). This kind of dissembling takes its name from Nicodemus, a Pharisee who believed in Jesus but came to see him only at night (304; see John 3:1–9). Eire speculates that Calvin might have been particularly infuriated by Nicodemites because he himself had once practised a similar subterfuge. Whereas Calvin thought deeply about art and wrote about it, the name Menno is now ironically attached to a group that for centuries has polished its image in the mirror as an example of plain style and literalism.

I concede that my biographical exaggeration takes a lopsided view of Mennonite history. If your interest, however, is in the "real and repressed past" that is not part of recorded history, then the image of Menno the clowning trickster is a useful link between centuries. I hear the legacy of this figure in lines from a poem by Patrick Friesen entitled "song of the sly one":

> I am a monk
> who slipped his vows
> and never prayed
> look behind you
> look ahead
> I'm standing in your shade (1987, 11)

Such contemporary escape artistry resonates with sixteenth-century ways of dealing with the double crisis of representation and identity. The survival lies of the Anabaptists did play a small part, after all, in the major shift in attitudes to representation that happened during the Reformation. In *The*

Culture of the Copy, Hillel Schwartz observes that "modern lying has its roots in the sixteenth century," when "religious beliefs had often to be dissimulated under threat of persecution" (1996, 331). Lies told to avoid martyrdom led to "equivocations in defence of contradictory dogma" (332). Although the connection should not be oversimplified, there is a link from the world of my lying Anabaptist ancestors to the world about which Appiah writes in *The Lies that Bind* (2018). The amorphous nature of tricksters, how they morph into clowns and fools, makes them a challenge to work with for any critic. In my own critical practice, I have found it useful to focus on clowning, and it became part of an aesthetic of failure that I spelled out in *Mothers and Other Clowns* (1992a).

Representation and the Challenge of "Ethnic Dialogism"

As the contemporary global scene shows every day, conflicts often erupt in contact zones where people "undertake to describe themselves in ways that engage with representations others have made of them" (Pratt 1991, 35). W.J.T. Mitchell's inimitable phrase "no representation without taxation" gets to the heart of the ethical dilemma (1990, 21). When it comes to representations of Mennonites, the tax is most often paid by the Amish. They are an easy target because their customs make them conveniently visible, and they don't fight or talk back. In the United States, they are often appropriated to represent difference itself. "Weird Al" Yankovic's brilliant parody of Coolio's "Gangsta's Paradise" (1995), for example, concludes "We're all crazy Mennonites / Living in an Amish Paradise" (1996). Here in Toronto, Mennonites make up a tiny fraction of the population and are not the most visible among the many minority groups in the city. Mennonites are perceived to be out in the country somewhere, riding around on their horses and buggies. The menu in my favourite Middle Eastern restaurant advertises the use of "Mennonite-farmed chicken," and a furniture store calls itself Urban Amish. Recently I had lunch in a gastro-pub and found that the menu included "Mennonite smoked duck," an oddity that resulted in jokes about ways of walking and quacking. Tourism represents the lowest common denominator of public responses to such stereotypes. What are tourists getting when they purchase dolls without faces in a tourist shop in St. Jacobs, Ontario? Does the fear conveyed by those blank faces say anything at all about how those who are urban and assimilated think about art? All of these questions have to do with representation.

In *The Predicament of Culture*, James Clifford (1988) isolates the illusion of authenticity as the most pernicious feature of such ways of marketing products. If he is right and it is the illusion of purity being sold and bought, then this has a peculiar relevance to a group that has a troubled history of trying to maintain a pure church community. The title of the 2017 CBC drama series *Pure* seems to indicate awareness of that fact. In his review of *Pure*, John Doyle (2017) wrote that "Mennonites absent themselves from the trappings and sins of the contemporary world" but that recently "some Mexican Mennonites—many with connections to Canada—have become partners with the canny and brutal drug cartels in Mexico." Unlike the well-researched 1992 CBC *Fifth Estate* program on this subject, *Pure* is the product of conspicuously shoddy research. Indeed, this was so obvious from the visual rhetoric used to advertise it that there was exasperation among Mennonites online long before the first episode aired. The title of a satirical blog post by Sherri Klassen (2017) captured the feelings of many: "O What Fresh Hell Is This?" Historians Royden Loewen and Sam Steiner watched the series and wrote online postings in which they provided corrections to the numerous historical errors in *Pure*, the most egregious of which was confusion between Old Order (Swiss) and Old Colony (Dutch/German) Mennonites.

The production and reception of *Pure* illustrate Clifford's (1988) view that a yearning for "pure products" comes up repeatedly against the contamination of those products. When this happens, the sparks fly in between groups. I was grateful for the corrections made by historians, but I noticed that after the dust settled there were many questions left that have the potential to spark dialogue with other misrepresented groups. If you substitute for the difference between Old Order and Old Colony Mennonites the difference, for example, between the Kitamaat and the Kootenay, it instantly exposes our collective Canadian habit of ignoring the separate histories of Indigenous peoples. Even harder for Mennonites to concede, however, is that such misrepresentations are routine *within* Mennonite communities.

Historian Hans Werner penned an editorial in 2016 for *Preservings*, a Manitoba periodical for Mennonite historians, imploring his readers not to watch *Pure*. He called on "like-minded colleagues to join in this protest" against a series designed to "sensationalize the story of Old Colony

Mennonite participation in the drug trade" (3). Werner praised the Old Colony people for their radical Anabaptist stance of separation from the world. This very stance, however, Hans-Jürgen Goertz has identified as the "anachronistic stance" that underlies "the crisis of the Mennonites" (1988, 3). It is precisely this, our foundational gesture, that fascinates non-Mennonites, as evident in *Pure*. To a casting director, it must look as if the "people apart" are ready-made for theatre, already dressed in costume like those in the real/fake Mennonite village in Miriam Toews's *A Complicated Kindness* (2004). The responses of outsiders to those Mennonite groups who choose to live apart from the modern world tend to split. On the one hand, viewers express admiration for and envy of these visibly "good" people who live simple lives apart from modernity. On the other, the group is seen as self-righteous, and there is *Schadenfreude* (delight in another's misery) when it is exposed as less than pure.

The reception of *Pure* shows that many of the barriers to dialogue about ethnicity and art have to do with illusions about representation that are not peculiar to Mennonites. In an essay about ethnic representation in film, Robert Stam observes that blocks to cross-cultural dialogue appear if we begin with an assumption of naïve realism. Questions are then reduced to the level of "pointing to 'errors' and 'distortions,' as if the truth of an ethnic group were unproblematic, transparent, and easily accessible, and the lies about that group easily unmasked" (1991, 252). Such a dialogue quickly becomes trapped in a futile insistence on "one-to-one mimetic adequacy to sociological or historical truth" (256). As an alternative to this model, Stam invokes Mikhail Bakhtin, arguing that "ethnicity is relational . . . between subjects existing in relations of power" (259). It follows that the task of the critic is to nurture "ethnic dialogism" (258) by calling attention to "the voices at play in a text . . . not only those [voices] heard . . . but also those voices distorted or drowned out by the text" (256). It is a daunting critical task. What does it mean to listen for unheard voices? As Stam concedes, there is always the danger of claiming that there is an "authentic voice" that can be identified. Does listening for the unheard voices of Old Order Mennonites in *Pure* lead inevitably to speaking *for* them? Is it enough to fill in the blanks and provide the history left out? The response to these vexing questions is often split. Some opt for formalism and excuse all errors in the name of art and entertainment. Others reject the art completely. My suggestion, as I have argued in the Introduction, is to pay attention to resonance. The critic should slow down, take a step back from the binaries, and learn from the art by studying how different artists negotiate the challenges of "ethnic dialogism."

How might an ethnic artist in a pluralist society respond when images of ethnicity are evoked as part of an authenticity game? This aesthetic challenge is faced by the members of numerous groups in Canada, and there are as many ways of responding to blocking stereotypes as there are artists. The first response is often satire, as illustrated by Sherri Klassen's blog posts on *Pure*. Aesthetic responses change in countless ways, however, depending on innumerable variables, among the most important of which are choice of medium and genre. Poet Dionne Brand (not to be confused with poet Di Brandt) takes on the stereotype of Aunt Jemima and makes a new kind of music in her moving poem "Blues Spiritual for Mammy Prater" (Brand 2014, 59). Thomas King (1999) deals with stereotypes of Indigenous culture by showing how his narrators are at the mercy of tricksters. All these examples support Clifford's view that our goal should be an approach that "does not see the world as populated by endangered authenticities" and that identity, "considered ethnographically, must always be mixed, relational, and inventive." We are "always, to varying degrees, 'inauthentic': caught between cultures, implicated in others" (1988, 9, 11). The answer to the fear of a loss of authenticity is not to shore up the walls that define Mennonites as "a people apart." The answer is to participate in the "ethnic dialogism" provoked by the work of artists who do the opposite—who walk through those walls.

It is an illusion, of course, to think that anybody can walk through walls. I make this obvious point to underline the major difference between dialogue that happens in the space created by art and dialogue that happens in ordinary discourse. Artists know that it is an illusion. They create on a boundary like the one in Robert Frost's "Directive" (1963), in which there is no pretence that art is not a "house of make-believe." The suspension of disbelief can happen, albeit in a more circumscribed form, when academics get together to debate and one person decides to be "the devil's advocate." Huizinga's (1970) ideas about the relationship between agon (conflict) and the ludic (play) resonate in academic contexts, in which playful debating is the order of the day. In the present political climate, there is a heightened sensitivity, however, and I am often taken aback when disagreements that were once an accepted part of serious but playful critical debate are met with collective repression.

I did not foresee this political climate in 1990, at the first conference on Mennonite writing in Canada, when I expressed the hope that the mock abrasiveness of a game would protect us from "that most paralyzing of Mennonite problems—our preference for what Melville has called the 'inoffensiveness of all to all'" (Redekop 1992b, 101). As part of my paper somewhat bizarrely entitled "The Pickling of the Mennonite Madonna," I invited the audience to play Button, Button, Who's Got the Button? As I remember playing the game, a button is put into the hands of one child in a row of children. The child who is *it* has to guess who has the button. After guessing correctly, that child gets to choose the next one who will be *it*—and so it goes, round and round. I would now use the model of "ethnic dialogism," but at the time I invited my listeners to imagine the conference as a Mennonite "family quarrel" (102). In his comments at the end of that conference, Robert Kroetsch (having been invited to share his perspective as an outsider) indicated that my wish had been granted when he described the conference as a "rather ferocious family quarrel" (Tiessen and Hinchcliffe 1992, 223).

All our visions are partial, and "ethnic dialogism" is an ongoing process, but still there is common ground. What we share is the fear of being trapped in a claustrophobic community or being excluded from a community altogether. Ongoing dialogue is the answer, and it can happen at conferences or in churches or in people's homes. These dialogues are most productive if we all remember that things are in play, that we are just making believe together. Art has a special part to play because of how it educates and exercises our imaginations. It authorizes a *Spielraum*, a playing space in which there is an opportunity for a dialogue that is deeper and more liberating than those that turn into family quarrels. In the next chapter, I will put forward selected case studies with the aim of showing how such a dialogue works.

2.

US AND THEM

REAL TOADS IN IMAGINARY GHETTOS

Eck en dü: Malasch küh.
Malasch äsel: daut best dü.

I and you: Miller's cows.
Miller's donkey (ass): that is you.

X Marks the Spot: "Almost the Same, but Not Quite"

On 14 January 2011, the *Globe and Mail* published a photo essay by Peter Power entitled "Hockey's Real Winter Classic." The images are of boys playing shinny on a homemade rink (Figure 7). The text identifies them as Mennonite, but some readers will be able to deduce that they are not Russian Mennonites in Manitoba but Swiss Mennonites in Ontario. "These are the young men of the David Martin Mennonites, one of the Old Order groups that call [the] rural Waterloo region home." In the text, the photographer describes the eerie silence of a cold winter day broken only by the sound of the skates and by fragments of a "distinctly German dialect [floating] across the field." He also remembers the sounds coming from a nearby barn, "the distinctive laughter of young girls drift[ing] over from a small window." The dialect Power heard would not have been the one spoken by Russian Mennonites. These children, however, would almost certainly know some Swiss Mennonite version of the mock insult in the Low German epigraph to this chapter. When we chanted that rhyme on the farm, we paid no attention to the glaring grammatical error. The Low German plural of "cows" is not *küh* but *kjiej*. Once again the collective mind of folk culture ignores grammar so that the repeated sound becomes like a finger pointing at *dü*, the *äsel* who is taunted for being different. While it captures the perpetual process of stereotyping, the rhyme also conveys the dynamic nature of the constant dialogue between *Eck en dü* that will be my focus in this chapter. In this case the photographer cannot tell us what the skaters are saying to each other. Since he does not take his camera into the barn, we also do not know what the girls look like, why they are laughing, or what they might have to say about being left out of the game. All sounds are muted in the still photographs. They speak a different language.

I begin with these images because they illustrate the important part that medium plays in my reframing of us and them. I will focus on the work of artists whom I assume to be non-Mennonite, such as Power, who position themselves as spectators looking in on a Mennonite community from the outside. Why are so many drawn to this subject? Why do they write about us, take pictures of us, and make films about us? What leads an individual artist to choose a particular genre or medium? Why do so many reach, as Power did, for a camera? My interest is not so much in the answers to these why and what questions as it is in exploring the how questions that follow from them. How does the Anabaptist vision of community stand up against the constant pressure of contemporary stereotypes about Mennonites? How do artists deal with the limits of a chosen form when they come up against the stereotypes? How does a particular artist transform the image of community to which he or she is drawn?

All these questions are about representation. The questions have changed, however, since sixteenth-century caricatures mocked the extreme individualism of Anabaptists (see Weimann 1996, 95). Contemporary representations of Mennonites reflect instead widespread fascination with communities that set themselves apart from the excessive individualism of Western modernity. All these representations take place in a highly charged "contact zone." To be accused of *othering* a person or group will now cause public shaming in social media. Even when stereotypes are

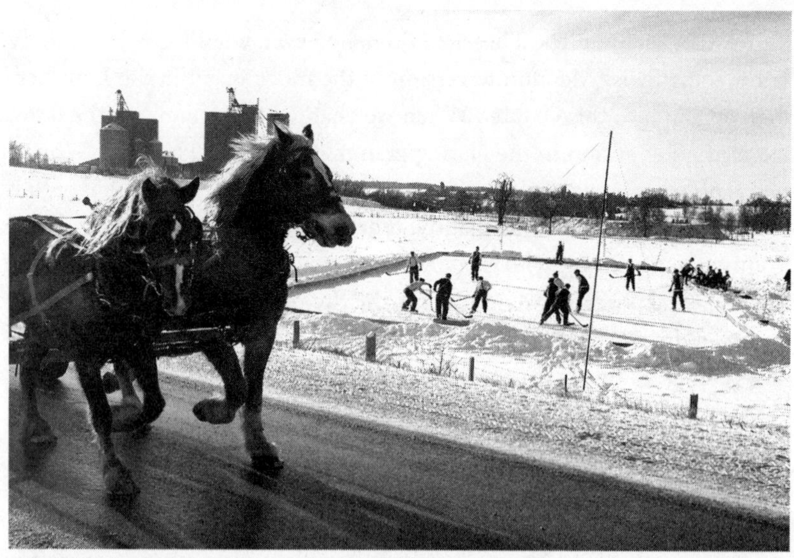

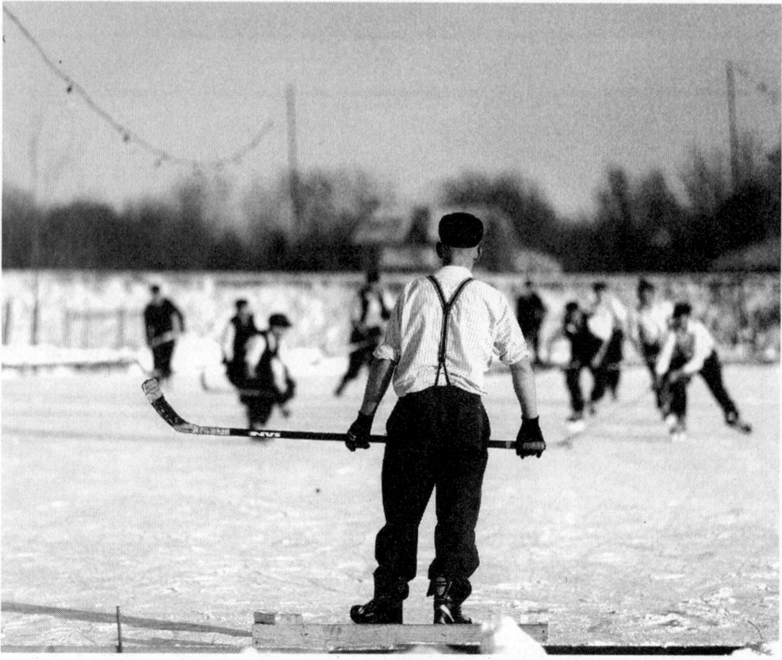

Figures 7 and 8. Mennonite boys playing hockey, 8 January 2011. Photographs by Peter Power. Courtesy of the artist.

fixed, however, the dialogue around them is fluid. This is a place where ethical and aesthetic problems come alive and cannot be separated, a point made succinctly by W.J.T. Mitchell with his mock slogan "no representation without taxation" (1990, 21). As glossed by Robert Weimann, who refers to it rather oddly as a "happy phrase," this means that there is no representation "without, that is, loss in the shape and presence of the represented" (1996, 196).* What are the different ways that an artist might respond to this moral dilemma? Here I consider that question in relation to representations that involve interactions between Mennonites and non-Mennonites. Once ethnic identity has been recognized as interactive, there is no fixed place to stand. This *Spielraum* is like the slippery surface of a skating rink. There is only the constantly destabilizing challenge of "ethnic dialogism."

Images and texts such as the ones that I have chosen demonstrate that, despite the "fixity" that is part of "the ideological construction of otherness," stereotypes do not offer "a secure point of identification." On the contrary, they are part of what Homi Bhabha calls "a complex, ambivalent, contradictory mode of representation" (2004, 69–70). In his brilliant essay "The Mennonite Thing: Identity for a Post-Identity Age," Robert Zacharias (2015, 106) draws on Slavoj Žižek's theories about "the inversion of ideology and the fetishistic structure of the 'Ethnic Thing.'" What is an "ethnic thing"? How is the "Mennonite thing" different from what we call stereotypes? Who is doing the fetishizing—or is it branding? Unlike Žižek, who fudges such questions, Bhabha, the theorist who first argued for "reading the stereotype in terms of fetishism" (2004, 74), deals directly with "the question of agency" (171). It is precisely because there is no essential identity behind the masks of identity (Mennonite or other) that it is so important to pay attention to how agency is shared. Nothing that I write here should be misconstrued as saying that only Mennonites have the right to create art about Mennonites. For all I know, Power might be Mennonite. What interests me is not biology but the aesthetic strategies

---

* I have explored this kind of taxation in relation to a cartoon by Stephen Pastis, part of the *Pearls before Swine* series, in which the bust of an Amish man pops out of a "catch-all drawer" and Rat concedes to Pig that it is something "a bit unusual" (Redekop 2015, 196).

that come into play when an artist such as Power implicitly poses as an outsider observing a Mennonite community.

The skating rink in his photo essay appears as a "contact zone" when it is combined with the accompanying commentary. This combination of visual and verbal representation is a *Spielraum,* a place where community is imagined and different ways of making believe coexist. Like all the communities imagined in this chapter, the skating rink is loosely connected to a real place that can be found on a map. When transferred to the *Spielraum* of art, however, the lines on the map are charged with the electricity of cultural difference. Us and them, like the puck in a hockey game, are put into play. No playground, of course, offers absolute freedom or safety, and each work of art (not unlike a hockey game) is constrained by countless variables, including the conventions of the chosen medium. As an introductory case study, however, a still photograph is a useful pedagogical tool because it seems to frame the problems so that they can be held still and studied. This is an illusion. If you take your time with Power's photographs, then you will experience movement on the skating rink. It is a slippery playground where us and them are looking for some kind of balance. The artist, his subjects, and the viewers of the art form a triangle that might appear, like a tripod, to offer some stability. The trouble is that the viewing audience is not uniform. Consider, for example, what would happen if I pointed out that every person in Power's photo essay is male. Who, then, are us and them?

Since "Hockey's Real Winter Classic" appeared in a newspaper, it invites a response based on naive realism. Familiar pastoral tropes are hidden out in the open, and most readers will use them as vehicles for borrowed nostalgia. The majority of readers will see the image of boys playing shinny as a representation of some kind of utopia. Others will see a dystopia. Such viewers will pity those poor boys and see them as skating in circles in a Mennonite ghetto. Neither group of readers, I suspect, would be much interested in history. Eyes will quickly glaze over if you contaminate the pastoral landscape with too many details about how these David Martin Mennonites might differ from other Mennonites. In some ways, photographs of minority groups do not even represent those groups but act instead as mirrors in which people from the majority group can see their desires and fears. Power's photographs construct an in-between space within which dialogue happens and community is constructed and performed, not as a static ideal but as a dynamic process. The obstacles to achieving such a representation are many, as are the possibilities of misinterpretation by viewers. Those Mennonites or Jews or Muslims who use clothing or customs to set themselves apart from the rest of the world are a minority within the larger world population of Mennonites and Jews and Muslims. Representations of the visibly separate portion of the larger group elicit ambivalent responses and sometimes fiercely protective ones from the more assimilated urban members of the same group.

Like Power, the other artists whose work I will consider deal with representations of a community that claims to be both "in the world and not of the world." Shinny is a good choice of game to photograph if you want to explore that riddle. It is played all over Canada without protective equipment and is free of the violence that has marred professional hockey. The pictures in "Hockey's Real Winter Classic" seem to say "it's a small world." But this evocation of the cliché of the global village sits oddly with the Mennonite stereotype. In that very oddity is the strength of Power's art because it nudges the viewer into participation, pushing past the commodification of ethnic identity and opening up a contact zone where ethnicity is a relational process. Power describes his session with the David Martin Mennonites as "a game of sorts," but he does not join the "young men" in the game of shinny. This sounds more like hide and seek. It seems likely that he first gained permission to play from some responsible adult. There is here none of that uncomfortable voyeurism that makes so many photographs of Mennonites creepy. Power's way of framing the images suggests that the game of photographing the other, like skating, has to do with finding balance on unstable ground.

One arresting photograph in the sequence frames an adult male with his back to the camera (Figure 8). His position on the ice suggests that he is the goalie. Like the boys he is watching, the man is wearing a white shirt and suspenders. He is not, however, wearing skates. Compared to the graceful shapes of the skaters, the legs of this adult body are planted inside rubber boots. The straps criss-crossing the man's back are like an X in the centre of the frame, set off against the horizontal line formed by the hockey stick that he holds loosely. It is a strong composition because of the tension held in balance within the frame. The stick is held ready to stop a puck, but the body stops viewers from seeing all the hockey players. As beholders, we are simultaneously drawn toward the X and pushed away from it by the body of the goalkeeper. The image moves us beyond the limits of newspaper reporting, and the suspenders act as a *punctum*, the word used by Roland Barthes for a detail in a photograph that punctures the denotative surface or *studium*. X marks the spot where a viewer might sense a meaning that cannot be intellectualized, a meaning that remains "persistent and fugitive," which Barthes calls "the obtuse meaning" (1985, 44). The effect in this case is like the experience of iconoclash or "ekphrastic fascination," which I will discuss in Chapter 6. When the subject photographed is an "other," however, viewers' responses are complicated by the fixity of stereotypes.

My admiration for the skill of the photographer whose composition evokes the obtuse meaning coexists with my irritation at those obtuse viewers whose borrowed nostalgia will erase the history of my people. But who are they, those people out there? And who are "my people"? And who am I to take umbrage when I cannot even begin to answer those questions? The Mennonite boys in Power's photographs seem to skate smoothly around all these troubling questions. We all know, these pictures seem to say, that technology is a necessary evil, but here, in this place both in time and out of time, there is a community so harmonious that even hockey can be played without violence. I take the *punctum* in this photograph as an invitation to push past this illusion and explore deeper levels of meaning. The X formed by those suspenders might seem fixed on the level of naive realism, but if you see it as a *punctum* then it turns into a "floating signifier" (Mehlman 1972). Loosening those suspender straps is as good a way as any to begin a chapter devoted to art about stereotypes since sartorial choices are related to cultural identities. The internet, for example, is overflowing with images and anecdotes—some mildly entertaining but many openly racist—regarding the question of whether or not it is possible to identify black Muslims by the bowties that they wear. Digital technology multiplies these images exponentially, but art asks us to slow down, to pay close attention as we attempt to create a space for dialogue in the contact zone.

The X in Power's photograph of the goalie brings into focus how our desires and fears about the other relate to recognition. I am thinking here not only about what Charles Taylor (1994) calls "the politics of recognition" but also about the deeper literary resonance of the term (see Cave 1988). Aristotle's definition of the word *anagnorisis* in *Poetics* (2013) usefully lights up literary texts from Shakespeare to Dickens in which the discovery of a scar or a birthmark, previously hidden by clothing, leads to a moment of recognition. In the photograph of the Mennonite goalie, the X of the criss-crossing suspenders is a signifier floating over the spot where we long for recognition and belonging. As a marker of Mennonite identity, however, suspenders fail. The reason is the same as the reason why suspenders are sexy in some movies. It is because they go on and come off so easily. When Harrison Ford dons suspenders in the 1985 movie *Witness*, the visual rhetoric is subordinate to commerce: sweetening the eye candy results in more money at the box office. Contemporary audiences are quick to see irony in sartorial performances of identity, and Susan Sontag's "Notes on 'Camp'" (1966) is still influential. Under our quick laughter, however, might be the fear that inside all the clothing and behind the floating signifiers there is no authentic identity at all. This fear is more primal than the fear that now leads so many critics (and I include myself) to emphasize that there is no essential identity behind the mask of mimicry.

It is easy to condemn naive realism, but it is much harder to perform the task that remains: to consider how representation works and to engage with the gaps and the inevitable failure of representation. Doing so involves taking on the challenge of "ethnic dialogism" that I defined in the preceding chapter. The line between art and "real life" is sometimes as blurry as the outlines of a makeshift skating rink when it starts to melt. My strategies for dealing with this challenge all go back to my introductory emphasis on the importance of play and on the space made by a collective act of making believe. A scene of children at play has metaphorical associations that will resonate throughout this chapter. I have been referring to the hockey players as boys, but I note that Power refers to them as "young men" and to the females in the barn as "young girls." This shape-shifting middle space, known as adolescence, offers unique opportunities for writers. Those on the skating rink in Power's photo essay are reminiscent of those in Alice Munro's "The Moon in the Orange Street Skating Rink" (Munro 1986, 132–61). In that story, the rinky-dinks control the rising of a fake moon, but the children sometimes seem to be at the mercy of a world full of adult fanatics. Colour it orange. The social interactions in Munro's story are complex, but the rink is a contact zone within which Munro briefly captures a play of us and them. In Power's photographs, the players happen to be Mennonites, and in Munro's story they are often Scottish Presbyterians, but the play is not at the deepest levels *about* Mennonites or Presbyterians. In both cases, the skating rink is a site for a theatre in which identity is performed on many levels.

Whether you refer to the hockey players as boys or young men, the fact is that they exist. I assume that they are going about their lives somewhere in the world. Simply insisting on such a blunt fact can be the best weapon against stereotypes. The "real toads in imaginary ghettos" of this chapter's title refer to a poem by Marianne Moore (1935) entitled "Poetry." The speaker in that poem seeks "a place for the genuine" that is "beyond all this fiddle" and "beyond all the high-sounding interpretation" that become "so derivative as to become unintelligible" (36). She finds it in poets who are "literalists of the imagination" and who create "imaginary gardens with real toads in them" (37). The shock of Moore's poem for many critics is in the blunt statement that "these things are important . . . because they are useful" (37). The "real toads" are useful, however, precisely because, once imagined, they are no longer real. That is a recognition that once again puts all the players on unstable ground. The search for balance, like life, goes on.

Reimagining Us and Them: "The Unending Orphic Task of Art"

"Can the world ever be home to all of us?" asks Ted Chamberlin, and he answers "I think so. But not until we have reimagined Them and Us" (2004, 4). From what I have already said, it must be clear that I see this reimagining as something never finally achieved. On the most basic level, the construction of otherness is a perpetual process—an inevitable part of how we create our identities. Sander Gilman writes that "the creation of a stereotype is a concomitant of the process by which all human beings become individuals" and argues that it is the product of anxiety (1985, 17). The shame culture of social media leaves the impression that "othering" is something done by wicked people who deserve to be called out, perhaps fired, or even jailed. The truth of the matter is more banal. In *My Name Is Lucy Barton*, Elizabeth Strout captures it in plain language: "I have said before: It interests me how we find ways to feel superior to another person, another group of people. It happens everywhere, and all the time. Whatever we call it, I think it's the lowest part of who we are, this need to find someone else to put down" (2016, 95). The "we" here excludes no human being. This is the lowness confronted by Jane Austen's Emma when she finally sees herself as a moral monster. Bigotry can take extreme forms and comes in various flavours, but the best satirists, from Jonathan Swift to Paul Hiebert, have always written from an unflinching awareness of the lowness in human nature: "It happens everywhere, and all the time."

Chamberlin's suggestion of a future time when "we have reimagined Them and Us," while not literally true, is vital to the ongoing process. If we are unable to envision a better world, then why would we be motivated to work toward one? Among the most powerful images of such an ideal future is the one that inspired the revolutionary poetry of William Blake: "And I John saw the holy city, new Jerusalem, coming down from God out of heaven, prepared as a bride adorned for her husband" (Revelation 21:2). The claims made for the human imagination by the Romantic poets might seem inflated, but the fact remains that no revolutionary movement happens without some double vision of an idealized past and an idealized future. The metaphor of bride and bridegroom remains powerful and suits my purpose here, to point out that the reimagining of "the other" contains an erotic charge—as my flirtation with suspenders demonstrated. There is a profound connection between our response to art and our response to otherness. Various versions of paradise can be constructed as metaphors for the goal of overcoming otherness, but in the real world apocalypse is forever postponed. W.J.T. Mitchell relates this kind of desire to our perpetual ambivalence about the power of images. "Iconoclash," the term used by art critics to refer to having an image and not having it at the same time, will come to the fore in Chapter 6 when I turn my attention to Mennonite responses to visual art. Mitchell sees this kind of aesthetic response as "grounded in our ambivalence about other people" (1994, 163).

In *Poetry and the Fate of the Senses,* Susan Stewart explores poetic representations of otherness and argues that "poiesis as a figuration relies on the senses of touching, seeing, and hearing that are central to the encounter with the presence of others" (2002, 3). In a move that I find compelling, Stewart goes on to envision the poet as taking on "the unending Orphic task of drawing the figure of the other—the figure of the beloved who

reciprocally can recognize one's own figure—out of the darkness" (2). It
is an analogy that resonates in many of the stories of Alice Munro, who
alludes frequently to the myth of Orpheus and Eurydice. In the seminal
early story "Dance of the Happy Shades," children perform at a piano
recital, and the recognition that they are different in some way comes gradually. All the children have Down syndrome, but the story foregrounds
one gifted child who performs the famous melody from Gluck's *Orfeo ed
Euridice* and, in a sense, plays the part of Orpheus. In a later story, "The
Children Stay," Munro challenges the gender bias of the original myth.
Cast in an amateur production of Jean Anouilh's *Eurydice*, Pauline has an
affair with the director of the play and "runs away" with him. Her husband
insists that the children must stay with him, an imperative echoed in the
title of the story.* Questions about guilt hover in between the lines. Where
are the children while the parents are off in some romantic underworld
playing at being Orpheus and Eurydice? I put the question so plainly
because it dramatizes the part that children play in my argument and anticipates their important role in *Irma Voth* (Toews 2011), my last case study.

Paying attention to the fate of the children is a useful moral guide
but not because children are inherently good. Their play is a good model
because it shows that it is possible to make believe with others, to make
mistakes and learn from those mistakes, to make up when quarrels happen
and move forward. In what follows, I will keep the children in mind as
I go about a critical version of "the unending Orphic task." If this is a kind
of lovers' quarrel, then it demands honesty, and I will voice my discon-
tent with misrepresentation and erasure when I sense it. My aim is to find
balance on the unstable ground of a contact zone, to engage in a lovers'
quarrel while still paying attention to the fate of the children. I will focus
on the movement in between the senses, particularly those of hearing and
seeing, because it has the potential to disturb the rigidity of stereotypes.
I will pay close attention to the art, to how representations of the other
change as you move from one medium to another. Despite my personal
involvement in this subject, I will make the constant effort to establish
critical distance. Given my focus in this chapter on art made by those who

---

* I offer a close reading of that story in "Alice Munro's Tilting Fields" (Redekop 2000, 353–55).

observe Mennonites from the outside, this means that I will be stepping back and observing the observer.

Have You Heard The Quiet in the Land? *Observing Glenn Gould*

Adaptation is a word most commonly associated with films based on novels, but as Linda Hutcheon (2006) has argued in *A Theory of Adaptation* the process has a wider application of particular importance to the study of cross-cultural art. I consider adaptation to be a form of translation, a way of exploring different aesthetic languages. Have you heard *The Quiet in the Land*? Have you heard the quiet in the land? If you remove the capital letters and the italics, the question sounds like a riddle, a little like the philosophical conundrum about whether a tree falling in the forest makes a sound. Glenn Gould's use of the phrase as a title for a 1977 radio program about Mennonites announces a paradox. If Mennonites are the quiet in the land, then how will their voices be heard on the radio? His choice of title holds up a mirror, reflecting back to Mennonites the phrase that has been used for centuries as a shorthand term encapsulating the foundational gesture of shunning the world. The word *quiet*, associated with pacifism, is useful as a way of reassuring those who might remember that some Anabaptists were violent. For an outsider to use the word as Gould does could be seen as a form of flattery, a way of assuring Mennonite audiences that they will be represented in ways that match up with their own self-images. The 1983 play by Anne Chislett, *Quiet in the Land,* uses the word in that way and does not do much to question the cliché. Gould's adaptation of it is more disquieting, and the questions that Gould raises are in tune with how many Mennonites are now questioning the phrase. The rubric of a 1995 conference on Mennonite women, for example, did so by adding a question mark: The Quiet in the Land? The conferences on music hosted by Carol Ann Weaver since 2004 at Conrad Grebel College have raised implicit questions under the umbrella title Sound in the Land.

The Quiet in the Land is part of Gould's *Solitude Trilogy,* a series of three hour-long radio documentaries produced by the Canadian Broadcasting Corporation (CBC) between 1967 and 1977. Howard Dyck has noted in a conversation with ethnomusicologist Doreen Helen Klassen that *The Quiet in the Land* is different from the other two programs in the trilogy, *The Idea of North* (1967) and *The Latecomers* (1969), because they portray a separateness that is geographical—the North and Newfoundland. The Mennonite community, in contrast, "was separate in a way yet was in the middle of things" (Klassen 2015, 182). According to Dyck, Gould "was intrigued with the idea of there being a community that lived within another larger community, in a larger context, in this case, Winnipeg, and deliberately chose Winnipeg because it has such a large Mennonite population" (182). Dyck himself was living in Winnipeg at that time and was one of the nine people whom Gould interviewed in August 1971. Gould also recorded rehearsals by the Mennonite Children's Choir during that visit and later, upon returning to Ontario, he made recordings in a Mennonite church.

Gould often said that he thought of the *Solitude Trilogy* as autobiographical. The questions about community in *The Quiet in the Land* circle around the solitary figure of a performing artist revered worldwide even as he shunned the world. The life and art of Gould comprise a visible example of how the technology of reproduction has intensified the dilemma of the solitary artist. When Gould made his famous decision to stop performing in live concerts, his intention was that mechanical reproductions should transcend the original productions. As Hillel Schwartz notes, however, "the culture of the copy muddies the waters of authenticity" (1996, 377). She describes Gould's choice as an example of how recording artists have to make a deal with a doppelgänger. In some ways, the disembodied voices of the Mennonites in his radio documentary played the part of his doppelgänger, and this was a role that listeners have had difficulty interpreting. Speaking to a conference audience in Waterloo in 2014, for example, Sabine Breitsameter, a German audio media expert, argued that *The Quiet in the Land* provides "an enlightening frame around the topic of worldwide homogenization" of sound (2015, 142). It was Gould's aim, she argued, "to reflect on the beliefs and practices of Mennonites who, at least in part, attempt to renounce a world dominated by machines, commercialization, and utilitarianism" (148). Her assumption is contradicted by the fact that the people whom Gould interviewed for the program were mostly urban Mennonites.

The difficulty of knowing what to do with the actual Mennonites involved in the making of the program has long been a problem for critics. To what extent is the program some kind of documentary? In a letter to

Elvin Shantz written during the planning stage, Gould described himself as creating a "rather poetic program." At the same time, however, he wrote that he intended to "capture the essence of the Mennonite communities and the life style of the peoples involved more faithfully than any recitation of historical facts possibly can" (1992, 194). This ambivalence has been part of the reception of the program from the time that it was first released, when Marshall McLuhan's influence was at its height. On the one hand, there is still an assumption that "The Medium Is the Message," the now famous phrase that is the title of the first chapter of *Understanding Media: The Extensions of Man* (1964). On the other, there is the claim that *The Quiet in the Land* contains some message about Mennonites. Breitsameter (2015) takes the message as offering a Mennonite antidote to the contemporary loss of "acoustic identity" (a term pioneered by R. Murray Schafer) but offers no details on how this might work. Nor does she acknowledge the exceptional challenge for listeners that results from the fact that Gould overlaps the speaking voices and adds various distracting sound effects. Like many other critics, Breitsameter sidesteps this practical problem and does not question Gould's attempt to aestheticize cross-talk. She describes Gould as having "subordinated his interview materials to the compositional principles of a fugue, which work on sonic . . . not semantic patterns. The characteristic voices of his interviewees can be followed by their pitch, their intonation, or their sentence melody, but only vaguely by their content" (142).

What happens to community when form erases content? During his conversation with Klassen, Dyck described the program as a "trio sonata, where you had a low voice, a high voice, and a middle voice" (Klassen 2015, 181). Klassen responded with a question: "Did Gould regard the three voices as a way of allowing the community rather than the individual to speak, or was this more a way of using technology?" (181). Dyck replied that Gould was "creating the illusion of a conversation" and added that "I'm not sure that by interposing the voices the result had any philosophical, theological, or sociological significance for him" (181). Be that as it may, the passage of time has drawn attention to all the content left over if you take a purely formalist approach. Geography is not so easily erased. Whatever they have to say, the voices in *The Quiet in the Land,* including that of Dyck himself, convey a powerful sense of place. All of them speak with a distinctive and identifiable Manitoba Mennonite accent.

Gould was supported in the making of *The Quiet in the Land* by his contacts at the CBC during the 1970s, a time when people in Winnipeg often joked about the presence at the CBC of the "Mennonite Mafia." Ben Horch was Gould's CBC contact in Winnipeg, and it was Horch who suggested the names of people whom Gould might interview, including his wife and his father-in-law. It would be useful to study the role of Horch in the creation of *The Quiet in the Land* and to compare it with his role with relation to *The Mennonite Piano Concerto,* composed by Victor Davies in 1975. Breitsameter ignores such regional contexts when she claims that Gould's Mennonites somehow open up possibilities for a "kind of listening" that subverts "the usual homogenized auditory patterns" (2015, 149). *The Quiet in the Land,* she argues, "celebrates the autonomy of the human auditory sense beyond being directed and 'made to listen'" (148). In itself this is a laudable goal. As Eric Leonardson notes, one of R. Murray Schafer's most useful ideas was that we are "co-creators of the soundscapes we inhabit" (2015, 154). But just whose autonomy is being celebrated? Is it that of the people whose voices are heard *in* the documentary? Or is it that of the person listening to *The Quiet in the Land*? And how do such questions change when the voices are disembodied—on air? Does that lessen the power of the maker of the documentary? Is he not still, at least to some extent, making us listen?

These are questions that come to the fore if you begin by assuming that art is relational and social. The critic who sets out to provoke a lovers' quarrel with the ghost of Glenn Gould must pay attention to the fate of all the senses—including those blocked by radio. The result of doing so is that facts from various social contexts crowd in around you as you listen. Along with this come the moral questions raised by Gould's manipulation of the voices of the real toads in his Mennonite ghetto. Gould himself dismissed these questions, but they have persisted. In "Glenn Gould's Manipulations," pianist Anton Kuerti (1994) offers a scathing denunciation of what he calls Gould's self-glorifying and "scandalously offensive" methods. Kuerti views the manipulations of musical text for which Gould is known as part of the same "perversity and moral turpitude" that led him to manipulate people during the making of his "bizarre documentaries."

Kuerti was bored by the banal content and reports that he "lost patience" and listened to only part of *The Quiet in the Land*. In contrast, Geoffrey Payzant listened carefully before observing (in a chapter entitled "Creative Cheating") that *The Quiet in the Land* includes "several 'imitations' in the strict musical sense, where words in one voice are echoed by another voice in a carefully measured interval of time, in another register and tone-quality" (1984, 133). Payzant concludes: "In this work Gould seems to have solved problems of combining complexity with clarity which were unsolved in earlier documentaries" (133).

I must confess that, if you are a Mennonite who registers social stratification in various accents, then it is impossible to stay with the "strict musical sense" while listening to *The Quiet in the Land*. Matters are made worse if you happen to recognize some of the voices as belonging to real people. On an intellectual level, I agree with scholars who have pointed out that we privileged Western scholars should not presume to call ourselves subalterns who talk back (see Morris 2010). Listening to the program in my apartment here in Toronto, near the corner of St. Clair and Yonge, I am just steps away from the building that Gould called home, part of the same bourgeois urban culture that he inhabited. The fact, nevertheless, is that I could not listen to *The Quiet in the Land* without wanting to talk back. The more I listened, the more curious I was about what Gould might have said to elicit the often peculiar comments that became part of the final program. Might the actual conversations help, I wondered, to understand the illusory ones in the documentary? Curiosity triumphed, and I ordered the taped conversations from the Mennonite Brethren Archives in Winnipeg, where they are held as part of the Ben Horch fonds. What I heard when I listened to them provided evidence to support Kuerti's (1994) observation that Gould, "while purporting to believe in absolute honesty and equality between people, . . . actually treated many people in the most manipulative and utilitarian manner."

Readers who knew the man will not be surprised to hear that, of all the people interviewed, Roy Vogt was the most resistant to Gould's manipulations. In his biography of Gould, Otto Friedrich reports that "Roy Vogt, a professor of economics at the University of Manitoba in Winnipeg, complained even before the tapes were edited that Gould was manipulating people" (1990, 198). Vogt wrote to Gould that "several times in our conversation . . . I was led to believe that my ideas would be used not as the expression of an individual but as a foil for the ideas of others. You can't abstract an individual much more than that, even in a totalitarian society. The musical analogy of counterpoint which you used very often reinforces this impression. Each person becomes a note in a larger symphony, which in social terms is perhaps as good a way as any of describing the underlying assumptions of a totalitarian state. The dictator is a social composer" (quoted 198–99). Josef Škvorecký's novel *The Engineer of Human Souls* (1977) had not yet been published when Vogt wrote that letter, but he obviously had in mind the phrase made notorious by Josef Stalin that the writer is "an engineer of human souls." Vogt invites a spotlight here because of the important role that he played in fostering the cultural renaissance that is the subject of this book. He was the founding editor of *Mennonite Mirror*, the forerunner of *Rhubarb*, but his influence on Manitoba writers goes beyond his institutional roles. Poet Patrick Friesen, for example, considers him an important mentor.

Nothing in official Mennonite responses to *The Quiet in the Land* even hints at humour, but Gould's interview with Vogt is charged with a repressed humour that reflects tension between Gould and his doppelgänger. In the tape of the original interview, Gould exhibits audible anxiety as the conversation turns to dancing. When Vogt speaks about preferring "rock and roll to the waltz or the fox trot," Gould's anxious voice interrupts: "May I caution you about your hands on the table?" Vogt obliges with "Okay" but instantly goes back to enthusing about the "exhilarating effect" of dancing and how it is "nice to feel close to another." I imagine Vogt's fingers dancing on the table when Gould responds with an exasperated *non sequitur*: "Why then do you want to start a magazine which will reaffirm the ghetto psychology of the Mennonites? . . . It strikes me as ornery to organize a magazine to reconsolidate the ghetto virtues, which I don't find all that virtuous." In some parts of the interview, Vogt seems to play the role of coyote in a tale by Thomas King, and this carries over into the finished documentary. When the unidentified voice speaks in that identifiable flat Mennonite accent, comparing the amounts of alcohol consumed by Mennonites and non-Mennonites at Winnipeg parties, I conclude that Vogt is pulling Gould's leg. Eventually this kind of comparison became too distracting, and I decided that it was impracticable to go back and forth between the tapes and Gould's composition. From what I had heard, I concluded that in many ways Gould was more Mennonite than any of the Mennonites whom he interviewed. I was content, in any case, to accept the fact that in *The Quiet in the Land* it is Gould himself who chooses to be quiet.

Attempting to exclude aspects of the social context from my response, however, only served to increase my exasperation with critics who ignore them entirely and respond on a theoretical and formal level. Matthew McFarlane (2002), for example, apparently views real people as raw material to be sacrificed by Gould to create a "unity of machinery and spirituality." Far from positing Mennonite communities as a utopian remedy for the loss of "acoustic identity," McFarlane wipes them out and along with them, for good measure, the city of Winnipeg. He assumes that Gould's recordings were done in "an isolated Mennonite community in Manitoba." He concedes that Gould was "criticized harshly by some for betraying his subjects by piecing together fragments of their conversations to create pseudo-fictional characters." It is his view, however, that the great man should be allowed to follow "his own spiritual and philosophical inclinations," and it is only right that he would have "no qualms about using technology . . . and thereby transcending the boundaries of reality." McFarlane concludes that the "pseudo-fictional characters" in *The Quiet in the Land* are more interesting than any of the real people, but he makes this judgement without any apparent knowledge of those people.

A telling moment in McFarlane's (2002) essay is his reference to an "example of one of Gould's rare editing mistakes." In the passage that McFarlane cites, an unidentified voice speaks of "those who preach about breaking up the ghettos, as some of them would refer to the smaller villages and the towns." "It is obvious," McFarlane writes, "that the word 'ghettos' has been spliced into this sentence; you can hear a slight click before the word, and the intonation does not correspond with the previous words. . . . The slight break . . . gives us insight into how Gould spliced in order to modify the meaning of an interview subject's comments."

When I first read this, I was outraged, as much by the calmness of the account as by what McFarlane supposed Gould to have done. When I listened to the recording of the interview, however, I discovered that McFarlane had jumped to the wrong conclusion. Not having listened to the tapes, he would not have known how Gould's manipulations worked, how often Gould introduced the word *ghetto* into his conversations in a transparent effort to get his subjects to use it when they responded. Many did so. On the original tape, Clarence Hiebert does in fact refer to "small ghettos." The perfectionist Gould deleted the extraneous adjective, which accounts for the click that McFarlane heard. He concludes that Gould was "attempting a king [*sic*] of healing process among his subjects. . . . Gould creates beauty out of the ruptures within the Mennonite community, . . . inventing harmony out of dissonance."

McFarlane's *worship* of Gould, to use Kuerti's (1994) word, ironically results in a failure to do justice to his achievement in *The Quiet in the Land*. Contrary to his claim that Gould attempted to harmonize the discord that he found, the evidence of the interviews shows that he was constantly attempting to provoke and even invent the discord. I think that Gould was listening for a back-and-forth rhythm not so much between the subjects as within each subject. I also think that he ended up recording his own ambivalence. The many overlapping voices create a poetic rhythm based on attraction and repulsion in response to the very idea of community. One of the most eloquent moments in *The Quiet in the Land* (Gould 1977) happens when a fellow musician responds to the riddle that obsessed Gould. How is it possible to be in the world but not of the world? The unidentified voice responds "And that's really what great art is all about, isn't it? I mean, that's what a fugue, ultimately, is all about—using, if you will, the techniques that the composer had at his disposal and making something of it which is really quite other-worldly." So familiar is the voice in Canada because of his role in the CBC that many Canadians listening will recognize it as that of Howard Dyck. When I listened to the tape of Gould's interview with Dyck, I was struck by the fact that Dyck appeared to be so absorbed in pondering the questions that he was oblivious to the manipulative ploys. Toward the end of the interview, Gould played the ghetto card and asked Dyck if Mennonites were moving in a more "universalist" direction or retreating into the "ghetto." Unlike Hiebert, Dyck ignored the word. To Gould's question "Which way are Mennonites headed?" he responded "In about fifty different directions!"

When I interviewed Dyck in November 2010, I asked him what, in hindsight, he thought it was that fascinated Gould so much about Mennonites.

He replied: "I think it was the whole aspect of being separate but not being separate. He saw himself so much that way. Here he was in Toronto all his life, but he lived in his own little bubble. That whole notion of separation fascinated him." I asked Dyck if he shared my own sense that Gould just did not *get* the very idea of community. His instant reply was "Yes! Yes!" Dyck mentioned that Gould often phoned him in the middle of the night regarding some detail of the composition of *The Quiet in the Land*. I imagine Gould alone in his apartment working with his machinery late into the night, seeking release from cerebral abstraction, and needing to hear a real, live human voice. The only way to understand community is to make it. You can try to do that in the middle of the night by phoning people, but an easier way is to sing together. And, if you get caught up in an intense lovers' quarrel, then it is always a good idea to remember the children. Gould would have better understood the power of community, whether Mennonite or non-Mennonite, if, after interviewing conductor Helen Litz, he had joined in and sung with the children in the Mennonite Children's Choir.

Have You Seen The Goldlandbergs? *Observing Emanuel Gat*

I was in the middle of puzzling over Gould's *The Quiet in the Land* when I was startled by the following headline in the *Globe and Mail*: "Choreographer Puts Gould's Radio Documentary into Motion." It was J. Kelly Nestruck's (2013) review of Emanuel Gat's *The Goldlandbergs*, performed for the first time as part of Berlin's annual dance festival. Nestruck describes the dance as "set primarily to Gould's mash-up of speech, music and ambient noise" in *The Quiet in the Land* (2013, 31). Having interviewed Gat in Berlin, Nestruck reports that the choreographer told him how for a year he listened to the program every time he went jogging. Unlike Anton Kuerti, he was not bored by it. It was "the music in his earphones that kept him moving." Nestruck describes how Gat traced sound waves with his finger on a table while talking: "It's really unbelievable, it's so well structured. . . . You can listen beginning to end. It's like hearing a symphony. It's like watching a movie. It's like reading a book." Gat's quick analogies to hearing, watching, and reading offer an intriguing glimpse into the creative mind of a choreographer. Paying attention to the fate of the senses in between those transitions when they are mixed up, however, requires a double take. "It's like reading a book"? Have you read *The Quiet in the Land*? Have you heard the Goldlandbergs dance? Nestruck sees the dance as "communicating through movements that look like an elaborate and elegant secret language."

Secret or not, this is an embodied language, not one that vanishes into thin air. What happens to an embodied Mennonite community when disembodied radio voices are performed by the bodies of an "extended family" of dancers? If we are being asked to translate the "secret language" of *The Goldlandbergs*, then the playfulness of the proper noun might be a clue. *Goldlandberg* is what Humpty Dumpty would call a portmanteau, combining reference to both Gould and the *Goldberg Variations*, but the word *land* inserted between them is a reminder, once again, of geography and of national identities. Is Gat, himself Israeli, playing with the slippage between Gould and Gold? Confusion about Gould's possible Jewishness lingers even though his parents were Presbyterians who changed the family name from Gold to Gould in 1939 to avoid being mistaken for Jews. Most reviewers appear to assume that the Goldlandbergs are a backward Mennonite family, but in which country do they live? Bach's *Goldberg Variations* do travel with great ease and have often invited dance adaptations. As Nestruck (2013) observes, however, *The Goldlandbergs* "attract[s] interest for having excavated a lesser-known part of the Canadian pianist's oeuvre"—the radio documentaries. What happens to community when Manitoba Mennonite voices are parachuted into Germany by an Israeli choreographer? Nestruck, the interviewer, is originally from Winnipeg, and his review suggests that he might have asked the choreographer about the reception among Mennonites. Referring to the people interviewed by Gould, Gat told Nestruck that "they really complained . . . that he manipulated completely what they said in the way that he edited it."

I write with reluctance about a dance that I have not seen live, but I venture to do so because the twenty-minute excerpt that I have seen online appears to have been edited by Gat himself.* It has a finished quality to it, beginning with the sound of children and ending with a curtain coming down. I now find *The Goldlandbergs* deeply moving, but my first

---

* See https://emanuelgatdance.com/previous-works-1/2017/1/26/the-goldlandbergs.

viewing of it did not go well. I began to watch before I remembered to turn on my speakers. The sheer beauty of the dance brought to mind the question asked by W.B. Yeats in "Among School Children": "How can we know the dancer from the dance?" (1963, 245). Belatedly I turned on the speakers. Instantly I felt disoriented. The sound that filled my room was of a congregation singing "Just as I Am without One Plea." To make matters worse, the singing faded to be accompanied by an earnest preacher's voice claiming to channel the voice of Jesus but speaking in a familiar Manitoba Mennonite accent. We must expect to be persecuted. It is inevitable that God's people must suffer—pronounced *soffer*. The single word triggered my recoil from definitions of Mennonite community as a "suffering church," separate from the world and, by implication, spiritually superior. Needless to say, while I was looking for an escape from the "bloody theatre" of martyr identity, I was no longer taking in the beauty of the dance. Those moving bodies on the screen might as well have been so many wriggling worms.

Eventually I watched the excerpt again. It helped that in the meantime I had read or heard an interview with Gat (I cannot now remember exactly where) in which he expressed an interest in "the gap between what we see and what we hear." My botched first way of watching it had intensified my experience of that gap. As I was sitting at my desk, it occurred to me that, if Mennonites are the people who don't dance, then all spectators are Mennonites. Except of course that the Goldlandbergs are dancing and Mennonite. Or are they? Who is us, and who is them? And what are we to make of those words spoken in a Mennonite accent while people dance? An online review of the Paris performance by Patricia Boccadoro (2014) leads me to believe that I am not alone in puzzling over the presence of real toads in this garden of dance. Her description suggests that she dealt with the gap between what she saw and what she heard by blocking out those distracting voices: "The eight dancers slid under their partners, climbed on top of each other, arms and legs emerging one after another within a group which moved and breathed as one." She adds that the religious references distracted from the dance movements, but nothing in those words seems to have helped her to make sense of the dancers' costumes. "Why," she wonders, "did one of the women harbour grey 'granny' bloomers with an unbecoming singlet, while a young male dancer remained on stage in dubious orange underpants a size too small?"

During all my viewings of *The Goldlandbergs*, I have felt a similar disjunction between what I was seeing and what I was hearing. Unlike Boccadoro, however, I have found that the deliberateness of these gaps, along with the fact that the dancers just keep on moving, provides access to a spiritual level that completely escaped me during my first viewing. The fragments from *The Quiet in the Land* that Gat selected for his soundtrack resonate with biblical allusions. When I read Boccadoro's puzzled response, indeed, I wondered if the men dancing in their underwear might be an allusion to the scene in the Bible in which David dances before the Lord "with all his might" clad only in a "linen ephod" (2 Samuel 6:14).

What I have concluded after repeated viewings is that in *The Goldlandbergs* there is no easy connection between word and image, but neither is it ahistorical or divorced from social contexts. This performance is consistent with Robert Stam's view that "ethnic dialogism" is not about "fidelity to preexisting truth" but about an "orchestration of discourses" (1991, 253). When I watch the dance on my computer now, I am able to abandon myself to Gat's "orchestration." This excerpt begins with the sound of children mixed with the sound of traffic. I feel myself transported onto the dance floor in spirit, as if the yellow rectangle of light is a magic carpet. By the time the organ begins to play the prelude to "Just as I Am," I am already in that *Spielraum*, and the dancers' bodies have already merged for me with the voices of the playing children. After that the preacher's voice, speaking about *soffering*, sounds soothing, and I remember that the preacher was Esther Horch's father. My eyes are on the dancers when the voice of Roy Vogt comes on talking about how he never really felt separated from the world and how music connects him with the rhythm of his being. I laugh a little when he says how his children are astonished when they come home and find their old man lying on the floor listening to Janis Joplin. It doesn't seem possible that these funny and endearing words were part of Gould's *The Quiet in the Land*, but they must have been. Gat's dancers guide us deep into that underworld where we all participate in "the unending Orphic task" of luring the shadowy other into dancing with us. Best of all is the way that Gat lures Gould into the dance. This Gould is not "the quiet in the land." Appropriately he is cast in the role of

Orpheus, playing not on a lute but on a piano. Bach's *Goldberg Variations* float in and out of the dance, disconnected from all the bodies and words yet somehow deep inside them. This is as close to perfect balance as an artist can get while working within his chosen art form to take on the challenge of "the unending Orphic task of art."

In the review that first alerted me to this work, Nestruck observed that Gould's "doc is about a religious group that at times has discouraged dancing among its members. . . . But when *The Goldlandbergs'* disparate elements suddenly seem to connect, and the voices of the Mennonites that Gould recorded in Manitoba over 40 years ago become the inner voices of the European dancers moving about in their underwear, there is a rush of joy" (2013, 31). By what magic do all the "disparate elements suddenly seem to connect"? Nestruck does not answer that question, but he concludes that Gould's radio documentaries "really stand up." To that he adds "and, thanks to Gat, now they dance, too." But who are *they*? Is it the Mennonites who are dancing? Or is it the "inner voices" of the dancers? Us and them are reimagined by Gat because he accepts a mixture of the actual and the imaginary and never loses sight of the real toads in his imaginary ghetto. In the abstract, dancer and dance might be one, but what is dance if not the relation of one's body to other bodies? Those dancers on my computer screen, moving to the sound of Mennonite voices, they too are real people, each just looking for a *Spielraum*. When the one who was assigned to wear the "orange underpants a size too small" goes home after the show, I imagine he is as relieved to take them off as any one of us would be.

The Red River that Gat imagines is more like Africa in Saul Bellow's *Henderson the Rain King* than like the muddy river that flows through Winnipeg and sometimes floods parts of it. Like *The Quiet in the Land, The Goldlandbergs* does not simply recapitulate a stereotype about Mennonite utopia or dystopia. Since my first troubled watching, I have watched the Goldlandbergs dance many times on my computer screen. At the time of writing, it had 8,595 viewings. I cannot say what others might make of the gap between what they see and what they hear. What I can say is that it was only when I acknowledged that gap that I was able to take a leap of faith into the *Spielraum* where Gat works his magic. My conclusions are influenced by the fact that I was watching as an isolated viewer sitting at my computer. I think it inevitable, however, that audience responses to *The Goldlandbergs* will vary depending on specific contexts. If the dance were ever performed in Canada, for example, it would surely evoke a different response in Winnipeg than it would in Montreal. In some ways, I now see *The Goldlandbergs* as a dance of diaspora in which different ethnic groups cannot be separated from each other without destroying the music. Only a dialogical aesthetic can account for the power of this kind of art. Together Gould and Gat perform "the unending Orphic task" of art in such a way that we are drawn into a perpetual reimagining of us and them. Willy-nilly, in or out of our underwear, we find ourselves dancing to the music of Bach.

Have You Seen Stellet Licht? Observing Carlos Reygadas

Stellet Licht, the Low German title of a 2007 film directed by Carlos Reygadas, is also referred to as *Silent Light* or *Luz Silenciosa*. If you do not use capital letters, then the question about reception, in any of the three languages, again invites questions about medium. Have you seen silent light? For those interested in ethnic representation, however, it is useful to begin by shifting the focus and asking have you seen the Mennonites in Mexico? "We see them, but we do not know them" (Janzen 2015b, 75). That is what Rebecca Janzen, a specialist in Mexican culture, reports that a Mexican friend of hers said about Mennonites in her country. *Stellet Licht*, I will argue, is a film in which the director's camera sees the Mennonites but does not know them. The camera invades the private lives of Low German Mennonites and even zooms in for close-ups of their faces. These Mennonites welcome the camera into their homes, but the community filmed remains inscrutable, somehow opaque.

The history of the Mennonites seen in *Stellet Licht* is not well known. Let me begin, therefore, by stepping behind the cinematic illusion and offering a sketch of the historical context. Mennonites arrived in Mexico in 1922 and settled in the state of Chihuahua, where *Stellet Licht* was filmed. They were Kanadier Mennonites from conservative Old Colony churches in Manitoba and Saskatchewan who left in response to the threat of losing control over language and religion in their schools. They were promised land and religious freedom in Mexico, but hardship followed as subsistence farming combined with a burgeoning population and poor education. Because of the group's apartness within Mexico (where the population now numbers about 80,000), and because members have dispersed to other countries (Argentina, Belize, Bolivia, and Paraguay), historians refer to them as Old Colony Mennonites or Low German Mennonites. A large number, about 70,000, have returned to Canada permanently and assimilated in various ways. In Mexico, however, Mennonites are a peculiar white minority separated from the larger *mestizo* or mixed-race population. This puts a unique and disturbing spin on the Mennonite foundational gesture of shunning the world. Janzen, whose great-grandmother was part of the first immigrant group, notes that "Low German Mennonites [in Mexico] deliberately resist being included in the national body" (2015b, 80). She also observes, however, that representations of Mennonites there are more positive than representations of other minority groups. They are seen as the harmless people who make and sell *queso menonita*. In Canada, the stereotypes about Low German–speaking Mennonites are class related, and Mexican Mennonites are seen as backward.

Carlos Reygadas, the director of *Stellet Licht*, has never pretended to have any interest in the history of Mennonites. During an interview with Karin Luisa Badt (2007), he was asked the inevitable question "Why Mennonites?" He replied "I am not particularly interested in Mennonites. I like that they are so uniform, so monolithic. They are all dressed the same. They are archetypes." Critics have mostly followed the director's lead. On his website, Roger Ebert (2009) describes the film as cast "entirely from the actual Mennonite community, which I believe will feel he played fair by them." Janzen reports that the "German-language Mennonite media in Mexico would disagree" with this assumption (2015b, 81). She has pointed to the numerous inaccuracies in the film and expressed the view that the characters are two-dimensional images onto which Reygadas projects his ideas. The majority of critics follow him in aestheticizing ethnic difference. Writing for the *Village Voice*, J. Hoberman (2008) refers to *Stellet Licht* as a "behavioral experiment . . . a unique amalgam of ethnographic documentary and 16th century psycho-drama." Although Hoberman calls the non-professional actors "devout performers," he implicitly mocks his own stereotypical assumptions when he adds "(who knew that Mennonites were allowed to act, let alone act out?)." By his account, Reygadas is a director who is "flirting with fraudulence and often working without a screenplay," a director who "orchestrates conditions where nonprofessional actors are compelled to expose themselves, sometimes cruelly, on camera."

If the acting is coerced participation, then is it not important to ask if anyone was hurt in the making of the film? That question has been directed at Reygadas's first two films—*Japón* (2002) and *Battle in Heaven* (2005)—and a few critics have hinted at it in relation to *Stellet Licht*. Jose-Luis Moctezuma (2009) points out that, in order to gain the cooperation of the local Mennonites, Reygadas showed a "willingness to forgo his usual dependence on raw sexual imagery" and made a "pact . . . with the Mennonites to respect the purity and decorum of their community." The happy result, according to Moctezuma, is that in this film Reygadas "separated what was obnoxious and profane in him from what was cinematically reverential." I do not doubt that the Mennonites refused to be photographed naked, but you do not need to have watched the CBC series *Pure* to conclude that the purity projected onto this community is illusory.

What are individual Mennonite viewers to make of *Stellet Licht*, positioned as we are on different diasporic threads of a complex history? I write as a Canadian conscious of my inadequate knowledge of Mexican contexts but intrigued by the presence in *Stellet Licht* of one of the stars of CanLit. Among the "devout performers," novelist Miriam Toews is a misfit, and this was apparent to Canadian viewers before the film was released. On 12 May 2007, Simon Houpt reported in the *Globe and Mail* that, when Reygadas saw a photograph of Toews on the jacket cover of *A Complicated Kindness*, he knew instantly that her face would be perfect for the part of the suffering wife in his film. Reygadas eventually persuaded Toews to take the part and make the trip to Mexico. Houpt's article was accompanied by a publicity photograph of Toews dressed as a Mexican Mennonite woman. The photograph of a Canadian urban assimilated Mennonite dressed as a "backward" Mexican Mennonite, to say the least, is a complex semiotic object.

For Mennonites of my generation, the problems faced by those Kanadier who left Manitoba for Mexico in 1921 are similar to those that we ourselves narrowly escaped because our families made the decision to stay. Recent reports about drug smuggling among Mennonites in Mexico have served to heighten that sense of escape. These facts are at odds with utopian stereotypes about Mennonites. The first time that I saw *Stellet*

Licht, as part of the Toronto International Film Festival in 2007, I was curious how this famous Mexican director would tackle such a charged subject. I was predisposed to like the film during the first seven minutes. Put simply, the camera records a sunrise. So spectacular is this opening that critics have vied with each other to find words to convey the power of it. Moctezuma (2009) writes that "this is the film's first miracle, when God said, 'Let there be Light.' And it was silent." There is plenty of time to think during those seven minutes. At that first viewing, I thought about the courage and humility in allowing the sun to rise without speeding it up. At the same time, by imperceptible degrees, I became aware of the controlling hand of the director and an increasing discomfort. That had to do in part with his decision to opt for diagetic sound, unlike a soundtrack in that it is connected to what is happening on the screen. While the sun rises and the stars fade gradually, the silence is punctuated by the sounds of farm animals stirring. Manohla Dargis (2008) writes about "the mesmerizing, transporting opener" as being "accompanied by an unsettling chorus of animal cries and screams (what's going on in there?)." Samuel Manickam (2013) writes that "the sound of animals braying and mooing seems more creepy than heart-warming" and is "suggestive of evil trickling into this ostensible paradise." Moctezuma (2009) thinks it to the director's credit that "these ancient creatures which so fearfully bellowed at the rising sun turn out to be just cows and bulls in their pens." All I ever heard was the urgent sound of cows demanding to be milked.

My first viewing became worse when the predatory camera moved inside the farmhouse after the spectacular sunrise. Instant claustrophobia combined with the discomfort of voyeurism, and this was complicated by the presence of Toews sitting at the foot of the breakfast table as Esther, the mother. I had not at that time met Toews and knew her only as a writer whose work I admired. As the family gathers at the breakfast table, the camera records their silent grace and then the near grunts that pass for table manners. In all my viewings of this scene, I have found it impossible not to identify with the children, whose silence feels coerced. I always want them to run away and am relieved when Esther leaves with the children. After which her husband, Johan (played by Cornelius Wall Fehr), is left alone in the kitchen. No explanation has yet been offered for the man's histrionic suffering. Johan slowly begins to break down; rather, he is an amateur actor trying to make it look as if he is breaking down. Ebert (2009) wrote that, "if you didn't know they were untrained actors, you would assume they had years of experience," and he described the performances as assuming "an almost holy reality." Ed Gonzalez, however, might have had this excruciating scene in mind when he wrote that "the director exploits the inexpressiveness of his obviously unprofessional cast, none of whom believably convey[s] even the *idea* of emotional anguish" (Gonzalez 2007).

The claustrophobia in that house is oppressive, but the mood lightens somewhat when Johan leaves it and drives in his truck to see his friend Zacarias (Jacob Klassen). From their stilted conversation, the viewer learns the reason for the agony of Johan: he is in love with a woman who is not his wife. He is trying to resist the temptation to go to her, but of course he fails. Marianne, the woman whom Johan "really" loves, is played by Maria Pankratz. Once dressed in the garb that makes Mennonites "uniform," those familiar archetypes, Madonna and Whore, are flattened out to be replaced by the archetype labelled Mennonite—or is it stereotype? We are supposed to believe that Johan's feelings for Marianne are too powerful to deny and that Johan cannot stop himself from hurting Esther. I did not believe it for a minute.

Esther finally dies of a broken heart, hugging a tree in the rain as she weeps uncontrollably. Surely even Gonzalez would concede that Toews's performance of this wrenching scene conveys anguish. The funeral that follows makes it clear, however, that the predatory camera is not finished with us, and we are subjected to a prolonged view of the open coffin. At my first viewing, no review had yet forewarned me of the moment (spoiler alert here) when the other woman, Marianne, leans over to kiss Esther in the coffin and Toews wakes up. Later I read Karin Luisa Badt's (2007) account of how this scene moved the audience at Cannes to give Reygadas, who was present, a thunderous standing ovation. People shouted "Bravo!" as they wept. According to her, it was "the only entry at Cannes that got such an intense response." To her, it offered proof that people are hungry for miracles and for belief in the transcendent. I have heard reports, however, of audiences in which there was laughter. My own response was to dissociate from the scene. I remember thinking about Sleeping Beauty and how it did not fit. Let me be clear: I am not saying that the film is not moving, only that I saw the beauty but was not especially moved by it.

The language in the film is estranged in ways that make little sense. Mexican Mennonites speak Low German, to be sure, in ways different from the Low German still spoken in southern Manitoba. Even so, I had looked forward to hearing my mother tongue used in everyday communication. It was a shock when the words coming out of the actors' mouths sounded like gibberish. Even when I could make them out, the subtitles were ridiculously inaccurate. People in costume moved around on the screen muttering things in a version of Low German mostly unintelligible. To me, they seemed to have been rendered voiceless and stripped of history. Afterward, when asked for my response, I expressed cautious reservations about the film to fellow Mennonites milling around in the lobby. One of them reproached me, saying "Maggie! It's an art film!"

I have sometimes wondered what it would be like to watch *Stellet Licht* as part of an audience of people who all speak Low German. I was intrigued to hear from ethnomusicologist Judith Klassen, who speaks Low German, that she had organized a private showing of *Stellet Licht* in Manitoba for her mother and several of her mother's friends and recorded their conversation while they watched it. Klassen, curator of cultural expression at the Canadian Museum of History, shared with me the transcript of the conversation. Laughter cannot be transcribed, but it was obvious that these women could not watch *Stellet Licht* without laughing constantly, in large part because of the absurd mistranslations in the subtitles. I take this as a sign that they were aware of the interethnic differences erased in *Stellet Licht*, differences that would humanize the "archetypes."

As Susan Sontag has observed, the technology of the camera militates against awareness of class. "Gazing on other people's reality with curiosity, with detachment," writes Sontag, "the ubiquitous photographer operates as if that activity transcends class interests" (1973, 55). From this position of distanced privilege, the viewer is "asked to look at what is really other" (Sontag 1973, 55). In his comments on the "gritty authenticity" achieved by directors who use amateur actors, Tobias Grey (2008) observes a "real desire among contemporary filmmakers to shed light on concealed environments" and "to realistically penetrate these worlds." But what if Reygadas, far from a naive realist, shares Marianne Moore's (1935) view of art? What if he inserted actual Mennonites into his ghetto/paradise the way that one might place real toads in a pretty garden? What if his cinematic art is more subtle and complex than suggested by his own commentary on it? Oddly I came closest to connecting with his deeper vision for the film when I watched it all alone in my own home and had the luxury of reflecting on such questions. Perhaps it was just that the crazy-making slow pace was more endurable with a glass of cold white wine in my hand. Or perhaps the claustrophobia was alleviated because I knew that if I wished I could get up and leave the room. During that solitary viewing, though not entirely charmed by the film, I could at least get past my irritation to a sort of melancholy intuition of what others might find enchanting in it. Take, for example, the title. I was surprised that I had not previously registered the distorted echoes of the High German carol "*Stille Nacht*" and the phrase *die Stillen im Lande*, "quiet in the land." The English title *Silent Light* also echoes the popular Christmas carol "Silent Night"—with the difference of only one letter. I now take these slippages of sound as an invitation to consider the fate of the senses in the film, and they draw attention to "the gap" that fascinated Emanuel Gat "between what we see and what we hear."

It helps to remember that *Stellet Licht* can be seen as an adaptation or translation of the 1955 Danish film *Ordet* (The Word), directed by Carl Theodore Dreyer. Like Dreyer, Reygadas opts for a slow-moving camera, and both movies contain a resurrection scene. In his comparative discussion of *Stellet Licht* and *Irma Voth*, Travis Kroeker invokes *Ordet* and sees these works as "bound together in a figural relation to the Gospel of John's sacramental hymn to the incarnation." Adaptation, when viewed as this kind of "scandalous displacement," makes of the artist a theologian, as Kroeker concedes: "This word through which all things were and are made—let's call it '*poiesis*'—is also named 'light' and indeed 'life itself'" (2018, 89–90). On a theoretical level, this helps to make sense of what Reygadas does in *Stellet Licht*, but I remain sceptical of interpretations that encourage transcendence of the inconvenient real toads in this Mennonite ghetto.

Commentators often invoke the image of paradise. Reviewing the film in *Mennonite Life*, Samuel Manickam (2013) writes that these Old Colony Mennonites represent "a simpler prelapsarian world illuminated by clear, silent sunlight." Manohla Dargis (2008) describes a family bathing scene as "a gorgeous, innocent yet sensuous scene" that offers "a glimpse of the prelapsarian with a hint of the viper." There is a palpable longing in such responses for a pure cultural product labelled Mennonite. Reading such commentary makes me want to tell the critics to listen to what the animals are saying. Those vipers are only cows needing to be milked. My protests, however, are muted by an awareness of my own blind spots. It took me a long time, for example, to realize that *Stellet Licht* might be a film made with a Catholic sensibility at odds with the Mennonite content. Writing about the resurrecting kiss, José Teodoro speculates that "maybe it's a Catholic thing, a way of rehabilitating the ritual of communion" (2009).

I now consider it fortunate that Reygadas cast Toews in a major role in *Stellet Licht*, thus igniting sparks in overlapping contact zones and opening up the possibility of crossover "ethnic dialogism" between Mexico and Canada. That does not mean, however, that I think the ethical questions about the casting of non-professional actors have easy answers. Tiago de Luca argues that people who say that non-professional actors are being tricked are "insinuating that these are people unable to take responsibility for their decisions." He flips the ethical coin and concludes that "it is the critic, not the director, who is taking up the position of 'condemned superiority'" (2014, 89). Surely the problem requires a more nuanced response. Are there not varying degrees of empowerment? Do not the ethical questions change when it is children, rather than adults, who are being used? There are good reasons to be disturbed by the much-admired scene in which children bathing in a creek look directly into the camera. And what are we to make of the puzzling scene in which Johan leaves his children with an apparent stranger—watching a Jacques Brel show inside a windowless van while he goes off to a rendezvous with Marianne? The children stay, to adapt Alice Munro's words, while the adults are away playing at being Orpheus and Eurydice. "I can't be the only one," writes Gonzalez, "who thought Johan . . . would find his children violated and/or cut to pieces after returning to the van. . . . But *Silent Light* never goes *there*" (2007). I put the spotlight on this scene briefly now as I turn my attention to *Irma Voth* because being concerned about the fate of the children is central to that novel's way of translating *Stellet Licht* into story.

Have You Read Irma Voth? *Observing Miriam Toews*

Have you seen *Irma Voth* (Toews 2011)? The question is anticipatory since I hope that a film adaptation of the novel will be made, thus continuing the back-and-forth dialogue that Reygadas and Toews have initiated. If you have read *Irma Voth*, however, the question can also be heard as a concern about the whereabouts of Irma. Has anybody seen Irma? Perhaps the most important thing to keep in mind about the behaviour of children is what was evident in Peter Power's (2011) images of a skating rink: they have a tendency to outgrow the fixed frames created for them. The implicit references to *Stellet Licht* (Reygadas 2007) in *Irma Voth* are many, however, as are the implied autobiographical links. The scene of ekphrasis that has the child-artist Aggie crying in front of the Diego Rivera mural in Mexico City, for example, sounds as if it might be based on Toews's own experience in front of that mural during her time in Mexico. Aggie's creation of a sky with stars as a gift for her sister could be interpreted as recreating the famous opening scene of *Stellet Licht*. These displacements might not seem scandalous, but the stories that reverberate in that scene refract it and invest Aggie's simple mimetic act with a charge that echoes down the centuries. The art is made with paper, echoing Matisse cutouts, but somehow the stories take us back to the shadows in Plato's cave, back to the prehistoric paintings at Altamira that awed Pablo Picasso, and, yes, back to the Bible.

As Toews did in *A Complicated Kindness* (2004), in *Irma Voth* she positions an adolescent narrator as a lens through which to refract the stories. By making the narrator a translator, however, she turns *Irma Voth* into a vehicle for exploring aesthetic questions that go far beyond anything in *A Complicated Kindness*. Added to this is the enriching fact that *Irma Voth* can be read as a parody of *Stellet Licht*—one of those parodies that pays homage to the earlier work of art. Toews deploys her own art of storytelling to move their shared quest into a kind of underworld where both she and Reygadas are engaged in "the unending Orphic task" of coming to terms with the shadowy figure of the other. In *Irma Voth*, Toews reimagines us and them while confronting and dealing at a deep level with the crisis of representation.

Literary critics often point out that one narrative technique especially resistant to film adaptation is first-person point of view. It is fitting, then, that Toews opts for that point of view as she reverses the typical scenario.

Many films are adapted from novels, but not many novels are adapted from films. In *Irma Voth*, our attention is frequently directed to the windows and doors of houses, bringing to mind a metaphor famously developed by Henry James to explain point of view: "The house of fiction has in short not one window, but a million. . . . At each of them stands a figure with a pair of eyes" (1975, 7). The adolescent translator in this "house of fiction" moves around a lot, making frequent ventures back through the cinematic frame and onto the set of a film thinly disguised but still recognizable as *Stellet Licht*. This backward movement exposes the cracks in any vision of a Mennonite community as a paradise. The laughter that I smothered while watching *Stellet Licht* is liberated here. On every page of *Irma Voth*, a reader might realize the truth of a point made by D. Diane Davis in *Breaking Up [at] Totality*, that us and them are "never given, never stable," and that it is laughter that breaks them up (Davis 2000, 3). As often happens in a novel by Toews, this laughter is mixed with tears, but there is always hope. Novelist David Bergen has observed: "She goes to dark places and yet she comes out leaning to the light." This, he concludes, is "what makes her writing so available" (Quoted in Barber 2011).

A central part of Toews's strategy in the novel is to keep the focus on the children. The love triangle in *Stellet Licht* is set aside and replaced by a triad of children: Irma, Aggie, and the baby Ximena, a name that puzzled me until my husband, Dennis Duffy, pointed out that it rhymes with cinema. As Anthony Doerr demonstrates in *All the Light We Cannot See* (2014), concern for the fate of the children can keep readers turning the pages even when it is nearly impossible to discern a linear narrative. The Mennonite children caught bathing in the frame of *Stellet Licht*, staring into the camera as if hypnotized, are here released. What is the fate of the children when Orpheus and Eurydice are busy acting out some romantic quest? Toews answers the question, to echo and invert Munro's title, by insisting that the children do *not* stay. They run away. It is an ancient story, the tale of babes lost in the woods. In this retelling of it, the children are lost in the urban jungle of Mexico City. The situation inverts the one in *A Complicated Kindness*. Events are precipitated not by a mother who abandons her children—*mater abscondita*—but by the children who abandon their mother. Hansel and Gretel come to mind, as do any number of other folktales in which children are at the mercy of powers around them and have to take care of each other.

Toews's adaptation of the story is subtle and designed to open up questions about art. Since one of the three children is an artist, the Orphic quest is revised to empower a little girl, but this revision of the myth is almost invisible, hidden in everyday details about childhood creativity. Unlike the plot of *Stellet Licht*, the stories in *Irma Voth* are not easily summed up. The novel has an anarchic quality. The crumbs that guide Hansel and Gretel seem to multiply exponentially, leaving no clear path through the shifting sets. Irma, still on the threshold of childhood, plays the role of the surrogate mother whose tenderness suffuses the book. As the eldest daughter in a Mexican Mennonite family, she has violated the us-and-them rules by falling in love with a Mexican man. Her tyrannical father punishes her by expelling her from the family home, and she takes up residence in a nearby abandoned house (the hapless lover having long since also abandoned her). A film crew moves into another abandoned house, and Irma is hired as a translator for Marijke, the German Mennonite who has been flown in to act in the film. Matters are further complicated when Irma's younger sister Aggie runs away from home to join her. Eventually they both run away to Mexico City, taking with them their baby sister Ximena.

The absurdity of it all sometimes resembles what you might find in a children's book by Robert Munch. Multiplication is central to Toews's comic strategy of reverse adaptation, and I experience it as a welcome antidote to the claustrophobic settings in *Stellet Licht*. Where Reygadas imagines a single-family home, Toews sketches in multiple farmyards and multiple houses. If you try to count the many haunted houses in *Irma Voth*, the novel begins to seem like a parody of a gothic novel. One of them is the abandoned farmhouse in which Irma lives after her expulsion from her parental home. Another is the one used by the film crew. These ghost houses and yards, left behind by Mennonites who have continued their wanderings, become the sites of unpredictable explorations not bound by gothic conventions. It is impossible to envision any one of those farmyards as a bucolic world inhabited by a Mennonite family somehow in the world but not of the world. All these houses show what the voice says in *The Quiet in the Land* and in *The Goldlandbergs*: We live in a real world of geography and the specific social contexts that come with one particular place. You can almost feel the grit of the soil of Chihuahua even as the clustering of houses on that land evokes larger historical contexts.

When some Kanadier Mennonites in Manitoba left for Mexico in the 1920s, they abandoned houses and farms. Some of them were inhabited by newly arrived Russländer refugees and then left empty again when those Mennonites moved to Winnipeg. Reflecting on the many "leave-takings" and escapes in *Irma Voth*, Armin Wiebe shrewdly notes that they touch on "something of a Mennonite thing. . . . Mennonites spent 450 years trying to escape from the world, but now there is no place left to escape to" (quoted in Prokosh 2011a). There is a consensus among Mennonites that the large migrations to Manitoba were the last possible settlements on sustainable land. Awareness of this colours how Toews reimagines us and them. Hers is an art that seeks out precarious crossings, her inner clown finding balance somehow on a high wire between laughter and tears, always adapting, always translating.

An adolescent focus is particularly well suited to an exploration of different kinds of translation. As George Steiner (1974) notes, adolescence is the time when languages are contested, a time when received rules about language are put through a filter of whatever vernaculars are dominant at the time. The gibberish version of Low German spoken in *Stellet Licht* is left far behind in *Irma Voth*, which feels more like a Tower of Babel than a ghetto. There are too many languages, too much noise, and too much information. In an essay entitled "He Stuttered," Gilles Deleuze (1998) argues that great writers test a system of language and make it stutter. This is an apt description of what Toews does in *Irma Voth*. She herself is a translator, working to move from the language of cinema to the language of storytelling. The future is never spelled out as a form of *translatio* or total metaphor but left deliberately vague, like the name of the baby, Ximena. In this novel, Low German is one language among many—not a remnant from medieval times put forward as a kind of exotic thing but simply the everyday language of the children. Spanish, a language nearly absent in *Stellet Licht*, also features prominently as the girls fight to survive in Mexico City.

The national contexts that are almost dissolved into archetypal designs in *Stellet Licht* matter deeply in *Irma Voth*. For example, whereas the children in the film are untroubled inhabitants of a utopian community, the children in the novel struggle with culture shock. Similarly, references to social context are almost forcibly absorbed into symbol by Reygadas, in contrast to how Toews exposes referential connections with a daring nakedness. This is notable, for example, when the words of Diego, the fictive director in the novel, are almost verbatim quotations of actual comments made by Reygadas. Phil Hoad (2007) reports, for example, that Reygadas spoke as follows about filmmaking: "But when the time comes, you have to be fully there and you have to be ready to risk your life. If you're not, you have to leave. It's commando mentality." In *Irma Voth*, Diego echoes this sentiment: "This is commando filmmaking," he tells the crew. "This is guerrilla filmmaking. . . . If you're not prepared to risk your life, then leave now. . . . YOU MUST BE PREPARED TO DIE" (Toews 2011, 43). Irma's mistranslation of it reads like a sly pacifist dissent. When Marijke asks Irma "What is he saying?" Irma replies "He wants us all to have fun, relax and be brave" (113).

The scene in the novel that comes closest to being emblematic of Toews's aesthetic involves a lowly cab driver called Gustavo, who plays the role of Orpheus with relation to the three children who are other. He plays it with the gusto suggested by his name, resembling a Good Samaritan figure who rescues the children lost in the urban jungle of Mexico City while acting as a clowning ferryman helping them across a threshold. Gustavo models a form of compassionate translation, but there is no pretence that a language barrier does not exist or that the differences between Spanish and English can be dissolved into archetype. In tacit homage to Reygadas and to the art of cinema, Toews creates a scene in which gesture is more important than either word or image. Gustavo's balancing act on a collapsing beach chair brings to mind other physical clowns, such as Mr. Bean. Irma cannot stop laughing: "I tried to. Ximena stopped wriggling and stared at me. Gustavo swore and turned around to look at me. One of the lenses in his sunglasses had popped out" (155). The partial vision of a clown is preferred here to the single eye of a visionary as a model for the role of the artist. Abandoning any effort to bridge "the gap between what we see and what we hear," this scene affirms the humanity of living in that gap. Art is made with gusto in the midst of the life that constantly destabilizes it.

Gustavo's clowning stunt embodies what is clearly, within the comic vision of Miriam Toews, the essential ingredient for acts of translation that aim for "ethnic dialogism": love. Love is not easily translated, however, and kindness is indeed complicated. In an earlier scene, the words to the song "Gott ist die Liebe" (God Is Love) are mistranslated, and there is a constant reminder in this novel that love, like kindness, is complicated. In this scene, however, Toews allows herself to celebrate in Gustavo the power of love. She does so with a maternal gesture performed by a man: "At the airport Gustavo held each of us close to his warm body, his beating heart" (157). What follows, however, makes clear that this gesture cannot be easily reduced to words or to the Word. Gustavo tells the girls to go to "the lake of echoes," where anything that they say will be "cannonballed right back at us clear as day. If you say, for instance, the name of the person you love, then the world will say it back to you as though it is confirming that it understands.... You can yell anything, said Gustavo, and the world will confirm it. You could yell *Vive mucho tiempo el muerto*! Or you could yell *Esto es una locura*!" (157). The phrases are not translated in the text, thus pulling the reader into participation. If you do not know Spanish, then you have no choice but to consult a dictionary or accept the opacity of the words. This is how "ethnic dialogism" moves forward, when the inevitability of inadequate translation is accepted as a given and we abandon the tempting illusion of some final certainty. Then us and them can join in a perpetual act of shared making believe, and love is celebrated as an ongoing act of mistranslation repeatedly forgiven. Toews does not present one dramatic act of forgiveness, such as the one that offers redemption in *Stellet Licht*. Forgiveness is refracted and multiple, an inextricable part of the life that surrounds this one text. We cannot stop ourselves from constructing us and them oppositions. We can only forgive each other for doing it and then reimagine them once again. Irma is every person, standing in for all of us as she translates and mediates the world around her.

"And a Little Child Shall Lead Them"

The central part that children have turned out to play in this chapter has been as much of a surprise to me as it might be to my readers. As I reflect on this, I think of Isaiah's prophecy about that place where "the wolf also shall dwell with the lamb ... and a little child shall lead them" (Isaiah 11:6).

Not long ago, at the Philips Gallery in Washington, I saw one of the paintings in the series by Edward Hicks known as *The Peaceable Kingdom*. When I turned my attention away from the splendid animals and the beautiful child and pondered the background scene of William Penn and "the Indians," I saw what looked like boys playing a game. The scene loops my argument back to the opening images of boys playing on a skating rink. Although the reality is that we play games together in various demarcated spaces on this Earth, we cannot and should not do so without visionary goals. The vision of a harmonious community that I see in the painting is consistent with what I was taught as a child to define as the aim of all our endeavours. So is the powerful vision of peace. The advantage of acknowledging the presence of real toads (and real cows) in imaginary ghettos is that, when the border between art and life is exposed as porous, there is at least the possibility of constructing a community that works toward such a vision.

The skating rink in Peter Power's (2011) photographs is a good image for the cultural interactions happening in a contact zone and for the perpetual reimagining of us and them. A healthy community is an open one, a place that allows for multiple crossings of the borders surrounding it, whether geographical or ideological. Utopias and dystopias are no places. We knew that, even in the church of my childhood. All the preachers were farmers, and there was a practical sense of community as something always in process. There was no systematic theology, only a repeated return to Bible stories. Community was something that you kept trying and failing to achieve, and then you tried again. Of course we knew that there was no utopia anywhere on Earth, least of all in our community. That was what heaven represented.

It has not escaped my notice that, among the artists with whom I deal in this chapter, Toews is the only woman, the only Mennonite, and the only comic writer. I did not plan for this to happen, but I now see it as reflecting my view that this kind of clowning is often part of a Mennonite sensibility. I realize, of course, that this counters the stereotype that Mennonites have no sense of humour. I nevertheless hear the hilarious mistranslations of Irma Voth as tapping into a tradition that includes the mistranslations of any number of other Mennonites who write in a place where languages intersect. I confess that I am sometimes amused and moved by the earnestness with which some non-Mennonites struggle to understand Mennonites. Although the vast majority of Mennonites have never lived in separated communities, this has only increased fascination with those who do. Because of Anabaptist history, there still seem to be more Mennonites than non-Mennonites who choose to live in anachronistic communities. Toews takes her art to that place of fascination and embraces the challenge of "ethnic dialogism." After reading *Irma Voth* I come away with the sense that all artists, at their best, touch on the deepest parts of our humanity when they open us and them up to dialogue. These examples of flawed and broken community are ways of reimagining us and them. It is an everyday task, not only a job for poets, to work at "drawing the figure of the other—the figure of the beloved who reciprocally can recognize one's own figure—out of the darkness" (Stewart 2002, 2).

CLOWNING WITH LOW GERMAN*

Dei ess nich oppem muel jefolle.

That one has not fallen on the mouth
(That one talks a lot.)

Sush (which rhymes with push) is a Low German nickname for Sarah. I came up with the name Sush Funk simply because I liked the sound of it, and after that a character began to attach itself to the name. Many years later, after I had clowned with masks, I saw how my adventures with Sush were one way of getting inside the paradox of plain style while indulging my desire to play with Low German. The many lessons that I learned from Sush cast a sideways but clarifying light on my

---

* With gratitude to the following clowns: my mother, Elizabeth Falk, my late husband, Clarence Redekop, Mary Lowery, Bruce Kirkpatrick Hill, Henry Schellenberg, Don Harron, Elsie Neufeld, Hildi Froese Tiessen, Paul Hiebert, Michael Kennard and John Turner (Mump and Smoot), and Walter de la Mare.

argument about making believe and on the problem of nostalgia that will be my focus in the next chapter.

Sush made her first appearance in 1998 when I was casting about for a way to help out at a fundraiser for the Pax Christi Chorale, a Toronto choir. I started with the idea that it might be entertaining to read to people from Paul Hiebert's *Sarah Binks* (1947). Remembering how much I had enjoyed amateur performances based on that book, I decided to pretend that I was the only living descendant of Sarah Binks. The Pax Christi Chorale at that time was still calling itself Toronto's Mennonite Choir, but Mennonite choristers were already in a minority. I was not certain how many people would even be familiar with *Sarah Binks*, still popular in Manitoba but not well known in Toronto. I invited my friend Mary Lowery, then teaching theatre at the Toronto French School, to join me. I had the idea that we would be a clown duo and that her British accent would be a foil to Sush Funk's Low German accent. I cannot now remember which lines I wrote, if any, for Mary. Probably she improvised. I asked a soprano chorister with a particularly sweet voice to sing Hiebert's translation of *"Die Lorelei"* ("The Laurel's Egg"), and the late Bruce Kirkpatrick Hill agreed to accompany her. He was our rehearsal accompanist and the husband of our conductor, Stephanie Martin. If memory serves, I even asked Bruce to pretend to be a farmer. He played along like the good sport that he always was, but I cannot remember whether or not he donned overalls or a straw hat.

My plan was simple. I would make an absurdly prolonged introduction to the performance of the song, during which I would read from *Sarah Binks*. Thinking about a costume felt like playing dress-up. I finally settled on a short-sleeved over-blouse made of heavy-weight cream-coloured brocade cotton. My mother had made it for herself, and I had seen her wear it not long before she died. When I put it on, it felt a little like a suit of armour. It did not occur to me to bother with makeup. I simply took off my glasses, pulled my hair off my face, held it back with a headband, and then tied a large flowered kerchief under my chin. When I looked in the mirror, it felt a bit off. That was not at all how my mother had worn her daily head covering, but I let it go. Why would I want to look like my mother?

On the day of the fundraiser, my stage fright was so intense that I prepared a copy of *Sarah Binks* to use as a prompt book, taping into it scraps of dialogue to read in case I was struck dumb. Mary Lowery recommended the old thespian trick of taping a penny underneath the arch of one foot. As it turned out, that worked like a charm. As I hobbled painfully into the room, I found myself catapulted into a space where a Low German accent came to me without effort. Sush talked about having come all the way from Pluetznaut, Manitouba (Sopping Wet, Manitoba). As I remembered it later, the audience response was muted, but it is possible that there was laughter and that I was too nervous to hear it. Certainly my late husband, Clarence Redekop, a Pax Christi bass, would have been laughing. Afterward a Mennonite friend marvelled at how I had been able to make myself look so ugly. More gratifying was the response of a woman whose name I have forgotten but who said that she had been born in Russia and was working as a translator in Toronto. *"Eckj ha mee meist dout jelacht!"* she said. I almost laughed myself dead.

Sush made her next appearance at a Schellenberg family gathering in Manitoba in August 2000. On that occasion, she was less attached to the text of *Sarah Binks* but still dressed in my mother's blouse and that ridiculous kerchief. My cousin, the late Henry Schellenberg, performed one of the songs. Sush talked about a recent gallbladder operation and proudly exhibited a jar with her gallstones in them. She also brought a long-stemmed artificial rose to present to my Aunt Agatha, then almost ninety, in memory of her sister Liesche. I had the idea that this would be a comfort to my aunt, a reminder of how much her sister loved flowers. Afterward, however, my aunt, normally a chatterbox, looked sad and said only that I looked exactly like my mother.

The gallstones that Sush displayed in that jar were perfectly shaped round pebbles that Clarence had gathered carefully on the shore of Lake Winnipeg that day, which he had done gladly so as to have some private time away from his rather overwhelming in-laws. I was told later that he was doubled over with laughter when I clowned with them. A few days later, right after our drive back to Toronto, he fell down on our front yard and died as the result of cardiac arrhythmia.

Several weeks later, when I was still in the first shock of grief, I convinced myself that Clarence would want me to keep a promise to have Sush Funk appear at the opening ceremony of the Isabel Bader Theatre at Victoria College. It has been said that grief is a form of insanity, especially when a death is sudden and untimely. That might account for some of the bizarre aspects of my performance at that gala event. The evening was planned with precision, and I was allotted precisely twelve minutes. While I was getting into costume in the green room, it was decided at the last minute that I should wear a wire. I remember thinking that I must really have looked like I felt, as if I had aged several decades after my husband's death. The students who helped to attach the wire treated Sush tenderly, as if she were made of glass.

I had persuaded those in charge to allow Sush Funk to stumble back and forth along the catwalk in advance of her entry. It was an idea that I got from having seen the duo horror clowns Mump and Smoot make an entrance while talking gibberish. I lacked their skill, but I reasoned that Low German would sound like gibberish to this audience. Accordingly, Sush walked along the catwalk shouting Low German insults down into the darkness of the auditorium while the master of ceremonies, Don Harron, was getting things started. There was laughter when Harron looked up at Sush and, sounding a lot like Charlie Farquharson, yelled "I think you want immigration." In spite of this discouraging response, Sush eventually appeared on stage, recognizable (I hoped) as a bag lady. She sat down on a park bench and extracted various objects from her assorted bags and eventually produced a document to prove that she had been born as the result of a secret love affair between Sarah Binks and Walter de la Mare. This was my private joke with my children, who were in the audience, and it alluded to a flat-footed shtick that Clarence did to make us laugh. The joke was based on the absurdity of the name and had nothing at all to do with the poetry of Walter de la Mare. It involved making an endless list of titles. If, for example, you chanced to comment that the weather was lousy, Clarence might say: "'Lousy Weather' by Walter de la Mare."

Just before her exit, Sush fished a bag of candies out of one of her bags and, as a farewell gesture, threw them out into the audience.

This *bescherrung,* or gift giving, was my way of connecting with the comforting spirit of my mother, whose most gleeful moments were on Christmas day in the afternoon when she distributed gifts to her grandchildren. My children, who had never met my mother, were in the audience. My idea had been to throw candy to them, on her behalf, but the theatre was dark, and I could not see back to where they were sitting. I could only see the front row, where the important people were sitting, so I aimed for Dennis Lee. Somebody told me afterward that one candy hit the forehead of the lieutenant governor of Ontario.

During the long years of grief that followed, I moved and downsized. I gave away Sush Funk's "costume" at about the same time that I recycled Clarence's clothes. It seemed to me that in a sense Sush had died when Clarence had died and that her performance in the Isabel Bader Theatre had been a little like how a chicken would keep hopping around in the barnyard even after my mother had chopped off its head.

My last performance of Sush Funk had a Lazarus air to it. It happened in response to an invitation from Hildi Froese Tiessen. When she retired, Conrad Grebel College asked Tiessen what she would like as a retirement gift. With characteristic generosity, she chose to ask the college to host a series of lectures, and her invitation to me came as part of that series. She requested that I perform as Sush Funk and then follow it with a lecture on clowning in Mennonite literature, a daunting challenge indeed. While emailing about it with my friend, the poet Elsie Neufeld, I told her that in the past Sush had done a candy *bescherrung.* This brought back to Elsie a vivid memory of the lobster candies given to children at Christmas in a brown paper bag called a *tüt.* The detail linked her up instantly to the tangled threads of her family history. I knew that her mother had survived untellable horrors as a result of multiple wartime displacements (see Neufeld 2018). To have continued the lobster candy tradition after that was surely no small feat. I, however, had never heard of lobster candies. My Kanadier nostalgia came in a different flavour. We called the brown paper bag a *lush,* not a *tüt.* After reciting a poem for my grandparents, I would receive a *lush* containing a handful of unshelled peanuts, an Oh Henry! chocolate bar, an orange, and a few striped peppermint candies. Because I had no memory of lobster candies and jokingly accused Elsie of making them up, she looped Hildi Froese Tiessen into our email exchange. Hildi confirmed that Russländer children also received lobster candies in a *tüt*. In due course, a large parcel came in the mail from Elsie with lobster candies for Sush to distribute in Waterloo.

Something about the nostalgia of my friends was intoxicating even though it was not exactly my experience, and this helped to inject life into the moribund body of Sush Funk. I was able to coax her into action by dint of a shopping expedition to a Goodwill store, after which she came to me as an elderly Mennonite from Altona who was losing her memory but spoke with a heavy Low German accent. I was surprised to find that I no longer needed *Sarah Binks* as a crutch. I did have a moment of panic while I was changing in the small room adjacent to the chapel at Conrad Grebel College, the location of the event. The plan was that Hildi would introduce Sush Funk while I changed, but when I opened the bag containing my costume I found that, during the drive from Toronto, the jar containing the gallstones had broken. There were bits of broken glass mixed in with the stones. I was nearly undone by a grief spasm, but the day was saved when a kind student fetched Paul Tiessen, who came up with a replacement jar.

The penny under my foot did the trick one last time, and I had brought a cane for good measure since by that time I was old enough to be aware of the need for fall prevention. After she had hobbled onto the stage, Sush apologized for not having anything to say about *Sarah Binks*, as Hildi's introduction had led the audience to expect. About Paul Hiebert she remembered *nuscht*. The audience was warm, and I saw many familiar faces, so it was difficult to stay in character. Each time Sush said "I don't belief it!" everybody laughed. When it came time to do the *bescherrung*, Sush produced the bag of lobster candies and gave them to Hildi Froese Tiessen to distribute to the audience. After which Sush made her laboured exit to change into clothing more appropriate for a professor giving a public lecture.

3.

RESISTING NOSTALGIA
Little Shtahp on the Prairie

Oost, vast—
Tüss es bast.

East, west—
Home is best.

Where We Come From

One Sunday morning in Toronto, geographer John Warkentin asked me
to point out exactly where I come from. We knelt together on the floor of
a friend's living room, and he unrolled a topographical map that he used
while writing *The Mennonite Settlements of Southern Manitoba* (2000).
I put my finger on the spot. There was our farm, halfway between Rosenfeld and Altona, down to the last meticulously drawn barn. Every building
on that yard has long since been torn down. All that remains is the familiar
tree line, but still I feel a deep connection to that place. When I was invited by Carol Ann Weaver to contribute something to her mixed-media

composition *Earth Voices*,[*] I thought of that spot on the Earth and came up with the following: "*Shtahp*. When my father worked on the field, we used to say he was *uppe shtahp*. The word comes from the Russian *steppe*, meaning prairie. If referring to a particular field of flax, the Low German would be *fleckj*, meaning patch. The same word, *fleckj*, could refer to a small piece of fabric used for mending. A *fleckj* is something you can own, no matter how small the patch, but nobody owns the *shtahp*. That's why my father went down on his knees in the dirt to give thanks for what grew on the *shtahp*." I was aware of my nostalgia even as I was constructing it. That bit about my father going down on his knees is not literally true. I only imagine him doing it because I was told at his funeral that my brother Peter did that every year at harvest time. Peter was the only one of my six brothers who chose to be a farmer. I was there when his three children buried him in the soil not far from his farm, near the town of Lowe Farm, which happens to be Warkentin's hometown.

It is also not true that "nobody owns the *shtahp*." That phrase was the product of my wish to harmonize with the chorus of voices that Weaver was assembling for the folks in California. I was not able to attend that conference, but I imagined *Earth Voices* as evoking solastalgia, a neologism coined to convey the distress felt as a result of the destruction wreaked on the planet that is our home. Land ownership remains an issue, however, and the emergence of Indigenous voices has unsettled the familiar narratives of settlement. A shift happened within me when I read Caroline Fraser's compelling account, in *Prairie Fires: The American Dreams of Laura Ingalls Wilder*, of the attempted genocide of the Dakota people (2017, 15–24). Our farm was just north of North Dakota. I wondered if some of the Dakota people once wandered over our *shtahp*. Then I realized that I do not even know the name of the language spoken by that group, and I heard once again that haunting reproach: "Are you not history knowing?"

My father expressed pride in his waving fields of grain to the extent that you can when humility is a cornerstone of your theology. Owning land was not something that his ancestors in Russia had taken for granted. Indeed, it was land that drew many of those Mennonites to Canada in the 1870s,

---

[*] *Earth Voices* was performed at the seventh Mennonite/s Writing conference on Movement, Transformation, Place, held at Fresno Pacific University, California, in 2015.

the situation in Russia having reached a point where there was a class division between those who owned land (sometimes large estates) and those who were landless. As W.H. New pointed out in *Land Sliding: Imagining Space, Presence, and Power in Canadian Writing*, "while the word *land* often functions as a familiar synonym for *dirt* or *earth* or *ground* or *loam*," it also resonates "with notions of ownership or social attachment (*territory, home, property, estate, plot, yard, grounds, region, nation, world*)" (1997, 5).

Shtahp. Among Kanadier, this Low German word has a double meaning, denoting both a field that is owned and prairie that is wild. Russländer Mennonites use the High German *Steppe* to mean only prairie. In High German, the word rhymes with the English *steppe* and *step* and evokes the kind of nostalgia pictured in the title of a memoir by Connie Braun: *The Steppes Are the Colour of Sepia* (2008). The words that I sent to Carol Ann Weaver for composition show how much I love the *sh* sound and the long *ah* sound in the middle, present only in Low German: *Shtahp*. Exclamations, writes Daniel Heller-Roazen, "mark an excess in the phonology of an individual tongue," where the onomatopoeia is a "calling out" by the human to "what is not human" (2008, 17–18). In this place of excess that signals an awareness of human limits, however, one tongue surely also cries out for contact with other tongues. *Ah*! Even as I sent the word *shtahp* out to Weaver, hoping that it would cry out for such contact, I was hugging it to myself, cherishing my specific memories of one particular place on this Earth.

I begin by exhibiting my nostalgia to make the point that it is impossible to study nostalgia at all when it is denied. On the basis of the words that I sent to Weaver, a listener could do little more than guess that my nostalgia has something to do with Low German and my attachment to the earth that the pioneers dug into in the 1870s to build the temporary sod shelters known as *semlins*. By itself, however, this did nothing to advance my understanding of nostalgia in a way transferable to readers in other cultures. To do that, I had to engage with numerous works of art, two of which will serve as case studies in this chapter. I have also learned from others who have studied nostalgia. Susan Stewart long ago referred to nostalgia as the "social disease" of our time (1984, ix). More recently, Svetlana Boym has described it in *The Future of Nostalgia* as being "at the very core of the modern condition" (2001, xvi). As Boym puts it, however, "the more nostalgia is there, the more heatedly it is denied" (xiv). Scholars in various disciplines approach this problem in different ways. Literary critics have tended to see their role as countering denial by studying the semiotics of nostalgia, showing how particular tropes and genres serve as vehicles (see Santesso 2006). My own discipline, in other words, focuses on the very questions about representation that are central to the argument of this book.

Nostalgia is not an academic question for anybody, but the place where literary criticism intersects with autobiography might be where something can be learned from recognizing that denial begins at home. It is easy for me to point to Russländer nostalgia because it is so obviously not mine, a human failing that Jesus pinpointed in the Sermon on the Mount when he reproached a hypocrite: "And why beholdest thou the mote that is in thy brother's eye, but considerest not the beam that is in thine eye?" (Matthew 7:3). Narratives associated with German national identity are now charged with a kind of electricity, and they are relatively easy targets for moral reproach. Kanadier narratives, however, are not immune to essentialist ways of thinking. Russländer collective memory might attach itself to tragic narratives of loss and images of orchards and mansions in Russia. In contrast, Kanadier collective memory clings to settler narratives and pastoral memories of a little *shtahp* on the prairie. Both genres can become vehicles for the dangerous kind of nostalgia that erases history. Boym suggests that not all nostalgia is bad. Instead of fuelling dangerous attempts to recreate a lost home on actual land, she suggests, "reflective nostalgia can foster a creative self. . . . Nostalgia can be both a social disease and a creative emotion, a poison and a cure" (2001, 354). Art is not her focus, and she does not engage with any work of art to test her hypothesis. At one level, that is what I will do in this chapter. My aim, however, is not simply to argue that nostalgia can be creative, nor do I think that art offers a cure. The best art, however, makes it possible to resist the dangerous kinds of nostalgia. It does so by heightening our awareness of differences, not by smoothing over them.

The differences that have guided my choice of case studies emerge from the Mennonite history that I sketched in the introduction. I have chosen two texts: Paul Hiebert's *Sarah Binks*, published in 1947, and John Weier's *Steppe: A Novel*, published in 1995. The asymmetry of these companion texts is deliberate. If I were comparing authors working during the same time period, then a more logical choice for a Kanadier parody of pioneer pastoral would be *A Complicated Kindness* (Toews 2004). With this rather odd juxtaposition, I hope to show that the earlier arrival in Canada of the Kanadier and the very different refugee experience of the Russländer have resulted in different narratives of assimilation and different genres. Nostalgia is a problem for Mennonites in all groups, however, and this is no surprise since, as Boym points out, nostalgia is a "rebellion against the modern idea of time, the time of history and progress" (2001, xv). Given our centuries-long effort to create communities set apart from both "the world" and history, nostalgia can become a last-ditch effort to preserve that separation.

The experience of nostalgia varies among the many different subgroups of Mennonites. After engaging closely with one work from each of the groups primarily responsible for the Canadian Mennonite renaissance— the Kanadier and the Russländer—I will conclude the chapter with comments about the varieties of nostalgia related to other Mennonite immigrant groups. This does not mean that I am recommending that works of art should be sorted out and put in cubbyholes designated for the particular subgroups to which authors belong. I do not know, for example, the family ancestry of Joanne Epp, nor do I need to know it in order to appreciate how her poetry plays with nostalgic tropes. I do not need to know exactly which place she herself comes from to follow her words to a place of making believe where she resists nostalgia in ways that reframe our way of seeing home. The old tropes come alive in Epp's poetry collection *Eigenheim* (2015). The word *eigen* means own. To call a place *Eigenheim* is an implied tautology, pointing to ambiguities regarding ownership and belonging. Epp's poem "Eigenheim," about the burial of an uncle's body, is in a long line of literary works that takes on familiar nostalgic tropes (flowers, grass, wind, graveyard) and pushes past clichés to reimagine our relationship with the Earth.

The Greek word *nostos*, meaning to return home, and *algia*, meaning painful condition, come together in the word *nostalgia*. The concept of home is present in every culture on the Earth: whether in the East or in the West, home is best. The truism in the epigraph to this chapter, however, requires a double take in relation to nostalgia. Stories about a *return home* vary widely depending on differences in histories. The structure most familiar in the West is the departure and return enacted in Homer's *The Odyssey*. The quest of a male hero whose Penelope is waiting for him at home is a convention deeply embedded in our culture. Such a relentless focus on an individual male quest, however, is missing from many other traditions, such as in the ancient Indian epic *Mahabharata*. It is also challenged by feminist texts such as Margaret Atwood's *The Penelopiad*. Within the multicultural fabric of Canadian life, it is further complicated by stories of immigrants from many different countries. When resisting nostalgia, however, the moral of *The Odyssey* remains a useful guide. Adam Nicolson spells it out: "As they pass the Sirens, Odysseus's men tie him even more tightly to the mast. . . . To live well in the world, nostalgia must be resisted: you must stay with the ship, stay tied to the present, remain mobile . . . , engage, in other words, with the muddle and duplicity and difficulty of life" (2014, 6). Almost without exception, I see all the artists from different Mennonite groups who are part of the renaissance as practising this kind of resistance.

Both texts that I have chosen for case studies in this chapter are rural based, and this doubtless reflects the bias of somebody who grew up on a farm. The same big sky looms over both the city mouse and the country mouse, and I can see that sky from my home here in a twelfth-floor apartment in Toronto. But it is on the prairie that you feel the full force of it, and that is where I come from. Because my life's work has been with words, I have a heightened awareness of the nostalgia known as topophilia and of the intense pleasure in the sounds of place names: Schoenthal (lovely valley); Schoenwiese (lovely meadow); Steinbach (stony brook); Rosenfeld (field of roses); Rosenort (place of roses); Weidenfeld (pasture field); Blumenfeld (flower field); Sommerfeld (summer field); Hochfeld (high field); Rosengart (rose garden). Many of these villages no longer exist.* Only their names remain, resonating with the pastoral tropes that lead, all too quickly, to that place where all the layers of history are erased. The way out of this dead end is to reject the search for *Lebensraum* that goes with nostalgia and to look instead for *Spielraum*. My first case study closely examines one such search.

---

* My sister, Mary Neufeld, has written the history of our father's home village. Entitled *Prairie Pioneers: Schönthal Revisited* (2016), it is part of a growing list of published histories of the Mennonite villages in what was known as the West Reserve.

Rewriting the Settler Narrative: The Case of Sarah Binks

In his 1957 history of Manitoba, W.L. Morton referred to Paul Hiebert's *Sarah Binks*, published in 1947, as being "rich with the soft laughter of the Mennonites." He ventured a prediction: "It is in such transmutations of folk cultures and genius into the vernacular English that the hope of Manitoba letters seems to lie" (470). The notion that laughter in a book can be identified by ethnicity seems quaint now. Morton, however, was an eminent historian who specialized in the settlement of the Canadian west, and he had read widely in Canadian and American literature (Wardhaugh 2013). The Mennonite literary renaissance seems to provide evidence that his hope was not misplaced. How strange, then, that Hiebert has been erased from Mennonite literary history and that this erasure was confirmed during the very time of that flowering. In 1972, when the first stirrings were just beginning in Manitoba, Jack Thiessen wrote an essay entitled "Canadian Mennonite Literature" in which he remarked: "to what extent Paul Hiebert's sketches in *Sarah Binks* (1947) can be called Mennonite literature is debatable" (71). After the full Manitoba flowering of the 1980s had passed, Al Reimer, in his 1993 survey of it, confirmed Thiessen's view, referring to *Sarah Binks* as an "isolated literary phenomenon" that can be "regarded only peripherally as 'Mennonite'" (20). I have never been content to leave it at that. In October 2009, during the closing panel discussion at a conference on Mennonite/s Writing: Manitoba and Beyond, I asked a question from the floor, wondering why Hiebert, since he was a Manitoba writer, was not part of our discussions. Rudy Wiebe, on the panel, replied that "Paul Hiebert never identified as a Mennonite." Nobody questioned that, but later over coffee a local resident told me that his conversations with Hiebert had given him the impression that the man was puzzled and hurt by his exclusion from the Mennonite community.

In a welcome turn, Robert Zacharias has questioned this repeated critical gesture. He observes that *Sarah Binks* is a text "set aside" because it is perceived as "not sufficiently attuned to Mennonite contexts," but this has happened "primarily because the various contexts for the emergence of Mennonite Canadian literature have been forgotten" (2013, 37–38). I will consider a few of these forgotten contexts before turning to this text that so often has been "set aside." One of these contexts is the culture that developed among Kanadier Mennonites during the nearly half century that they lived in Manitoba before the Russländer arrived. These fifty years often vanish mysteriously when Mennonites talk about Manitoba history. During the time that Hiebert was growing up in Manitoba, there were, to be sure, many Kanadier who were "backward," an ethnic slur often applied to the entire group: poor, living on farms, resistant to education, and hanging on to Low German. My own family could be seen as fitting that description. Many more, however, were already assimilating (as was Hiebert's family) into mainstream English culture. How many assimilated writers are hidden behind this blind spot is impossible for me to say, but one example does come to mind. A.E. van Vogt, an influential writer of science fiction, was born in 1912 on his grandparents' farm near Gretna, just a few miles south of our farm. He spoke Low German as a child, and his name then was Alfred Vogt. His first and most famous novel, *Slan*, was published in 1946, one year before the publication of *Sarah Binks*.

Although I never had the pleasure of meeting Paul Hiebert, I have always felt as if I know the man who wrote what I call a "direct oversetting" of Heinrich Heine's "Du bist wie eine Blume":

> You are like one flower,
> So swell, so good, and clean,
> I look you on and longing,
> Slinks me the heart between. (Hiebert 1995, 40)

How could the man who wrote that not be Mennonite? I don't remember anybody giving that question much thought during the 1950s. His speech did betray Hiebert. I have written in "Farm Animals' Desertion: In Which Puss in Boots Learns that the Kota Is Full" (2013a) about how I made the mistake of naming my calf one year and then paid the emotional price when it was slaughtered and I had to eat it. Sarah's elegy to a calf gave voice to my feelings: "Oh calf, that gambolled by my door. . . . Oh calf, calf! Art dead, art dead?" (Hiebert 1995, 24–25; see Redekop 2013a). My experience contradicts Margaret Atwood's view that farmers by definition would not find humour in *Sarah Binks*. Atwood reads the book as based on the "assumption that there is something intrinsically unpoetic about Saskatchewan and especially about farms." She asks, "what is so funny about Saskatchewan? . . . Laughter and audience are educated, they are from somewhere else, they are not provincial. A reassuring thought, except, of course, for those in Saskatchewan" (1982, 182–83). Doubtless that last line gets a laugh from Atwood's educated audiences, but perhaps the joke is on them.

My first glimpse of what kind of man Hiebert might have been came about, in fact, as a result of my yearning to get an education. I saw him through the eyes of my aunt, Agatha Schellenberg, the same aunt presented with an artificial rose by Sush Funk in the clown interlude preceding this chapter. My aunt was a remarkable woman who, against seemingly insurmountable odds, including severe physical disability, achieved the rare feat for her generation of acquiring a university degree. She was living proof that it could be done. On one visit to our farm, she told me that she had met the author of *Sarah Binks*. He was invigilating a German exam that she was writing, and when she met him at the entrance to the exam room he gave her a chocolate bar and told her that it was brain food. Many years later, after hearing from poet Di Brandt and ethnomusicologist Doreen Helen Klassen about his kindness to them, I deduced that Hiebert would instantly have seen in my aunt the qualities that I see in those two women. When I learned that Hiebert and his wife were childless, I suspected that he longed for a daughter, as my late husband and I did during years of infertility. In other words, I think of Hiebert as a man who took pleasure in watching mischievous young women outsmart the older men who were then in positions of undisputed authority.

My impression was confirmed by something that happened when I was an undergraduate, probably in 1964. I was asked to join a symposium of students who would be filmed for a CBC program about the range of student religious beliefs at the University of Manitoba. Fresh off the farm, where we had no television, I was terrified. At the studio, my anxiety was heightened when I discovered that we would be filmed while eating lunch. Table manners had not been a priority on the farm, and I was still learning how to use a fork and knife the way that people in Winnipeg did. Despite these distractions, I was determined to speak my mind. As it turned out, that was no easy matter. Each time I began to speak I was interrupted, not by a student, but by the staff person who was the head of the Student Christian Movement. He assumed, in advance, that he knew what I was going to say and took it on himself to educate me about my supposed fundamentalism. When the moderator finally insisted that I be allowed to speak and the giant camera swung in my direction, I made a comment to the effect that Jesus was a way of imagining how we could be better people and that other religions had other ways of imagining how to do that. Days later, when I was still recovering from the shock of that exposure, I met a fellow student on campus who told me that he had just spoken with Hiebert. Professor Hiebert had seen the CBC program, and in his opinion the student who had "made the most sense" was Magdalene Falk. After this indirect affirmation, it was always unlikely, to say the least, that I would agree with those feminists who believe that Hiebert makes fun of women.

The quickest way to suggest the many forgotten contexts that inform the text of *Sarah Binks* is to refer to the life of Paul Hiebert. Unfortunately no scholarly biography of him has been written. What emerges from the fragments that I have pieced together is a picture of somebody living in between worlds. This is true on many levels, from a childhood dislocation to his choice of career. Even within the large panorama of Mennonite history, the life of Hiebert falls in between two major Mennonite renaissances. He was born in Canada in 1892, when a Mennonite renaissance was at its height in Russia, the country that his grandparents had left. He died in Canada in 1987 at the age of ninety-five. That year the Mennonite renaissance was at its height in Canada, but for all the contact that he had with it he might as well have been living in another country. If the story of Hiebert's life is ever written, then a scholar might want to go back to the questions that T.S. Eliot raised in "Tradition and the Individual Talent." Here was a man of extraordinary genius whose life and writing do not link up in obvious ways with linear literary histories.

His literary writing happened while Hiebert was pursuing a career in between the fields of chemistry and philology. He was eighty-four years old and looking back at that career when he wrote *Doubting Castle* (1976). In that "spiritual autobiography," he described himself as "a Canadian boy, monolingual and unaware of any foreign roots or of any ethnic background different from those of my playmates at school" (13). The period of his earliest childhood he describes as "the transition phase of western prairie history in which the frontier was beginning to give way to modernity" (13). His earliest years were spent in Pilot Mound, Manitoba, and his father was a businessman. Pity for the plight of Indigenous people later informed his satire, and it had its origins in what Hiebert observed as a boy:

> My father bought many carloads of buffalo bones which still lay
> on the fields and shipped them east to be used in the refineries for
> bone meal. Families of Indians in carts drawn by a single shaginappe
> wandered into town from the near reservations and we boys used
> to welcome them at the town nuisance-grounds and watch them
> kill and skin a dog for their dinners and hang some of the flesh
> upon sticks to dry. They sold willow baskets and wild fruit to the
> townspeople and begged for food and milk for their unhealthy
> children, for they were miserably poor. (13)

His family was "very churchy" (17), and Hiebert remembered the Presbyterian Church that they attended as being dominated by fear. The "strong streak of religiosity" in his nature, he speculated, was "probably inherited from those far Anabaptists whose beliefs and piety had been kept alive by Mennonite ancestry" (14). When Hiebert was seven, his parents moved from Pilot Mound to Altona, "this all-Mennonite town of my boyhood"—a "prairie town" that he describes, with barely concealed irony, as having "an amazing charm" (34). In *Altona: The Story of a Prairie Town*, Esther Epp-Tiessen (1982) provides an intriguing glimpse of how the child Paul Hiebert experienced being in between worlds while looking, literally, for playing space. Quoting from her interviews with him, Epp-Tiessen writes that "Paul Hiebert remembers that when his family moved from Pilot Mound to Altona in 1899, he was stunned to discover that the children did not know how to play London Bridge or Pom Pom Pull-away or other games. At recess they stood around with hands in their pockets" (92). The missing perspective in this picture is language. What Hiebert could not have known, as a seven-year-old child, was that, though Mennonite children played Low German games at home in 1899, they would not have done so at school. I know this from my mother, who grew up in Altona. Only English was allowed in school, and those children would not have known the English games. They too were in between worlds but at a later stage of assimilation into mainstream English-speaking culture.

Looking back, at the age of eighty-four, Hiebert offered a nostalgic, idealized version of his first experience with Mennonite churches in the Altona area. As a result of "the return of my parents to their Mennonite background," he writes, he experienced "new cultural and religious

environments." In the Mennonite community there, he saw, in contrast
to the Presbyterian Church in Pilot Mound, a faith based not on fear
but on a calm acceptance of God's ways. The spirit of "these unpreten-
tious Mennonite folk," he writes, was "characterized by something which
could almost be called a blessedness" (1976, 33). He remembers the
hymns sung on Sunday mornings "as a gift from my ethnic background"
(35). He describes how he quickly learned Low German: "It is a lovely
language, simple and to the point and much like English, differing from
that convoluted High German in which I was later to major at college."
The "simple, uncluttered language," he writes, went along with an "uncluttered faith" (36).

Hiebert was about the same age as my father, a preacher in one of those
churches, but he does not say at what age he learned Low German. What
is unusual is that he took the trouble to do so, during the time when the
newly arrived Russländer were leading a concerted effort to stamp it out
completely. I like to imagine Hiebert and my father meeting and joking
together in Low German. Although his love of the language endears him
to me, it is important to remember that Hiebert did not grow up with the
Low German oral culture, as he would have done had he been born in a
Mennonite town in 1892. He grew up, rather, on a borderline.

Hiebert was sixty-five years old in 1957 when the Brunk Brothers
revival campaign came to Manitoba. It is interesting to note that, twenty
years later, in his old age, he still felt anger about it. He laments the fact that
the "uncluttered faith" of these "folk" was destroyed when fundamentalist American evangelicals came into the region, bringing with them "the
sound and fury of the American Bible Belt" (1976, 31). Like James Urry,
in comments I have already cited (quoted by Arnason 1992, 214), Hiebert
ignores the complicating fact that the supposed villains in this story were
also Mennonite. Although useful, Hiebert's autobiography should be read
with attention to other forgotten contexts. The most important of them is
the Second World War. The war is not mentioned in *Sarah Binks*; however,
as Ruth Panofsky (2004) has documented, its publication was delayed
because of paper shortages resulting from the war. Hiebert spent the years
from 1940 to 1947 revising the manuscript. Conflicts among Mennonites
in Manitoba are not mentioned in his autobiography. As a philologist,
however, Hiebert must surely have been keenly interested in language

conflicts, especially when they played into different responses to the war. Pro-Nazi articles and letters written by prominent Russländer leaders were published at that time in *Der Bote*, a German-language Mennonite newspaper. Hiebert's friend John Warkentin has told me that Hiebert sometimes joked darkly about Mennonite "brownshirts."* This shameful history is absorbed obliquely into the darkest layers of *Sarah Binks*, and the satire at that level is directed at the assumptions about narrative that eventually came to inform orthodox Mennonite literary history. R.T. Robertson calls *Sarah Binks* "a fable in the form of a satire of the local poetess and the local literary historian" and reads the book as satirizing the assumptions that lie at the base of "every assertion of national identity in early national literary studies" (1973, 76). *Willows Revisited*, the sequel to *Sarah Binks*, was published in conjunction with the 1967 centenary celebrations, just as CanLit was being born. Having expressed his visceral distaste for German nationalism in *Sarah Binks*, Hiebert lived long enough to see the development of Canadian nationalism, which he satirized in the sequel.

Despite his extraordinary contribution to Canadian literature, Hiebert's erasure from CanLit is as total as his erasure from Mennonite literary history. It is tempting to speculate, given how all discussions now revolve around identity, that this is the result of the deracination of Hiebert. To *deracinate*, my dictionary tells me, is to pull up by the roots and thus to alienate a person from his or her "native" environment. The metaphor draws attention to the part that Hiebert played in his own erasure. Roots are a recurring target of satire in *Sarah Binks*. The Author asks us to make believe that the genius of the Sweet Songstress of Saskatchewan is rooted in the soil of that province. The alliteration alone conveys his contempt for such notions of identity. It was his effort to distance himself from such ideas that led Hiebert, in my view, to displace the book from his home province of Manitoba to Saskatchewan. In search of *Spielraum*, he chose, as Nathaniel Hawthorne did, to work in a "neutral territory . . . where the Actual and the Imaginary may meet" (1978, 31). He did teach for a time in a desolate part of Saskatchewan, and Warkentin's memory is that the experience made a deep impression on his friend. Understandably

---

* I am grateful to John Warkentin for permission to share this detail from our conversations about Paul Hiebert and for permission to quote from the unpublished letters.

intrigued as a geographer by the displacement, Warkentin asked Hiebert about it. Hiebert wrote back: "Don't for the love of Pete destroy my good opinion of you by suggesting that . . . . am 'hard' on Saskatchewan. No one is meant, no person, no province, no place."*

"No one is meant, no person, no province, no place." I repeat these words because they are an antidote to the literalism of our own time. Even when I read *Sarah Binks* on the farm in the 1950s, however, I did not think that Hiebert was making fun of farmers, or of people in Saskatchewan, or of women. I have come to believe that he is perceived as a *persona non grata* because people are taken in by his persona, which remains somehow alive alongside the character of Sarah Binks. The irony that happens for me when I read *Sarah Binks* is related to class in ways that I will never fully understand, but the Sweet Songstress of Saskatchewan came to my mind often during the years that I was writing about James Hogg, the Ettrick Shepherd. Like Hogg and like Robert Frost, Hiebert helped to create the rustic persona behind which his achievement is hidden.

The popularity of Hiebert's persona is captured by the opening sentence of *Peter Gzowski's Book about* This Country in the Morning: "When I grow up I want to be Paul Hiebert." In his book about the CBC program that he hosted for many years, Gzowski expresses affection for the author of that "small Canadian masterpiece" (1974, 11), and he includes in his book a letter from Constance E. Dwyer, who remembers her former chemistry professor as a "little gray and brown gnome" (224). In a 1984 article on his "contented retirement," Mary Enns describes him living with his wife in a "little brown house" and Hiebert as "a diminutive man in a large armchair and wearing a brown velvet smoking jacket." The interior of the house was filled with little things, "every cornice and shelf and antique cabinet . . . laden with collectables [*sic*]" (6). Collectibles also feature in a tribute by poet Di Brandt, who describes how she and her twin sister, Rose, met Hiebert in the Carman Museum: "Being teenagers, we weren't terribly interested in the assortment of old things laid out in the museum. But there was a little old man walking around in the museum, telling the most animated, funny stories to museum visitors. . . . He asked us who

---

* Paul Hiebert to John Warkentin, 1967; quoted with the permission of Warkentin.

we were, why we were there, & next thing we knew, he had whisked us off to his cottage, called 'The Burrs,' where his wife, Mrs. Hiebert, made tea for us" (1999, 43). In this magical space, anything could happen. At any minute, the "little old man" could change into a white rabbit. If the child drinks the tea, then perhaps she will grow up in an instant and be Paul Hiebert. Brandt describes the house as "quite a small, even shabby little house, filled with book-lined shelves . . . & rows & rows of little glass knickknacks in the windows, collected by Mrs. Hiebert" (43). All these adjectives signal a turn to nostalgia. In *On Longing,* Susan Stewart's study of nostalgia, Stewart describes miniatures, "knickknacks of the domestic collected by elderly women," as "located at a place of origin (the child-hood of the self . . .)" (1986, 33). It is my sense that the cumulative weight of those adjectives—*little, small, diminutive, tiny*—has contributed to a diminished view of Hiebert's literary achievement. It is almost as if the man metamorphoses into one of those garden gnomes that people steal or collect. Metamorphosis can be frightening. *Sarah Binks* plays on anxiet-ies about authority, and Hiebert begins the book by playfully abdicating his authority. Readers might enjoy the illusion that they can control "the Author"—that this unthreatening souvenir can be kept in the pocket like a little gnome. The satire would then heighten the shock, as if the gnome has changed into a malicious dwarf.

Far be it from me, given the man's lifelong efforts not to be pinned down, to welcome Paul Hiebert like a lost sheep to the fold of Mennonite writers. I delight in the literary pyrotechnics that show how blessedly free he was of the anxieties about play that infect so much Mennonite writing. Like Samuel Taylor Coleridge, Hiebert was a chemist, and scientists are good at making believe. When one hypothesis does not work out, they simply imagine another one. It is no wonder that Hiebert was drawn to pastoral form. As William Empson argued in *Some Versions of Pastoral* (1935), one lesson of the pastoral is that we should not take our fictions too seriously. Although I have no desire to drag Hiebert into the mire of our contemporary obsession with identity, the peculiarities of his recep-tion tell me that his supposed freedom from ethnic identity did not happen without effort and that he paid a price for it. Only close attention to the text of *Sarah Binks* can correct the misperceptions that stand in the way of doing justice to his literary achievement. A number of blocks have accumulated around that text, however, so the first step of any critic must be to deal with them.

Ironically, one of those blocks is made visible by my account of clowning as Sush Funk. Like many a hapless amateur, I succumbed to what Gerald Noonan described as the "quality of nostalgia [in *Sarah Binks*] that directs the reader's response toward shared enjoyment, not contemptuous laughter" (1978, 267). This invitation to participate goes back to Hiebert's disingenuous accounts of the accidental nature of the composition and his disavowal of sole authorship. "These bits of 'bad poetry,'" according to Eileen Pruden, "were begun as time-killers . . . by Hiebert and his brother, Ernest. They were constructed for amusement between chores in the store their father had in Altona, Manitoba" (1988, 5; see also Epp-Tiessen 1982, 58). Some collaboration was evidently part of the writing of *Sarah Binks*; however, as Ruth Panofsky points out, Hiebert's claims of collective improvisation are belied by the publishing history of *Sarah Binks*, which she describes as "one of the most protracted publishing ventures in all of Canadian literature" (2004, 72). Hiebert spent seven years repeatedly revising the printed text of the book while continuing to do spontaneous public performances. Elizabeth Porter writes that her parents remember him at gatherings pulling out a piece of paper from a vest pocket and announcing that he had received it recently from that new poetess in Saskatchewan (1982, 107).

The participatory reception of *Sarah Binks* has been varied and continues to this day. It is like a noise around the text that cannot be ignored. In 1968, Don Harron chose "the funniest book written in Canada in recent years" (279) to mount a show with Jane Mallett called *Here Lies Sarah Binks*. In his memoir, Harron wrote that, "in all my years in the theatre, I don't think I've ever had so much fun in a play" (280). In 1979, Eric Donkin toured with a one-man show called *The Wonderful World of Sarah Binks*. The highlight of the show was his drag performance of Rosalind Drool, one of many absurdly named literary critics in *Sarah Binks*. Such entertainments are not a thing of the past, and it is not my aim here to suggest that they should be. Sometime in the 1990s, I had the pleasure of hearing Roy Thomson Hall in Toronto fill with laughter when Mary Lou Fallis sang "Hi, Sooky, Ho, Sooky," a poem about pigs sung to a tune composed by John Greer. A reliable source assures me that Greer is at work on a bestiary songbook based on *Sarah Binks*. I confess that these high-art shenanigans give me pleasure because they make me feel as if the people in the concert hall are dimly aware of the existence of the *shtahp* from which I come. Or at least the existence of pigs. As Terry Eagleton pointed out in "The Critic as Clown," however, pastoral form often presents us with "a spurious harmonization of class struggle" (1988, 622).

Class conflicts also complicate my response to feminist readings of *Sarah Binks*. Much to my chagrin, given my admiration for the text, many feminist critics are now following a pattern of evading *Sarah Binks* the text while responding to Sarah Binks the character. This template was created by Carole Gerson in an article entitled "Sarah Binks and Edna Jaques: Parody, Gender, and the Construction of Literary Value" (1992). According to Gerson, *Sarah Binks* is a parody of Edna Jaques, "Canada's most successful real-life folk poet," who lived from 1891 to 1978. Gerson begins by wondering "whether the creation of Binks was inspired by Jaques—a possibility enhanced by the similar sounds and identical rhythms of their names" (66, 62). From this wisp of speculation, she then leaps to an assertion of it as fact. In her otherwise well-researched study of "poverty narratives," Roxanne Rimstead follows this template. She never questions the "fact" that Sarah Binks is based on Edna Jaques. *Sarah Binks* the text, however, is not listed in her bibliography. Rimstead (2000, 64–65) joins Gerson in lamenting that Hiebert's parody of Jaques is "better known in Canadian culture than Jaques herself." Five years later an essay by Candida Rifkind echoed this lament: "While Binks retains currency as a stereotype," Rifkind concludes, "Jaques has receded from cultural memory" (2005, 114).

Parody, to put it simply, is a form of repetition that returns to an earlier text and changes it (Hutcheon 1985). If Hiebert were in fact making fun of Jaques, then the result might be called a burlesque or caricature but not a parody. Since the argument against Hiebert veers into an ad hominem attack, it is only fair to let the man speak for himself. During an interview with cellist Reynold Siemens, Hiebert protested,

> Well, for one thing, I never debunk anybody. I object very, very
> much to the suggestion that I'm trying to debunk.... I was very

much annoyed when a Canadian author mentioned that I had written *Sarah Binks* as a takeoff of *Edna Jakes* [*sic*]. I was simply furious. I cut my association with the Canadian Authors completely. At that point I said I will have nothing to do with a group that takes such a nasty view of one of their fellow authors, that he should be so mean as to write about another writer with an acid pen and try to show him up as being poor" (quoted in Siemens 1977, 69).

I hear this vehement denial as a mark of sincerity. Another reader might think that Hiebert protests too much.

As a feminist, I ask myself why I have never had any serious "feminist trouble" with *Sarah Binks*. Part of the reason is that I read it as aligned with the feminist aesthetic that I find in the stories of Alice Munro. In "Who Do You Think You Are?" (Munro 1978), the names Milton and Homer, both literally blind, evoke centuries of literary history that celebrate the artist as a blind seer, someone who can see with a third eye in the middle of his or her forehead. Milton Homer, the clown in that story, is a feminine mimic in the sense that we would now call queer. So is Almeda Joynt Roth, the poetess in "Meneseteung" (Munro 1996, 492–514). Hiebert told Siemens that he planned at first that his poet would be "a country bumpkin by the name of Henry Hayfoot," but then decided that it would be "a bit more fascinating" if the poet was a girl (1977, 66). With that gender switch, he undermined orthodox assumptions about literary history. Indeed, *Sarah Binks* reads like an anticipatory challenge to Harold Bloom's *The Anxiety of Influence: A Theory of Poetry* (1973). Like Erasmus, Hiebert portrays folly as a woman and praises her. *Sarah Binks* is a mock encomium directed at the idea that literary history moves forward "by means of antagonism and strife" (Perkins 1992, 167).

An absurd poetry competition is the cause of her martyrdom because Sarah Binks swallows the prize: mercury from the horse thermometer. The trickster Mercury, rendered bathetic, makes visible how her female receptiveness and passivity are a satire of dominant male models. Over and over again, the female perspective serves Hiebert's purposes by bringing freshness to hackneyed ideas and by allowing a female voice to subvert male authority. The preacher in Ecclesiastes 3:7, for example, has had a gender change before writing these lines: "Oh it's time for this and it's time for that / For mending unending and tending the brat. . . . To-morrow's another day" (Hiebert 1995, 96). This echoes the famous last line of Margaret Mitchell's *Gone with the Wind*: "After all, tomorrow is another day" (Mitchell 1961, 1037). A plethora of domestic details in *Sarah Binks* draws attention to a point made by Susan Stewart that the "impersonation of the feminine" in the form of camp makes it "available to parody" and "reveals the feminine as a surface" (1984, 168). The Author marvels at Sarah's "sympathetic nature and essential womanhood" (Hiebert 1995, 34). The poem that illustrates this is about a man who has his ear pecked off by a "cursed duck":

> But a woman came, and she loved the man,
> With a love serene and clear—
> She loved him as only a woman can love
> A man with only one ear. (34)

To my feminist ear, *Sarah Binks* undermines essentialized definitions of the feminine. When I studied Betty Friedan's *The Feminine Mystique* in 1963, the year that it was published, I thought that I had been prepared for it by having read *Sarah Binks* as an adolescent. I remain open to feminist readings different from mine if they are based on the actual text of *Sarah Binks*. At least eighty poems are interpolated into the narrative, covering a range of styles and forms and alluding to a large number of poets, British, American, Canadian, and German. Romantic poetry is a primary target, and the ersatz British Romanticism of the Canadian Confederation Poets comes in for frequent mockery. The text as a whole can be read as a parody of settler narratives or of pioneer pastorals, but it could also be read as a structural parody of Alfred Lord Tennyson's *The Princess: A Medley* (1965, 154–202). Had Gerson, Rimstead, and Rifkind been less sweeping in their judgements, they might have noticed that there is at least one poem in *Sarah Binks*, entitled "The Wedding Dress," that sounds like a parody of a poem by Edna Jaques entitled "I Love New Things" (1974, 14).

After academic quarrels pass, we always have the literary text left over. I cannot give the text of *Sarah Binks* the kind of close reading that Hiebert mocked and that it so richly deserves. As with any text, however, it is always a good idea to start at the beginning. The first edition of *Sarah Binks* contained the following prominent note before the title page: "ALL

THE CHARACTERS IN THIS BOOK ARE FICTITIOUS INCLUDING THE
AUTHOR." The note appeared again before the title page in the 1964 New
Canadian Library edition, again in all capitals. When the New Canadian
Library edition was reprinted in 1995, however, this warning was displaced
and appeared in italics at the top of the copyright page with a note to say
that it had "appeared in the original edition." I consider this editorial inter-
vention unfortunate, since subsequent reception has confirmed Hiebert's
presupposition that readers would need this reminder. The announcement
signals the fact that the book is the work of an artist who, to adapt Richard
Poirier's description of a self-parodic writer, "won't allow any element . . .
to become stabilized or authoritative" and who himself "cannot be located
in most of his writing" (1992, 43). That absence is confirmed by the first
poem, a parody of free verse. The Author introduces it by raving about
how Sarah captures in her "net of poesy . . . the flatness of that great province" of Saskatchewan. She wanders on the prairie and sings

> Hark! Like a mellow fiddle moaning,
> Through the reed-grass sighing,
> Through a gnarled branch groaning,
> Comes the Poet—
> Sylph-like,
> Gaunt-like,
> Poeming—
> And his eyes are stars,
> And his mouth is foaming. (Hiebert 1995, 12)

To which the Author adds the note "Thus, Sarah herself, in the divine
frenzy" (12). This poet is instantly recognizable from Romantic anteced-
ents such as the figure in Coleridge's "Kubla Khan": "Weave a circle round
him thrice, / And close your eyes with holy dread" (Coleridge 1994, 45).
The Author's claim that Sarah sees "with the prophetic eye of the poetess" (Hiebert 1995, 21) echoes jarringly with the words of Ralph Waldo
Emerson: "I become a transparent eye-ball; I am nothing; I see all" (1957,
52). The admirable moral of this famous Transcendentalist message is that
egotism must be abandoned. The problem for a woman is that the poets
thought to have achieved the goal of acquiring a "transparent eyeball" are

invariably male. That is why it is truly "a bit more fascinating" to imagine "the prophetic eye" in a poetess.

Sarah is a female version of the figure, made familiar during the Romantic period, of rural bards such as the Ettrick Shepherd, idealized as a natural poet even as his embarrassing vulgarity undermined that ideal. Bucolic verse is repeatedly evoked, and nostalgic tropes are put in play, only to be flattened by that dangerous girlish enthusiasm:

> Spring is here, the breezes blowing,
> Four inches of top-soil going, going;
> Farm ducks rolling across the prairie;
> Spring is here—how nice and airy! (Hiebert 1995, 67)

Unexpected incongruity in the last line is a tool that Hiebert frequently used. "Ode to a Deserted Farm," for example, begins with a quatrain, the first three lines of which could have been written by any one of the Confederation Poets. The fourth line abruptly inserts a machine into the garden:

> How changed and bleak the meadows lie
> And overgrown with hay,
> The field of oats and barley
> Where the binder twined its way! (21).

The poem's title echoes Oliver Goldsmith's poem "The Deserted Village" and the undertone is reminiscent of Goldsmith's anger about rural depopulation. The anger is buried deep under sentimental nostalgic tropes, but once again they are undercut:

> With doors ajar the cottage stands
> Deserted on the hill—
> No welcome bark, no thudding hoof,
> And the voice of the pig is still. (21)

In the last line can be heard an echo from Tennyson's "Break, Break, Break": "And the sound of a voice that is still!" (Tennyson 1965, 116).

Such twisting of pastoral tropes makes up the entertaining surface of *Sarah Binks*. Beneath this surface is a sustained and prescient satire that works on two levels simultaneously: outrage at the attempted genocide of Indigenous people and outrage at fascism and German nationalism. Both

are conveyed on the vehicle of Sarah's girlish voice, working in tandem
with the sly Author's supposed admiration of Sarah. In his afterword to
the New Canadian Library edition of *Sarah Binks*, Charles Gordon speculates that "one of the deeply hidden jokes of the book is that [Sarah]
may be a rather nasty piece of work and Paul Hiebert doesn't care for her
much." Gordon adds that this is "up for debate" (1995, 170). The question might not be "up for debate" if Hiebert had not repeatedly protested
his love for Sarah. He is not alone among satirists in trying to repudiate
satire because of an assumption that it is malicious, but the unfortunate
result has been that some readers have assumed that he approves of her
charming racism. Ruth Panofsky, for example, laments the fact that *Sarah
Binks* "employs stereotypes and reflects biases that readers now find regret-
table" (2004, 84): "I contend that *Sarah Binks*, for all the discomfort it
causes today's readers and critics, remains appealing for its 'command of
a large bag of tricks': in particular, Sarah's evocative poetry; its distinctive brand of irony; and its nostalgia which, as critic Gerald Noonan has
noted, 'keeps us interested in opposing views and . . . (relatively) unper-
turbed by conflict'" (84–85). This is damning with faint praise, as if the
job of the literary critic were to protect the book from charges of racism
and sexism by pointing to the author's "bag of tricks." The implication is
that hidden behind "the Author" is a racist who has to be forgiven because
people didn't know any better in those days.

The confused reception of *Sarah Binks* draws attention to the limitations of conventional definitions of satire. We usually assume that
the satirist has "a firm perspective from which to correct . . . vices and
follies, . . . 'real standards' in which to ground moral outrage" (Bogel 2001,
53). Fredric Bogel has put forward a different theory. What happens, he
argues, "is not that satirists find folly or wickedness in the world and then
wish to expose that alien something. Instead, satirists identify in the world
something or someone that is both unattractive and curiously or danger-
ously like them, or like the culture or subculture that they identify with
or speak for, or sympathetic even as it is repellent—something, then, that
is *not alien enough*" (41). This view of how satire works helps to account
for the ambivalent responses to Sarah Binks: she is *"not alien enough."*
The result is that readers might catch themselves in the act of performing
racism. Bogel points out that satire has long been associated with "social

rituals of purification, casting out, and scapegoating" (46). Sarah, however, is like a cartoon figure in a situation comedy, always bouncing back to familiar habits and never growing in depth. She is the racist inside us who cannot be exorcized.

What is "up for debate," in my view, is *how* Hiebert responded to the racism that he saw. Wordplay is the thing wherein Hiebert doth catch the conscience of his readers. It is no easy task to see how this trick works, but it helps if you begin with the presupposition that Sarah is "a rather nasty piece of work." If you accept the basic rhetorical technique of point of view, then the stereotypes that Panofsky abhors are constructed by Sarah and the Author. The refraction of racist formulations through these filters is of a dazzling complexity that tests the limits of theories about play. Confronted with such daunting complexities, I am tempted to emulate Rosalind Drool, who marvels at the poetry offered by Sarah and gives up: "One wonders how she does it" (Hiebert 1995, 28). I offer instead one small example of an alternative critical response, a focus on how the rhetoric of *Sarah Binks* changes constantly as Sarah's racism, already filtered by her education, gets filtered and distorted through the eulogizing lens of the Author. Underneath the sticky sweetness of the surface, words cluster together as if compelled by some invisible force, but this is not improvisational or random. It is the result of Hiebert's craft.

Take, for example, the repetition of words associated with *Blut und Boden* thinking. That nationalist slogan, meaning Blood and Soil, celebrated rural identity as opposed to corrupt Jewish nomadism and fuelled the Nazi search for *Lebensraum*. It is hard to think of a potent collective fiction more perfectly designed to expose the dangers that can come with the pastoral form. In *Sarah Binks*, the actual phrase is never spoken, but as a result of wordplay it vibrates in between the lines. I hear it like a drumbeat that accompanies Hiebert's dismantling of dangerous illusions such as the Author's view of literary history, which echoes that of Johann Gottfried Herder. Herder envisioned poets in just the way that Sarah's biographer envisions Sarah—as the creator of a nation, a voice for the *Geist* or soul of the people. The most disturbing moments in *Sarah Binks* are when pastoral commonplaces slide into *Blut und Boden* rhetoric. An undertow is set up, and the words *soil* and *blood* have a cumulative impact. "Sarah Binks was the product of her soil and her roots go deep" (Hiebert 1995, 10). She is "the unspoiled child of the soil" (13), and "the soil of Saskatchewan has been enriched and fertilized" by her songs (60). The Author observes that "the blood of the Vikings flowed in Ole's veins, and from Ole's veins to Sarah's verse was but a step" (35). Sarah "rises to splendid heights of pure patriotism" with the vow that "not while yet the blood of Christopher Columbus / Flows in our veins, shall these our foes, succumb us" (42). Who are these "foes"? What is the home being defended? Who are "they" and "us"? In the foreground, always, is the dubious charm of "the sweet songstress," girlishly showing off how she can multiply nostalgic tropes. It is notable that when Sarah exhibits her fascist tendencies the references to dirt veer toward scatological humour.

The fascist rhetoric that vibrates throughout the Author's enthusiastic celebration of Sarah's poetry blends smoothly into the pastoral tropes that are the vehicle for racism against Indigenous people. The Author's efforts to make Sarah's "Red Brother" fit into farm life are so painful that it is hard to imagine any reader laughing. Sarah's "Red Brother" is like a ghost that bleeds into the text. In many passages, the "prairie Indian" resembles a pet on a leash or a slave, and the word *home* acquires an ironic edge. "On the reservation or off it," the Author writes, "Sarah never permits the Red Brother to wander far from the farm. When he goes astray, as in West Wind, where Squawking-Hawk goes to town with his treaty money for 'a bottle of lemon and three of vanilla,' she quickly brings him home" (Hiebert 1995, 139). Hiebert does not evade the problem of alcoholism, but the target of the satire is not the "Red Brother." It is the rhetoric of the Author, the poetry of Sarah, and the self-delusions that they conceal.

There is bitter irony in the poem that Sarah uses to bring her slave home. She speaks not to him but to the wind:

> Blow him, West Wind, that his going,
> May be coming back to me,
> Speed him, West, or he'll be blowing
> All he's paid for being Cree. (Hiebert 1995, 140)

The apostrophe to the West Wind echoes an ode by Percy Shelley, but the familiar image from a British poem is rendered literal and located in the Canadian west. An apostrophe is a rhetorical strategy that involves turning away from the living to address the dead, but this ancient tool is wielded with savage intent in this case. It is a turning away from Indigenous people and a denial of their very existence. The poem is also a parody of a lullaby in Tennyson's "The Princess"—"Sweet and low, sweet and low / Wind of the western sea" (1965, 167)—but the lulling of the poetic rhythm jars deliberately with the racist content.

Hiebert draws attention to the part played by the Canadian system of education in shaping Sarah's racist assumptions. Echoes from the school textbooks of the time surface repeatedly, and Sarah apes the poems as she constructs Romantic stereotypes of Indigenous life. It is her cheerful belief that in writing about him she owns her "Red Brother" and that this ownership is confirmed when her poetry is published for schoolchildren. The most significant of these poems is "Little Papoose," a parody of Duncan Campbell Scott's famous 1898 sonnet "The Onondaga Madonna" (1926, 230). Critical neglect of Hiebert's parody is scandalous given the amount of critical attention that has been devoted to the poetry of Scott, an architect of what we now view as cultural genocide in Canada. Once again Hiebert's prescience is uncanny, and his parody opens up the racism in Scott's poem for all to see. Like the baby in "The Onondaga Madonna," the one in "Little Papoose" refuses to go to sleep. In Scott's famous poem, the mother is a "woman of a weird and waning race, / tragic savage lurking in her face." The infant in "the shawl about her breast" is "paler than she" but still savage. A "primal warrior" gleams from his eyes: "He sulks, and burdened with his infant gloom, / He draws his heavy brows and will not rest" (230). In "Little Papoose," the image of the infantilized "noble savage" is undermined by an exaggerated emphasis on the body of the baby being stuffed with food—food that is deliberately incongruous and does not fit with Romantic stereotypes of what a "Red Brother" ought to eat:

> Little Papoose, the twilight creeping,
> Draws its shadows across the skies—
> Another hour and you'll be sleeping—
> Here's a pickle, close your eyes. (Hiebert 1995, 139)

As "the night grows blacker," the baby will be "full of bread and molasses, / And stewed dried apples and tinned sardines." This voracious baby, "round as a young balloon" (139), is a wakeful infant represented with what Mikhail Bakhtin called "grotesque realism" (1968, 1–58). The technique renders absurd the idea that there is any difference at all between Indian and non-Indian babies, and it mocks the classical idealism of Scott's image of the ever-awake warrior.

"Eagle Feather" sets out to sing an "appropriate requiem" for "silent, inscrutable, Eagle Feather," but the rollicking meter communicates an overheated vicarious nostalgia (Hiebert 1995, 142). The killing off of "the Indian" is complete, but the story of it is told with a girlish enthusiasm. The Author marvels at the fact that Sarah gets a poem out of it: "For one brief moment [in that poem] the page of history is again lifted, and across it stalks Eagle Feather, splendid, confident, arrogant, a symbol again of Saskatchewan's most glorious past. Nor has Saskatchewan failed to recognize its greatness. Year after year, with unfailing regularity it has been placed on the List of Supplementary Reading for the Schools" (143). With this piece of pedagogical puffery, the "glorious past" of the "Red Man" is eliminated and replaced by a silly poem.

Among the most pointed examples of Hiebert's parody of the pioneer pastoral is his satire of the myths surrounding the Mound Builders, a fascination doubtless related to his early years in Pilot Mound. Bizarre theories circulated widely before scholars finally conceded that in fact the 100 or so mounds scattered throughout southern Manitoba were created by ancient North American Indigenous societies. Unable to believe that the complex structures could have been created by "savages," scholars invented a mythical Mound Builder race assumed to be European (Rempel 1994). Sarah writes *Up from the Magma and Back Again* in Mound Builder, a language that does not exist.

Examples of such specious scholarship accumulate in *Sarah Binks* and constitute an ironic version of a process known as *translatio studii*—the transfer of learning from one place to another. Karlheinz Stierle (1996) has deployed the term as a means of exploring "the translatability of cultures" in other contexts, but it seems useful in this context. It is a concept, after all, embedded in early North American culture, where it was assumed that learning moved from east to west and where it could become part of *translatio imperii*, the transfer of rule that leads to imperial domination. There is in *Sarah Binks* a growing awareness of a westward expansion that leads not to enlightenment but to increasing darkness as it threatens to wipe out Indigenous people. Sarah herself is blind to this horror, yet her descent into a "Dark Hour" during a trip to Regina, "at that time the Athens of Saskatchewan" (Hiebert 1995, 91), feels like a bizarre enactment of it on the level of metaphor. Here, where she should be receiving the light of culture, "the sudden change from the pastoral simplicity of Willows to the teeming marts of men . . . threatened for a while to extinguish the divine spark and leave her forever dumb" (91). Behind the absurdity of the pastoral cliché, the metaphor speaks to a deeper horror, and I found myself thinking of *translatio studii* as an ironic cover for *translatio stultitiae*, the corollary metaphor that informs Alexander Pope's *Dunciad* (1728) (Pope 1966, 723–49). The literary critics in *Sarah Binks* resemble the dunces in that satire. Sarah presides over this gathering darkness like the goddess Dulness, who rules Pope's mock-heroic poem.

If you read *Sarah Binks* as the Canadian *Dunciad*, then the most important among all the targets is our collective refusal to see our own racism. The varieties of it that can be attached to Kanadier or Russländer myths are only a small part of this larger picture. On the surface, *Sarah Binks* appears to resemble the lightness of Stephen Leacock's *Sunshine Sketches of a Little Town* (1912). On deeper levels, it is even darker than Leacock's *Arcadian Adventures of the Idle Rich* (1914). When I come to the place where I experience the terrible darkness that threatens to engulf the sunny pastoral tropes in *Sarah Binks*, I puzzle over the relationship between Hiebert's Christian faith and his satire. One particular poem invites a closer focus than I can give it here. It is "Hordes of Sheep," for which Sarah wins the prize that is the cause of her death. Poetry competitions are an ancient pastoral convention, going back to the classical model established by shepherd poets. Hiebert adapts this convention in ways that resonate with the German tradition of *Meistersinger* or master singers, and parody the singing competitions romanticized by Richard Wagner in his 1868 opera *Die Meistersinger von Nürnberg*. Hiebert satirizes the assumption, common in Mennonite educational institutions during the time he wrote *Sarah Binks*, that German poetry by definition is superior to all other poetry.

Despite the densely allusive nature of all the poems in *Sarah Binks*, allusions to the Bible are extremely rare. In "Hordes of Sheep," Hiebert (1995, 122–23) brings all the pastoral tropes in the book into an intense focus on the central metaphor in the Bible: Jesus as the Lamb of God. He twists that trope in ways that attack the assumptions of settler narratives, and he does so by asking an implied question. What if we imagine Jesus as Indigenous? The poem begins with an echo of the Christmas carol "Silent Night," but the meter evokes the panicky voice in Johann Wolfgang von Goethe's "Erlkönig." As the anapestic beat gallops along, it sets up a longing for the melody of the carol to return. What emerges in the mind's eye is an implied nativity scene that anticipates those in William Kurelek's *A Northern Nativity*. Kurelek displaces the scene of Christ's birth into an igloo, a fishing village, and other places designed to jar viewers out of their mental sets. Hiebert's iconoclasm is more violent. The effect is as if a crèche has been shattered. This is Sarah's racism run amok, so it is not pretty. The God that descends to be incarnate in Jesus is the white man who uses an Indigenous woman as his temporary spouse, only to leave her and their children behind.

In its very savagery, "Hordes of Sheep" testifies to the depth of the religious vision that informs Hiebert's satire, and in this it invites comparison with the satiric vision of Jonathan Swift. Such a violent repudiation of what *is* happens only when there is a powerful vision of what *ought to be*. Although parodies of the nativity scene are not rare, this one is unusually daring. To find an analogous example, we would have to reach back to the medieval miracle play in which Mac's wife hides a stolen sheep in her cradle and pretends that it is her newborn child. "Hordes of Sheep" is not, however, a loveless poem. The presence of embodied love becomes increasingly apparent as the babies multiply and the mother "Grabs her child, and another and another" (Hiebert 1995, 122). Grotesque realism is once again the means of destroying the death in life of classical realism. In the midst of this chaos is the presence of maternal love. This happens to be an Indigenous mother, but that is not the point. She is just there in among the broken pieces of the crèche as an affirmation of love incarnate.

Almost twenty years after the publication of *Sarah Binks*, Hiebert was urged to write a sequel as part of the 1967 Canadian centenary celebrations. In a letter to John Warkentin, he described the writing of *Willows Revisited* as part of a deal with McClelland and Stewart. If he gave the company a sequel to *Sarah Binks*, then it would publish *Tower in Siloam* (1966). The fact that Warkentin took the time to read *Tower in Siloam* and respond with a thoughtful letter clearly meant far more to Hiebert than the predictable reception of *Willows Revisited*. My strong impression is that Hiebert had grown weary of living inside the constricting persona that he himself had helped to create. As the title suggests, *Willows Revisited* replicates the pastoral convention of a place revisited that structures Wordsworth's "Tintern Abbey." The title is a parodic echo of "Tantramar Revisited," a poem by Confederation Poet Charles G.D. Roberts, but *Willows Revisited* is no gentle scene of departure and return. It is a revisiting of an old playground that clearly stirred bitterness in Hiebert. Although he does not spell out the Mennonite associations, I cannot resist, as a Mennonite, reading between the lines. On the one hand, there is a continuing intense distaste for nostalgic German-based approaches to Mennonite ethnic identity associated with the Russländer. On the other, there is an equally strong distaste for the nostalgic settler narratives associated with the Kanadier.

Revisiting his parody of "The Onondaga Madonna" in *Willows Revisited* shows that Hiebert had not changed his views about Duncan Campbell Scott, whose literary reputation had been established by then. As part of the centennial celebrations, a poet called "Wraitha Dovecote" wins an award for a poem called "Mother's Song" (Hiebert 1967, 65). The mother in Scott's poem is a "tragic savage," but her baby is "paler than she" (1926, 230). The mother in Hiebert's poem, in contrast, is given a voice. She sings "So blessings on your little head, / Barefooted boy—at least you're red!" (Hiebert 1967, 65). Hiebert ties Sarah's racism to the educational system. "It is apparent here," notes the Author, "that Wraitha's knowledge of the Indian nature, despite her own distant ancestry, was at second hand, and that she was reflecting her high-school point of view." The deputy minister of education, when he awards her a prize for the poem, chucks her under the chin and says "'Honey, you don't know your Indians.'" Despite this, Wraitha's poem "has been included in the school readers of Saskatchewan" (65).

The satire in *Willows Revisited* is sharpest and most scatological when *Volk* is watered down to *folk* and German and Canadian nationalisms overlap to become targets. The Canadian government is described as paying tribute "to various contemporary ethnic groups for the contributions they were making towards the enrichment of western culture in the matter of folk-dances, folk-costumes, and folk apple cake" (Hiebert 1967, 37). The Author appeals to "the great German critic and historian, von Hinten" (German for from behind). Like Herder, von Hinten sees history and poetry as having a shared nationalist goal, the effort not to lose "the soul-spirit, the *Poltergeist*" (47). "The history of the people lies not so much in the *Zeitgeist*, or record-of-events, as it does in the strength-through-interpretation-given-to-events, that is to say in effect, the *Wienerschnitzelgeist* of the poet" (47). This parody of the Nazi slogan *Kraft durch Freude*, Strength through Joy, is not particularly subtle. Allowing for the fact that irony does not happen to everybody and that no reader will hear all the allusions, it is hard to imagine how any reader could be in doubt about where Hiebert stood on questions of racism.

Whether Hiebert was Mennonite or not, his make believe Author is a consummate trickster. "Every group has its edge, its sense of in and out," writes Lewis Hyde, "and trickster is always there" crossing the boundaries and confusing distinctions (1998, 7). In a complex and not easily definable way, Hiebert, as W.L. Morton (1957) suggested, transmuted the oral culture around him. What Homi Bhabha termed the "space of the translation of cultural difference" is a troubled space indeed in *Sarah Binks* (2004, 224). It is a space, however, that scholars would do well to consider closely if they aim to understand nostalgia within Mennonite contexts. I take from my close reading of the text a lesson that will serve me well as I turn my attention to contemporary texts. The lesson is that the best art by Mennonites does not come from inside the safety of an ethnic or religious community. It is not an art set apart to be enjoyed by a people apart. The best art, rather, happens at the crossing places where tricksters are active and where different visions of community are contested.

Rewriting Epic Tragedy: The Case of Steppe: A Novel

The lessons about nostalgia learned from *Sarah Binks* can be applied to all the art by Mennonites that is part of the renaissance. As a Kanadier reader, however, I can best put these lessons to the test and show how "ethnic dialogism" works by looking closely at a contemporary text that is self-conscious about Russländer nostalgia. My rereading of *Sarah Binks* required me to clear critical ground and then fill in some "forgotten contexts." Reading John Weier's *Steppe: A Novel* (1995), in contrast, is like stepping onto familiar ground because the contexts are contemporary. My goal is to find common ground while respecting differences, and for this purpose I find it useful to use a model put forward by Michel de Certeau. He compares reading a literary text to renting an apartment. There is a "play of spaces" as "a different world (the reader's) slips into the author's place" (1988, xxi). How might a Kanadier reader slip into the place of a Russländer author? De Certeau suggests an answer when he writes of making "the text habitable, like a rented apartment. . . . Renters make comparable changes in an apartment they furnish with their acts and memories" (xxi). This analogy, though useful, does not convey the possible dangers. What happens if the apartment turns out to be haunted? How do you deal with the skeletons in the closet? What if they start to talk back? And·how will you respond if another reader enters the same space and takes issue with your choice of furniture? Reading, in other words, happens in that contact zone where sparks fly.

I find it helpful to think of this challenge as related to hospitality rather than the more neutral image of rented space. As I enter the text of *Steppe*, I feel as if I am being welcomed into a room that contains a Bible and a storytelling father. The book opens with the following arresting sentences: "Is this the beginning? A story should have a beginning. Something must be planted, born. Is this how the words started, where the world began? My father's story. The things he told and told and told" (Weier 1995, 1.1). As Robert Zacharias (2013, 4) notes, Weier begins by turning the opening statements of Genesis and the Gospel of John into questions. With a dense, one-page reading of it, Zacharias puts *Steppe* forward as an introductory illustration of his thesis that the fall of the "Mennonite Commonwealth" in Russia functions "as a mythological beginning, or origin story, for the Russian Mennonite community in Canada" (4). Even his brief reading of the text shows, however, that Weier is unmaking that myth by means of a confrontation with nostalgia. The narrator is "an everyman character who is left without a name," but at the same time he is a son "deeply suspicious of his father's nostalgia" for the lost world of the Mennonite Commonwealth in Russia (4). As Hiebert parodies the Kanadier genre of pioneer pastoral, so Weier parodies the Russländer genre of tragic epic.

The reader who happens to be Russländer will have a special connection to that variety of nostalgia, just as I do to some of the varieties found in *Sarah Binks*. Hildi Froese Tiessen could have offered this as an example of a text that identifies her to herself (2012, 13). I take *Steppe* as a case study here, however, not because it "identifies me to myself" (though I accept that it might do so for other Mennonites), and not because it dismantles a Mennonite myth (though I agree with Zacharias that it does), but because it overtly encourages the kind of dialogism that I advocate in this book. It is worth quoting again Tiessen's account of what might happen if texts that identified her to herself no longer existed. What if, Tiessen wonders, "the new 'Mennonite' literary text were to prove to be, simply, utterly *everyone's* text—the normative 'universal' text—what might remain to allow the Mennonite reader to say that *this text is particular*; in fact, it 'identifies me to myself'?" (2012, 14). She answers by suggesting that what remains is a "trace," but her tone is wistful. My own reading experience tells me that the same text can do both and that all we ever have are traces. Both *Sarah Binks* and *Steppe* are texts that might identify some readers to themselves, and at the same time they are both "simply, utterly *everyone's* text." It is dialogue, in response to the traces or accents, that makes them so. I begin not with the goal of extracting an ethnic identity from the text but with the goal of engaging in "ethnic dialogism."

This is easier said than done given the complex generic hybrid that Weier has constructed. I take as my starting point that Weier rejects tragic epic and replaces it with the density of lyric poetry. Zacharias hears in *Steppe* an emphasis on how "the process of narrative representation is central to the construction of origins" (2013, 4). I concur with that statement only with reference to the kind of layered storytelling that Walter Benjamin defined as part of "oral tradition" (Benjamin 1969a, 93). In *The Story Species: Our Life-Literature Connection* (2002), my mentor, the late Joseph Gold, celebrated this kind of storytelling as part of life itself. It is a dynamic activity that happens on every page of *Steppe*. "Something must be planted, born" (Weier 1995, 1.1), and Weier sprinkles the seeds of stories liberally, generating an explosion of more stories. Narrative in this text, in the sense of a linear representation of events moving along in time, is more an obstruction than a construction. Before I even read *Steppe*, the sheer brevity of it looked like a playful challenge to Rudy Wiebe's famous imperative that a writer must master the prairie with "great black steel lines of fiction. . . . No song can do that; it must be giant fiction" (1995, 4). *Steppe* is like a singing stone thrown by David at gigantic Mennonite novels. It can be read as a parody of Arnold Dyck's *Verloren in der Steppe*, a canonical novel published in translation as *Lost in the Steppe* (1974) and listed by Weier as a "source."

The forceful rejection of linear narrative locates this book in the messy middle of the crisis of representation. The speaker confronts that crisis at every turn as he tries to make sense of history. The layout—absence of pagination and plenty of white space—brings to mind what W.J.T. Mitchell refers to as an "image/text," a combination of the visual and the verbal that signals "a problematic gap, cleavage, or rupture in representation" (1994, 89). There is in *Steppe* a collapse of *all* narrative, not just the "originary myth," and as the narrative collapses in on itself other forms of representation are tested. Nostalgic photographs are described repeatedly only to be mercilessly punctured. *Forever Summer, Forever Sunday: Peter Gerhard Rempel's Photographs of Mennonites in Russia, 1890–1917* (Rempel, Rempel, and Tiessen 1981) is listed as a source, indicating that linear narrative is not the only form of "realistic" nostalgic representation that Weier is questioning.

His everyman is a pilgrim feeling his way over the shards of history, demonstrating the truth of Michel de Certeau's comment that "history begins at ground level, with footsteps" (1985, 129). Weier pulls the reader along with him, using urgent imperatives. On the first pages, the father's voice is heard: "*Listen* . . . he said" (1995, 1.1). On other pages, the reader is pushed away: "What are you doing here? You, the reader, what do you want with my story?" (1.16). The rhythm of push and pull between the first person and the second person, the I and the you, is like a hinge opening a door into the space of *Steppe*. Together, like pilgrims going hand in hand, I and you stumble over the rubble of history, confronting absurdities and chaos but also some profound questions. Is our world born of a mother or made by a father? What kind of book is this exactly in which a son begins with his father's story but then disowns it? *Steppe* contains the formulaic disclaimer: "This is a work of fiction. The characters are works of the imagination and do not represent actual persons, living or dead." This statement appears opposite the copyright page. The contents of this "novel," however, reveal the word *represent* to be less easily understood than such denials suggest. This is clearly not a "novel" in the same sense as David Bergen's *The Time in Between* (2005), also about being haunted by the ghost of a father. Some would call it a memoir, a subgenre of filial narrative known as patriography (Couser 2012, 154). Many would call it metafiction. I respond to it as a kind of ghost story, one example of what I think of as varieties of Mennonite gothic, but I also think of it as a long poem. Weier, after all, is a poet. Five volumes of his poetry sit on my shelf.

It is difficult to define the genre of the book because Weier writes self-consciously on that "equivocal site" where we confront questions about making believe. In this unstable territory, belief is not the certainty of dogma, but facts acquire a peculiar anarchical force. Whether or not the father who speaks in the book is in fact the author's father is related to what we do when we believe. As Thomas Couser points out, "because the memoir is not supposed to require fiction's willing suspension of disbe-lief, readers invest in it differently" (2012, 17). James Frey learned that lesson when he decided to call *A Million Little Pieces* a memoir in order to get a more lucrative contract from his publisher. When the "facts" were exposed as "fictions," his readers felt betrayed (Couser 2012, 16–17). An unspoken contract of some sort had been violated.

What, then, should we make of the results when an author, conversely, writes about his actual father but asks us to think of it as a form of make believe? I take it as an invitation not simply to suspend disbelief but also to think about belief in that shared and unstable space in between unreli-able memory and the facts of history. We do not do this alone as part of a subject/object or I/world binary but as part of what Martin Buber called the I/Thou relationship. With that relationship comes moral responsi-bility. With an evangelical urgency that I hear as a Mennonite accent, the speaker in *Steppe* insists that there is no escape from confrontation with agency. His occasional exasperation suggests that he knows better. "Is it evening? Are you stretched on the couch? . . . Would you like me to sing you to sleep? . . . Listen to me. Reader, are you there?" These urgent appeals are interwoven with apostrophes to the dead father: "Father, were you never lonely in Tiegerweide?" (Weier 1995, 1.16). Clearly "the time is out of joint," but this son is not a hero like the one in Act I, Scene V of Shakespeare's *Hamlet,* who laments "the cursed spite/ That ever he was born to set it right!" Instead, he urges readers into a space filled with a chorus of ghosts that threatens to drown out the voice of the father: the peddler, the hungry peasant, Onkel Jakob, Onkel Abram, Katherine the Great, Nestor Makhno, Joseph Stalin, Christopher Columbus, and many more. Luckily the dramatized I/thou dialogue creates a strong rhythm that keeps a reader turning the pages.

When I inhabit the space of *Steppe*, either as a renter or as a guest, I hear music. This does not surprise me. As Chapter 5 will show, music tends to be what Mennonites turn to when they confront the crisis of representation. It is not with narrative but with song that Weier communicates hope. At those places in *Steppe* where music offers a response to the crisis, there is also the tension between song and word that will be my focus in a later chapter. One page contains a list of the different ways the father taught his son to make a whistle, with a blade of grass, with a willow branch, with two fingers between your teeth: "Mother (father's mother) finds all these different whistles so annoying. Why don't you sing, she says. Come, let's sing a hymn, mother says, a nice hymn" (1995, 1.9). For readers who, like Weier, are the children of Russländer survivors, the music in *Steppe* will almost certainly be sad, and the reading experience might become part of ongoing attempts to deal with collective trauma. Cathy Caruth emphasizes the inherent belatedness of trauma, how it is "not locatable in the simple violent or original event in an individual's past, but rather in the way that its very unassimilated nature—the way it was precisely *not known* in the first instance—returns to haunt the survivor later on" (1996, 4). The result is that it is later generations who are haunted, which Weier dramatizes by talking to the ghost of his father. The reader does not need to be Russländer, however, to be riveted by that conversation, any more than you need to be Danish to find yourself drawn into Hamlet's exchanges with the ghost of his father.

I am most conscious of myself as a Kanadier visiting the home of a Russländer when I read the last section of *Steppe*, entitled "A Song and a Judgement." Where is the song? What is the judgement? Must this music have a message? In the middle of a jumble of historical facts, Weier indulges, as I have done, in a *schmaltzy* romance with the word for prairie: "*Steppe*. Say it! No, not like that. Like my father says it. Make it sound German, well, Mennonite. *Steppe*. Here, listen. Sh . . . te . . . ppe . . . Sh . . . te . . . ppe. . . . Yeh. Like that. Say the *ehh*, a soft vowel, say both of them. Both of them, *ehh*, like step, just like in the English. You can tell my father loves the word, the way it slips off the tongue. *Steppe*. The German word for prairie. Almost like a prayer" (1995, 5.7). There is no way to tell from the spelling how the word should be pronounced, and the imperative "Here, listen" is ironic since we cannot hear the father. It is generally assumed that words in the mother tongue are learned when infants mimic a caregiver, usually the mother. But there is no mother here to show us how it should be done.

After repeated readings, I remained disturbed, as does the speaker, by the yawning gap between the father's nostalgia and the mother's silence. The voices of father and son are bouncing off each other somewhere in this space, but what language do they speak? I found myself thinking that, if the mother were allowed to enter the text, she would have her feet on solid ground, but of course I don't know that. Into the gap, where there is no mother, I was projecting my own earthy, talkative mother, who for sure would be speaking Low German. To use de Certeau's metaphor, I was furnishing Weier's apartment with my own memories. The reader who becomes aware of doing this must go back to the text, to the actual words on the pages. There the son describes his mother's silence as a gift: "Silence belongs in a woman's world. Still, I claim it. Silence. This is the gift she gave me. . . . Hear, listen, mother isn't talking" (Weier 1995, 5.10).

Although a move into extraliterary territory always comes with the risk of reductive interpretation, the ambiguity of this genre is likely to make readers wonder how the details in *Steppe* match up with those in the life of John Weier. In his essay "Home Place" he reveals that his parents "wandered from [Ukraine] nine years after the Bolshevik Revolution to southern Manitoba" (Weier 2004, 97). *Wandered?* That oddly gentle word, used to describe the journey of traumatized refugees, speaks to me about how the numbness of shock is passed on to second and third generations. When Weier was six months old, his parents moved to the fruit belt of Ontario, where he grew up. Only High German and Low German were spoken in his home: "English wasn't tolerated in our house; that was the rule." Weier refers to Low German as "the language of our origins" but remembers his embarrassment about how language betrays ethnicity (99). Later, as an adult, Weier moved back to Manitoba. I wondered how, then, to account for the absence in *Steppe* of the Low German word *shtahp*. Weier ends his meditation on the word *steppe* by announcing that "this is our common love song. This is our creed" (1995, 5.7). Far from joining in the recitation of this Mennonite creed, this one-word song, I want to protest. How could you? How could you replace the strong *ah* sound of *shtahp* with the "soft vowel" *ehh* in *steppe*? Curiosity eventually pushed me to write to Weier to ask for clarification. I was not surprised to learn that in his family, as in many Russländer homes, the parents spoke Low German to each other and High German to their children. He expressed shock at the possibility that the Low German *shtahp* might refer to both prairie and field.

My brief exchange with Weier confirmed my sense that *Steppe* makes visible a place where our inevitable failure with words leaves us with fragments of music interwoven with the I/you of dialogue. I say *shtahp*. You say *steppe*. With this small distinction, I anticipate the questions about shibboleth/sibboleth that will concern me in the next chapter. In all my explorations, however, I will insist on a return to the text and on the need to pay attention to the words chosen with care by the author: "A Song and a Judgement." It is all too easy to sit in judgement of other people's nostalgic songs if you yourself have not lived through the trauma that those people endured. What is important is not which myths we construct to evade or erase history but that we move forward together through the rubble of history, finding strength in singing together. In *Steppe*, I hear a pilgrim telling stories and a poet listening for songs. This maker is one man, both an everyman and this particular man, taking steps on the steppe with the reader. *Steppe*, made by a poet who is also a luthier and a birder, resonates like a newly crafted violin made from old found objects. Even as the poet tries to get the sound right, he knows that he will get it wrong. Nonetheless, Weier ends up claiming a gift in the first person: "Father, the steppe. Mother, the silence. These are the gifts I own" (1995, 5.13).

Within the limits of this book, it is not possible to offer the kind of comparative study needed to explore the varieties of nostalgia and anti-nostalgia that I hear and see as part of the fabric of Mennonite culture. I have found them in more texts than can be listed here and in visual arts and music. I can do no more than close this chapter by gesturing toward three texts that would reward comparison with *Steppe*: Andreas Schroeder's *Renovating Heaven: A Novel in Triptych* (2008), Vern Thiessen's play *Back to Berlin* (2006), and Miriam Toews's *Swing Low: A Life* (2000). Each of these fictions confronts the problem of how to talk to the ghost of your father, but each father is from a different Mennonite immigrant subgroup.

If each of these texts is "simply, utterly *everyone's* text," then why pay attention to the differences? I hope that my engagements with specific texts so far have demonstrated that easy pieties about supposed universals do not lead to productive dialogues. My specific engagement, as a Kanadier reading a Russländer text, tells me that Dominick LaCapra was right to warn against the "appropriation of particular traumas by those who do not experience them, typically in a movement of identity-formation" (2001, 65; quoted in Zacharias 2013, 146).

In *Steppe*, a question about land is repeated like the burden of a song: "Whose land is this? Who lives here? Who owns this land?" (Weier 1995, 1.25). The focus is not on land but on the *questions* about land written into Mennonite history because of our pattern of dispossessing other people. The challenge of coming to terms with history goes far beyond the loss of actual land. I choose to envision each work of art as a *Spielraum*, a space of making believe, but this does not eliminate the existence of real places and real times. The truth is that, wherever you settle on this Earth, the land is haunted. "Every site," writes de Certeau, "is haunted by countless ghosts that lurk there in silence, to be 'evoked' or not. One *inhabits* only haunted sites" (1985, 143). Making believe together is fraught with dangers, including the borrowed nostalgia that leads us to mourn the past of people whose history we have not bothered to learn. Despite major differences among Mennonite groups, the artists from all of them have in common what also unites Paul Hiebert and John Weier, a search for a *Spielraum*, a place of making believe within which to find new ways of exploring old questions.

WITNESSING A NEW PHENOMENON

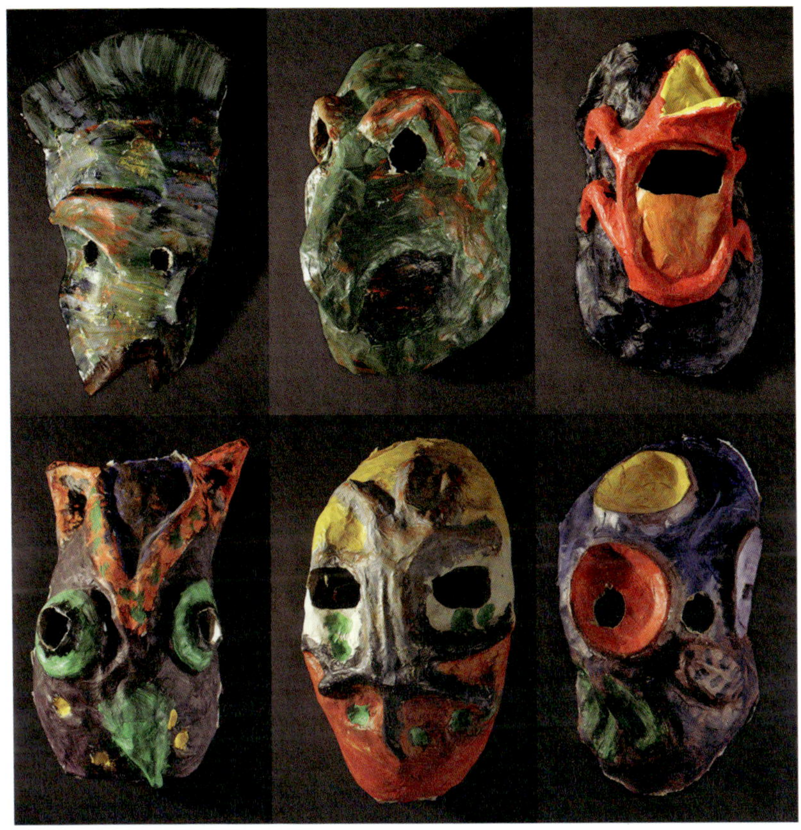

Plate 1. Magdalene Redekop, *Pochinko Masks* (2008), papier-mâché. Clockwise from top left: *Fesh*/Fish; *Naze*/Nose; *Kjniepa*/Bug; *Loch*/Hole; *Boum*/Tree; *Foss*/Fox. Photograph by Peter Legris, 2018. Courtesy of the artist.

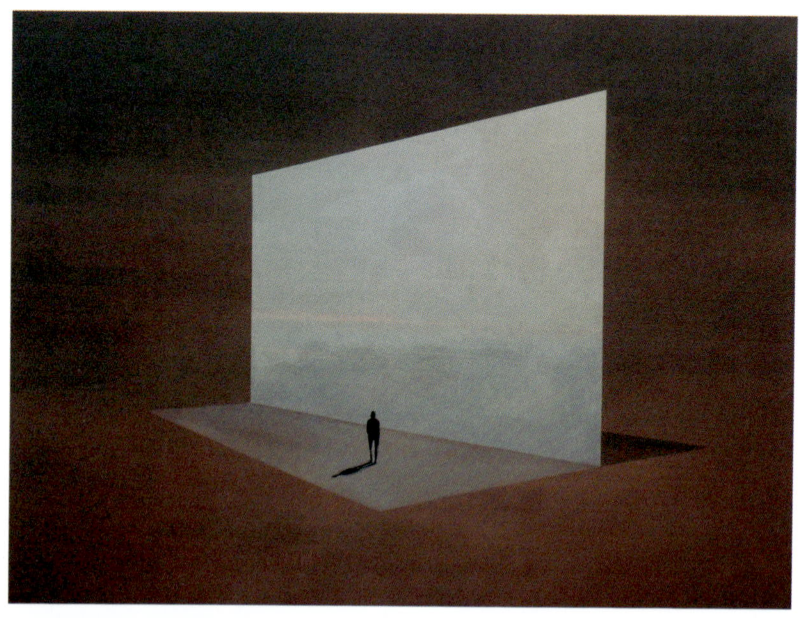

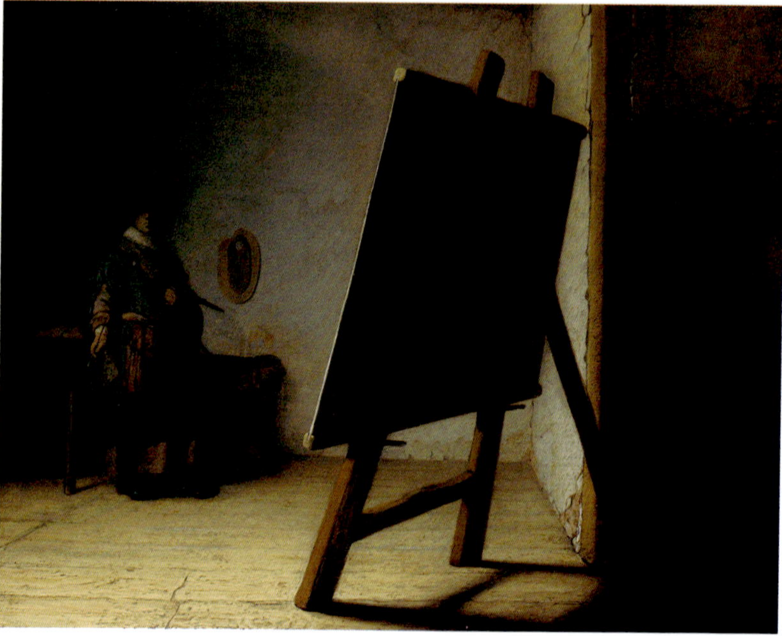

Plate 2. Wanda Koop, *Untitled* 2010, from *Hybrid Human.* Copyright Visual Arts CARCC, 2019. Courtesy of the artist.

Plate 3. Rembrandt van Rijn, *Artist in His Studio,* c. 1628, oil on panel. Photograph, 2019, Museum of Fine Arts, Boston.

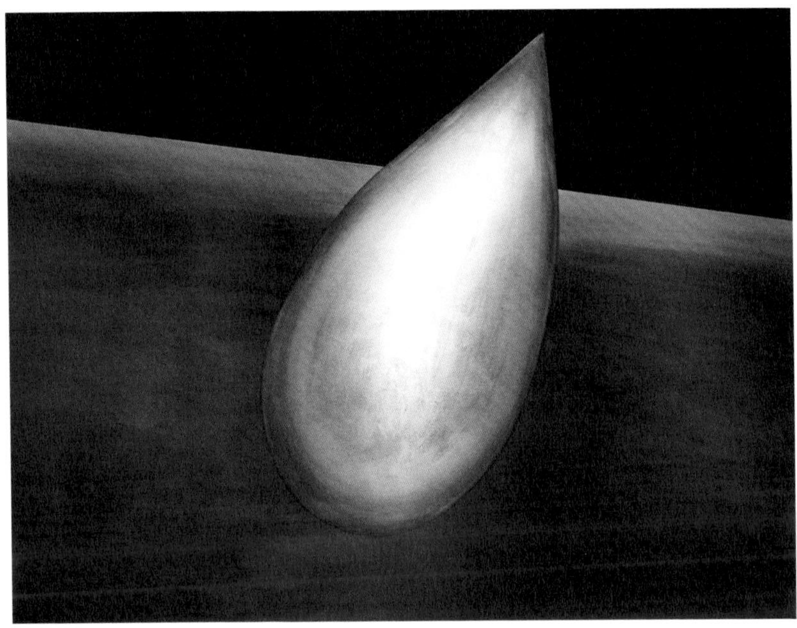

Plate 4. Wanda Koop, *Tear,* 1996 (*See Everything/See Nothing*). Copyright Visual Arts CARCC, 2019. Courtesy of the artist.

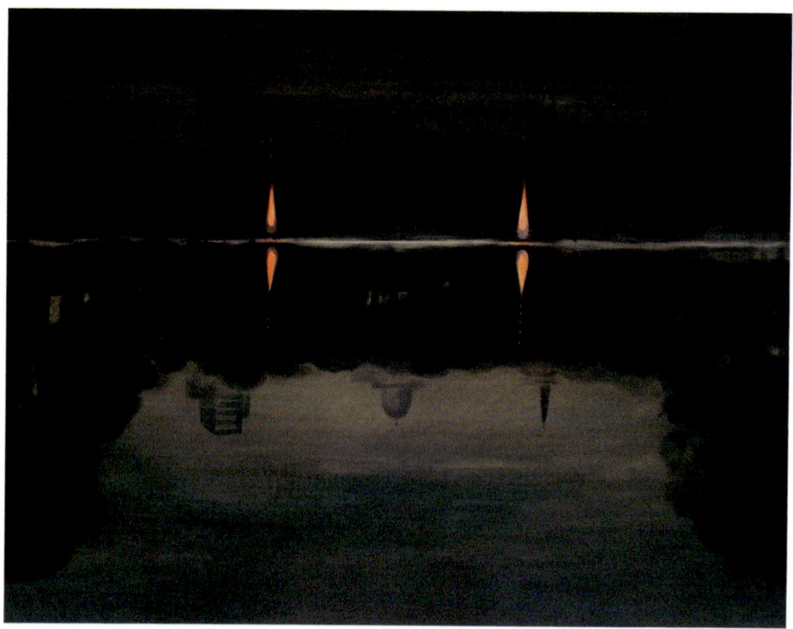

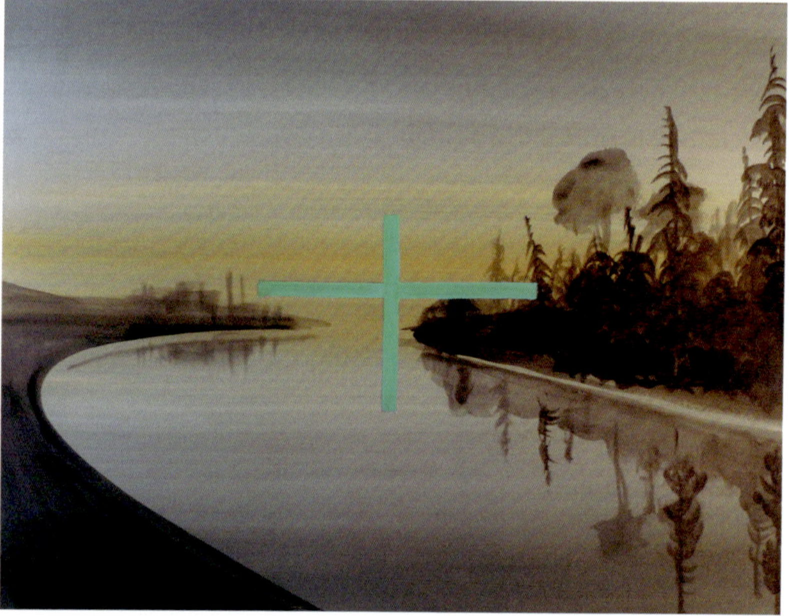

Plate 5. Wanda Koop, *Untitled (Native Fires)*, 1996 (*See Everything/See Nothing*). Copyright Visual Arts C A R C C, 2019. Courtesy of the artist.

Plate 6. Wanda Koop, *Sightline – Green Crosshair*, 1999. From the collection of Jeff Neufeld and Katrina Lee Kwen. Courtesy of the artist.

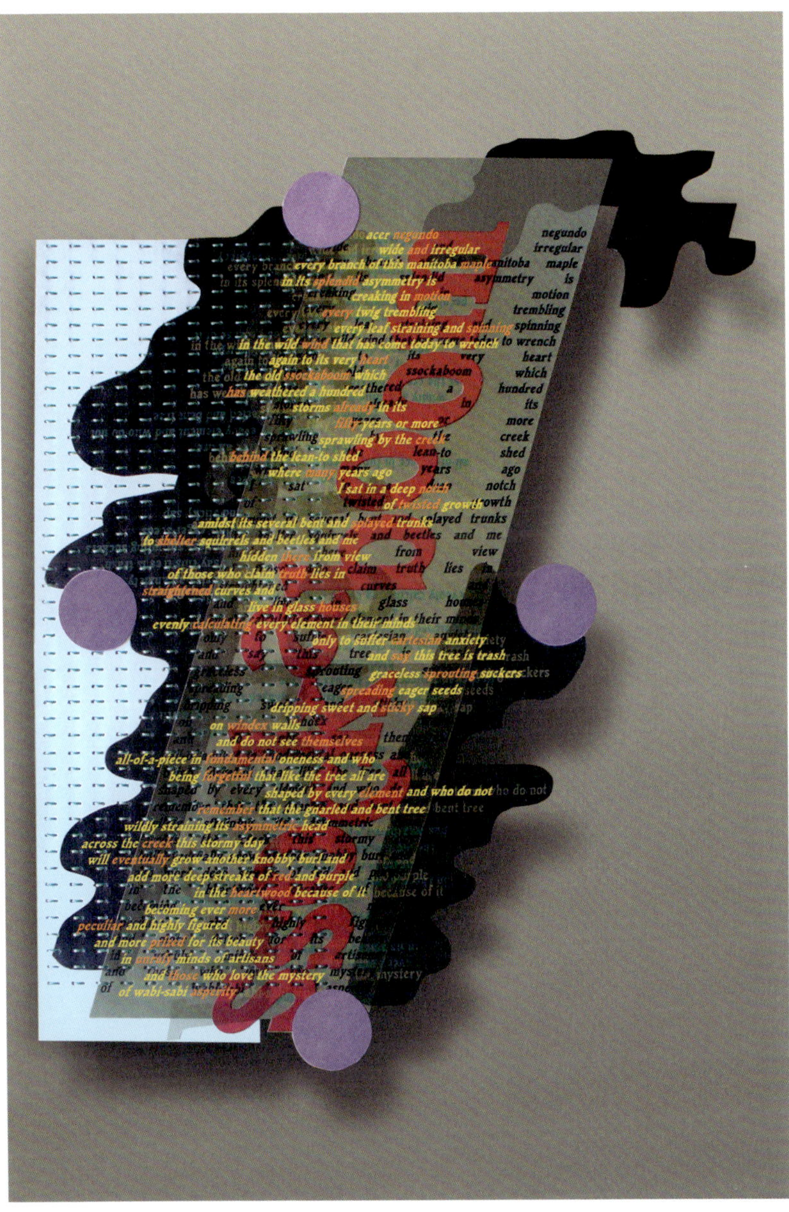

Plate 7. Norman Schmidt, *ssockaboom typoem*, 2012. Hand-printed paper, cut and pieced. Courtesy of the artist.

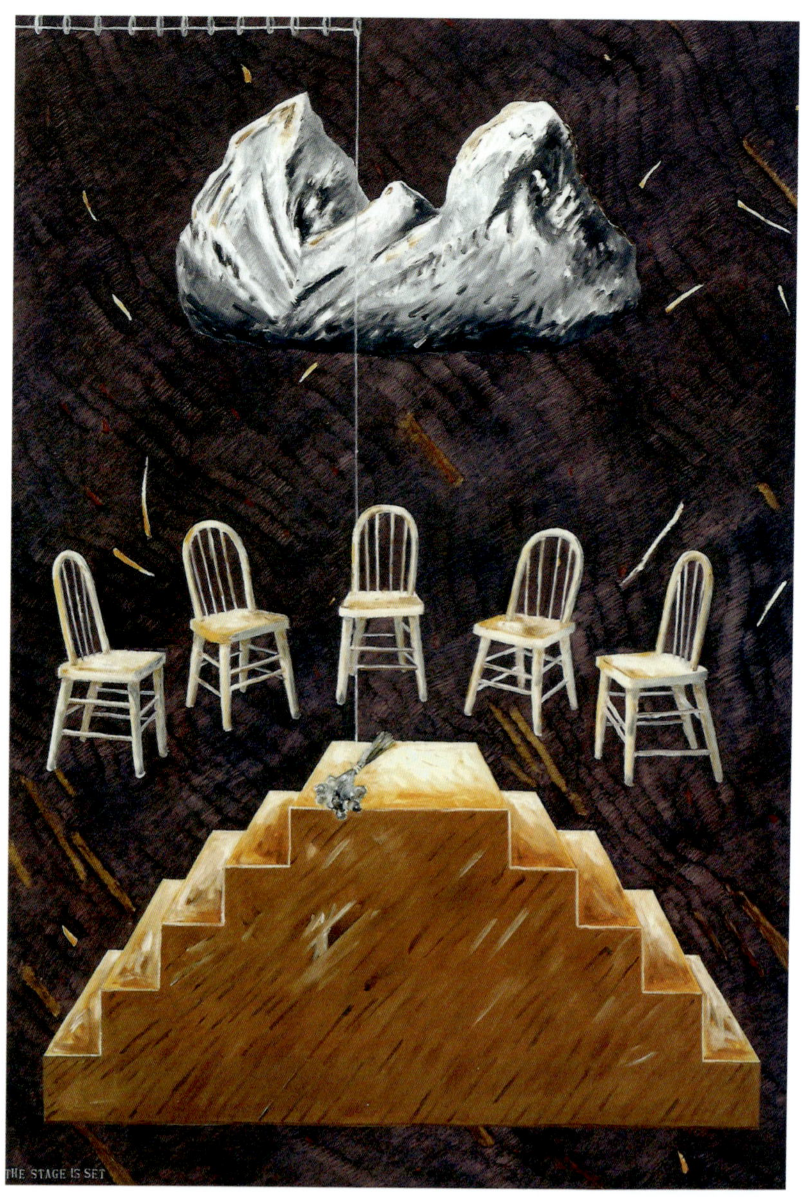

Plate 8. Gathie Falk, *Development of the Plot III #1 The Stage is Set,* 1992, oil on canvas, 228.6 x 160.0 cm. Photo by Teresa Healy, Vancouver Art Gallery. Collection National Gallery of Canada, Ottawa. Courtesy of the artist.

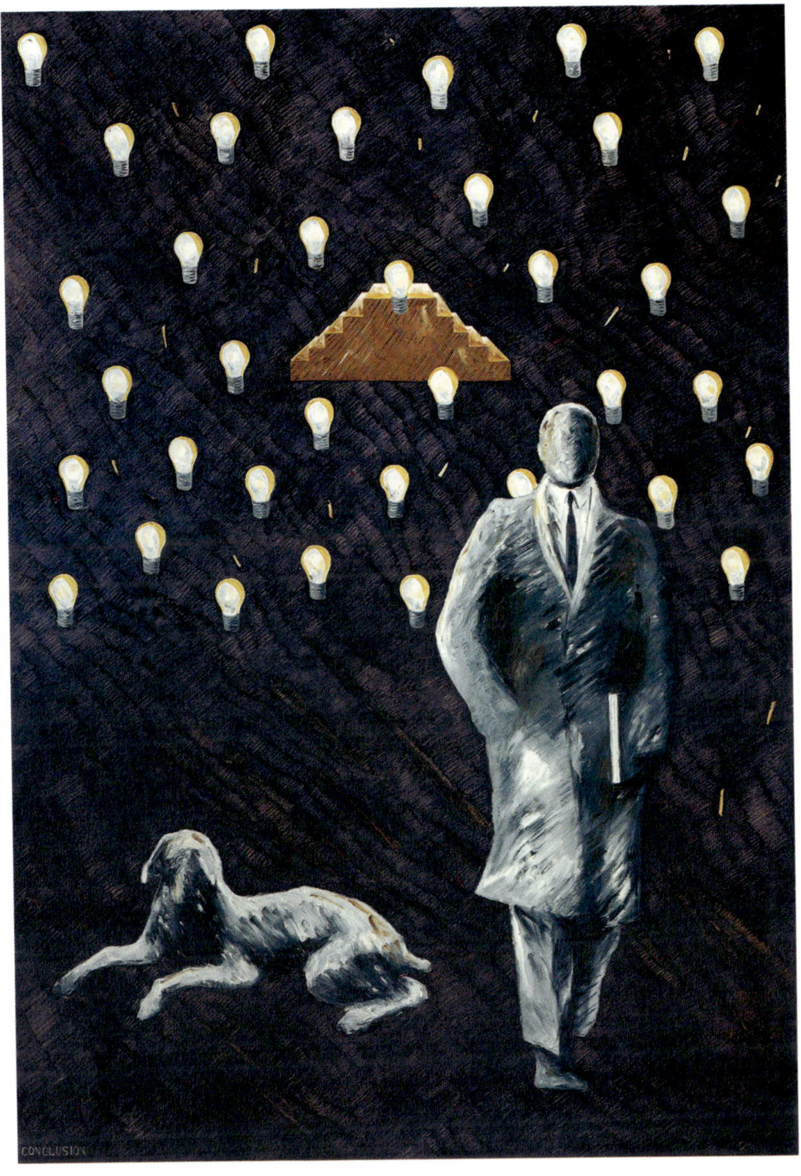

Plate 9. Gathie Falk, *Development of the Plot III #8 Conclusion,* 1992, oil on canvas.
Photo by Teresa Healy, Vancouver Art Gallery. Collection National Gallery of Canada,
Ottawa. Courtesy of the artist.

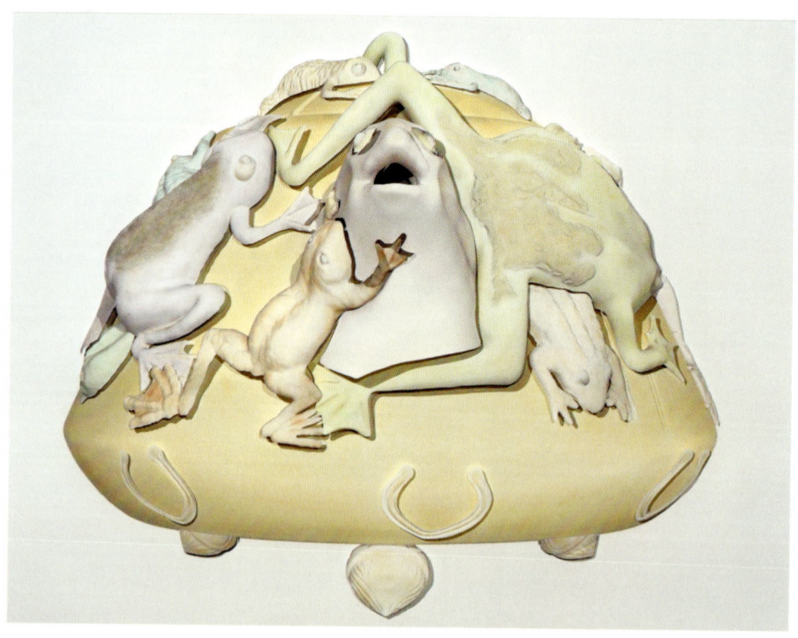

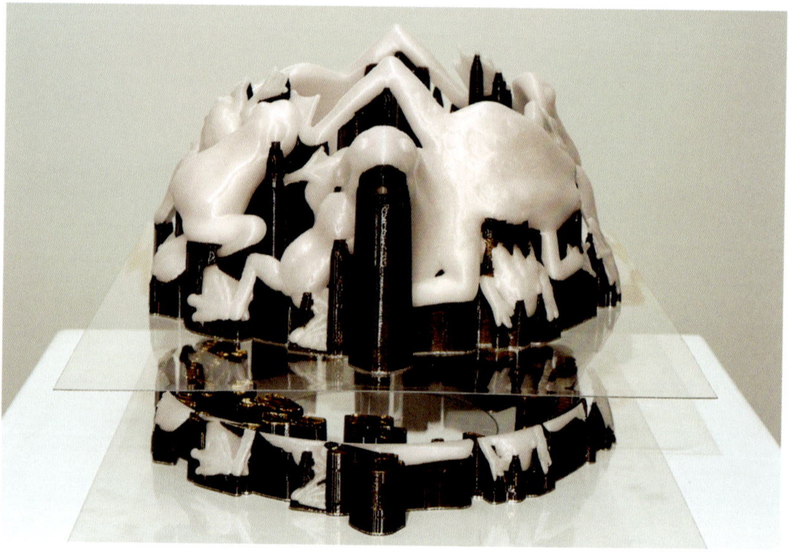

Plate 10a. Susan Shantz, *Creatures in Translation*, A G G V Website 3D, Frog Print Paper Tolle, 2011–12, mixed media on paper (mounted on gatorboard), 167 x 112 x 13 cm. Collection of the Regina Public Library. Courtesy of the artist.

Plate 10b. Susan Shantz, *Creatures in Translation*, A G G V Website 3D, Print Fragment (Frog Crown), 2011–12, thermoplastic, 18 x 35 x 35 cm. Collection of the Saskatchewan Arts Board. Courtesy of the artist.

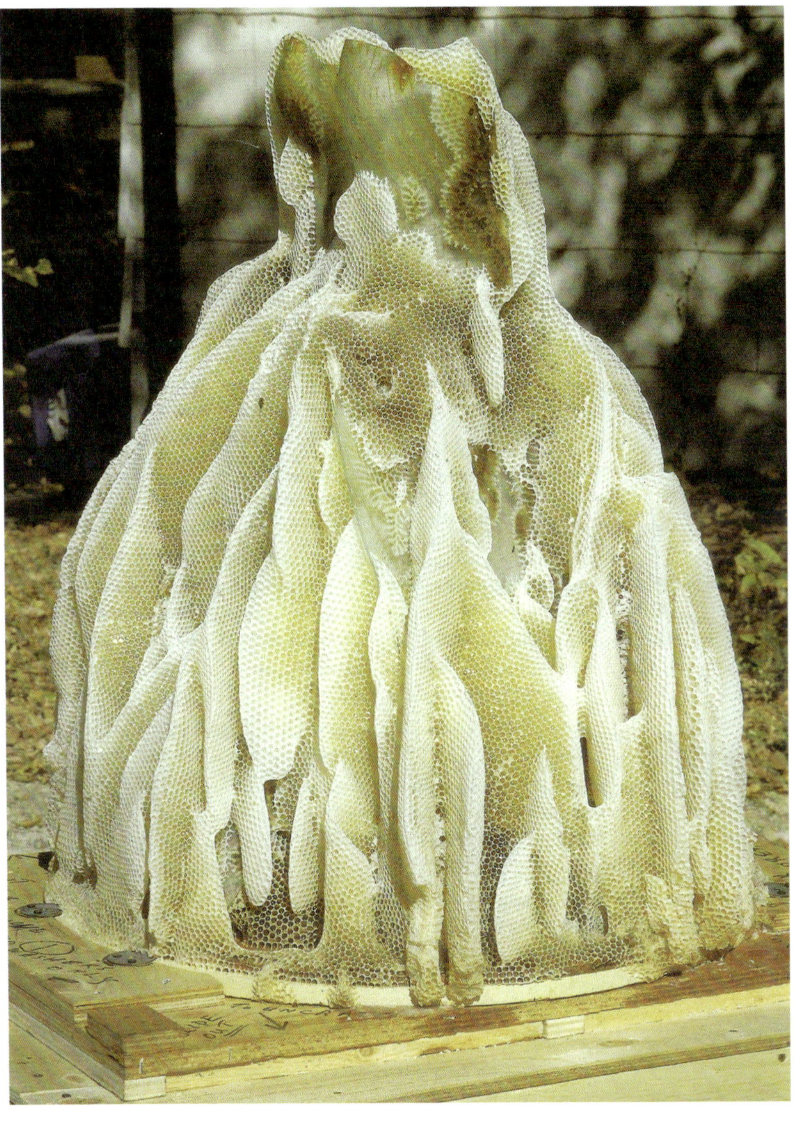

Plate 11. Aganetha Dyck, *The Glass Dress: Lady in Waiting* (1992–98), glass, pearls, honeycomb (wax and honey), wood. Photograph by Peter Dyck. Collection National Gallery of Canada, Ottawa. Courtesy of the artist.

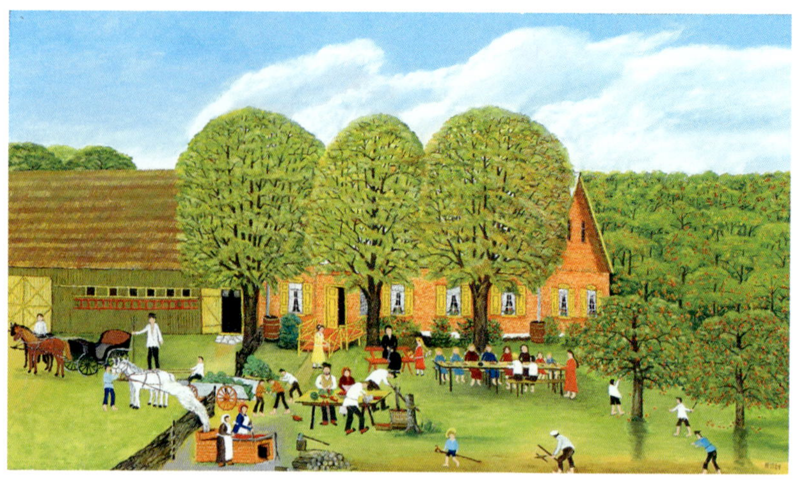

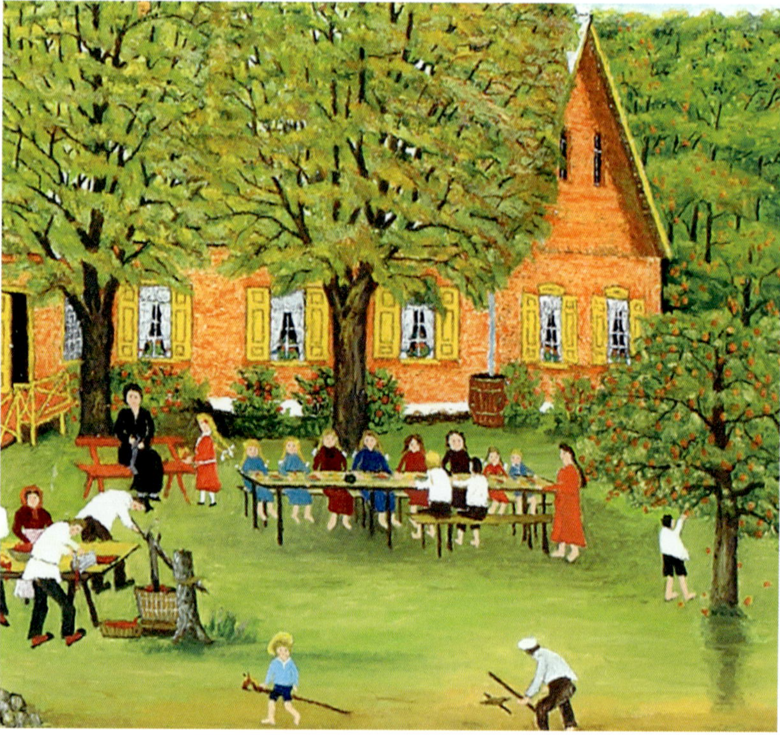

Plate 12. Henry B. Pauls, *Watermelon Syrup Cooking,* 1984 (with detail below).
Collection Canadian Museum of History, 84-82, D2005-20217. Courtesy of the family
of Henry Pauls.

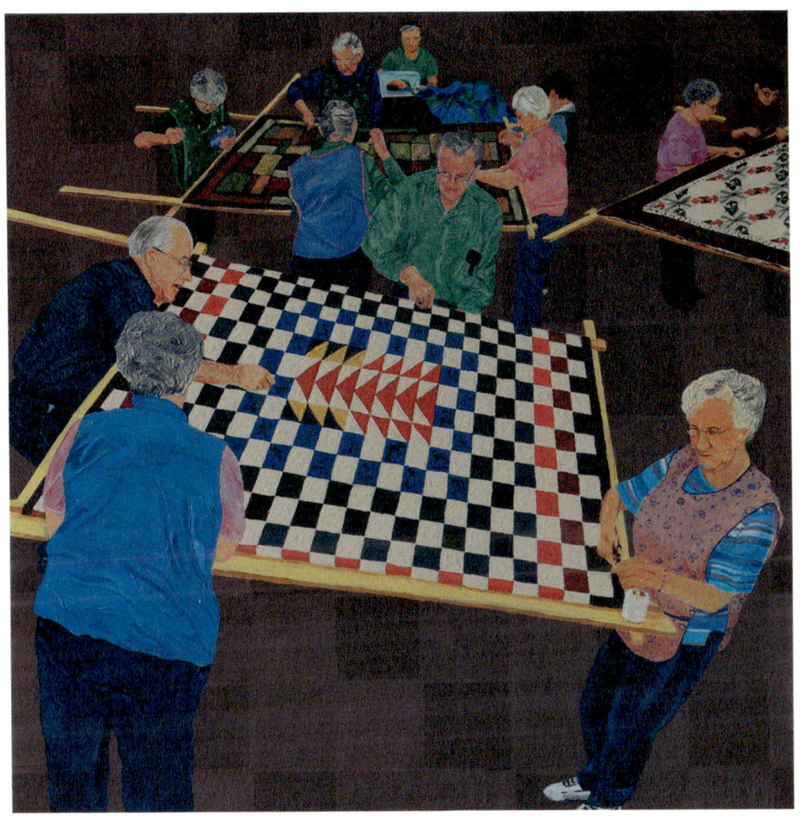

Plate 13. Margruite Krahn, MCC *Quilters*, 2010, acrylic and latex house paint on canvas. Courtesy of the artist.

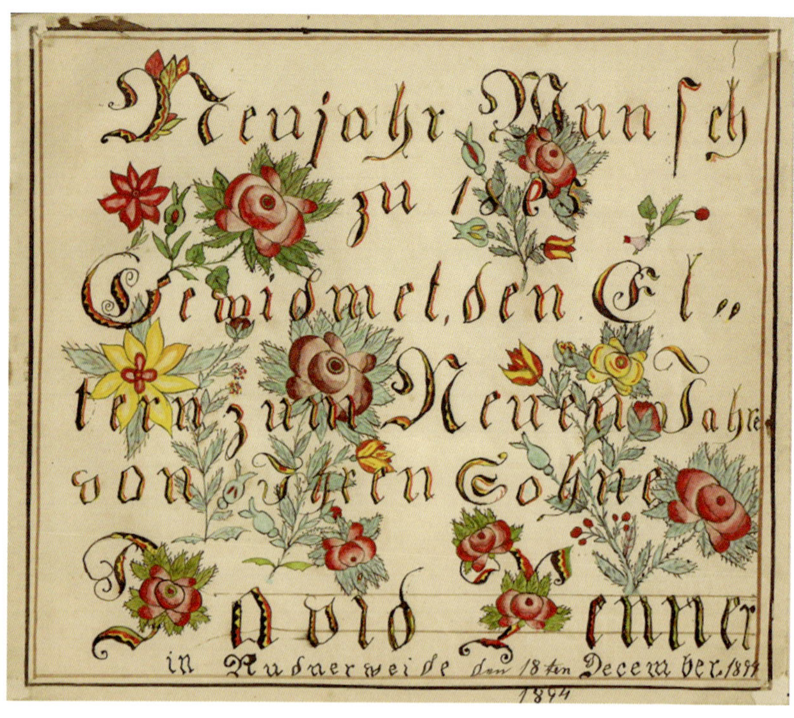

Plate 14. David B. Penner, *Fraktur,* 1896. Courtesy of Ruth Stoesz.

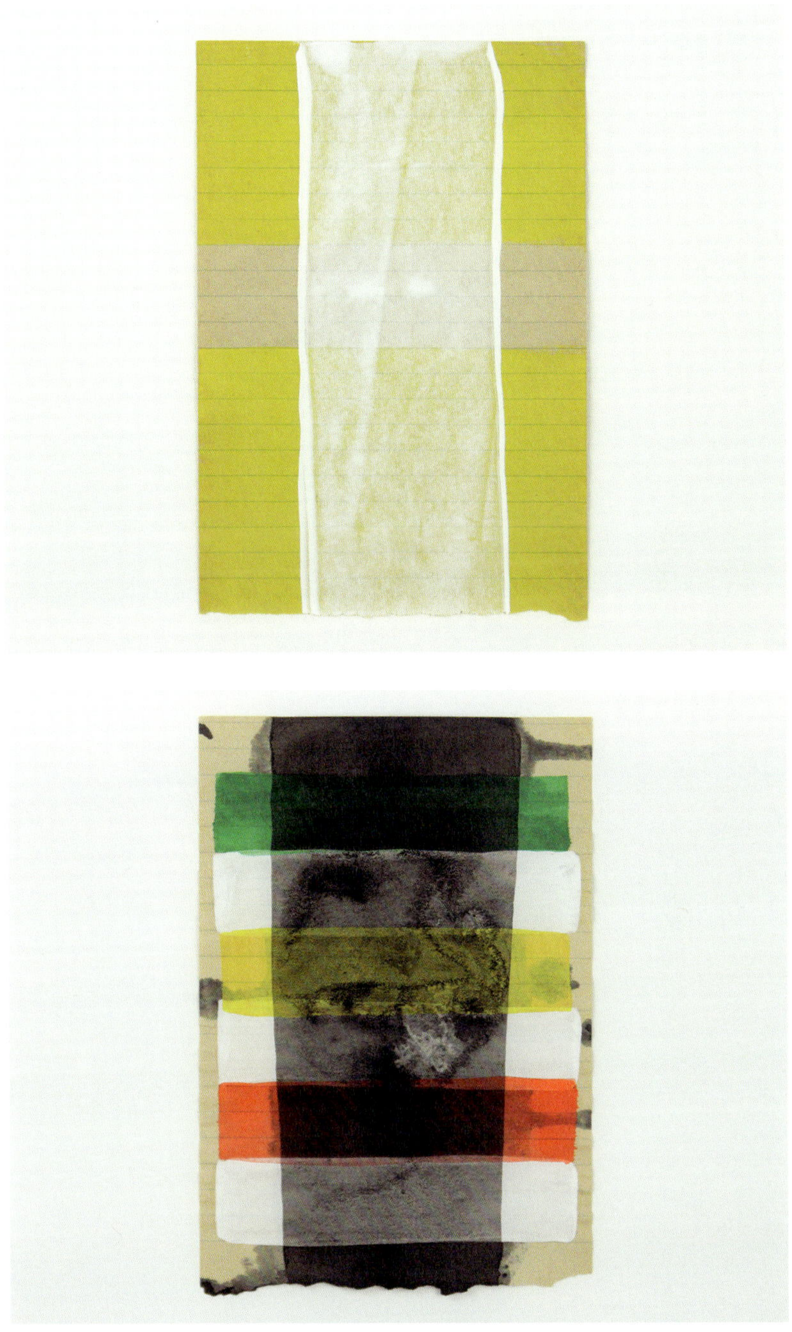

Plate 15. Douglas Witmer, *School Papers,* 2011–13, mixed media on found paper. Courtesy of the artist.

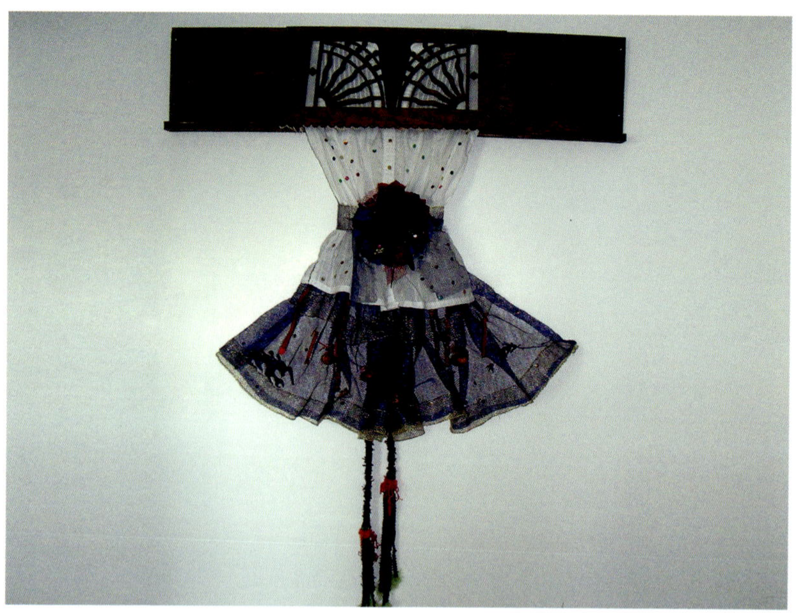

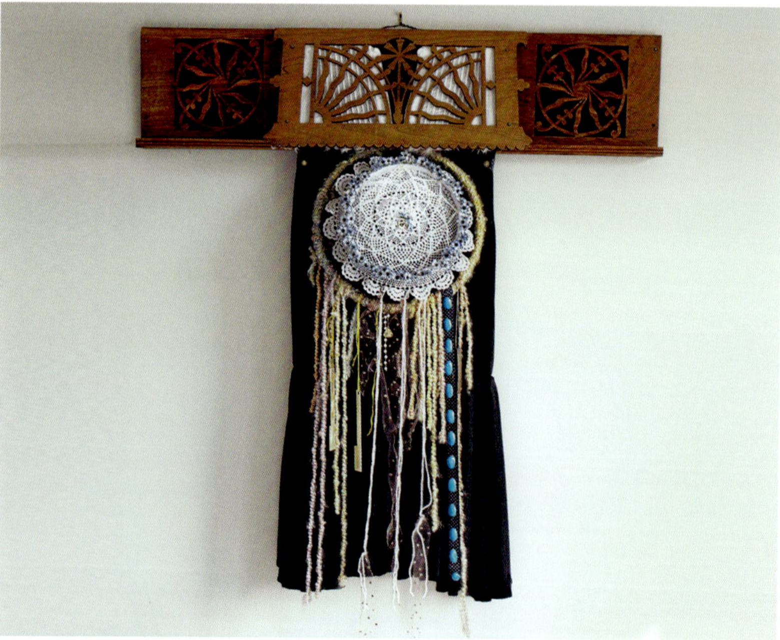

Plate 16. Elizabeth Falk, *I'll Fly Away*, 2008, fabric and found objects. Courtesy of the artist.

Plate 17. Elizabeth Falk, *I'll Fly Away*, 2016, fabric and found objects. Photograph by Laurie Salter. Courtesy of the artist.

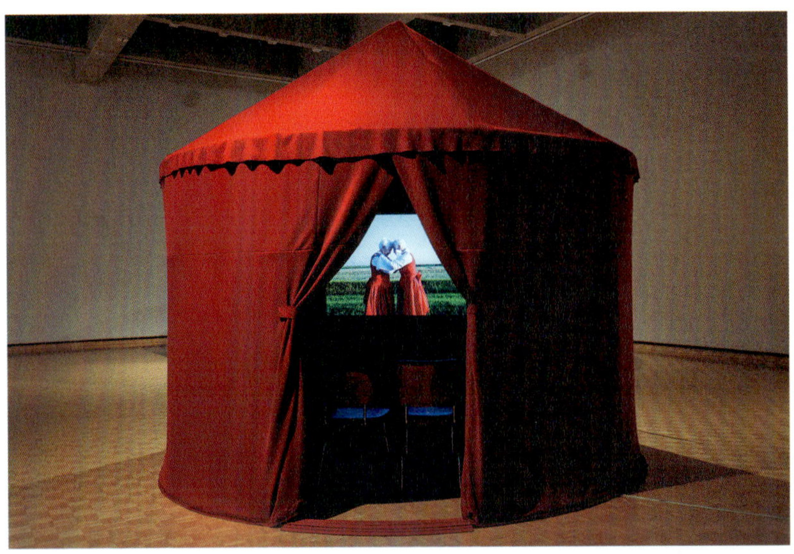

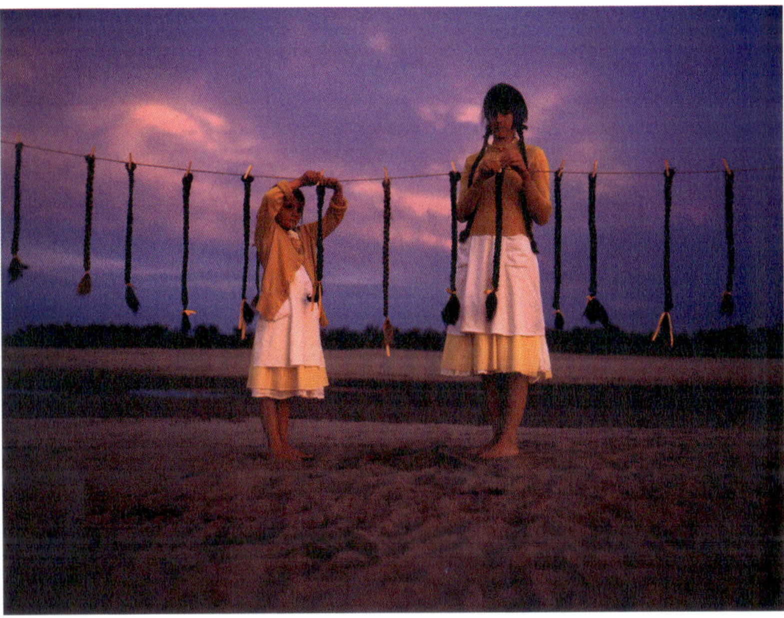

Plate 18. Amalie Atkins, *Embrace,* installation view, Mackenzie Art Gallery, 2014. From "We Live on the Edge of Disaster and Imagine We are in a Musical," an ongoing mixed-media project. Photo by Trevor Hopkin. Courtesy of the artist and MacKenzie Art Gallery.

Plate 19. Amalie Atkins, *Hanging Braids 11,* 2013. From "We Live on the Edge of Disaster and Imagine We are in a Musical," an ongoing mixed-media project. Courtesy of the artist and MacKenzie Art Gallery.

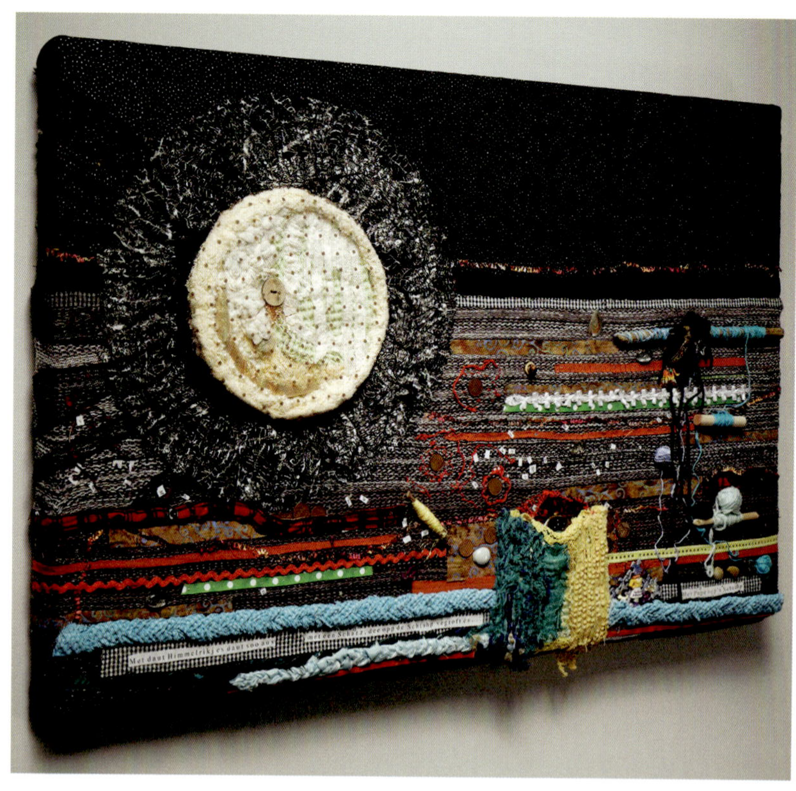

Plate 20. Elizabeth Falk, *Met Pahpe opp'e Shtahp*, 2018, fabric and found objects. Photograph by Peter Legris. Courtesy of the artist.

4

LOCATION, DISLOCATION
HARVESTING A LITERARY BUMPER CROP

Chemt teet, chemt rote.
Chemt zodelteet, chemt zote.

Comes time, comes wisdom.
Comes seedtime, comes seed.

Dealing with a Bumper Crop

As I turn my attention in this chapter to the literary part of a larger Canadian Mennonite cultural renaissance, I am overwhelmed by the embarrassment of riches. It helps to think of myself as playing one small part with others in harvesting a "bumper crop." The agricultural term is useful because it conveys the mixed feelings experienced by farmers who have to deal with an exceptionally large harvest. There is the thrill of abundance, but it comes with anxiety when the harvest exceeds the storage space available. For my father, there was added worry because he could not afford to buy a combine and had to wait until a neighbour was finished harvesting to borrow one. When our *shpikka* or granary was full, it was time to transfer grain to make room for more, and this process was mysterious to me when I was a child. I knew only that there was anxiety in my father's voice when he told my mother "*Dei kota ess voll.*" In "Farm Animals' Desertion" (Redekop 2013a), I wrote about how I was puzzled because *kota* was Low German for tomcat. In fact, my father was using an English word. The *quota* is full. This word was linked in some way to the mystery of grain elevators, those odd structures that then dotted the prairie landscape. *Bumper* was also a baffling word. As a child I imagined tractors pulling wagons heaped with grain, travelling bumper to bumper on the highway to our local elevator. Now I know that a bumper is a large cup filled to the brim with wine, which happily echoes Psalm 23: "my cup runneth over." On the rare occasions when we drove into Winnipeg, I was fascinated by the Golden Boy perched at the top of the legislative building holding a sheaf of wheat. In my mind, this figure of the trickster Mercury now overlooks the field in which some of us are trying to harvest this bumper crop.

Over the years, I have followed the work of other harvesters on the field and been particularly helped by the invaluable interim reports provided by Hildi Froese Tiessen. Even so, I have never been able to keep up. I have downsized several times since the books first began to multiply, with the result that my MennoLit bookcase is bulging with books. The pile of *Rhubarb* magazines jammed into the bottom shelf shows, all by itself, the challenge that this bumper crop presents. *Rhubarb* (which folded in 2018) was a Manitoba periodical published by the Mennonite Literary Society since 1998. The forerunner of *Rhubarb* was called *Mennonite Mirror*, a title that suggests collective self-reflection. *Rhubarb* mostly lived up to its name—adding tartness to the self-reflections—and it helped me to keep in touch from a distance with what was happening in Manitoba. I read it alongside other journals, among which *Border Crossings* was especially important, but *Rhubarb* was a way to stay tuned in to conversations among Mennonites. Although the quality of the writing was uneven, as happens inevitably with such publications, *Rhubarb* was a nurturing ground that generated new talent, invited the cracking open of fixed ideas, and encouraged Mennonites to clown with each other in public.

In the previous chapter, I laid the groundwork for this one by reaching back to 1947 and including Paul Hiebert's *Sarah Binks* as part of a Mennonite literary legacy, and I will continue to keep that legacy in mind.

It was undeniably Rudy Wiebe's *Peace Shall Destroy Many*, however, that broke new ground in 1962 by proving, for the first time, that it was possible for a Mennonite to represent a Mennonite community in fiction and get away with it. Wiebe's continuing influence on younger writers is reflected in a recent moving tribute to him by Miriam Toews (2016). To continue the agricultural analogy, it could be said that later writers such as Toews work on ground first cultivated by Wiebe. In the words of Al Reimer, his first novel opened up "a Mennonite literary world that other Mennonite writers could enter and explore. . . . And that has led directly to the efflorescence of 'Mennonite' writing we enjoy today" (in Tiessen 2002, n.p.).

As Robert Zacharias has noted, "Mennonite Canadian literature as a body of literature was explicitly framed in its emergence by its relation to the nationalizing project of Canadian literature as an institution—hence Mennonite *Canadian Literature*" (2013, 27). That institution clearly did not know how to make room for *Sarah Binks*, and certainly not for *Willows Revisited* (Hiebert 1967), a book that put itself out of the running by satirizing "the nationalizing project." It was the historical fiction of Wiebe that came to represent the Mennonite contribution to the larger mosaic of early CanLit, which included the fiction of Margaret Atwood, Robertson Davies, A.M. Klein, Margaret Laurence, and many more. In those days, there was much talk of our "colonial mentality," and collective insecurity prevented critics from claiming that there was a Canadian renaissance that followed the American renaissance. CanLit, in any case, is the self-derogatory neologism that stuck in the academy as something with which we could live, however uncomfortably. To me it has always conveyed an odour of something canned too hastily. By this I do not mean the literature of the time but the speed with which critics leaped to make absurd generalizations about it. To this day, the common misperception is that all Canadian fiction is rural and claustrophobic, a ridiculous generalization if you consider the heterogeneity of the actual fiction. Recently CanLit has morphed into a strange kind of monster, and a hasty rush to judgement is now often followed by the shunning of an author but seldom by the careful reading of literary texts.

As I tried to show in the previous chapter, close reading of a selected text can help to counter the inevitable falsifications of literary history. In this chapter I will have no choice but to range more widely among texts so as to offer an impression of the larger phenomenon. Distortion will be inevitable and will reflect my bias, but I begin with a consensus stated clearly by Hildi Froese Tiessen: "We cannot speak of contemporary Mennonite writing in Canada without placing at its centre Manitoba, where it began" (Tiessen 2010, 9). I will rely heavily on the published proceedings of a conference on Mennonite/s Writing in Canada that took place in 1990 at Conrad Grebel College in Waterloo. It is important to note that this conference (although eventually hosted by Hildi Froese Tiessen) was not initiated by Mennonites, but by the editorial board of *The New Quarterly*—Kim Jernigan, Peter Hinchcliffe, and others. With the help of funding from various Canadian government agencies, writers and critics from across the country—Mennonite and non-Mennonite—gathered in Ontario to talk about what had happened, mostly in Manitoba, during the preceding decade. Literary ferment continued among Mennonites in Canada after that. The presence of a small number of American writers enlivened the 1990 conference and in the years that followed, a literary flowering happened also in the United States and it too is still ongoing. Mennonite/s Writing conferences took place in 1997 and 2002 at Goshen College, Indiana, and in 2006 at Bluffton College, Ohio. Almost two decades passed after the memorable 1990 conference, however, before a Mennonite/s Writing conference once again took place in Canada. During this time it became, in the words of Robert Zacharias, a "well-established principle in the field" that "Mennonite/s Writing" transcends "national boundaries." As Zacharias notes, the result of this has been that we have tended "to gloss over the ways in which the field has been structured differently in Canada and the United States" (2015, 3).

Differences among Mennonites were out in the open at the first 1990 conference in Waterloo, and the sparks that flew in various "contact zones" helped to ensure that the writers who emerged in the 1980s would go to their various homes and keep writing in their many different ways. Because of the glossing over that Zacharias describes, however, open differences now seem to be viewed as unseemly scratches on the smooth finish of transnational Mennonitism. I must confess, nevertheless, that I felt like a fish out of water during a moment at the Bluffton College conference in 2006 when Hildi Froese Tiessen felt it necessary to explain to the Americans in the audience what we mean in Canada by the term "secular

Mennonite." It is at least possible that the Americans who attended the 2009 conference on "Manitoba and Beyond" at the University of Winnipeg felt similarly dislocated. I remember one American expressing to me his disapproval of the Manitoba focus because, as he put it, we should have long since moved beyond "provincialism." I take the caution seriously, as the title of this chapter shows. To be "provincial" is to see and value only your own local reality. At the border crossings—where dislocation reveals difference—is where the sparks fly and renaissance can happen. My own paper at the 2009 Winnipeg conference was entitled "St. Mary at Main and Other Prairie Crossings." This title alluded to a poem by Patrick Friesen and reflected my sense of being in the vicinity of crossings where tricksters were at play.

Fortunately, poets and novelists do not wait for academic conferences to authorize their writings. Although I have never understood exactly what was meant by the interpolated slash mark, I do not believe that there is something called "Mennonite/s Writing" that transcends inconvenient differences between Canada and the United States or between Swiss Mennonites and Russian Mennonites. Although the deepest roots of Anabaptism do indeed grow across all national boundaries, I share Zacharias's view that "scholars have yet to fully explore the ways in which questions of Mennonite identity and cultural difference . . . have been negotiated through starkly different regional, denominational, and national contexts" (2015, 3). What follows is an account of how one woman witnessed a Mennonite renaissance while negotiating her own nostalgia along with the stark differences of her own experience.

H is for Harvest: Preparation for an Untaught Course in Canadian Mennonite Literature

My quota is full and "my cup runneth over." When confronted with such an embarrassment of literary riches, I tend to use my teaching experience as a guide. I remind myself that the rubric of any literature course assumes that students and teachers will act as if the titles can be separated out from the larger body of literature that presses in on them. I therefore began this chapter with a plan to adapt Northrop Frye's strategy in "Preface to an Uncollected Anthology" (1971) and imagine what I might do if I were asked to teach a course on Canadian Mennonite Literature. As I soon discovered, this was not a method without risk. Since I have never taught such a course, it felt a little like one of those recurring nightmares that haunts retired professors—being told that you have to teach a class for which you are totally unprepared and, predictably, inappropriately dressed. I then considered writing a more direct adaptation of Frye's essay. It was tempting to rewrite his prefatory note: "The author imagines that she has collected her ideal anthology of Canadian Mennonite Literature, with no difficulties about permissions, publishers, or expenses, and is writing her preface" (adapted from Frye 1971, 163). I came up immediately, however, against the probable reasons why no scholar has yet ventured to make up such an anthology. New voices are emerging constantly, and their diversity makes a critic reluctant to impose on them what Hildi Froese Tiessen referred to in 1990 as a "masquerade of coherence" (Tiessen and Hinchcliffe 1992, 20). An imagined teaching assignment has remained useful, however, as a way of achieving critical distance. I will attempt a rough inventory of the harvest. To some extent, I will sort out the fruits into bushel baskets labelled according to genre.

I once again begin by reminding myself of the advice of Fredric Jameson: "Always historicize!" (1981, 9). This would influence my choice of an introductory text for my imaginary course. Yet no such text should be offered as a point of origin. In any case, the only text in Mennonite culture that might deserve to be elevated to that position is the Bible. What I would look for is something published in the midst of the material culture of the particular place where the phenomenon started. I imagine this as a graduate course, and I would hope to have at least a few students interested in book history. As a lure for such students, I might choose *Harvest: Anthology of Mennonite Writing in Canada, 1874–1974* (De Fehr et al. 1974). This book has the advantage over my imaginary anthology in that it actually exists. It is material evidence of a moment when early voices were gathered together in a real time and a real place. Published in 1974, *Harvest* commemorates the 1874 arrival in Manitoba of the Kanadier, that group of Mennonites that included my grandparents. In hindsight, *Harvest* sounds premature as a title. A more appropriate title would have been *Seedlings*. A one-page introduction by G.K. Epp ends with a prediction that has come true: "Canadian Mennonites have reached their land of final destination and can look forward to an era in which outstanding Mennonite writers will be encouraged by their own people to create literature of the first rank" (viii). Some writers in the anthology are now well known, but they appear alongside names of writers now unknown. *Harvest* is included by Joseph Pivato in a list of other ethnic anthologies (2003, 58) and by Carole Gerson in a similar list in volume 3 of the *History of the Book in Canada* (Gerson and Michon 2007). Since Gerson's 1992 debunking of *Sarah Binks* turned a blind eye to Paul Hiebert's ethnicity, it is not surprising that she did not point out his inclusion in *Harvest* and that she concludes: "Rudy Wiebe was the first significant Mennonite writer to publish in English" (Gerson and Michon 2007, 97).

In his brief but cogent reflections on *Harvest*, Robert Zacharias draws attention to the contradictory aims of the anthology, noting that it claims to reach out to "an imaginary Canadian public" but includes "some eighty pages of text in Low or High German. . . . Significantly, it repeatedly opposes the Mennonite community against an imaginary Canadian public to whom it appeals, implicitly excluding Mennonites from the national narrative and thus reinscribing the very alterity that it seeks to address" (2013, 39). Zacharias concludes that *Harvest* has had "no obvious lasting impact on the field of Mennonite literary studies" (39). That is true in the sense that it does not appear to have directly influenced the writers or critics who emerged in the years that followed. The contents of the book, however, suggest to me that on a less obvious level it could be a rich resource for scholars wishing to do just what Zacharias recommends we do, to interrogate "the unspoken presuppositions that commonly guide discussions of Mennonite Canadian literature" (38). Such a study, however, would be productive only if the investigators paid attention not only to what is in the anthology but also to what is not in it.

The gaps in *Harvest* are relatively easy to spot in hindsight. Although the collection ostensibly commemorates the 1874 arrival in Manitoba of Kanadier Mennonites, for example, there is little mention of that event. I went through the book in vain looking for descriptions of the sod houses, or *semlins*, that the Kanadier pioneers built on the prairie when they first arrived. In his "global survey" of traditional structural forms, Allen Noble includes *semlins* in his account of "semi-subterranean structures," describing how "German-Russian Mennonite settlers entering the largely treeless prairie provinces of Canada in the mid-nineteenth century resorted initially to the old dwelling forms called the *semeljanken* or *semlin*" (2007, 128). Ukrainian settlers, Noble comments, built similar structures called *zemlyanka*. I thought of them when I read, in Robert Pogue Harrison's *The Dominion of the Dead*, about various subterranean structures that Harrison offers as examples of the "humic foundations" of our civilization. They show "that the new must repose on, or literally renew, the foundations of the old" (2003, 43). This is a powerful anachronic image, this semi-subterranean dwelling that reminds us of the houses we construct for our dead so that we can go visit them. The absence of *semlins* from the anthology anticipates how, in the decades to come, a majority of Kanadier writers would share Al Reimer's view that our history, compared to that of the exotic Russländer, is "utterly devoid of drama or glamour" (1988, 257).

As it turned out, I did find in *Harvest* a single glancing allusion to sod houses in a poem entitled "Patriarchal Light" by "Pat" Friesen. In the lines of that poem can be heard the emerging voice of the now-seasoned poet Patrick Friesen:

> I did not know the patriarchs,
> I am not sure which was their light.
> I was not born in a simlin [*sic*]
> though my feet lovingly touch the ground (1974, 85)

Friesen's first collection of poetry, *The Lands I Am*, was published two years later (1976). The deceptive ease with which that title incorporates the bold words *I am* anticipates his spare style and his insistence on his right to "blaspheme." The radical identification with the land, with the actual ground that one's feet touch, stands in contrast to Russländer nostalgia for the steppes of Ukraine. It was the Russländer story, however, that was soon put forward by literary critics as the one worthy of the highest forms in the hierarchy of genres: tragedy, epic, and elegy. *Harvest* foreshadows this with the contribution by Reynold Siemens (1974), a lament for the death of a Russian Mennonite cellist replete with tropes of nostalgia such as the ruin. A reader of this anthology, however, would have had no way of anticipating that this story would become the basis of an "originary myth." All the authors are on a level playing field, except perhaps Frank Epp, given precedence as a historian. There is an excerpt from Wiebe's *Peace Shall*

Destroy Many (now in the canon), but it is on a level with an excerpt from Hiebert's *Willows Revisited* (now seldom read).

Since I myself have only recently identified pioneer pastoral as the genre that conveys Kanadier varieties of nostalgia, I cannot fault the editors of *Harvest* for not giving Hiebert's parody of that genre special status in the anthology. That Hiebert was included at all among other Mennonites draws attention to his nearly total erasure since 1974. His parodic mistranslation of Goethe's "Heidenröslein" is included, accompanied by notes "from Professor Wotan Scheisske's *Bilderbuch des Deutschen Volksmischmasch for Colleges*" (De Fehr 1974, 92; Hiebert 1967, 174). This satire, as I argued in the previous chapter, is directed both at Mennonite glorifications of High German culture and at shallow celebrations of multiculturalism that took place during the Canadian centenary year. Although it is hard to fathom, given the scatological *Scheisske* that conveys Hiebert's disgust at any celebration of *Volk*/folk, his inclusion in this collection might well have been a reflection of such shallowness.

Such complex questions about reception cannot be addressed without a fuller account of the historical contexts than I am able to offer here. Various contexts, for example, contradict the apparent assumption by the editors of *Harvest* that only Russian Mennonites are important to the development of Canadian Mennonite literature. Notable among those left out is BC writer Andreas Schroeder, who had already published two books of poetry in 1974. Schroeder was born in Germany and is not a Russian Mennonite. The absence of women's voices in *Harvest* is also noteworthy, especially since the earliest publication by a Mennonite in Canada was not by a Russian Mennonite man but by a Swiss Mennonite woman. Bertha Mabel Dunham's 1924 novel *The Trail of the Conestoga* tells the story of the migration of Mennonites from Pennsylvania to Ontario. There is no way that the editors could have foreseen that Edna Staebler's writing would acquire the status of folk literature (see Verduyn 2005), but the popular *Food That Really Schmecks* appeared in 1968. A more notable omission is Barbara Smucker, an American writer who moved to Canada in 1969 and wrote children's fiction that is an important part of the Canadian Mennonite literary legacy.

Rudy Wiebe and the Rewriting of Frankenstein

How the fiction of Rudy Wiebe relates to the larger Mennonite phenomenon that he preceded is not an easy question to answer. In an article entitled "Why Rudy Wiebe Is Not the Last Mennonite Writer," Maurice Mierau takes a tongue-in-cheek approach to the question. He claims that he first intended to title the article "Why Rudy Wiebe Is the Last Mennonite Writer," and when Wiebe objected he revised the title because of his "weak character" (Mierau 2004, 2012). Surely Wiebe was right to protest against being set up as a straw figure of authority and slotted as the last in a linear literary progression. If this model of history were accurate, then we might as well take a leaf out of *Sarah Binks* and have Wiebe "stuffed and mounted and presented to the Nation" (Hiebert 1995, 79). I prefer to meet a writer on his own territory, and in the case of Wiebe that is the genre for which Linda Hutcheon coined the term "historiographic metafiction" (1988, 61–77). His major achievement has been in this genre, and *The Blue Mountains of China* (1970) is the novel in which Wiebe applied his innovations to Mennonite history. That novel is difficult in a modernist way that has limited its readership, but it shows how dialogue takes the form of constant translation in response to Mennonite dislocation. Peggy Van Toorn was right to note that my use of the term "direct oversetting" in my essay on that novel (Redekop 1981, 98) was meant to refer, in her words, to "a very literal translation designed to accentuate rather than negate the disparities between two social/ideological worlds" (Van Toorn 1995, 70).

The poetry of the 1980s, as I will show, is in part a resistance to a well-known manifesto by Rudy Wiebe. It appeared in Wiebe's "Passage by Land," an essay first published in 1971 and then reprinted in a collection called *Writers of the Prairies* (Wiebe 1973b). "To touch this land with words," Wiebe wrote, "requires an architectural structure; to break into the space of the reader's mind with the space of this western landscape and the people in it you must build a structure of fiction like an engineer builds a bridge or a skyscraper over and into space. A poem, a lyric, will not do. You must lay great black steel lines of fiction, break up that space with huge design and, like the fiction of the Russian steppes, build giant artifact. No song can do that; it must be giant fiction" (1973, 130–31). The rhetoric here is vintage Wiebe, the language building on itself like the grand design about which he speaks. In reality, however, his own way of writing "giant fiction" was to break it up by using poetic or figurative language. Those "great black steel lines" cannot, in any case, be lined up neatly with what Al Reimer called the "tragic curve" of Mennonite narrative (Reimer 1988, 263). It is my view that Wiebe's response to the traumatic events experienced by one group of Russian Mennonites, his own, is not the most important bridge connecting Wiebe to the writers who followed him, both Mennonite and non-Mennonite.

When viewed in retrospect, through the filter of the later flowering, it is his struggle with the crisis of representation that anticipates it. Writing about Indigenous history drew Wiebe inexorably into confrontation with that crisis. The resulting aesthetic complexities are inseparable from political conflicts about appropriation. Wiebe, it must be said, has not shied away from those conflicts, as evident in his public quarrel with W.P. Kinsella about the representation of Indigenous people in Kinsella's "Hobbema stories." Although he often appears to speak "on behalf of" Indigenous people, Wiebe always does so while identifying clearly as a Mennonite. He does not represent them in the sense of pretending to be one of them; he does represent them in the sense of attempting to portray their lives. No matter how many documents Wiebe consulted to be accurate in his representations, no matter how gigantic the fictions, there are always places in his novels where his lament for the loss of lives and for the dispossession is inseparable from a lament for his failure to represent those lives without falsification. *The Temptations of Big Bear* (Wiebe 1973a) and *Where Is the Voice Coming From?* (Wiebe 1974) are texts that have resonated with so many readers not because they succeed in representing Indigenous history but because of the ways in which Wiebe deals with that failure.

This failure is conspicuous in his obsessive engagement with the story of Albert Johnson, the name assigned to a trapper in the North who, in 1932, led the RCMP on a foot chase that lasted more than a month. Eventually there was a shootout, and Johnson was killed before his true identity was known. Something about this mystery gripped Wiebe and would not let him go. In 1973, he wrote "The Naming of Albert Johnson" (Wiebe 1994; 74–91), and he returned to it in 1980 with *The Mad Trapper,* a novel written in as plain a style as Wiebe has ever used, as if in an attempt to lay the story to rest. But Johnson returned in *Playing Dead: A Contemplation Concerning the Arctic:* "I've written a story, several articles, a movie script, a novel about that man and now he has returned to haunt these essays!" (Wiebe 1989, 52). In that essay, Wiebe related his obsession to the round song: "My name is John Johnson / I come from Wisconsin" (53), a round "in which you can circle forever" (54). The image evokes the pursuit at the end of Mary Shelley's *Frankenstein or The Modern Prometheus*, in which pursuer can no longer be distinguished from pursued (Shelley 1831). Like that final pursuit, the one in *The Mad Trapper* blurs the boundary between the maker and the creature that he made. Here on this boundary the very act of representation can become charged with something that I have come to think of as a Frankenstein effect.

Wiebe's fiction, however, does not leave me with the sense of futility evoked by the ending of *Frankenstein*. On the contrary, it is dialogic in a way that reflects a central value dramatized by Mary Shelley: hospitality. That novel would not exist were it not for the hospitality of a blind man who welcomes the "being" into his home and listens to his story. On one level Shelley is setting a test for her readers. How hospitable would you be? Would you be like the blind man or would you be like his children, who respond with terrified rage? A similar test of hospitality is confronted by readers of Wiebe's novels, in which an affirmation of storytelling is matched by the urgent importance of story listening as he embarks on the "Orphic task" of courting the shadowy figure of the Indigenous other. Hospitality is a central value for Mennonites, as it is also for Indigenous people, and this shared value forms a meeting ground so that dialogue becomes a form of gift exchange. This is not to say that simply affirming the value of hospitality makes communication easy. The German word for poison happens to be *Gift* and the gifts in Wiebe's novels are often toxic. Conflict is never smoothed over in *A Discovery of Strangers*, nor is there any sense that differences can be transcended. Dialogue nonetheless moves forward towards the hope of reconciliation even when it sometimes feels as if the blind are leading the blind. The epigraph to that novel is a quote from Rainer Maria Rilke and suggests a telos, a place where there is a merging of past and present, self and other: "*Strangely I heard a stranger say, I am with you.*" Although the novel explores a journey without arrival, this moment of epiphany offers a spiritual vision that resonates with a familiar Bible verse: "Be not forgetful to entertain strangers: for thereby some have entertained angels unawares" (Hebrews 13:2).

The Manitoba Seedbed of the 1980s: The Rise of Poetry

Mennonites are so few in Toronto that it would be absurd to even calculate a percentage. From this distance, the growing list of Mennonite writers in Manitoba looked very impressive indeed as it developed during the 1980s. I lived in Japan during the first year of that decade, and when I returned to Toronto I turned my attention to the study of Alice Munro. I was not paying close attention to literary happenings among Mennonites. The exception was a reading in Toronto in August 1986 as part of a Harbour-front Mennonite Festival weekend of cultural events planned as part of a year-long bicentennial celebration of the first arrival in Ontario of Swiss Mennonites. When I accepted the invitation to organize a reading by Mennonite writers, I was uneasily aware that the writers who came instantly to mind were not Swiss Mennonites, whose bicentennial it was, but Russian Mennonites. Although it did not occur to me at the time, my situation was similar to the one faced by the editors of *Harvest*. As it turned out, Rudy Wiebe was not available, and the readings were done by Di Brandt, Patrick Friesen, Anne Konrad, and Armin Wiebe. The Brigantine Room was packed, and the atmosphere was electric. Brandt read from manuscript pages—poems from the soon-to-be-published *questions i asked my mother* (1987). Her breathless style, which afterward became familiar, was new and mesmerizing. Friesen, already well known as a powerful performer, read with his usual intensity. Konrad delighted us with stories from *The Blue Jar* (1985), written in her distinctive plain style, and Wiebe moved us to tears and laughter with a scene from *The Salvation of Yasch Siemens* (1984). In the years that followed, similar events have happened countless times in Winnipeg and Waterloo. That celebration nevertheless remains in my memory as a moment when a Mennonite literary phenomenon briefly touched down in Toronto.

As the novelty wears off, the first thrill of a new phenomenon is replaced by calmer study. My reflections keep returning to the 1980s as a time when something resembling a literary revolution was happening among Mennonites in Manitoba. It happened not in separation from the larger culture in that province but as a result of individuals who took advantage of opportunities available there at that time. As David Arnason put it, "the fact that Mennonites led in a number of ways in that community is a reflection of what happened in writing in the province on a much broader level: there were a lot of other people, non-Mennonites as well, involved in this" (1992, 217). Within this larger context, however, surely it would have been apparent even to a casual observer that among Mennonites in Manitoba there was a crisis. A crisis, as I indicated in the Introduction, is not inherent in events but appears in how human beings respond to events. As I have already indicated, I see the crisis created by Mennonites in Manitoba during the 1980s as a restaging of the crisis of 1957.

It is a well-known aspect of trauma that you always know afterward what you should have done. At the time of abuse, there is numbness and dissociation. To say that the teenagers who felt that they were at the mercy of evangelists in 1957 were grown up and ready to fight back in 1980 is an oversimplification, but it helps to account for the intensity of the anger that can be heard, for example, in Victor Jerrett Enns's *Jimmy Bang Poems* (1979). Of course, the poems are much more than that, and no poem should be reduced to the rage that gave birth to it. Innumerable other forces came into play, and each individual artist experienced them in different ways. This revolution was facilitated, moreover, by the fact that writers could borrow the energy that came from other movements happening in Canada at the time. Postmodernism was asking questions about the different languages of representation, and postcolonialism was asking new questions about the representation of identity.

People who construct a crisis usually do so because they want change. The poets and novelists found words to define the crisis, but in fact change had also been happening for Mennonites in the other arts. Music has always been the most available art for Mennonites, and it was music that helped Gathie Falk to pioneer a breakthrough to painting in the 1960s. Although the literary phenomenon has now spread across the continent, I have found it useful, as a way of bringing the crisis into focus, to bracket one decade. A chronological list of titles published during the 1980s, most in Manitoba, acts like a framed snapshot of a seedbed for future flowerings:

1980 Patrick Friesen, *The Shunning* (long poem)
1980 Rudy Wiebe, *The Mad Trapper* (historical fiction)
1982 E.F. Dyck, *The Mossbank Canon* (poetry)
1982 Sandra Birdsell, *Night Travellers* (short stories)
1983 David Waltner-Toews, *Good Housekeeping* (poetry)
1983 Rudy Wiebe, *My Lovely Enemy: A Novel* (novel)
1984 Patrick Friesen, *Unearthly Horses* (poetry)
1984 Andreas Schroeder, *Toccata in "D": A Micro Novel* (musical novel)
1984 Sarah Stambaugh, *I Hear the Reaper's Song* (novel)
1984 Armin Wiebe, *The Salvation of Yasch Siemens* (novel)
1984 E.F. Dyck, *Pisscat Songs* (poetry)
1984 Paul Hiebert, *Not as the Scribes* (non-fiction)
1984 Sandra Birdsell, *Ladies of the House* (short stories)
1985 Victor Jerrett Enns, *Correct in This Culture* (poetry)
1985 Anne Konrad, *The Blue Jar* (short stories)
1985 Al Reimer, *My Harp Is Turned to Mourning: A Novel* (novel)
1986 Lois Braun, *A Stone Watermelon* (short stories)
1986 Andreas Schroeder, *Dustship Glory* (historical novel)
1986 Audrey Poetker, *I Sing for My Dead in German* (poetry)
1986 John Weier, *After the Revolution* (poetry)
1987 Patrick Friesen, *Flicker and Hawk* (poetry)
1987 Di Brandt, *questions i asked my mother* (poetry)
1987 Vern Thiessen, *The Courier* (play)
1988 Sarah Klassen, *Journey to Yalta* (poetry)
1988 Harry Loewen, ed., *Why I Am a Mennonite* (essays)
1989 Douglas Reimer, *Older than Ravens* (short stories)
1989 Sandra Birdsell, *The Missing Child: A Novel* (novel)
1989 Dora Dueck, *Under the Still Standing Sun* (novel)
1989 Rudy Wiebe, *Playing Dead* (non-fiction)

This list is not exhaustive, but it is useful to linger over it with genre in mind. What I notice first is that eleven of the titles are collections of poetry and that a poetic sensibility is evident even in the narrative-based books. Having just emerged from my immersion in the mixture of poetry and narrative that appears in *Sarah Binks*, it is sad to find on this list a book by Paul Hiebert in which he turns his back on his own astonishing achievement. *Not as the Scribes*, written when Hiebert was ninety-four, is a laboured effort by a scientist to find a way to salvage his faith. Although it shares with the work of the younger writers on this list a resistance to fundamentalism, Hiebert's title is sadly out of tune with "the age." His more important presence on this list might be indirect. Since Di Brandt has written about him as a mentor, it is interesting to note that the mischief in *questions i asked my mother* resonates with the playfulness of *Sarah Binks*.

I see this list as documenting the rise of poetry as a major challenge to the centuries-old dominance of Mennonite historical and theological narratives. This development is directly related to the fact that many of the books on this list were published by Turnstone Press, founded in 1976 in Winnipeg to publish chapbooks by Manitoba poets. Mennonites took up this opportunity to use poetry as a vehicle to challenge the literalism of fundamentalist thinking. This movement was often characterized in political terms. Although not entirely inaccurate, such an emphasis does not do justice to the achievements of the poets. At their best, lyric poems do not have agendas but challenge authority on the level of close-to-the-bone intimacy. As Ben Lerner has argued in *The Hatred of Poetry* (2016), lyric poetry is powerful because it fails deliberately. The rejection of master narratives is most profound in this place where there is no mastery at all. As John Weier showed in *Steppe* (1995), the deliberate failure of lyric poetry can act as an effective resistance to the nostalgic myths that grow out of collective memory.

Rudy Wiebe's forceful advocacy of epic narrative softened over time as Wiebe interacted with the many young Mennonite writers who clearly held him in high esteem. His own fiction is written at the edge of narrative where music is about to take over. In his long poem *Seed Catalogue*, Robert Kroetsch engages in playful dialogue with Wiebe about genre, dividing up the famous passage I have already quoted, to make it look like free verse:

> Rudy Wiebe: "You must lay great black steel lines of
> fiction, break up that space with huge design and, like
> the fiction of the Russian steppes, build a giant
> artefact. No song can do that." (1977, 59)

Like much of Kroetsch's writing, this is a metapoem that questions its own status as a poem, but Kroetsch's challenge to Wiebe's denigration of poetry, published in 1977, should not be underestimated as an important influence on some of the Mennonites writing poetry at the time. However, opposition to the excesses of postmodernism continues to this day among Mennonite poets, and it is still Kroetsch who is associated with them. In his eloquent monograph on Patrick Friesen's poetry, Maurice Mierau describes Friesen as influenced more by "European modernism" than by "American notions of a radically local and un-European postmodernism." Mierau describes the "regional postmodern" as something brought to Winnipeg by Kroetsch in 1978 when he joined the faculty at the University of Manitoba (2018, 18).

Every title on this list is shaped by complex historical and autobiographical contexts that should not be reduced to some Mennonite agenda. I do not intend to suggest that narrative was replaced, but seeing the poetry titles appearing among the narratives should lead critics to consider the implications of this major shift in genre. One implication is that lyric poetry may be uniquely suited to perform "the unending Orphic task" that Susan Stewart described as "drawing the figure of the other . . . out of the darkness" (2002, 2). Rudy Wiebe's *My Lovely Enemy* (1983), as the title shows, is a novel on this list that performs that task using narrative. Perhaps his most experimental novel, it features a historian called Dyck who embarks on adventures both philosophical and erotic. As I suggested in my review of that novel, however, Wiebe seemed to be reaching beyond the limits of what narrative can do (Redekop 1983). A song might have done it better.

Patrick Friesen had already published two volumes of poetry in the 1970s, but *Unearthly Horses*, published in 1984, was a breakthrough collection. A series in that volume entitled the "pa poems" was likely foremost among the reasons that Arnason referred to Friesen at the 1990 conference as "one of the four or five best poets in this entire country" (1992, 216). The "pa poems" were always riveting, but I reread them now through the lens of Alice Munro's story "Royal Beatings" (Munro 1996, 119–42). The voice in these poems takes us down into a basement near a furnace where a child is being *strapped*, a word that Friesen prefers to *beating*, which to him suggests uncontrolled spontaneous rage.* The father in these poems performs a ritual that he himself hates but enacts out of obedience to some higher authority. "pa poem 1: firstborn" begins in the third person:

> pa dropped the baby
> when he heard it speak
> scared as hell to hear the young one talk
> thinking of the devil
> and the tongue that can take you anywhere (15)

As the series progresses, the I and the you go through transformative stages to an I/Thou place where the son addresses the father as "you" and is released into song. There is a story that resembles a parable, but it is dissolved into a new kind of ode that involves a rereading of the language of the Bible. In "pa poem 4: naked and nailed," a monster takes shape out of a conscious cliché: the parent who claims that "this hurts me more than it hurts you":

> but you not spoiling the child
> and you swung that leather high
> me twisting to look up your arm flung out
> seeing you naked and nailed like a child to a tree (18)

The adult son wonders "how could there be so much love?" With this reversal, the child becomes the loving father and expresses pity:

> you one-eyed monster
> you saw more than you let on
> maybe more than you ever knew
> but you couldn't find the words for me (18)

This act of compassion is a turning point. As so often happens in a Friesen poem, it resonates at levels far deeper than the immediate scene. It is true that Friesen's father was blind in one eye, but this feels like that turning point in Coleridge's "Rime of the Ancient Mariner" when the mariner blesses the water-snakes: "A spring of love gushed from my heart,/ And

---

* Patrick Friesen, email to the author, 17 February 2019; cited with permission.

I blessed them unaware" (Coleridge 1994, 57). When the albatross falls from the son's neck, there is music. In "pa poem 5: singing elijah," the poet moves through words to music:

> just thought I'd let you know
> I'm starting to sing   no one's really heard me yet
> and I'm not singing jerusalem
> I'm singing 'beulah land'   I'm singing elijah
> because I see ahead where I shed my clothes
> maybe hang them in a closet
> and disappear (21)

When Friesen was growing up, spanking or strapping was a widespread practice and not only among Mennonites. The risk of raising this volatile topic is that it can lead to unsupported generalizations about Mennonite practices compared to those in other communities. I am dubious about claims that abuse of various kinds is more common among Mennonite communities than other communities. I am not a sociologist, but I have not seen statistics to support such generalizations. There seems to me, however, no question that violence of this kind might be *felt* more acutely in a community that identifies itself as pacifist. What might be particular about the Mennonite versions of these strappings is that they were attached to the Word of God, as if somehow it could be beaten into the child. The particular Bible verse being obeyed was Proverbs 13:24: "He that spareth his rod hateth his son, but he that loveth him chasteneth him betimes." In the "pa poems," biblical language is dispersed by the carefully arranged fragments. Other scenes from the Bible play over this one, including the crucifixion and the moment when Abraham almost kills his son Isaac in obedience to God's command (Genesis 22).

For people in Friesen's generation, these strappings were often experienced as efforts to enforce the message of the revival meetings. In an email to me, Friesen wrote that "I felt more fear at revival meetings than I did of strappings. . . . That terror may have had a longer-lasting traumatic effect than strappings. That was spirit/soul stuff, not physical."* My

---

* Patrick Friesen, email to the author, 17 February 2019; cited with permission.

primary focus here is not on his life but on how, as a poet, Friesen uses the ancient tools of prosody and rhetoric to respond to a crisis. The ties between art and life, however, cannot be cut, no matter what the formalists say. I now see these poems as an oblique manifesto because they are a dramatic staging of the crisis of that time. When the Bible has been used as a weapon against you, it is no small feat to go back to it and find in it the resources that you need to fight back. Friesen tells me that during a long period after the revival meetings he refused to sing at all. I did not stop singing, but I experienced a similar shutdown in my response to the Bible, which seemed to me an object of terror. Even now, when people start reciting verses from the Bible in some innocuous scholarly context, I can feel muscles in my body tensing up.

In my readings of the titles on this list, I note how often the poets indicate some awareness that they are part of a counter-awakening. "The tongue that can take you anywhere" is a dangerous thing, and it recurs as an agent of transformation. *Correct in This Culture* by Victor Jerrett Enns contains a poem entitled "Tongue and Cheek." The poem evokes an underlying image of death in life, as if a moribund body is in need of awakening. Irony is the tool used by the poet, who displaces powerful tropes from "A vast book / of Martyrs":

What we hold
is silence. Afraid
to speak, our tongues
frozen, stuck
to the metal of success. (1985, 32)

The tongues of Anabaptist martyrs were sometimes screwed to the roofs of their mouths to silence them before burning so that they could not sing praises to their God while dying. Enns blurs this story into a frightening experience that I remember from my own childhood. If you lick metal on a very cold day, your tongue will stick to the metal. That happened to me only once, but I remember it as the purest terror that I have ever known. With this kind of ironic wordplay, Enns and Friesen seek to awaken the communal body to a new kind of song.

These poetic methods resonate with the trickster ways of the sixteenth-century Anabaptists who joined with others in developing the art of dissembling. Tricksters are certainly at play in the pages of Di Brandt's *questions i asked my mother*, published in 1987. At almost the centre of the book are six "missionary position" poems. The poems announce a literary revolution written in the very flesh and bones of the female body, but the vehicle is breath—the breath of life that is also the key to Brandt's prosody. The first of the poems, "missionary position (1)," begins thus:

> let me tell you what it's like
> having God for a father & jesus
> for a lover on this old mother
> earth

From there the words flow on a single sustained breath with no punctuation other than the shock of imagining God as an old man who "demands bloody hard / work he with his rod" and Jesus as "a good enough lay" (28). There is no mistaking the political punch. One poem in the collection promises that "i will dance mighty ones i will dance" and, in the same breath, threatens to throw words "stone by stone" into the "ancient teeth" of the "mighty ones" (48).

In her afterword to the 2015 reissue of *questions i asked my mother*, Tanis MacDonald writes that the book "leapt straight from a sixteenth-century separatist community into late twentieth-century women's writing, drawing with it a series of revelations about silence and speech" (72). I take MacDonald's description as her way of registering what I have described as a sensation of time warp and it locates Brandt at the heart of anachronic renaissance. Whatever the complex details of Brandt's particular background, however, Brandt did not grow up in "a sixteenth-century separatist community." I speak with some confidence about chronology in this case since, as it happens, Brandt and I share a church background, alluded to in the opening lines of "missionary position (4)":

> these things are really true
> Mary is my mother & her favourite
> colour is blue my grandfather
> Peter was a firm believer &
> founded a church (Brandt 1987, 31)

The grandfather in question was Peter Zacharias, and the church in question was the Rudnerweider, which he and two other preachers co-founded with my father, Wilhelm Falk. I did not meet Brandt until the day that she came to read at Harbourfront in 1986, but the differences in our experiences, despite having been members of the same church, are a useful counter to the persistent assumption that there exists a single Mennonite community. Even within one relatively small church there are major differences. In an "Author Profile" written for a series published on the website of *Quill and Quire*, Donna Bailey Nurse (2004) reports that "books were frowned upon" in Brandt's home. "They were not something people had around, says Brandt. The only book Brandt's father allowed in the house was the Bible."

This leap from one father's decree to a generalization about "people" fits with MacDonald's image of Brandt as a poet who "leapt straight from a sixteenth-century separatist community," but it does not fit with my experience. I cannot speak, of course, for other people who grew up in this church. However, since my father was a traditionalist and the Ältester, a few facts about him—things that are "really true"—can provide perspective. Although his formal education stopped after grade eight, my father had a sizable collection of German books in his little study, and my mother was a voracious reader of fiction in English. My father disapproved of fiction but he did not forbid it. There were never enough books to satisfy my appetite, but this had to do more with shortage of money than with religious prohibition. Brandt told Nurse (2004) that she loved the Bible, the only book in the house. Here too my experience was very different. I found ways to avoid the Bible as an adolescent, having been filled with fear of it by fundamentalist threats after the 1957 Brunk Brothers revival campaign. Perhaps our names tell the tale. Brandt reflects on her name in a three-page poem that ends with "the advent of Lady Di" and a fantasy about being a princess (1987, 16–18). Magdalene is not a name that lends itself to such upward mobility. I was more likely to plot escapes from my nightmare of being trapped in one of those zippered Bibles that contains hidden clues in Armin Wiebe's *Murder in Gutenthal: A Schneppa Kjnals Mystery* (1991).

One Menno can often recognize the survival tricks of another. The international reception of Brandt's first book shows that such tricks resonate far outside "the Mennonite community." MacDonald comments that the "surprise" of *questions i asked my mother* is that "the book offered not only a window onto resistance in female Mennonite lives, but also a look at women's speech outside of the traditional community, holding the mirror up to what it meant to be female and silenced anywhere in the world" (2015, 72). Brandt has said that her commitment to poetry derives from the fact that "poetry is an ecological language because it is relational" (Nurse 2004). This relational quality is reflected in collaborations with other poets and with musicians. They are too numerous to list here but include a memorable piece entitled *Awakenings*, which pianist Carol Ann Weaver and jazz singer Rebecca Campbell performed in 2003 for my poetry students at the University of Toronto.* Composed by Weaver, *Awakenings* is based on a poem by Brandt entitled "Waking Up" and a poem by Dorothy Livesay entitled "Awakening" (published as a chapbook in 1991). The title fits with my own sense of Brandt's contribution, her nurturing of the many alternative languages that are part of the larger collective counter-awakening.

The Fate of Narrative

One question raised by the emergence of poetry is what impact it had, if any, on the narrative genre attached to an "originary myth" about Mennonite literary history. In the previous chapter, I broadened and reframed that question by also including the genre attached to Kanadier settler narratives. These two narratives were clearly identified by Robert Kroetsch in 1990 during his survey of genres. He began by commenting that "we, all of us in a community or in a culture, work with a story which we don't recognize or which is hidden from us and it's what we call a master narrative" (224). He went on to relate this to the question "where is home?" and to a description of two master narratives that he had heard "operating" at the conference. "On the one hand there is a story of the fall from a golden age (the departure from an ideal world somewhere in the past which was apparently Russia).... Against that, however, is another and contrary story,

---

* *Awakenings* premiered at the conference Wider Boundaries of Daring: The Modernist Impulse in Canadian Women's Poetry, co-hosted by Di Brandt and Barbara Godard at the Scarab Club, Detroit (as part of Detroit 300), and the University of Windsor, October 2003. The text appeared in the multimedia anthology *Re:Generations: Canadian Women Poets in Conversation*, edited by Brandt and Godard (2005).

the story that we left something bad and have come to a garden. Another group of immigrants, apparently, is responsible for this" (225). For that audience, there was no need for Kroetsch to say which of these narratives was Russländer and which Kanadier.

Kroetsch's division corresponds to the genres that I have identified as epic tragedy and pioneer pastoral. Given the current dominance of the former among literary critics, the first question that comes to mind is what impact does the rise of poetry have on what Al Reimer saw as "the tragic curve of all Mennonites" (quoted in Zacharias 2013, 13)? I began to answer that question in the previous chapter by identifying that master narrative as particular to the Russländer experience and showing, with my case study of *Steppe*, how poetry undermines it. *Steppe* was published in 1995 and can be seen as the fruition of the seeds planted during the previous decade. During the 1980s, however, only one title, Al Reimer's *My Harp Is Turned to Mourning* (1985), dealt in long narrative form with the Russländer experience. In my paper at the 1990 conference, I spoke about how the nightmare images in that novel show Reimer parting company with utopian ways of looking at Mennonite history. It is a *Bildungsroman* that opens itself up to ironies that undermine the picture or the *Bild* that Reimer constructs. The nightmares of the boy Erdmann Lepp are inhabited by grotesque images of "shrieking female devils and witches" and even a "plump, frog-white hag" (Reimer 1985, 174). These slimy passages are small parts of the grander historical fiction, but they seem to me to threaten that larger structure. For me, there was a sense that, if the poet were to bless these slimy creatures, then the albatross of the master narrative might fall away (Redekop 1992b, 120).

Reimer's novel on this list is the exception that proves the rule. Although "the tragic curve" of the Russländer narrative does not dominate, however, it is an implied presence in several collections of poetry on the list, including John Weier's *After the Revolution* (1986). David Waltner-Toews's *Good Housekeeping* (1983) contains a poem entitled "Roots," which imagines Rudy Wiebe as a character digging for his own roots and finding a dry bone that takes on a life of its own. The ways of taking on the Russländer narrative are not always that direct, but always the poetry comes sideways at that tragic arc, breaking it up and releasing meaning on other levels. Sarah

Klassen's *Journey to Yalta* contains a poem entitled "Origins," but it pictures Mennonites engaged in a search for an origin that cannot be found:

> On Khortitz Island
> we fall to our knees
> searching reluctant undergrowth
> for evidence of our having been there. (1988, 3)

In a poem entitled "Legacy," the stabilizing image is a "set of stays" that the mother "claims were made from fishbone. / She says her mother stitched them into waistlines" (41). A corset seems like a frail alternative to "great black steel lines of fiction" only if you discount the power peculiar to the genre of lyric poetry, a power based on an aesthetic of failure rather than mastery.

I am not suggesting, of course, that there will be no more rewritings of the many Mennonite immigrant stories in the form of narrative, only that the writing during this decade signalled an increasing liberation from martyr myths and an increasing diversification. Dora Dueck's *Under the Still Standing Sun* (1989), for example, tells the story of one woman's life that also brings to life a Mennonite settlement in Paraguay. The genres that come with Kanadier settler narratives are dispersed, and it occurs to me that perhaps Paul Hiebert was a bigger influence than I allowed in the previous chapter. Andreas Schroeder is not a Kanadier, but his *Dustship Glory* (1986) reminds me of Hiebert's satirical approach to the little *shtahp* on the prairie. Schroeder's prairie classic is a biofiction and tells the story of the life of Tom Sukanen, who set out to build an ocean-going ship on a Saskatchewan wheat field. It runs counter to the master narrative that informs pioneer pastoral. Schroeder imagines his way into the life of a man whose acts of making believe become inseparable from the literal act of making something.

Oddly, given the fact that Sandra Birdsell was not seen during the 1980s as a central participant in the Mennonite phenomenon, it is *The Missing Child* (1989) that most clearly embodies what I have been calling anachronic renaissance. This is not surprising, upon reflection, since Birdsell, having a Mennonite mother and a Métis father, writes on the borderline between identities that I have described from the beginning as the in-between place where the renaissance is most evident. *The Missing Child* was

Birdsell's first novel, but it was preceded during this decade by two collections of her short stories. The presence of short-story collections on the list—by Birdsell and then by Anne Konrad, Lois Braun, and Douglas Reimer—reflects the influence of Alice Munro. Whereas Munro stayed with short stories, Birdsell went on to write long fictions that embody the movement back and forth in time that is a feature of anachronic renaissance. Minnie Pullman, the eccentric protagonist of *The Missing Child*, can remember back to a time before she was born and has a prophetic ability to sense the melting of an ancient underground glacier. In the town of Agassiz, there is also a boy called Hendrick Schultz, "who had been born, it seemed, with the entire words of the Bible miraculously committed to memory" (14). The circular time frame that I see as a feature of Mennonite sensibility is made explicit in *The Missing Child*: "Minnie wondered what would happen once they got right back to the beginning of history. Start again? Was it all a circle?" (164). Historical Mennonite narratives have not been replaced by such fantastical stories, but they are now happening alongside them. Even Rudy Wiebe's *My Lovely Enemy* has a fantastical quality, reflecting (as does *The Missing Child*) the influence of magic realism.

When considering the long-term fate of Mennonite narratives, the significant text on this list is Patrick Friesen's long poem *The Shunning*, published in 1980. In the words of David Arnason, "Friesen's emergence was immensely important to Mennonite writing . . . the critical reception of his work across the whole country, his specifically immediate and local work, and the fact that he came onto the scene right at the time when things were beginning to happen across the Prairies" (1992, 215). It was *The Shunning* that brought Friesen's influence into focus. The protagonist in that poem, Peter Neufeld, dies by his own hand after being shunned by his church community for not believing in hell. The poetry and the ritual push that story down and back into the ancient past, but not as a search for some master narrative or theological answer. I have written that the iconoclastic impact of *The Shunning* derives from a radical revision of the martyrdom story (Redekop 1993b). The iconoclasm in the poem is not some superficial rebellion against orthodoxies. It comes in the form of iconoclash, which I will explore in Chapter 6 in relation to visual images. Iconoclash happens on a borderline where you experience having the icon and not having it at the same time. *The Shunning* is like a literary version of paintings by Gathie Falk in which there both is and is not a cross. This might seem like a Kanadier displacement of Russländer tragedy, but the poetry prevents the narrative from getting attached to linear time. History is present, to be sure, but in a way that anticipates Friesen's ironic use of it in *a short history of crazy bone: long poem.*[*]

Friesen's own choice of title for *The Shunning* was *Tomorrow It Gives Rain*—a "direct oversetting" of the Low German consolation proverb *Morje jeft daut Rejen.* In an interview near the time of publication, Friesen called the publisher's choice *The Shunning* a "sell-out title . . . because it cashes in on a big thing." "To me," said Friesen, "the most important part of the book is the second half, not the first. All the love and eroticism is in the second half. The scenes of the shunning are insignificant" (Reimer and Tiessen 1985, 250–51). As if deliberately echoing Friesen twenty-four years later, Miriam Toews chose *A Complicated Kindness* as the title of a novel that includes a shunning story. Fortunately, her publishers allowed the ambiguous title to stand. Although shunning rituals resonate at deep levels of Anabaptist history, they are dismissed by most middle-class Mennonites as something only done by "backward" Mennonites. It was "secular" or non-Mennonite reception that turned Friesen's *The Shunning* into a landmark text. Those scenes that Friesen called "insignificant" became central to the dramatized version of *The Shunning*, and it was in this form that the text remained in public consciousness throughout the decades to come. Following its 1985 stage premiere by Prairie Theatre Exchange, a one-hour radio adaptation was produced for CBC Radio in 1990 by John Juliani and further stage productions appeared in Kitchener and Michigan (1992), in British Columbia (1993), and in Nova Scotia (1995). The performance that I remember most vividly was an adaptation by the Motus O Dance Theatre at the Tarragon Theatre in Toronto in 1995. The suicide of Peter did not happen as an offstage gunshot, as it does in the Prairie Theatre Exchange adaptation, but by a hanging onstage, a change that made for

---

[*] *a short history of crazy bone* premiered as a play at Le Cercle Moliere in Winnipeg on 27 March 2018. With Tracey Nepinak in the title role of the trickster, "history" was transformed into a dance inspired by a Japanese style called *butoh.*

a powerful closing dance. If I remember correctly, the performance was wordless, but there must have been music. What I remember to this day is how the last scene embodied something inarticulate and haunting at the heart of the story.

The Shunning opened up new territory for other writers and for Friesen himself. This is signalled on the last page, blank except for these words: *"O dass ich tausend Zungen hätte"* (Friesen 1980, 99). This is a translation of a famous hymn by John Wesley: "O that I had a thousand tongues to sing my dear Redeemer's praise." It appropriates the biblical story of the Pentecost, but the tongues of flame are ignited with a regenerative power in a new context. Friesen had little involvement in the various productions of *The Shunning* and moved on, often working in collaboration with dancers and musicians as he honed his poetic craft—a spare musical style based on modulation of complex rhythms. His escape artistry is captured in a poem entitled "Song of the Sly One" that appeared in *Flicker and Hawk*, published in 1987. The last stanza of that poem reads thus:

> I am a sly one
> who slides through the net
> that every jesus cast
> show me an icon
> show me the text
> I will show you where I passed (11)

As the founding president of the Manitoba Writers' Guild in 1981, Friesen was a respected cultural leader in Winnipeg whose magnetism crossed boundaries and allowed non-Mennonites access to previously hidden aspects of Mennonite culture. In 1985, the same year that *The Shunning* was premiered by the Prairie Theatre Exchange, Friesen hosted an event called The Missing Mennonite Cabaret. Allan Safarik's account describes Friesen as a "bizarre MC in a loud check jacket. He was behaving like a sleazy night club comedian" (1992, 57). Writing to Victor Jerrett Enns at the time, Friesen explained that "The Missing Mennonite is the one we can't hear. At a reading, in church, anywhere where two or three are gathered. The Missing Mennonite must be a child of the future. The old, old child who knows the world intimately and dares to sup with the great spirits" (Enns 1992, 52). This figure of an "old, old child" who sups with spirits brings to mind Lewis Hyde's description of the trickster as "the wise fool, the gray-haired baby, ... the speaker of sacred profanities" (1998, 7).

"Acts of Concealment": Writing about Myself

During his closing comments at the 1990 conference, Robert Kroetsch began by talking about autobiography, using as his example a reading that I had done with my sister Elizabeth Falk on the first evening of the conference: "Maggie and Elizabeth introduced us to this. That curious pretence at revealing things, and the incredible act of concealment that is going on—I think that kind of tension makes for very interesting writing. So, questions of autobiography—Di Brandt, of course, has worked with this—these might be interesting questions in the future" (223). The editors of the volume of essays based on that conference chose to foreground Kroetsch's comment in the title: *Acts of Concealment.* The title implicitly gestures towards memoir, which seems to be the genre of our time—as the long novel was for Victorians and the lyric poem was for the Romantics. The body of autobiographical writing by Mennonites calls out for serious scholarly attention of the kind that I cannot give it here. On one level *Making Believe* is, as I have conceded, an exercise in life writing. As soon as I begin to write about autobiography, however, I find myself dealing with the ambivalence that Kroetsch observed. As a critic I look for literary contexts and these have taught me that my experience is shared widely as a result of a long history of Protestant invasiveness. I remember the exact moment when I came to that realization. I was reading Nathaniel Hawthorne's *The Scarlet Letter* (1850) for an undergraduate course when Roger Chillingworth, also known as "The Leech," literally sent chills through my body. I recognized him instantly because of what I had experienced as an adolescent during revival meetings. This prying figure has literary relatives in numerous novels by both Mennonites and non-Mennonites. In *A Complicated Kindness* he appears as a cartoonish monster called "The Mouth." On the day of the closing panel in 1990, a quarrel about mirrors happened as a result of combined efforts to release the tensions that surrounded this subject. Patrick Friesen spoke for me and, I suspect, for many others in the room when he asked: "Why should I answer questions that want to know the state of my soul?" (1990, 234).

Giving testimony in public is a form of discourse that can cause fear and trembling among Mennonites. Privately many Mennonites keep journals and diaries. Whether or not they are published and how they are edited comprise a complex issue, one that I dealt with at that conference in relation to *The Diaries of Anna Baerg* (Redekop 1992b). Aside from occasional bits of poetry, my first experience of writing about myself was for the collection *Why I Am a Mennonite* (1988). My contribution to that volume was the essay entitled "Through the Mennonite Looking Glass." Harry Loewen's invitation catapulted me unexpectedly into a belated confrontation with the grief that had gone underground since the death of my mother in 1978. My anger about her death (the result of malpractice) became inseparable from my feeling that her silencing was writ large in the invisibility of women in Mennonite history. I remember how enraged I was when I looked at a published collection of photographs of Mennonites in Russia and found that the captions listed only the names of the men. The women were there, smiling out from the pictures, but their names were missing, just as their stories had been left out of the published histories of Russian Mennonites. Since that time, the erasure has been remedied to some extent, most notably by historian Marlene Epp (2000), but maternal silence was a powerful force in novels and poems by Mennonites during the 1980s and into the next decade.

The stories that Robert Kroetsch referred to as an illustration of "acts of concealment" were part of an interactive writing project with my sisters that absorbed me for almost a decade. It all began when W.H. New wrote to me to ask for a contribution to a special issue of *Canadian Literature*. I retrieved an unpublished story, entitled "Still Life with Menno," and sent it to him. It was a story about a photograph in which my sister and I are sitting on either side of an open coffin in which is the body of our stillborn brother Menno. New had already accepted the story when, during a visit from my sister Elizabeth Falk, I gave it to her to read. Her response to it led me to write New back and ask him to withhold publication until she had written her story from the other side of the coffin. That story was entitled "No Stone." This "duet," published in *Canadian Literature* (Falk 1990b; Redekop 1990b), was so well received that we decided to try it again, only this time she would go first. The process turned out to be agonizing because both of us are endless revisers, and the back and forth of revisions tied us up in knots. We did eventually complete another set of stories. Hers was entitled "The House," mine "The Little Dipper," and the joint title was "Moving." It was from these stories, eventually published in *Prairie Fire* (Falk 1990a; Redekop 1990a), that we read at the conference.

Motivated by our long experience of singing as a trio, The Falk Sisters, Elizabeth and I eventually persuaded our sister Mary Neufeld to join us. With great difficulty, we completed a trio, but it was never published, in part because we became so intensely aware of the four additional older sisters who also had stories to tell. Not to mention our five brothers, all still living then. As anybody who has ever written a family history of any kind knows, when siblings tell family stories, it can seem as if each sibling has a different father and a different mother. The ease with which we harmonized while singing turned out to be unattainable in writing. When the conflicts became intolerable, we abandoned the project by mutual agreement and moved forward with separate creative projects while respecting each other's boundaries. Mary went on to research and write a biography of our father, *A Prairie Pilgrim: Wilhelm H. Falk* (Neufeld 2008), using interview material from all our brothers and sisters. Elizabeth moved increasingly into fabric art, and some of her work will appear in my imaginary art gallery in Chapter 6. The first story that I wrote solo after this experience was entitled "Making Up" (1998). It was a response to a near-death experience that I had after a fall on 1 December 1990. Retroactive amnesia made it necessary for me to reconstruct my identity, and this process turned into a plea to be allowed to make things up without having to make up afterward.

The Return of the Repressed: Traces of the Mother Tongue

In 1986, as the Mennonite renaissance was in full swing, *Border Crossings* published a forum convened by Robert Enright that featured Sandra Birdsell, Di Brandt, Patrick Friesen, and Rudy Wiebe. When Enright asked about the "perverse" sense of humour that leads Mennonites to "undermine the place out of which you've come," Friesen responded "You have to use the critical terminology if you want me to talk about that. It's called *jehn on*" (Enright 1986, 28). A direct translation of that term might be the word *contrary*, and the pronunciation is easier with Herman Rempel's spelling, *jääjenaun* (1995, 69). The release of this Low German expression led to a comparison of translations. Wiebe defined the term as meaning "you push against something all the time." Brandt compared it to being *"ein koppich,* which means you always want to do everything your own way." Friesen explained how these terms differ: "See if, for example someone would say, 'that wall is solid' and you were *jehn on,* you would say, 'No, I'll walk through it.' But with *ein koppich,* you'd just be stubborn. You wouldn't walk through it, you'd just keep saying, 'It's not solid, no, it's not solid.'" Enright pressed the point and asked "So *jehn on* comes through opposition, not through having a position. Is that right?" Friesen's succinct reply: "It's process" (Enright 1986, 28).

This discussion illustrated a problem raised by Hildi Froese Tiessen (1988) in an article entitled "Mother Tongue as Shibboleth in the Literature of Canadian Mennonites," in which she pointed out that interpolations of Low German words in an English text can function as a "shibboleth" to keep outsiders out. This problem is complicated by the inconvenient splits between us and them that happen within Mennonite culture. Most significant with relation to language is the split that resulted in Low German becoming a marker of class that separated the Kanadier and the Russländer. The resulting conflicts support Tiessen's (1988) view that there is a need for caution, but the historical contexts also show that there is no simple solution to the problem. Simplistic solutions, in fact, are precisely what the original story about shibboleth should teach us to avoid. Shibboleth is a Hebrew word, pronounced *sibboleth* (Judges 12:5–6), that distinguished one group of people from another, but there are more recent examples of the dangers that it represents. The most shocking is the Parsley Massacre of 1937 in which at least 12,000 Haitians in the Dominican Republic were murdered because they could not pronounce the Spanish word for parsley. On a less horrific scale but still disturbing is the case of Mennonites who escaped Europe after the Second World War because speaking Low German was taken as proof of their Mennonite identity. With my reading of Weier's *Steppe* (1995), I have already indicated my response to this dilemma. I say *shtahp.* You say *steppe.* In between is dialogue. It was dialogue at Enright's forum (1986) that prevented the phrase *jääjenaun* from acting as a shibboleth. It was the total *absence* of dialogue during the Parsley Massacre that made the word for parsley dangerous. Trying to pretend that differences in language do not exist is not the answer. If it were, then the Swiss Mennonite evangelists at the tent meetings would have been on the right track when they urged us to forget about Low German so as to better evangelize the heathen in Africa.

On the question of whether or not interpolated Low German words can act as a shibboleth in an English text by a Mennonite, my answer is that it depends on the particulars of that text and its contexts. Take, for example, David Waltner-Toews and his way of mixing up English, High German, and Low German in the voice of Tante Tina. I deduce that Waltner-Toews did not speak Low German growing up, from the fact that he writes *Tante* instead of *Taunte*. His speech doth betray him. This slippage, however, like the *steppe/shtahp* one, is the place where dialogue happens. What I respond to in the Tante Tina poems is the poet's way of searching for a connection with his mother's mother tongue, hidden as it is underneath layers of repression. What resonates for me is his sensitivity, as a Russländer, to the class differences that separate High German from Low German. Tante Tina reproaches Haenschen for referring to Low German as a "pile of manure." She threatens that "I will surround you with Low German. / I will piles of it to you be speaking" (1983, 19). The threat is hollow, but what comes across is the voice of a woman whose syntax shows that she still thinks in Low German even though her sentences are in English.

There is no question that when I hear the sound of my mother tongue it sets up an undertow pulling me away from literary texts and toward a nostalgic memory of my oral culture. Anthropologist James Urry offers a useful bridge back to literature in "From Speech to Literature: Low German and Mennonite Identity in Two Worlds" (1991). He draws attention to the major part played by Kanadier writers in the flowering of the 1980s and notes that many of them moved directly from Low German to English. Urry inverts Tiessen's hypothesis, suggesting that Low German "can threaten religious aspects of Mennonite identity" and become "a means of challenging the dour image of religious Mennonitism, to attack the sacred shibboliths [*sic*] of the community, and to puncture the pretensions of the 'learned' who stress High Culture" (251). This inversion is appealing now that Low German is being celebrated belatedly by Mennonites who were once embarrassed by it or who have never spoken it. I am old enough, however, to remember when friends and relatives responded to the sound of it as if recoiling from the smell of a pigsty. As a result, I sometimes hear these celebrations as a nostalgic exercise gleefully announcing the death of the language I love.

While reflecting on "the forgetting of language," Daniel Heller-Roazen asks "what is the 'certain point' at which a ghostly tongue finally comes to an end?" He goes on to suggest that the futile attempt to determine that point is "motivated by a powerful, albeit unstated, wish . . . of those who would be its keepers, who seem often desperately in search of the assurance that a language has truly been laid to rest, buried in a grave from which it will never rise again" (2008, 64). On the list of books published in the 1980s, Armin Wiebe's *The Salvation of Yasch Siemens* (1984) is the text that demonstrates how alive the language still is and what a powerful weapon it can be in the fight against fundamentalist thinking. As Di Brandt has observed, "it was impossible to say anything abstract or even earnest in Plautdietsch" (2007, 112). The power of Low German lies not in some special onomatopoeic effect that Mennonites sometimes ascribe to it but in the resistance to abstraction that throws the listener back onto the sheer sound of the words. It is a literalism that challenges fundamentalism, so to speak, on its own ground.

Robert Kroetsch touched on this power when he asked, in 1990, "how do you make writing out of oral tradition?" He identified what he called a "wonderful paradox": "How do you write Low German as English?" Kroetsch was doubtless thinking of *The Salvation of Yasch Siemens* when he said "as we watch that kind of translation taking place we see writing itself becoming an act of translation. . . . And one I think a Mennonite writer can engage in pretty honestly. He doesn't have to deal with the question of lying, which is the old question from Plato on" (Tiessen and Hinchcliffe 1992, 226). Writing becomes a constant act of translation—constant because it always fails, and it is this failure that informs Armin Wiebe's comic vision. This involves much more than simply interpolating foreign words. It is the broken syntax that does the trick, as heard in the opening sentences of *Yasch Siemens*: "The year they built the TV tower I was heista kopp in love with Shaftich Shreeda's daughter, Fleeda. I was only almost sixteen and Fleeda was almost sixteen, too, and I had been in love with her all the way since we were only almost fourteen when she looked at me in her little pocket mirror from where she was sitting in the next row in school and I just went heista kopp in love" (Wiebe 1984, 1). Eric Friesen refers to that passage in his account of his last meeting with "Wild Willy" (a.k.a. Bill Kehler), a popular broadcaster "still revered as the voice of the Calgary Stampede" (2010, 122). Kehler and Friesen had been boyhood friends in Altona and then grown apart. After Kehler died, Friesen remembered the last time that they had met, in the late 1980s at a high school reunion, at which time Wild Willy greeted Friesen "by reciting from memory the brilliant opening page of Armin Wiebe's novel *The Salvation of Yasch Siemens*, with its delicious mixture of our Low German dialect (of which Bill was a master) and English" (119).

Friesen's story does not pretend that mutual nostalgia is not part of the pleasure. Do such experiences suggest, then, that the Low German in this particular text is a shibboleth keeping out non-Mennonites? I have taught *Yasch Siemens* a few times, and my students (all of them non-Mennonite) have told me that the interpolated words can be distancing, but at the same time they create a kind of intimacy. Although my evidence is anecdotal, I suspect that most readers would agree with the words of Josef Škvorecký from "Red Music" quoted in the epigraph to the novel: "My God, how we adored this buggering up of our lovely language for we felt that all languages were lifeless if not buggered up a little" (Wiebe 1984). The pleasure of *Yasch Siemens* comes from how Wiebe refracts language by putting it through a filter. In the second chapter of the novel, the English language is subjected to time warp as we view Mennonite New Year's Eve mumming customs through the eyes of Yasch. These rituals resemble Halloween trick-or-treating and involve loud music accompanied by a makeshift drum called a *brummtupp*: "Brumm. Brumm. Dummheit, Muttachi said. Old dummheit from Russlaund. Russische dummheit. Brumm Brumm" (15). I take this wordplay as an example of what happens when a writer moves past the assumption that Low German is a quaint language spoken in some mythical sixteenth-century community. This is what happens if you take it as a given that Low German is a living language and that it therefore keeps changing as it comes in contact with English. At this level of pure sound, there is no sense that the words reinforce ethnocentricity. Indeed, the sound effects here are a reminder that this play with language was happening at a time when the Canadian group of poets known as The Four Horsemen were performing sound poetry. The *brumm brumm* of the *brummtupp* resonates with the poetry of bp Nichol, Canada's leading concrete poet at the time.

Although I am too close to recent events to say for sure, it is my impression that new poetic ways of releasing the repressed mother tongue are very different from the poetry of the 1980s. In *Songen*, for example, Patrick Friesen (2018) pushes the English language to in-between places where the sound of Low German cannot be separated out from the sounds of Old and Middle English. High German is dissolved in a similar way into the poems based on hymns in Amanda Jernigan's *Years, Months, Days* (2018). In Nathan Dueck's *he'll* (2014), Low German is at once dismembered and re-membered. The translator in *he'll* is called Nada, and he is charged with the task of investigating the death of a postman called Roman Dyck, whose body is discovered among a pile of undelivered letters. These are literary ruins, but the familiar pastoral trope invites in-depth exploration. Low German also appears as a tantalizing trace in Jessica Penner's *Shaken in the Water* (2013). In it, a Mennonite woman gives birth to a child with a birthmark known in Low German as a *tieja kjoaw* or tiger scar (16).

The texts in which Low German appears as materiality support Kwame Anthony Appiah's view that the insertion of foreign words is not always about meaning in a literal sense. Appiah's notion of "thick translation" is part of his criticism of an "easy atmosphere of relativism" that has resulted in the loss of "the rich differences of human life in culture" (2000, 423, 427). Appiah views a rejection of linguistic difference as a "lazy liberalism" that rationalizes a "refusal to attend to how various other people really are or were." With the rejection of transparency comes a "thick description of the context of literary production" as a way to begin the "harder project of a genuinely informed respect for others" (427). Appiah refers to his work with his mother on a collection of over 7,000 proverbs written in Akan, a dialect spoken in Ghana, as his contribution to a "thick and situated understanding" of the oral literature of his people (428). I have attempted, in a small way, to do something similar with my "thick translation" of Low German rhymes. I am grateful to Victor Carl Friesen (1987) for his work in collecting them and for the rare honesty of his account of how Mennonite class conflicts relate to Low German.

Residual traces of Low German in the writing of people who no longer speak it might seem nostalgic to some, but I take them as signs of something much deeper that connects with anachronic renaissance on a level that does not set Mennonites apart. I have previously quarrelled, in "The Mother Tongue in Cyberspace," with those who take the opposite approach and find in Low German oral culture a link to an essential Mennonite identity (2009). Since that article is available online, I will not revisit my argument here except to say that I still believe Martin Heidegger has a lot to answer for. With relation to the Canadian Mennonite renaissance, in any case, it is important to remember that the loss of a mother tongue is an experience multiplied countless times in various groups. The larger body of Canadian literature, of which these texts are all a part, provides evidence that Dante's opening definition in *De vulgari eloquentia* is still useful: "I call 'vernacular language' that which infants acquire from those around them when they first begin to distinguish sounds; or to put it more succinctly, I declare that vernacular language is that which we learn without any formal instruction, by imitating our nurses" (Dante 1996, 3). Where the term "mother tongue" originated is not clear, and Dante appears to take the definition for granted (13). In common usage, however, "mother tongue" now tends to refer to the language we acquire without "formal instruction." Whatever the term used for it, this language, when it is different from English, can be a pressure that works from the inside of a literary text outward to the printed English surface. Space does not permit comparative study here, but there are innumerable fictions by Canadian authors from various groups showing that the Mennonite situation is not unique. The problem is not that any of these mother tongues will be used as divisive shibboleths, a danger that seems implied in Jeff Gundy's warning against the use of "obvious and easily manipulable cultural markers like Lowgerman [*sic*] and Zwiebach" (2005, 49). Ethnic markers can and are indeed used as shortcuts in any number of texts. The problem with such remnants is that they are *not* dangerous. Like other endangered mother tongues, Low German is unthreatening in the context of Canadian multiculturalism and the dominance of English. There is, however, plenty of evidence in Canadian literature that when deployed as traces, the bits and pieces of a mother tongue can resonate on deep levels. I have heard Tomson Highway say that Cree is the funniest language on earth, a deliberate hyperbole that echoes how many Mennonites talk about Low German. Cree cracks open new ways of seeing in Highway's plays because of the privileged status he allows it to have in his comic vision. To offer just one additional example, in M.J. Vassanji's *The Gunny Sack* (1989), Kutchi, a version of Gujarati, plays a particular role because it is Vassanji's mother tongue. Like countless other Canadian novels, *The Gunny Sack* is a powerful fiction not because any one language contains some essential ethnic identity but because of the dialogue and translation going on in a space between all the languages.

Proliferation: 1990 and After

As Robert Zacharias once observed to me, the remarkable thing about the Mennonites who first published fiction and poetry during the 1980s is that almost all of them "had legs." Indeed, many of them have been prolific. Notable also is the fact that writers continued to experiment by shifting into different genres. David Waltner-Toews, for example, wrote more poetry but also went on to write fiction, and is now best known for his writing on ecosystems. Poet Sarah Klassen went on to publish fiction and both Armin Wiebe and Patrick Friesen branched out into playwriting. The limits of this chapter do not allow for coverage of these many publications. Among the new writers who emerged in the 1990s, however, David Bergen stands out. His fiction would reward close study of how a writer confronts the crisis of representation by adapting a tradition of plain style in ways that yield richly multilayered fiction. Although explicit allusions to Mennonite themes are infrequent in his fiction, an ethical urgency acts like a force pushing from the inside out at his signature plain style. The title of his first collection of stories, *Sitting Opposite My Brother* (1993), contains a dissolved allusion to the biblical question "Am I my brother's keeper?" (Genesis 4:9). As Morley Walker (2005) has noted, it is significant that the trip to Vietnam that forms the basis of Bergen's Giller Prize–winning novel *The Time in Between* was originally undertaken on behalf of the Mennonite Central Committee, the foreign aid organization for which Bergen was working at the time.

Bergen's fiction resists being attached to Mennonite contexts, however, despite such formative experiences. The same is no longer true of the fiction of Miriam Toews even though her first two novels contain no references to Mennonites. The event that transformed her writing was the death of her father, who took his life by walking in front of a train. In *Swing Low* (2000), Toews appropriated her father's point of view to reinvent his life within the Mennonite community in Steinbach. The raw courage that it took to write that book deepened the comic vision in *A Complicated Kindness* (2004). In an essay entitled "Translating Grief," Françoise Lionnet argues that "the work of grief and the articulation of a grievance must go together for freedom to be achieved" (2005, 320). Toews would not claim to have achieved freedom. What is apparent to me, however, is that her fiction is compelling because of an "unresolvable tension between grief and grievance" (320). After the death of her father, her grief was channelled in *A Complicated Kindness* into a grievance about shunning. After the death of her sister, who imitated their father and walked in front of a train, she wrote *All My Puny Sorrows* (2014), a novel in which her grief is part of a grievance about assisted suicide. What lifts both novels above the grievances that they attack and the grief that they express is the comic vision of Toews, which I see as prophetic—not in the sense of being predictive but in the sense of shedding a revelatory light on where we all live. I imagine Toews as having an inner clown whose movements are guided by this vision and who is brave enough to keep going no matter what obstacles appear.

The art of a Miriam Toews novel is often closer to that of drama. It is brisk dialogue that keeps hurtling the reader forward through her texts. It has always been my impression, however, that resistance to drama as a genre is strong among Mennonites. I was therefore startled when, at the 1990 conference, Robert Kroetsch predicted that "perhaps the play is going to be very available [to Mennonites] as a communal art form at some point" (Tiessen and Hinchcliffe 1992, 223). Drama has never been "very available" to radical Protestants. Robert Weimann argues that plays are particularly suspect because they have the "dangerous ability to 'slip the anchorhold of authority'" altogether (1996, 19). For the reader in need of certainty (as response to *A Complicated Kindness* shows), it is easier to hold the author responsible for the views in a novel (even when those views come through the filter of first-person point of view) than not to be able to identify where the voice is coming from. When he made his prediction, Kroetsch might have had in mind the dramatized version of Friesen's *The Shunning* (1980). Well-known playwright Vern Thiessen has spoken of the influence on his writing of *The Shunning*, calling it "a Canadian masterpiece of poetry and theatre" (quoted in Prokosh 2011b). It is also possible that Kroetsch was thinking of the relationship between drama and Mennonite oral culture, which he would have been aware of after moving to Manitoba. Amateur Low German plays were performed in schools during my childhood, and they were likely an influence on Armin Wiebe's play *The Moonlight Sonata of Beethoven Blatz* (2011).

Kroetsch's reference to plays as a "communal" form, however, draws attention to the questions raised by Mavis Reimer (1997) with regard to the relationship between community and genre. Unlike published texts that allow a reader to participate in an imagined community, dramatic performances, whether in the amateur form of The Missing Mennonite Cabaret or in the form of a professional theatre production, are events that happen in front of a particular audience that might or might not constitute a community. The regional factors that partly account for the "Mennonite miracle" are more important in theatre than in any other genre for this reason. I am acutely aware of this because of my geographic distance. That is not to say that plays are a communal Mennonite form in Winnipeg. To be sure, there is now a company called Winnipeg Mennonite Theatre, but there is constant movement in between different companies such as the Prairie Theatre Exchange and the Manitoba Theatre Centre. Added to them is the annual Winnipeg Fringe Festival, managed for some years by my nephew Jason Neufeld, one of whose most popular performances was a one-man mixed-media act called "Confessions of a Repressed Mennonite."

It might be significant that the most prominent Canadian Mennonite playwright, Vern Thiessen, is neither Kanadier nor Russländer but from the much smaller group of Mennonites who found their way to Canada from Germany after the Second World War. Thiessen has been Artistic Director of Work Shop West in Edmonton since 2014, but the scope of his work is more international than regional. The three plays by him that I have seen suggest something of the range of communities to which they appeal. I saw *Lenin's Embalmers* at the Harold Green Jewish Theatre Company in Toronto, *Shakespeare's Will* at Stratford, and *Of Human Bondage* at Soulpepper in Toronto. If Kroetsch was right in seeing drama as a newly available "communal" genre, then it might be the one to watch in the future as regional dramas by Mennonites move outward from their local communities to performances in other communities whose locations are dictated more by the box office than by any sense of coherent ethnic identity.

Mennonite Gothic

As the many texts blur into each other, I have noticed a recurrence of what I call Mennonite gothic, a genre that I now take as a visible sign of anachronic renaissance. Oddly this genre first occurred to me as being of possible importance to Mennonites because Robert Kroetsch failed to identify it in my writing. After he gave his lucid account of available genres at the 1990 conference, Di Brandt pointed out to him that he had made no reference to the "questions of gender and violence in Mennonite writing" that had come up at the conference (Tiessen and Hinchcliffe 1992, 235). In his response to her, Kroetsch commented that "it's interesting that women were more experimental in a certain way in terms of form. They were working in forms such as Maggie and Elizabeth are working on. I was struck, listening to Maggie and Elizabeth, on the place of the house in their world. They presented it as a place of security, whereas in much Western Canadian writing at least the house is a place of terror" (Tiessen and Hinchcliffe 1992, 236). I remember how startled I was by this comment and how I wondered if perhaps Kroetsch had not actually been there. At the reading to which he referred, I read the first few pages of my story "The Little Dipper." Those pages are a record of how I try hard but fail to overcome my terror and enter the house in my sister's story "The House." Later in that story, I find myself already in the house without having consciously crossed a threshold. At that point, I deal with memories of violence, including the throwing of a "little dipper" and a glass of milk. If there is a "place of security" in that story, then it seems to be in the night sky, where the Little Dipper can be counted on to stay in the same place. It was no easy process for me to arrive, in that story, at the conclusion where I imagine my father planting flax in a field where my mother is able to see it from their bedroom window. I imagined him doing this out of love for her because the flax blooms early in the morning in her favourite shade of blue. I got that idea from a story by

Alice Munro, and it taught me, once again, about the comforts available to us if we let ourselves make believe.

Kroetsch's generalizations about houses and horses in relation to gender were well known at the time and somewhat notorious among feminists. That might be why I let it go and did not protest his misrepresentation. Afterward, however, I wondered how he could have missed the gothic echoes in my story that now seem obvious to me, though I was not aware of them while writing. Gothic forms have a particular fascination for women writers, as is apparent from the novels of the Brontë sisters. It might be that gothic forms are also appealing to Mennonites because they offer a way of dealing with time warp. Given the constant temptation of the kind of nostalgia that erases history, gothic is a genre that might appeal to writers who want to counter nostalgia by digging up embarrassing anachronistic customs. Friesen's *The Shunning* (1980), for example, could be seen as a gothic text. An individual writer might circle back again and again to the same haunted site. The best writing sometimes happens when a writer is open to dislocation even as she digs deep into local history.

One example of such Mennonite gothic is Christina Penner's *Widows of Hamilton House* (2008). Location, location, location. Penner begins on the everyday level of that real estate mantra, as does Alice Munro in "The Progress of Love," but then moves on, as does Munro, into deep dislocations by reinventing the gothic cliché of the haunted house. *Widows of Hamilton House* is a queering of gothic. Along with the pleasurable sense of transgression comes the delight of consciously making believe while playing with facts. Hamilton House is an actual house in Winnipeg, said to have been visited by both Arthur Conan Doyle and William Lyon Mackenzie King. When Ruth meets the landlady of Hamilton House, Ruth "takes a tiny step back" because the woman "articulates her consonants with unusual vigour, and the space around her sparkles with saliva" (Penner 2008, 16). The landlady's name is Mrs. Redekop. She tells Ruth that the house is "two short blocks from Concord College" (formerly Mennonite Brethren Bible College) and close to the Elmwood church and cemetery. The proper nouns evoke familiar pastoral tropes while locating the reader comfortably in Winnipeg. Mrs. Redekop extols the location on Henderson Highway: "She opens both hands, as if celebrating a successful magic trick. 'It's such a good place for young Mennonites to meet each other'" (16). Location, location, location. And dislocation. The referents in the novel have a flattening effect, as if we are touching the surface of a map. The wordplay leads down below that surface into a place where concord and death coexist.

An element of gothic is also present in David Elias's darkly funny *Sunday Afternoon* (2004), a tour de force play with the technique made famous by James Joyce in *Ulysses* of having an entire novel take place in one day. Comedy takes an even darker turn in Corey Redekop's *Husk* (2012). I feel pride at the aplomb with which my nephew works from inside the husk of formulaic fiction and brings it to life in the form of a zombie called Sheldon Funk. Such monsters are now familiar from films such as Guillermo del Toro's *Pan's Labyrinth*, but they have a long history going back to *Frankenstein*. The novels that confront the crisis of representation and self-representation in this way find ways to connect with the human subject that lives inside the objectified freak. An urge to respect difference is the moral kernel of many stories about monsters. This is certainly the case for del Toro, who never tires of showing that the human heart holds horrors beyond any visual ugliness that we can imagine.

The fiction that deals with otherness in radical ways is also often embarked on the kind of time travel that I have defined as part of a Mennonite sensibility. In *Little Fish*, a novel by Casey Plett published in 2018, the main character, Wendy Reimer, a thirty-year-old trans woman experiences time warp. The road definitely becomes *shtuckrich* or bumpy when Wendy learns that her Opa, her Mennonite grandfather, might have been trans. Plett embraces the challenge with dialogue and a relational aesthetic. A group of women converse in the present, but the novel begins with a discussion of how age is experienced differently by trans people than by cis people. New ways of looking at time travel similarly recur in the novels discussed by Daniel Shank Cruz in *The Queering of Mennonite Literature* (2018). The small Mennonite flowering of queer writers happening within the larger Mennonite renaissance is part of a renaissance of queer writing happening all across the continent, providing evidence of the deep resonance of anachronic renaissance.

Beginning Again and Again

As new writers continue to emerge, they play on borderlines between identities in ways that make it impossible to generalize about something called "Mennonite writing." Nothing I have written here should be taken as support for the notion that readers should actively look for what is Mennonite about a particular text. Every text should be taken on its own terms. The fact remains, however, that for purposes of writing this book I have necessarily had to separate out books written by authors with Mennonite names and that while doing so I have repeatedly registered Mennonite accents in the writing. When I look at my MennoLit bookcase, I see that it is bulging with books, and more are arriving in the mail soon. I am reminded of Robert Frost's words in "After Apple-Picking":

> For I have had too much
> Of apple-picking: I am overtired
> Of the great harvest I myself desired. (1963, 53)

I remember that I will soon be forced to do yet another downsizing, and then I hear the concluding lines of Frost's poem: "One can see what will trouble / This sleep of mine, whatever sleep it is" (53). Storage is indeed the problem with bumper crops. Should I order a copy of the latest new book by a Mennonite? Or will I need to give away the ones I have? At the moment, my MennoLit bookcase is in our bedroom, with the result that my sleep is sometimes troubled when the voices begin to speak to each other. One night I could have sworn that I heard the ship of fools in *Dustship Glory* (Schroeder 1986) whistling through the air on its way to land in the glacial valley of *The Missing Child* (Birdsell 1989).

Every harvester in this field will be able to name important writers whom I have not even mentioned. The embarrassment of riches can be acute for literary critics. While *Rhubarb* was still arriving in the mail, I noticed a tendency to try to predict the future of Mennonite writing and almost a hope that it might stop. Perhaps I am not the only one with inadequate space for this bumper crop. Maurice Mierau, for example, speculated about the future of Mennonite writing in an ironic mock-gothic Q&A published in *Rhubarb* in 2012. Mierau has the ghost of his ancestors ask this question: "If the only Mennonites left live in Belize, Paraguay, Mexico, etc., what are the odds that those exotic Mennos might produce uppity artists too?"

Mierau replies thus: "Close to zero. Rigorously depriving your children of education is a guaranteed way to never have artists in your community" (29). If I were to enter that graveyard, I would urge that facetious ghost to question the presuppositions behind his predictions. Just as the Russländer once lumped together all Kanadier as backward, so too this ghost, like most Canadian Mennonites, now lumps together all the Mennonites in "Belize, Paraguay, Mexico, etc." and calls them backward. I have no trouble at all imagining that the next flowering might happen, for example, in Mexico. I only have to imagine one woman irritated at the role that she was tricked into performing as a little girl swimming in the imaginary Mennonite ghetto of Carlos Reygada's film *Stellet Licht* (2007). I imagine her talking back, and then another woman joins in and urges a third to do the same. It's what Patrick Friesen said about The Missing Mennonite Cabaret: it can happen "anywhere where two or three are gathered" (Enns 1992, 52).

As climate change makes it increasingly obvious that our species might not survive what we have done to this planet, apocalyptic fictions will surely continue to multiply. What they will do to all the genres remains to be seen. As long as Mennonites keep on writing, however, all the new generic developments will continue to resonate with various Mennonite aesthetic accents. Like the tramps in *Waiting for Godot*, we will continue to comfort or torment each other no matter how uncertain the future. If, in my nightmare about teaching a course for which I am unprepared, a student were to insist that I say what the individual fruits have in common, I might say that most are bittersweet. They contain the quality characteristic of anachronic renaissance: the urge to go deep into the past, confronting skeletons and talking to ghosts, and the desire to savour the sweetness of new growth as you move forward and begin all over again.

To such a student, I might offer, as a final example, a novel that I have just finished reading: Miriam Toews's *Women Talking* (2018). I happened to see the Soulpepper production of Caryl Churchill's *Escaped Alone* (2016) in November 2018, shortly after reading *Women Talking*, and I picked up a resonance. In both, women talk to each other about how to deal with disaster. Both echo the biblical story of the messenger who comes to tell Jonah about horrors that he alone escaped. The difference of genre shapes them differently of course. *Escaped Alone*, like the plays of Samuel Beckett, deliberately strips the action of any reference to history. In contrast, *Women*

Talking is a response to the real-life dilemma of women in a Mennonite colony in Bolivia who desperately need to escape their rapists. To convey that dilemma, Toews adopts a deliberately awkward narrative apparatus, involving a male translator. Since the women are illiterate, there are drawings to represent the choices available to them. Despite these differences, the talking of these women seems to happen in the same play space as that of the women on the stage in *Escaped Alone*. In *Women Talking*, however, I see a gesture that resonates with sixteenth-century Anabaptist history. The women are in touch with an Anabaptist vision that always insists on beginning again and again. To do that, they must create a crisis, and with the help of a translator they manage to do so. Compassionate clowning is emblematic of Toews's aesthetic. The awkward male translator in *Women Talking* is called August Schellenberg. Add an e to August and it echoes the name of the red clown called Auguste—pronounced Aw Goost. Like Gustavo, the clownishly maternal man in *Irma Voth* (Toews 2011), August affirms the value of just being with others in a place where we make believe together.

5

MELOS AND LOGOS
TALKING ABOUT MUSIC

Schockel, schockel, scheia
Oustre ät vie Eia
Pinjste ät vie vittet Brout
Stoav vie nijch dann voa vie grout.
Stoav vie doch dann foa vie em Loch.
Keekeree! Dei Hohn es dout!

Rock-a rock-a riester
We eat eggs at Easter,
Pentecost we eat white bread
If we live, then we grow big.
If we die we go in the hole.
Cock-aroo, the rooster's dead.
(translation by Jay Macpherson)

Making Music in This World That Is Our Home

In 1957, the year that I turned thirteen, the Russians launched a rocket into
space. Shock waves from this seismic event could be felt even on our farm

in southern Manitoba. The word *sputnik* means satellite or fellow traveller in Russian, but to the Low German ear it sounds like *Shputt nich.* Mock not. In our house during that time, we would often joke *Sputnik. Daut mutnik.* (Mock not. That must you not.) My father was convinced that the Russians were lying. Our only sources of information were a local weekly, the *Red River Valley Echo,* and the CBC daily news report *The World at Six.* Every day my father insisted that my mother listen to the report and translate it into Low German for him. After she turned off the radio, he would announce "The world is sick." Those were among the few English words that I ever heard him say.

Being in the world but not of the world: that was our Mennonite goal. Achieving it was made a little more challenging the same year, 1957, when radio station CFAM began to broadcast "worldly music" out of Altona, a town three miles south of our farm. For Christmas that year, my mother (who had a knack for finding exactly the right gift in the Eaton's catalogue) gave me a small red-and-white plastic rocket radio. Attached to it was something that looked like an umbilical cord that led to an object resembling a baby soother. To my astonishment, when I put that object in my ear, only I could hear the sound. The tip of the rocket was a metal antenna that could be pulled up and down to change stations. The only one that came through, because of our proximity to the tower, was CFAM. That must have been a relief to my parents. Classical music was bad enough. For me to listen to the popular music on the Winnipeg station CKY would have been worse—a little like when the devil, disguised as a squat toad, whispers into the ear of Eve in Milton's *Paradise Lost.*

Thoughts of the devil bring to mind the revival meetings that also took place in Manitoba in 1957, the same year that CFAM was launched. I was startled when I did the fact checking and confirmed that these two events took place in the same year. I have cited the tent revival meetings as a root cause of the Mennonite renaissance and counted myself as one of the terrorized adolescents. My brain seems to have slotted the memory of that event into a separate compartment that has nothing to do with my enjoyment of my rocket radio. I am not sure what this means. Perhaps it just shows how desperately I needed my privacy during that year.

My brothers invented a new and untranslatable word for the music that was on CFAM: *fiddlejeqvirk*s. I did not share their aversion to classical music, having already experienced the first thrill of it when Handel's *Messiah* was brought to Altona by Ben Horch, a charismatic conductor who will feature prominently in this chapter. Several more years would pass, however, before learning to love the *fiddlejeqvirks* of Vivaldi became part of falling in love with Clarence Redekop, an exotic Russländer from Winkler who was a violinist in the Mennonite Community Orchestra (see the history by Bertha Klassen 1993). As a teenager on the farm, I was enthralled by my first taste of folk music. I savoured the private joys of transgression after bedtime, in the darkness of my room, listening to *Songs of the Nations*, hosted by Hans Andriessen. Charmed by songs about Loch Lomond and other Scottish places, the names of which often sounded Low German, I abandoned myself to borrowed nostalgia and fell hopelessly in love with the music of Scotland. Equally intoxicating were the songs of Stephen Foster and other American melodies that prepared me for that time, early in the next century, when (after the death of my first husband) I would fall in love with Dennis Duffy, an exotic Irish American from Kentucky. Many a night I would go to sleep with the "Tumbling Tumbleweeds," a song composed by Bob Nolan in the 1930s and made famous by Sons of the Pioneers. I was enchanted by the extra e in "tumbeling" and, lying alone in the darkness, I was comforted to know that "deep in my heart" was a song, "drifting and drifting along."

What could possibly be dangerous or sinful about such a pretty tune? What exactly is worldly music? Historian Ted Regehr writes that one of the objectives of Ben Horch, the first music director at CFAM, was to "divert young Mennonite listeners from the rock and roll played on most AM radio stations" (1996, 297). I knew about rock and roll because my older brothers, who had moved to Winnipeg, were fans of Elvis Presley. One of my brothers brought home a Chuck Wagon Gang record, rightly assuming that the rousing country beat would be acceptable because songs such as "This World Is Not My Home" contained a "gospel message." In contrast, the music on *Songs of the Nations* was in a grey area, and my rocket radio did not come with instructions on where to draw boundaries. I now see the problem that I confronted as related to the questions that Glenn Gould asked repeatedly of the people whom he interviewed in the 1970s when he was creating *The Quiet in the Land*, a case study in Chapter 2. Again and again, often using the word *ghetto*, Gould probed at the heart of what

I am calling the Mennonite foundational gesture—the act of shunning the world. What does it mean to be in the world but "not of this world" (John 8:23)? How does this stance relate to the making of music?

When I unpack the gift that my mother gave me in 1957, I discover that my *sputnik* contains the very questions about music that I will explore in this chapter. How has the foundational Mennonite gesture of shunning the world shaped our ways of making music and of listening to music? Does our Reformation history help to explain why music has been the art form strongly preferred in most Mennonite communities? In what ways has it been restricted and why? Does music provide an escape from the crisis of representation or only the illusion of escape? How do we reframe all these questions when technology changes how we make music and how we listen to it? How do our class differences and our diverse experiences of immigration and assimilation play into the answers to all these questions? Can music represent our faith? Can it represent us as a people? Can it have a Mennonite accent? If so, then how does that accent change in different times and places? And how, finally, does music deal with the pesky problem of nostalgia?

On the face of it, my teenaged love affair with Scottish and American folk music shows the failure, at the outset, of our foundational gesture. It shows how easily melodies travel via *sputnik*, my fellow traveller, through the walls of an ethnocentric community and how borrowed nostalgia is instrumental in the crumbling of those walls. This was true long before the development of digital technology. Folk songs have always been promiscuous, travelling across national boundaries in mysterious ways and creating mixtures of genres long before the word *hybrid* became fashionable among theorists. In hindsight, I can see that *Songs of the Nations* was pulling me inexorably into modernity—into a future that Roland Robertson calls "accelerated, nostalgia-producing globalization.... The world as *the place* in which we all live is being increasingly promoted on all kinds of fronts" (1990, 53, 56). For urban Mennonites, immersed as we are in a global electronic culture, it is easy to scoff at more traditional Mennonites who fear worldly music. Is it even worth paying attention to different musical traditions when we all live in a "global village"?

These are unresolved questions that I carry forward from previous chapters, but they seem more daunting when I take them into a discussion of music. From how vehemently I have insisted on respect for the text in the previous chapters, readers might deduce that the absence of a text presents a major problem when a literary critic turns her attention to music. I will offer a case study of the *Mennonite Piano Concerto* but not by dealing with it as a text. My focus instead will be on the dialogue *around* that concerto. Dialogism, in short, will necessarily take a different form in this chapter. Much of it will be impressionistic as I share, from my biased perspective, what I hear when Mennonites talk about music. The absence of texts makes me aware of the stronger undertow of my own nostalgia, which is why I have begun, as I did at the start of Chapter 3, by self-consciously foregrounding that nostalgia. I ground my discussion on the same *shtahp* because I am conscious of stepping outside the box of my own discipline. When I think about the pastoral tropes in those folk songs, however, I see that I have one foot in my own literary field. The awkwardness of the metaphor seems appropriate in this case.

While it acknowledges nostalgia, my opening story about my rocket radio is also located in a particular place, the same spot on the map to which I pointed in my chapter on nostalgia. Feet on the ground, so to speak, I aim to challenge assumptions about the "otherworldly" nature of music. I have come a long way since I wrote, in "Through the Mennonite Looking Glass" (Redekop 1988), about how painful I found my mother's love for songs about heaven, but I still experience the same ambivalence. In the previous chapter, I took my discussion of literature up to a point where writers give up on words and allow music or dance to take over. In this chapter, I will reflect on the same inescapable tension between words and music and show how, when it is acknowledged, it can help to shed light on the material conditions that shape the making of music.

Since I am not an ethnomusicologist, the social history of Mennonite musical traditions is beyond my knowledge and ability to provide. Why did singing in four-part harmony become a signature of Mennonite identity? Such a question demands research beyond what I can offer. My responses are based on my own experiences, on my interviews with Mennonite musicians, and on my study of poetry. As in any interdisciplinary study, it is sometimes possible for literary scholars to see problems that have been unnoticed by musicologists. A literary critic, for example, is more likely to notice that barriers to productive dialogue about music are created,

ironically, when people are effusive about their love for music. Roland
Barthes asks "how then does language manage . . . when it must inter-
pret music?" and answers "alas, badly—very badly, it seems." He observes
that, when critics talk about music, their response "is invariably translated into the poorest linguistic category: the adjective" (1985, 267).
The adjectives—*otherworldly, ephemeral, ineffable*—are conspicuously
weak, moreover, because they contrast with the perfectionism of musical
performance. The resulting hierarchies feed into a celebrity culture that
generates still more adjectives. The voice of Ben Heppner, a Canadian
tenor who happens to be Mennonite, is frequently labelled *incompara-
ble*—an adjective that announces its own defeat. This kind of rhetoric
leads quickly to a dead end for the curious scholar, as I discovered when
I was contemplating an interview with Heppner. I asked a colleague, a
passionate opera fan, what she would ask him if she had the chance. Her
quick response: "Will you marry me?" Heppner himself, now that he has
retired from singing opera, talks about how he enjoys singing the gospel
songs that he remembers from his childhood.

Many Mennonites who perform classical music speak openly about
their Christian faith in ways that assume it is a simple thing that enriches
but does not complicate the making of music. This reflects the conditions
under which those who perform classical music work. They devote endless
hours to achieve perfectionist goals, and the time spent reading music does
not leave much time to read books. Lack of interest in questions about belief
and music, however, is not the norm when you talk to Mennonites who
are composers or music educators. Outside classical music, when composition is often collaborative, there is evidence of thoughtfulness among
Mennonites about what we do when we make believe using music. I think,
for example, of the Royal Canoe song "Today We're Believers." I do not
know how many members of that band are Mennonite, but as it happens
the lead composer for Royal Canoe is Matthew Schellenberg, the son of
my cousin the late Henry Schellenberg (a music educator and conductor),
who was the son of my uncle Henry Schellenberg (a piano tuner). Most
Mennonites who make music can trace a similar family musical lineage.
Because music itself seems so ephemeral, it is easier to tell stories about it
than to talk about the music itself, and these are often family stories. Where
the verbal arts overlap with music is a rich area within Mennonite culture

now, and sometimes this overlap includes translation from oral storytelling traditions. Armin Wiebe tells me that stories about my piano tuner uncle were an inspiration for his creation of the pianist in *The Moonlight Sonata of Beethoven Blatz* (2011). I will keep such stories in mind in this chapter as a way of resisting the powerful illusion that music transcends our miserable human lives.

The difficulty of describing or representing music in words can lead to the conclusion that music itself does not represent anything. In *Musicophilia: Tales of Music and the Brain*, for example, Oliver Sacks writes that "music, uniquely among the arts, is both completely abstract and profoundly emotional. It has no power to *represent* anything particular or external, but it has a unique power to *express* inner states or feelings" (2008, 8; emphasis added). When music is taken in context, however, the questions related to representation come back with a vengeance. Shared musical expression is regularly seen in cultures—whether high, low, or middlebrow—as *representing* the identities of groups and not only of those groups assumed to be living in ghettos. Unlike birds, people do not sing as a result of a biological imperative. They do so as part of a culture in which identity is created interactively. Music is linked to the high value given to community in Mennonite culture, as it is in many non-Mennonite communities. Despite the constant overlap of communities, and despite assumptions about the otherworldly nature of music, "ethnic dialogism" occurs in music as it does in literature. Borrowed nostalgia, when we buy into it, sidesteps interethnic conflicts over music, but *Songs of the Nations*, after all, was connected to the histories of groups other than mine. The complexities of such histories tend to be obscured when music is turned into a commodity. As I eventually discovered, people of Scottish ancestry differ in their responses to Sir Harry Lauder and to sentimental songs presumed to represent them.

We can sing songs together, and we can listen to the same songs and pay no attention to differences, but when we begin to talk *about* the songs we relate them to our own lives and to the places from which we come. Those ways of talking, because of differing histories, contradict the assumptions about "music's autonomy from the social world" that have long been dominant in our thinking about classical music (Said 1991, xvi).

Many Mennonites who perform classical music have expressed to me the view, quoting Ben Horch, that "all music is a gift from God" (Klassen 2005, 92). Further discussion usually reveals that by this they mean classical music and perhaps a small number of hymns with music written by Bach. It often seems to go without saying that jazz and rock cannot be gifts from God and that metal is of the devil. As it happens, I have a vested interest in this subject since my son is a virtuoso guitarist in a metal band. Whatever his personal tastes, in any case, Ben Horch was open to bending rules because of his role as a mentor to countless Mennonite musicians who needed a theological justification for music during the 1960s and 1970s, when the after-effects of the 1950s revival movement were most strongly felt. A major block to music was the print literalism that came with fundamentalist thinking. Horch likely intended his idea that music is a divine gift to be a theological rationale to sidestep that block. I would argue, nonetheless, that such a statement itself can become a block because it suggests that music transcends problems such as class differences.

If music has meaning only within particular contexts, then which meanings do Mennonite ways of making music have in relation to the contexts that I have laid out in earlier chapters? The possible answers to that question seem to me less locally based than they are in relation to literature. American hymnodist Mary K. Oyer, for example, has noted a worldwide trend in Mennonite churches toward "growing ethnic diversity" and an "expansion of musical styles" (2005, 28). This has happened in part because of the influence of the music performed at Mennonite World Conferences by musicians from non-European Mennonite churches. Geraldine Balzer cautions, however, against a tendency to see music as a quick way of transcending local differences. "When singing songs from Latin and South America and Africa," she notes, "North American Mennonites are relieved, if temporarily, of their role as colonizers and settler invaders, and [they] can see themselves as part of the global collective, inclusive and open to difference" (2015, 288). The larger global developments do not eliminate the importance of particular places to the making of music and certainly not to our ways of talking about music. Indeed, they seem to be heightening it. Manitoba, for example, remains a central musical focus for me even though I have not lived in that province since 1966. I have not had the opportunity to take in the events of the annual New Music Festival of the Winnipeg Symphony Orchestra, which has sometimes featured the work of Mennonite composers and often involved Mennonite performing groups. When I start talking about Mennonites and music, I nevertheless find myself dealing with nostalgia and the presence of my own shadow on the Manitoba *shtahp*.

Nostalgia often draws me back to one Low German Mennonite folk song that strikes a deep chord for me. "*Schockel, schockel, scheia.*"* The translation that I provide in the epigraph was done for me at my request by my mentor, poet Jay Macpherson. In her pioneering study *Singing Mennonite: Low German Songs among the Mennonites*, Doreen Helen Klassen reports that no "equivalent or variant" of this song "has been found in European folklore collections, so it may be an original Mennonite folksong" (1989, 29). The song, however, echoes any number of children's songs from any number of countries. The words suggest a scene of children being taunted with the knowledge of death. A direct translation of "stoav vie doch" would be "if we *do* die"—*doch* meaning do—and the brutal rhyme of *doch* and *Loch* (hole) evokes the infant deaths so common during my childhood that many people buried babies in their gardens.** Macpherson's translation helps to draw me back from nostalgia because it shows that music, like writing, is translation and that all these creative processes happen as dialogue among people.

Despite its ephemeral nature, music takes place, as do all the arts, in the muddled world where cultures meet and clash. I do not hear the strength of Mennonite music traditions as being in any one kind of song or in any one ethnocentric body of music. It lies, rather, in something nomadic that goes with diaspora, something that moves into the places where cultures clash, something that welcomes cross-fertilization of different song traditions (see Redekop 2011). That said, I listen for those accents that communicate

---

* The first time that I reflected on this song in public was during a lecture at the University of Winnipeg in 1992 entitled "*Schockel, Schockel, Scheia*: The Making of Mennonite Song." I returned to the topic at a conference on the literary heritage of Northrop Frye. That paper, entitled "Charms and Riddles in the Mennonite Barnyard," was published in a collection of essays to honour Frye (Redekop 1993a).

** Three of my siblings died before I was born, and one was stillborn when I was a child, a death that I have written about in "Still Life with Menno" (Redekop 1990b).

a Mennonite sensibility, and I do so for reasons that have to do with where I come from. I still have my rocket radio, in the original cardboard box, made by Miniman Company in Japan. When I took it off the shelf recently, it reminded me of Susan Stewart's reflections on miniatures in *On Longing* (1986). This mute object tells me that history is a useful antidote to nostalgia and that, despite changes in technology, we continue to make music in this world that is our home.

Melos and Logos: Learning in the "Singing School" of Poetry

Conflicts over music take widely varying forms among Mennonites, but I see all of them as related in different ways to an ancient battle between *melos* (song) and *logos* (word). As Eleanor Cook has noted, this conflict has identifiable pre-Reformation roots in Saint Augustine. In an essay entitled "Melos Versus Logos, or, Why Doesn't God Sing?," Cook observes that "Augustine's beautiful meditation on his own susceptibility to music ('melos omnes cantilenarum suavium') is the *locus classicus* of this fear of music's distracting power" (1998, 169; see Augustine *Confessions* 1992, 207–8). Although Plato saw music and the soul as kindred, Henry Chadwick notes: "There was deep disagreement in the churches of North Africa at this time [when Augustine wrote] whether any music should be admitted to worship and, if so, what kind" (Augustine 1992, 208). E.H. Gombrich describes the conflict between *melos* and *logos* as pervading "the whole history of music." He articulates some of the basic questions: "Which is to be the master? The words or the music? The meaning or the form? The tensions can be productive of much artistic ingenuity, but they also lead to violent debates" (2012, 290). Within the largest aesthetic context, these are debates about power, about who controls meaning. In *Freedom and the Arts: Essays on Music and Literature*, Charles Rosen describes how words hem us in and threaten to trap us with the "imposition of meaning." Music offers "a partial freedom of, and from, meaning" (2012, 8).

When I look for grounded ways to talk about Mennonites and music, I turn to poetry. The densely allusive verbal music of poetry has the power to counter the sentimental nostalgia that saturates ethnocentric approaches to music. In "Hymns from Detroit," Di Brandt creates a potent mixture of nostalgia and satire. On a page beside the lyrics for the gospel song "This World Is Not My Home" is a poem by Brandt about a world being destroyed by pollution. In that context, the line about how "I can't feel at home / In this world any more" acquires ironic new meaning (2010, 111). The poem ends, however, with an affirmation of dialogue that lightens the dark tone. Brandt's last lines run counter to the rollicking refrain of the gospel song: "O Lord, you know, / I have no friend like you, / If heaven's not my home, / Then Lord what will I do?" (111). Brandt locates her closing vision firmly on the ground of this world that is our home with a radical change in the apostrophe—substituting for an address to "O Lord" an address to "Dear friends":

> Dear friends, you know
> I'm here because of you.
> Ten thousand shades of green
> Under the churning sky,
> And you, and you, and you. (2010, 110)

The metric feet try to hop along to the rhythm of the original song, but the word *churning* works against rigidity and against the tropes that evoke a lost green pastoral world. The echo from *The Sound of Music* in the last line is ironic, collapsing the sentimentality of the gospel song into that of a musical, but it does not quite dissolve into corrosive cynicism. I read the lines as offering the hope of dialogue that can become the nucleus of possible community.

A similar emphasis on music as a vehicle for dialogue is apparent in the poetry of David Waltner-Toews. In his popular "Tante Tina" poems, he constructs dramatic monologues that loop the reader into participation while providing distance from nostalgia. In an often-quoted poem entitled "Haenschen Remembers Winnipeg," the speaker constructs a version of nostalgia that ends with music: *"The Real Messiah will come singing / Handel to Winnipeg, reeking of borscht"* (2004, 33). This messiah will be *"a baritone, a fine baritone, . . . and after him a whole cherubic chorus / singing kernlieder / singing the Hallelujah Chorus"* (33). In the concluding section, the poet imagines hearing "the exquisite consummation: / Bach's Magnificat / in Low German" (34). The specific allusions to Mennonite history here prevent the poem from dissolving into a global soup of nostalgia. In other poems in this series, Tante Tina talks back, and the reader is free to do so. As it happens, I myself had a Taunte Teen (Low German for

Tante [Aunt] Tina). I can imagine her looking puzzled and asking exactly the question that many readers will have: "Vaut zent *Kernlieder?*" (What are *Kernlieder?*) It is a question to which I will return. I raise it here because it points to the fact that the variety of nostalgia in this poem is Russländer. Of course, we can ignore such inconvenient differences while we sing Hallelujah together. When you bring music down to this world that is our home, however, you become aware that there are particular histories and geographies that shape our ways of experiencing it. Haenschen, after all, is remembering Winnipeg.

It is often noted that music is the preferred art form among Mennonites. This might have to do with a view expressed by George Steiner, who claimed that, though "language is close-woven with lies," music does not lie. "Music can boast, it can sentimentalize, it can release springs of cruelty," he wrote. "But it does not lie" (1974, 94). When the birds make music, they do indeed sing without lying, but to be human is to be part of a world of deceit and mimicry. One lesson that I have taken away from the poetry and fiction written by Mennonites is an awareness of how music challenges the linear narratives that we construct about ourselves. Although Penny Van Toorn (1995) has argued that Rudy Wiebe's fiction is logocentric, it seems to me that a challenge to *logos* from *melos* is insistent in Wiebe's fiction. Again and again the linear narratives that Wiebe sets up crumble and give way to music. A consistent emphasis in his novels, furthermore, is the location of musical acts in social contexts that encourage dialogue. In *Playing Dead*, a collection of essays that he published shortly after the death of his son in 1985, Wiebe quotes an Inuit called Orpingalik: "All my being is song, I sing as I draw breath" (1989, 115). At the end of that book, Wiebe describes himself as trying to "walk into the true north of my own head," but he turns away from solipsism and affirms an I/Thou dialogue: "If I do, I will get a new song. If I do, I will sing it for you" (119).

In *Come Back* (2014), Wiebe returns to his son's death. At the heart of that novel is music. "Human song," the narrator speculates, "must have begun with the howl of lament; which became prayer; which became hope. O Living God, let your mercy shine on us pitiful sinners" (265). This cry for mercy links a Low German lullaby, "*Schlop, kliena, schlop* / Sleep, little one, sleep" (265) to the classical music that resonates throughout the novel: the "Kyrie eleison" of Bach's *Mass in B Minor* (129), the "Erbarme dich" aria in Bach's *St. Matthew Passion* (166), and Gregorio Allegri's *Miserere*. Such allusions to music open up cracks in the texts of Wiebe's novels. You could say that this is where an extraliterary musical context floods in and destabilizes the printed word, moving dialogue to a non-linguistic level. I venture to say that this tendency, to appeal to music in a verbal text, could be called an aspect of a literary Mennonite sensibility. A random sampling of titles by other Mennonite authors shows how widely the tendency is shared: Lynnette Dueck, *Sing Me No More* (1992); Maurice Mierau, *Ending with Music* (2002); Rosemary Deckert Nixon, *Mostly Country: Stories* (1991); Audrey Poetker, *I Sing for My Dead in German* (1986); Al Reimer, *My Harp Is Turned to Mourning* (1985); Miriam Toews, *Swing Low* (2000); Armin Wiebe, *The Moonlight Sonata of Beethoven Blatz* (2011).

My Shadow on the Shtahp

Ethnomusicologist Jonathan Dueck has described life stories about music as being geographical and resembling "a fractal or web, branching out and returning as memories of place, understood in part through the intense and sensual experience of music" (2005, 159–60). With geography comes an awareness of the "sociability of musical production." Like Dueck, I am interested in "how and why people come together at a particular place and time to make music" (160). Since I am not trained as an ethnomusicologist, however, my minimal "fieldwork" does not make it possible to exclude my bias at any point. My interviews with musicians, mostly done in 1998, left me with a box full of tapes, each one jammed with fascinating stories.[*] Listening to the stories of others has heightened my awareness of my own bias. I find it helpful to envision my exploration as happening in the setting evoked by the title of a 2008 collection of essays, *Shadows in the Field: New Perspectives for Fieldwork in Ethnomusicology*. Whether I intend it or not, my shadow will fall over the field that I explore. I therefore need to make sure that I am accountable to the other shadows on that field. Let me gesture toward three of them as a way of offering perspective on the nostalgia of my opening anecdote. All three are fellow Kanadier, a choice that I hope will counter the tendency to homogenize that contributes to stereotyping.

---

[*] Excerpts from the interviews used in this chapter are included with the kind permission of the subjects interviewed. For a list of musicians interviewed, see the references.

Contrasting my experience with that of conductor Howard Dyck is useful because of his prominent role as a former music commentator on CBC, known from his years of hosting *Choral Concert* and *Saturday Afternoon at the Opera*. Although Dyck has long lived and worked in Ontario, he grew up in Manitoba. Because of his high achievement in music, I had always assumed that he was a *schtauts bengel*—a town boy— and a Russländer. It was a surprise to discover, when I interviewed him, that like me he grew up on a farm and is a Kanadier. He went to school and church in the town of Winkler, where he and my late husband were classmates and played together in the Mennonite Community Orchestra. Both were from Mennonite Brethren families, and both therefore benefited from the concentrated presence in that town of Russländer musical leadership. There surely were few small towns in Canada at that time that could boast about having a symphony orchestra. As Dyck put it, "I think we always were seen as a rather snotty-nosed bunch!" The rich music culture in Winkler at that time is reflected in an oft-told anecdote about a prominent music professor in Detmold, Germany. When asked (sometime in the 1970s) if she had been to Winnipeg, she answered: "Is that someplace near Winkler?"

Like Howard Dyck, Eric Friesen is well known from his broadcasting career at the CBC, though both are now retired. Friesen, who like Dyck got his first experience in radio at CFAM, was my high-school classmate in Altona, one grade behind me. Like the majority of people in that town, the Friesen family was Kanadier. There was in those days good-natured cultural competition between the neighbouring towns of Winkler and Altona. The Friesen family, members of the liberal Bergthaler Church, were responsible not only for CFAM but also for numerous other cultural initiatives in Altona, including the well-known printing press and, more recently, an art gallery. In a moving essay about the "fierce and unmoving particularity" of his father's musical tastes, Eric Friesen remembers Ted Friesen, an extraordinary self-educated man, encouraging "the great sacred choral tradition, mostly German, and its secular kin, classical music, also mostly German. *Verboten* was rock 'n' roll and jazz. Viewed with suspicion was anything romantic or emotional. . . . Beneath our contempt was country music, guilty on all counts" (2010, 115). Friesen describes his failed effort to persuade his father to listen to Tchaikovsky (dismissed by his father as *schmaltz*). Such struggles of younger generations against the tastes of their elders are perennial.

Meanwhile, on the other side of the river near Steinbach (*Jantsied*, as we used to say), the Kanadier experience was still different. Patrick Friesen remembers hearing Beethoven symphonies on the family record player and his adolescent efforts to get his parents to accept rock 'n' roll:

> First, I bought them an album of the Blackwood Brothers Quartet. My thinking was that these guys were Christians singing Christian songs, but they kind of "rocked." . . . Well, my father didn't like the quartet at all. He objected, I remember, to one of the songs referring to God as "the man up there." God was not a man, he said. Still I kept trying. I played "Hey Jude" for them. It was a slowish ballad, maybe they'd like it. As soon as the song started my father said, "When do they scream?" Which really pissed me off because, of course, halfway through the song McCartney screams.[*]

When I step further back from my mental picture of shadows on a *shtahp* in southern Manitoba, the outlines become blurry. As a teenager, I imagined Winnipeg to be a large glittering jewel spread out on the prairie, just outside my line of vision. During the 1970s and 1980s, when there were heated conflicts about music among Mennonites in Manitoba, I was already living in Toronto. My interviews with Winnipeg musicians have given me glimpses of those years and of the complex ways in which the lives of individual Mennonites making music in that city are intertwined with the histories of various institutions. The CBC has played a prominent role in creating cross-country links within Mennonite music culture. Mennonite educational institutions across the country, meanwhile, have not only provided opportunities for Mennonite musicians but also created obstacles. The histories of these institutions are complex and beyond the limits of this study. I am less interested here in the institutions themselves than in the stories of individuals who, in their determination to find *Spielraum*, have taken idiosyncratic paths through them to do so. The shadows on the *shtahp* might be highly individualized, but the conflicts

---

[*] Patrick Friesen, email to the author, 24 April 2015; quoted by permission.

are recurrent. Studying these conflicts and tracing their ancient roots can help to dispel the illusion that music is an easy escape from the problems associated with representation.

Sing unto the Lord at Home

The diversity of individual experiences makes it all the more noticeable when there are experiences shared by individuals from many different groups. I sense a deep feeling of loss (at least among many in my generation) about the practice of singing in the home. The form that the practice takes surely varies among families. Notwithstanding the many variations, it remains true for large numbers of Mennonites from all groups that singing at home was where music education began even if the parent was not an educator. Older siblings often taught younger siblings how to play instruments or how to sing in four-part harmony. I did not then think of four-part singing as distinctively Mennonite, nor did I know that this was not a common practice in non-Mennonite families. I now suspect that these home schoolings in music might account for the large number of Mennonites from that generation who took up positions of music leadership in educational institutions across the country. Here in Toronto, for example, Rennie Regehr served as dean of the Glenn Gould School in the Royal Conservatory of Music (1997–2006), and my University of Toronto colleague Lee Bartel is the founding director of the university's Music and Health Research Collaboratory. The Winnipeg examples are too numerous to list. Often they are linked with Mennonite institutions, but increasingly institutions, such as Westgate Mennonite Collegiate, draw students from outside Mennonite communities because of the strength of the music programs.

For many Mennonites, regardless of the subgroup, the rare occasion when we sing grace in four-part harmony at family gatherings stirs up both joy and painful nostalgia. Conductor Henry Engbrecht described unaccompanied singing to me as something that he "heard in the womb. I mean I learned that before I was born—four-part singing." Tenor John Martens, who grew up on a farm in Manitoba, described music for Mennonites as something "essentially homemade." Not all Mennonites, however, look back on those days with pleasure. When I asked one friend whether or not they sang in the home, she said "Of course. There was nothing else to do." She told me of her impatience as a teenager when her father, terrified of thunder storms, would gather the entire family to sing together until the storm passed. Since theirs was a church that did not allow harmony, they sang verse after endless verse in unison. Miriam Toews explores the darker side of this Mennonite family practice in a scene in *Irma Voth*. A mother gets her children to sing "Gott ist die Liebe" (God is love) together repeatedly as a distraction from the fact that in another room the father is beating one of the children (2011, 95–96).

Urbanization has had the same effect in Mennonite communities as in many other cultures, and singing no longer happens regularly in the majority of homes. My evidence for this, like my knowledge of Mennonite music traditions, is more anecdotal than research based. An anecdote in a "Lives Lived" column in the *Globe and Mail*, however, provides a glimpse of the residual power of this Mennonite tradition and shows how it surfaces during times of grief. The article is about the mother of Wanda Koop, whose art will be my focus in the next chapter. When her mother died in April 2015, at the age of ninety-five, the last hours of her life were spent this way: "With more than 20 family members gathered in her hospital room, and having expressed her love for each one, she then exclaimed, 'Don't just sit there all quiet—sing to me!'" She spent her final hours "surrounded by love and the sounds of her favourite hymns, all sung in four-part harmony" (Finnigan 2015).

As a child on the farm, I absorbed the idea that *making* music was of higher value than *listening* to it but also that making music with instruments was somehow riskier than singing words that came out of the Bible. We knew that our father, Wilhelm Falk, had started a new church for reasons that related, at least in part, to music. He had played the fiddle at dances in his youth but put all that behind him when he became *Vorsänger* (song leader) in the Sommerfelder Church. Using instruments and singing in harmony were not permitted in that church. My father's leadership as a singer led to his election as a preacher, a typical progression that might explain why the style of preaching in a Sommerfelder Church is a lot like singing. When my father was elected as Ältester (bishop) of the newly formed Rudnerweider Church, he left behind not only his youthful repertoire of dance tunes, whatever that was, but also the style of singing that he had learned back in the Sommerfelder Church. By the time the name of his new church was changed to Evangelical Mennonite Mission Conference

(EMMC), my father had been ousted from his position as Ältester. By that time, music was being used to evangelize people and therefore had to be done in English, a troubling change for my father. The fact remains, however, that for our family it was his leadership that won for us the permission to sing in harmony, accompanied by instruments.

It has been noted often that what was once forbidden gains a heightened value. Carol Ann Weaver, who is both a composer and a virtuoso keyboardist, was born in Harrisonburg, Virginia. She told me gleefully about her memory of the day when "the Brunks lifted their ban on pianos." She said her father went out immediately and bought two pianos, one for himself and one for his daughter. Luckily that ban was unknown in Manitoba during my childhood. Even before we had electricity on the farm, we had a pump organ and a piano. There was never enough money to have plumbing in the house, let alone for the luxury of piano lessons, but as I walked to and from the outhouse I could usually hear one or the other of my sisters playing the piano. It was our good fortune to have an uncle who was a piano tuner and who kept our Heintzman perfectly tuned in exchange for *faspa* of our mother's fresh buns and strawberry jam. The most formative musical experience for me was singing with my sisters Mary and Elizabeth as a trio, The Falk Sisters. We sang in various churches, in hospitals, at street meetings, at weddings, and at funerals. We sang on CFAM as part of a weekly Rudnerweider Church program called *The Gospel Message*. We sang while doing chores in the house and in the barn. We sang to comfort our parents whenever they asked us to sing, and we continued to do so after they retired on the rare occasions when all three of us were at home together. During those times, our parents would go into a kind of trance, as if the world and all its troubles had gone away briefly.

There were rules, of course. We did not need to be told to stay with the gospel message and to avoid any beat so regular that it might tempt a body to move in time to the music. Above all, however, there was the need to avoid the sin of pride. One year, flushed with our success, we practised for many weeks the trio piece assigned that year at the Southern Manitoba Music Festival, "Lift Thine Eyes," from Mendelssohn's *Elijah*. The lyrics of the song exhorted us to lift our eyes to mountains that were nowhere in sight. We could sing it from memory while milking the cows, but in the end we could not muster the courage to register for the competition.

Fear of failure was part of it, but the more serious danger was that our egos would get in the way of the gospel message. Confronted by these various limitations, we simply responded, as have countless musicians, by compromising. Even now those compromises seem to me a small price to have paid for the deep joy of singing in harmony with my sisters every day. There was also a certain empowerment in our local fame, not of small importance during adolescence. Since our voices were heard on CFAM, we had a public presence of sorts but only as a unit. Often we were mistaken for triplets. When we had all left home and it was obvious that we would have to stop performing, we took the time to make a record: *The Falk Sisters Sing unto the Lord*. Later still we devoted a lot of time to writing the interactive memoirs about which I wrote in the previous chapter.

Somewhere in the world The Falk Sisters are still singing. The recordings made for CFAM's *The Gospel Message* have been digitized and circulated by the EMMC to rural Mennonite communities in South America and other locations where there is a demand for German singing. We were not consulted for permission, and I am not sure what my response would have been had I been asked. What I felt when I first heard about the distribution is something for which R. Murray Schafer coined the term "schizophonia"—the split between an original sound and its acoustic reproduction. When my voice is reproduced and thrown far away into some other country, is that still me singing? What sort of community is being constructed on air? Where is home? What is the message? Who controls the message? If those songs are taken to represent "my people" in some way, then am I still a Mennonite? Since my reproduced voice will go on singing even after I die, will *I* still be singing?

Sola Scriptura: The Burden of Our Song

The extraordinary flowering of literary and visual arts in Manitoba since 1980 demands some account of what part music has played in relation to them. In *From Russia with Music: A Study of the Mennonite Choral Singing Tradition in Canada* (1985), Wesley Berg (who happens to be my cousin) traces a history that runs mostly parallel to the account given by Harry Loewen of the early literary history of Mennonites in Canada. Berg documents how the determined leadership of musicians from the Russländer subgroup nurtured the choral tradition and led to significant achievements of conductors, soloists, and eventually instrumentalists (see also Regehr 1996, 273–85). There was no way that Berg could have anticipated the emergence of Mennonite composers in Canada from all the different groups. This new development is the most visible musical parallel to the literary renaissance, and, as is the case in literature, it has happened as a result of interactions among all the groups. Much research remains to be done, but the developments in all the arts since Berg wrote *From Russia with Music* invite a reframing of the history. Berg offers few details about what kind of music the Kanadier were making during the fifty years before the Russländer arrived in Manitoba. A fuller account would need to move beyond the important research done by Doreen Helen Klassen (1989) on the Low German singing traditions of the Kanadier. The Kanadier were not all backward Low German–speaking farmers in need of Russländer enlightenment. Like the family of Paul Hiebert, for instance, the family of composer Glenn Buhr must have been assimilating before the Russländer arrived. Research has not been done on the different music traditions of the two groups, but, as with literature, the music being composed does not support the idea that there is a single foundational narrative that accounts for the vibrant music culture of Mennonites in Canada.

I was rather surprised, given the diversity of music practices among different Mennonite groups, at the repeated painful conflicts that I heard about when I interviewed musicians active during the 1970s and 1980s. One vocalist saw a split between "the Mennonite community" and "the artistic community" and concluded that "Never the twain shall meet." She described her separation from the former as so painful that she could still feel the shrapnel in her voice. She added the poignant detail that she had learned to make good use of the shrapnel. An accompanist told me that she felt like murdering the theologian who asked her to play quietly "so that the message could get through." I stress that this was not a unanimous response and varied depending on the specific church involved and on the age of the musician. Often it involved conflicts in particular educational institutions. It happened often enough, however, that I wondered what might be causing such anger. I thought I heard at least a partial answer to that question in Howard Dyck's comment to Glenn Gould: "Music with a message is the problem that Mennonites fight all the time" (Gould 1977). Doreen Helen Klassen, writing about her time at Mennonite Brethren

Bible College (MBBC), commented on the assumption that music must be "at the service of the lyrics, or 'the message'" (2005, 85). These are conflicts about power and meaning. Who is controlling the message of the music?

When *logos* threatens to silence *melos*, it is surely no surprise that musicians will protest vehemently. I hear these protests as echoes of those heard in the poetry and fiction of Mennonites. Many musicians have spoken to me about preachers who obstructed their work as music leaders. In fiction also creative freedom is often embodied in the preachers who wield the Word of God. Deacon Block in *Peace Shall Destroy Many* (Wiebe 1962) and The Mouth in *A Complicated Kindness* (Toews 2004) are sinister figures because of their fanatical attachment to the Word of God. My own father was a preacher who also sang and who cared enough about music to found a new church in part so that we could play instruments. Needless to say, these caricatures do not sing. When I think of the deepest historical Mennonite root of conflicts in all the arts, I visualize the portrait of Menno Simons by Arend Hendriks (Figure 6). He appears with a copy of the Bible, and one gigantic finger points to the text. *Sola scriptura*, Latin for by scripture alone, is only one of the five Reformation *solas* and a foundational principle for other Protestant churches. The revival movement of the 1950s is a recent root that twists around and distorts the older Reformation root of *sola scriptura*, and music was and remains a vehicle for that twisting.

The Brunk Brothers brought powerful music with them when they came to southern Manitoba. Like a travelling circus, the brothers moved their gigantic tent from place to place in 1957, targeting those parts of Canada where Mennonites were concentrated. One song used repeatedly during "altar calls" was "Just as I Am." When I reminded Patrick Friesen of that song almost fifty years after that time, he wrote "that [the] hymn represented every fear I had as a teenager in the home church. And anger. . . . I assume pretty much every teenager (and some adults) had to have felt that manipulation, that internal wrenching."[*] Another song used regularly for the altar call was "Softly and Tenderly Jesus Is Calling." Jesus was not singing. He was calling. The fact that he was doing so "tenderly" was disturbing in ways that I could not define, but the entire show was designed

---

[*] Patrick Friesen, email to the author, 24 April 2015; quoted by permission.

to coerce people into moving forward down the aisle to the altar to be saved. The Brunks were American Swiss Mennonites and hence exotic visitors in southern Manitoba, previously known primarily from a CFAM program called *The Mennonite Hour*. For many of us, it was our first experience of hearing four-part harmony sung a cappella with the high quality for which the Swiss Mennonites are known. There was plenty of Mennonite content on CFAM, but as the title of that show suggests, these plain-style Swiss Mennonites seemed more pure, more authentically Mennonite, than our mixed bunch on the prairie. Of course, this was a stereotype. There's nothing plain about singing in four-part harmony, and the Brunks, by the time they arrived in Manitoba, had abandoned the rule against pianos. As I remember it, however, the presumed purity of their brand of Mennonite identity was a big part of their appeal, as was their fluency in English.

It is one thing to use music (as has been done from time immemorial) to intensify individual religious experience or to help others release their grief. It is quite another to use it coercively as a tool to impose your religious dogma on others. Individual responses to this abuse of music must have varied depending on numerous factors, and among them the customs of different churches would be a particularly important variable. During the purges that happened in the Holdeman Church near Steinbach in the 1960s, for example, it was cause for excommunication to sing in four-part harmony. Imagine the intense conflict that must have ambushed an adolescent from that church drawn to the excitement of a Brunk Brothers revival meeting on a warm summer evening in 1957. How must it have felt to hear the four-part singing of a song urging you to avoid hell when your own church leaders preached that singing in four-part harmony would send you to hell?

If I am right to see the Mennonite renaissance in the arts as a counter-awakening of sorts, an antidote to fundamentalism, then this raises the question of what part is played by music in that cultural awakening. I am not qualified to answer that question fully, but from my interviews with musicians I learned that the fervour and literalism that came with the revival meetings of 1957 acted as a block to Mennonite musical development during the decades that followed. Musicians fought back. Since conductors had long been highly respected figures in Mennonite communities, it is not surprising that they often acted as lightning rods in a charged cultural scene. In 1970, for example, when Howard Dyck was serving as interim music director at MBBC, Victor Adrian, then president of the college, not only objected to the choir singing in Latin but also was reluctant to approve the performance of the Bach cantata *Ein Feste Burg* (A Mighty Fortress) in German. Dyck told me that Adrian expressed the view that, "If you want to preach the gospel, you should be singing in English." Such intense conflicts have receded into the past and been replaced by a more liberal atmosphere in Mennonite educational institutions across the continent. The stories that I have heard from individual musicians have nonetheless sometimes seemed to me like fragments that, if not exactly shrapnel, are shards of painful repressed histories that suggest a deep affinity between Mennonites who work in the language of music and those who write fiction and poetry exposing the dark underside of our culture.

Sing unto the Lord with Harp: The Word of God and the Fear of Instruments

If the burden of our song is made up of a literal verbal message, then what happens if the words are taken away altogether? What happens if you just "make a joyful noise unto the Lord" with harp, timbrel, and tambourine (Psalm 97:12; Psalm 149:3; Psalm 81:2) or with piano, organ, fiddle, mouth organ, washboard, or whatever other instruments come to hand? Why were and are musical instruments viewed as dangerous in some Mennonite churches? Is the answer to that question related in any way to the piano burnings now sometimes part of performance art? In 2003, Michael Hannan, for example, performed a piece entitled "Burning Questions" that featured a piano set on fire while it was being played. Why do rock musicians sometimes smash their guitars on stage? What are those burning questions?

The usual reaction among musicians to questions about the fear of music seems to be evasion. When I asked a group of Swiss Mennonites why they sing a cappella, for example, they offered a playfully disingenuous reply, claiming that they do so because it makes a finer sound. Perhaps, like The Falk Sisters, they made compromises and then discovered that the results were more than adequate to make up for whatever loss was suffered. When I pay attention, however, to the place where words and

music are in conflict, I wonder how the perceived threat of purely instrumental music relates to our foundational gesture of shunning the world.
If the people in a group sing words to each other, words that have been
previously agreed to and approved by God, and sing them within a closed
circle that shuns the rest of the world, then they reaffirm their identity as
a church. But where does that leave all the instruments?

Although fear of musical instruments is not peculiar to Mennonites,
our history does invite reflection on the matter. Centuries have passed
since the organist at the Zurich cathedral stood by in tears as the pipes
of his organ were smashed. A consideration of how those attitudes have
carried over through centuries into more recent Mennonite practices is far
beyond my study here. I did find it fascinating, however, to pay attention
to the trajectories of particular individual lives while interviewing musicians. Doing this left me acutely aware of how challenging it can be for an
individual Mennonite artist to deal with time warp as he or she makes an
entry into modernity. One story about a musician looking for *Spielraum*
has stayed with me since the day that I heard it. It was told to me by Bill
Derksen, a Winnipeg violinist, conductor, and composer. When I asked
him for his earliest memory about music, during my interview with him
in 1998, this was his response:

> I think I was five. Being in a very strict Old Colony home, I had
> never heard an instrument played anywhere. We didn't have
> instruments in the home. It would not have been allowed. I could
> not have heard part singing. . . . So there was one wintry evening
> when our father, who was an Old Colony singer, produced out of
> his pocket a mouth organ and played amazingly well. He had us
> enthralled. He had just bought it, but we found out that he used
> to do this on a regular basis and had, I suppose, repented of it.
> A delegation of ministers had come to the home where he grew up.
> They had smashed his instrument. He was playing an accordion at
> that time. There had been a very formal and serious cleansing—a
> purging of the group composed of four people who formed the
> band. So this must have been a moment of weakness when he
> picked up a mouth organ and entertained his children one wintry

evening. That mouth organ was thrown out of the house. Mother took the appropriate action, probably the next day.

When Derksen formed a secret band with his brothers to play gospel and country music, they had to do so "on the sly," he said. "The violin was hidden in a sock drawer. Hidden from my mother. Mother was the spiritual police." He laughed at this memory and added that "She also managed to be a dearly beloved and respected mother." Derksen ran away to Regina, where he joined his brothers and made music with them. When his brothers converted during the Brunk Brothers revival movement when it went to Saskatchewan, it created another crisis and led to another twist in the narrative. Derksen then returned to Manitoba, where he discovered, for the first time, the joy of singing in four-part harmony, which, he told me, he found more exciting than any bluegrass ditty. He went on to complete a doctorate in music, much to the horror of his mother, who walked miles along a dusty road to see the bishop and ask for reassurance that her son was not going to hell.

Horch! The Case of the Mennonite Piano Concerto

Peter Letkemann's absorbing biography *The Ben Horch Story* (2007) resonates with ironies about the extraordinary man who commissioned the *Mennonite Piano Concerto*. It was important, as I remember it, that there was not another Mennonite with the unusual name Horch. The German word *Horch!* can mean Obey! It can also mean Listen! One affectionate story (a variation of a famous Abbott and Costello comedy shtick) was told to me by my father-in-law, Henry Redekop, who taught with Ben Horch at the Winkler Bible Institute from 1943 to 1944. The story goes that a member of a concert audience whispered to the person next to him "Who's the conductor?" That person whispered back "Horch!"

Of Lutheran origins, Horch was born in 1907 in the village of Freidorf in South Russia and was two years old when his parents came to Canada, where he attended a private school in a Lutheran church (see Klassen 2005). He was nineteen when he joined the North End Mennonite Brethren Church in Winnipeg and twenty-five when he married Esther Hiebert, the daughter of a Mennonite minister. His German origins, not surprisingly, meant that he was in tune with Russländer celebration of German culture and to some extent shared their presuppositions about music and ethnicity. As an adopted member of the Russländer musical group, Horch lived, like so many of the most creative "Mennonites," on a borderline between identities. During a year in Detmold, Germany, in 1950–51, he was particularly drawn to *Volksliedkunde* (folk song studies). Sometimes he jokingly referred to *Kernlieder* as "corn songs." The term was used in nineteenth-century Germany to refer to "chorales that stood at the 'core' of the Lutheran faith; chorales such as 'Ein feste Burg'" (Letkemann 2007, 233). According to Letkemann, the term was used at first by Mennonite Brethren hymnologists to designate chorales but then gradually became associated with "the German Pietist movement" and American gospel songs (234). *Kernlieder* have become a vehicle for a variety of nostalgia definably Russländer. If, on the one hand, your ancestors were from that group—refugees who escaped Russia, leaving behind everything except their songs—then those songs will be charged with meaning. If, on the other, your ancestors were Kanadier—immigrants who never heard the word *Kernlied*—then those songs will come to you second hand and with less emotional impact.

As Letkemann shows, Horch "came to view *Kernlieder* as Mennonite folk songs, as a true expression of the Mennonite *Volk* (people), even though practically none of the songs he included in this classification had been written or composed by Mennonites" (2007, 235). The Russländer "thought of themselves as a '*Völklein*,'" and *Kernlieder* came to be defined as songs expressive of "feelings of nostalgia for their lost homelands" (235). As a way of preserving "the essence of the faith expression they embod-ied for his beloved Mennonite people" (236), Horch conceived the idea of commissioning a piece of music that would incorporate the *Kernlieder*. His original plan was to have a concerto commissioned by the CBC, but in the end it was financed by the B.B. Fast Foundation and composed by Victor Davies. In "A Non-Mennonite Writes a Mennonite Piano Concerto," Davies (2005) describes how Horch approached him in 1973 and gave him a long list of hymns but freedom to transform them. Davies writes that he "had no idea what Mennonite hymns were and knew little about Mennonites," but when he received the list he "learned from Horch that these pieces were largely Victorian English hymns and American gospel songs that the Mennonites had appropriated and adapted with German lyrics during their travels" (95). Davies adds that he "knew nearly all of the hymns from my United Church background and realized in later years that engaging with these hymns during the composition of the concerto was a musical homecoming for me" (95).

According to Davies, Horch wanted to test his thesis that the hymns themselves were not sacred and outside the context of worship could be completely secularized. By his own account, Davies "only looked at what [the material] could become musically" and thought that he was "able to transform it without the emotion of tradition attached to it" (2005, 98). This formalist approach echoes that of those who hear Glenn Gould's *The Quiet in the Land* (1977) as pure form. According to this model, the composer makes use of Mennonite content as raw material, but the formal result renders that content irrelevant. The question remaining in this case is what kind of meaning is left in the *Kernlieder*? Do the tunes, stripped of words, represent ethnicity in some folk or *Volk* way independent of religious faith? Whatever uneasiness there was among Mennonites about that question was hidden behind responses to more technical matters such as tempo. The songs might have been familiar to Davies, but perhaps he was not aware that Mennonites sing them slowly. If you imagine "Amazing Grace" sung quickly, it provides some idea of how a *Kernlied* sounds to Mennonite ears when the tempo is increased.

The *Mennonite Piano Concerto* premiered on 27 October 1975 with pianist Irmgard Baerg and the Winnipeg Symphony Orchestra under the direction of Bill Baerg. In his review of that performance, Al Reimer wrote that the concerto, "for all its tunefulness and zest, was a disappointment" because "it does not succeed in capturing the essential Mennonite spirit and vision" (quoted in Letkemann 2007, 416; Reimer 1975, 15). Members of the Fast family were upset at first that the old hymns were "jazzed up," but Letkemann reports that they gradually "came to like it" (416). As have countless other radio listeners. The recording of the concerto that features Irmgard Baerg on the piano with Boris Brott conducting the London Symphony Orchestra has been "a frequently requested work on Canadian Broadcasting Corporation (CBC) radio, and is also a regular favourite on classical music radio stations in the United Kingdom, Europe, Australia, and the United States" (Davies 2005, 98). The enthusiastic reception of the concerto seems to prove Horch and Davies correct in their joint assumption that songs are not sacred in themselves and can be transformed into "a completely secular form" when detached from the worship context (98).

But where does that leave the question of ethnic identity? The concerto invites comparison with compositions produced in the United States during the time of Roosevelt's New Deal. Roy Harris's *American Symphony* (1938), for example, similarly used a medley of tunes to popularize and package national identity. A measure of Horch's success in this regard is that the concerto is now associated with the "originary myth" of the Russländer as a result of being the soundtrack for a docu-drama entitled *And When They Shall Ask* (1984). As the train carrying the refugees who make a harrowing escape from Russia in the 1920s comes closer to the boundary that will mark their freedom, they sing a *Kernlied* about taking refuge under the soft feathers of God: "Unter deinem sanften Fittich." The song is a translation into German of a hymn composed by W. Warren Bentley, a nineteenth-century American composer, entitled "In the Rifted Rock I'm Resting." The singing of the song in the film happens in normal tempo, making it all the more striking when the tune speeds up and instrumental music drowns out the community singing. For me, this "worked" the first time that I saw the film. It seemed fitting that the familiar melodies would be defamiliarized to become a strangely racing tune during the nightmare journey of escape in which Mennonite refugees are jammed into cattle cars. When I saw the film again, however, I was not so sure. There is a showbiz sense in the concerto that anything goes. Even Gershwin's *Porgy and Bess* join in the fun at one point. When I heard it performed live by pianist Irmgard Baerg, very belatedly, I was thrilled. When I hear snatches of it on the radio here in Toronto, however, I am often less than thrilled, annoyed by what feels like a glib distortion of musical history.

Can the melodies, stripped of their words, still be heard as representing the faith of a particular group of people? Is the fate of the songs related to the fate of the people who sing them? What are we to make of deliberate Mennonite accents when they become part of a medley? One indication of the wider influence of Horch's views on Mennonites and folk songs is apparent from the work of ethnomusicologist Kenneth Peacock, a well-known scholar of the music of ethnic minorities in Canada. Peacock was on the staff at the National Museum of Man (predecessor of today's Canadian

Museum of History) in Ottawa when he recorded the music of what he then called "the Plains Indians" and the folk music of Newfoundland. During a trip to Winnipeg in 1962, he also recorded *Kernlieder*, and it was Ben Horch who served as his guide and arranged a recording session in the Mennonite Brethren Church in North Kildonan. It is worth quoting at length from Peacock's notes to those recordings because they provide an admirably succinct account (doubtless acquired from Horch) of the convoluted genealogy of *Kernlieder*:

> The Mennonite Kernlieder are actually American gospel songs which migrated from America to Mennonite groups in Russia over the past two hundred years. The songs were, of course, translated from English into German which often meant altering melodic stresses to fit the new language. After the Russian Revolution most of the Russian Mennonites migrated to Canada and brought their hymns with them. They are now in the process of being re-translated from the German back into English by some of the more progressive Mennonite groups in Manitoba. The original English versions are not used. The Kernlieder are so named because they contain the kernel, so to speak, of the gospel truth. . . . The four-part harmony is similar in feeling to the Lutheran chorale, but there are also overtones of the Wesley-type English hymn. (Peacock 1962, 116)

There is much that remains unclear to me in this account about how this migration of music happened.

For Horch, the success of the concerto must have been gratifying. I am tempted to think of it as his victory over the fundamentalists who kept blocking his musical career by insisting on "music with a message." But was Horch correct in seeing *Kernlieder* as Mennonite folk songs? Folklorists tend to think of folk songs as the product of collective and anonymous authorship, but all the *Kernlieder* that I know have micro-histories related to the lives of particular composers. Horch seemed to go, instead, by a definition like that of Hans Joachim Moser, a German musicologist: "Folk song is that which the people sing constantly and regard as their treasured possession" (quoted in Letkemann 2007, 236). The distinction between sacred and secular music is problematic to begin with, but can a sacred song be made secular, or turned into a folk song, simply by leaving out the words? Within Mennonite contexts, all such questions draw attention to the fault line between ethnic and religious identity that runs deep in Mennonite history.

Hindsight is easy, but the organic metaphor that Horch used to describe his "corn songs" slides easily into essentialized descriptions of ethnic groups. When they are applied to the history of any *Volk*, they can set up a further slide into *Blut und Boden* thinking. Loose definitions of folk music often tap into the deep roots of German nationalism. It would be surprising if Horch, during his year of folk song studies in Germany, was not influenced by the writings of Johann Gottfried Herder, who coined the term "folk song" and developed a new way of talking about music and history (see Herder and Bohlman 2017). I find myself wondering whether Paul Hiebert and Ben Horch ever met and whether they talked about music and language. As a philologist with an aversion to German-based Mennonite nationalism, Hiebert would surely have found Herder's writing problematic. My impression is that Horch was ambivalent—both attracted to and repelled by ethnic definitions of music. Toward the end of his life, he seemed to commit himself with increasing evangelical fervour to the project of multiculturalism, with a focus not on Mennonites but on reaching out to other cultures.

Like Hiebert, Horch was Mennonite but not Mennonite enough, his creativity located on that boundary where sparks fly. Repeatedly, in spite of a remarkable strength of character and resilience, he had what we used to call nervous breakdowns. His role at MBBC finally ended when he himself defined it as the place where his vision for music exceeded the theological limits set by the college. The enormity of his contribution to music culture in Manitoba is beyond my telling here, but the successes and failures of his efforts on behalf of Mennonite culture make for poignant reading if, as I do, you think of them as part of a complicated love story.

It is important to keep in mind the larger historical context of the *Mennonite Piano Concerto*. Treating tunes as if they are independent of words has been common practice in church history for centuries. Hymn books are full of well-known tunes with new words written for new contexts. The meaning of any song depends on particulars of both text and context, as suggested by Maureen Epp in an essay on the sixteenth-century

Anabaptist hymnal called the *Ausbund*. With her close analysis of several songs, Epp challenges the idea, put forward by Rosella Reimer Duerksen, that the various available melodies "transcended" religious differences. For the Anabaptists, according to Duerksen, "a tune was not to be associated with a specific group or a specific doctrine, but the common property of all" (quoted in Epp 2005, 46; Duerksen 1956, 116). This is much the same position as that taken by Horch and Davies with relation to the tunes used in the *Mennonite Piano Concerto*. Epp demonstrates clearly that, for at least some of the *Ausbund* hymns, their "borrowed melodies do not 'transcend the realm' of differences between the Anabaptists, Lutherans and Catholics so much as carry with them residues of earlier meanings" (46–47). The same tune when used in a Lutheran church or a United church or a Mennonite church is bound to be accompanied by residues of meaning that vary with the contexts. Even when stripped of all words, as in the *Mennonite Piano Concerto*, a tune has historical resonance as soon as it is performed in a particular place. As Epp suggests, "sometimes a tune [is] more than just a tune, more than a neutral vehicle for conveying a set of words" (46).

The questions about the inception and composition of any work are bound to resonate most in the particular place where it was created. I was therefore curious, when I interviewed musicians in Winnipeg, to hear their responses to the concerto. I found that any question on the topic tended to evoke an evasive response. This is understandable since, in the absence of a clearly defined aesthetic context, there is always the risk of personalizing the conflict. There was widespread concern not to disrespect the composer, Victor Davies, and even more profound reluctance to badmouth Ben Horch, referred to by one person as "a saint." When pushed, however, one musician finally conceded that "I hate the *Mennonite Piano Concerto*." Another described it as "tacky." A third said that it was a "travesty" that Horch threw a couple of favourite Mennonite hymns at a non-Mennonite composer and said, in effect, "Here. Make something for us with these." The most thoughtful response to my questions came from Howard Dyck, who has conducted the *Mennonite Piano Concerto* four times: in Kitchener, Ontario; in Sofia, Bulgaria; in Kunming, China; and in Winkler, Manitoba. In an email to me on 30 December 2017, Dyck wrote that "although I've always had my reservations about the piece . . . it has nevertheless steadily grown on me. It may just be that it is Davies's 'non-Mennoniteness' that allows him to uncover aspects of those Kernlieder that we Mennos would not have seen, encrusted as those hymns are with decades of emotional and historical significance for many of us. . . . I've come to believe that it's precisely the courage to venture (on Davies's part) where angels fear to tread that makes the concerto so strikingly original, enduringly popular, and strangely 'authentic.'"*

Whatever their different opinions of the concerto, none of the musicians whom I interviewed suggested that Victor Davies was appropriating Mennonite music. That would be an absurd accusation since the *Kernlieder* are songs that Mennonites themselves have stolen from other groups. There is no escape from the promiscuity of musical traditions. That said, there is surely no point in pretending that the history of particular groups (whether Lutheran or African or Mennonite) is not important. Nor is there any point in pretending that we do not have strong feelings about the songs that resonate with the history of our people. The mistake is in assuming that it can be engineered, as Horch attempted to do. To label the music and sell it as a Mennonite product is to turn it into a commodity. Stories about exile and music lend themselves all too readily to romantic packaging; however, even if the texts are taken away and everybody is humming along to the same melody, the histories of the different people who sing the same song are not irrelevant. Geraldine Balzer has observed that songs become part of a "cultural narrative" (2015, 286). Just how this happens is not clear to me, but the reception of the *Mennonite Piano Concerto* shows that there are many competing cultural narratives, even within a single ethnic or religious group.

As Paul Gilroy (1991, 127) has pointed out, group performance of music "can produce the *imaginary* effect of an internal racial core or essence" (quoted by Graber 2005, 67; emphasis added). The important word in that sentence is *imaginary*. An "imaginary effect" is created when Mennonites sing a hymn known to many as "606," which refers to the song's page number in the *Mennonite Hymnal*. The hymn is a particular setting of the doxology "praise God from whom all blessings flow." I have

---

* Howard Dyck, email to the author, 30 December 2017; quoted by permission.

heard it often referred to as "the Mennonite anthem," but I did not hear that version of the doxology until I met American Mennonites at conferences. Balzer observes that "606" is "part of the rhetoric of belonging, the story Mennonites have chosen to tell," but that as a "marker for those who belong" it can also serve to "marginalize others" (2015, 287). Such differences are not to be lamented. On the contrary, they are a useful reminder that a community that appears to be monological while singing is in fact, if it is a healthy community, dialogical.

I come back, then, to my opening questions, the ones that go to the heart of our foundational gesture. If Mennonites are in the world but not of the world, then how does this relate to how we make music? BC composer Larry Nickel's *Requiem for Peace* is a choral piece suggesting that Nickel has given this question a lot of thought. He is the son of Mennonite missionaries to India. His *Requiem* appears untouched by the anxieties about music and message that motivated the commissioning of the *Mennonite Piano Concerto*. Far from abandoning words, Nickel collected them. The *Requiem* is based on the texts of pacifist poetry in thirteen languages, not only the English, German, and Latin familiar to choristers but also Farsi, Mandarin, Dutch, Swedish, and other languages. The piece premiered in 2005 in Vancouver, and in 2012 it was performed by the Orpheus Choir in Toronto, under the direction of Robert Cooper. In the program notes, Cooper stated his belief that "choral performance must express the social condition and strive to be a transformative force." He added that, "with Nickel's deep Mennonite faith, strong pacifist beliefs and beautiful lyric score, 'Requiem for Peace' does this and more."

When I asked Randolph Peters about his creative process, he referred to Bruce Chatwin's book *The Songlines* (1987), an account of what Chatwin learned from the nomadic cultures of the Indigenous people of Australia. Peters summed up Chatwin's paradigm for me: "The whole world is a labyrinth of songs. They tell you where you've been and where you're going." If the "you" referred to designates a tribe or religious group, however, then this paradigm raises as many questions as it answers. Certainly the concerted effort to identify and preserve the songs of the Mennonite *Volk* and affix them to the history of all Mennonites has demonstrated the exact opposite. Perhaps it remains possible to think of the *Kernlieder* as songs that tell one immigrant group, the Russländer, where they come from and where they are going. Even then, however, there is no neat alignment between historical narratives and what songs "tell" us about our past. The musical dispersion that accompanies a Mennonite geographical diaspora cannot be packaged. If you try, then the songs escape.

"Sing unto the Lord a New Song": Going Solo

While trying to determine whether or not there has been a change among Mennonites who make music that could be seen as parallel to the literary renaissance, it occurred to me that perhaps the single most important thing is not the content of their music but the fact that some musicians have been willing to go solo. Anxieties about representation are embedded in questions about belonging to a community, as Mavis Reimer made clear when she observed that musicians, unlike writers, produce their art "within the discipline of the community" (1997, 118). On the basis of this assumption, she concluded that "the fracture of sender from message can be terrifying" for writers because it is at the same time "a challenge to the notion of a Mennonite community and a logical extension of Mennonite theology" (120). In fact, however, it is rare for musicians to stay put in one particular community, and even if they do the music itself is reproduced and travels. As for terror during creation, writers are not alone in that regard. Making music by singing in a choir is one thing. Singing solo is a step beyond that in terms of potential performance anxiety. To go solo by composing music is another story altogether.

Community values have long been expressed through choral singing, and many of the composers write choral music. It might be more difficult for musicians than for literary artists to go solo. During an interview with ethnomusicologist Jonathan Dueck, singer-songwriter Cate Friesen gave expression to the enormity of this challenge. She described herself as having to "make a break with the Mennonite church" in order to become a songwriter. To "write from my own voice and tell my own story, and put myself on stage, not as part of a choir . . . but as my own voice . . . involved a 'fight against . . . that whole sense [that] the community and family come first and individual needs come second'" (Dueck 2005, 164). The sin of pride looms for musicians who excel within Mennonite communities. Conductor Henry Engbrecht remembers people saying *Dei meint zick uck vaut.* He means himself also something. Which is a Low German way of asking: Who do you think you are?

An important distinction needs to be made, in this regard, between performance and composition. Going solo as a classical performer has not been a serious problem, judging by the number of Mennonite singers who have won the coveted Rose Bowl competition in Winnipeg's annual music festival. Going solo by composing music, however, was almost unheard of among Mennonites until after 1980 and is not mentioned in Berg's (1985) history. During roughly the same time as the literary renaissance, there can now be discerned a smaller but distinct phenomenon—the emergence of composers from various Mennonite backgrounds. To the names of recognized composers such as Glenn Buhr, Leonard Enns, Stephanie Martin, Larry Nickel, Randolph Peters, and Carol Ann Weaver (Janacek 2005, 144) should be added the names of individual singer-songwriters who perform either alone or in various groups. The dispersal of the music scene and my distance from Manitoba makes it impossible to provide a list of these performers. For every name I might list here there would be a dozen I do not even know about. Hybrid forms are increasingly common as composers dare to cross the boundary separating classical from all other kinds of music. An advertisement for the Elora Festival in the spring of 2015, for example, captures the range of Glenn Buhr's compositions: "When he's not composing for the Elora Festival Singers, Montreal Symphony Orchestra, or The Verdi String Quartet, Glenn Buhr is bringing the house down with his Button Factory Band. This four-piece group is an energetic blend of vintage blues, jazz, country, roots music and art-rock."

A mixed style also characterizes the work of Carol Ann Weaver, a prolific composer whose cultural translations are shaped by her travels. Most compelling about the body of her work is her commitment to collaboration and her willingness to move into and out of various communities, as if in an embodiment of her name: Weaver. As a Swiss Mennonite born in the United States, Weaver has also facilitated cross-border dialogue, often working in collaboration with both American and Canadian poets. Her influence is widespread as a result of a series of conferences that she hosted at Conrad Grebel College under the title Sounds in the Land.

As I have argued in relation to literature, Mennonite accents do not make up some sort of template that can be imposed on art but result in a resonance that sometimes makes one aware of a Mennonite sensibility. I heard Mennonite accents, for example, at the 2016 premiere of Stephanie Martin's *Babel*, based on the text of a poem by her sister Cori Martin. The accents came through to me as a result of the conscious exploration of the tension between *melos* and *logos*. I heard a different variety of Mennonite accent during a Good Friday concert by the Toronto Mendelssohn Choir in March 2016. The concert included both old and new works, and one of the latter was by Leonard Enns. It was a choral piece based on the text of Psalm 121, which begins "I will lift up mine eyes unto the hills, from whence cometh my help." The accent that I heard came from Enns's interpretation of those familiar words. There was a questioning that reminded me of the Jesse Nathan essay "Question, Answer" (2015), in which he hears accents that result from an Anabaptist tradition of dissent. I am not suggesting that anybody else in that cathedral heard this as Mennonite or should have done so. Readers with greater musical sophistication likely heard musical echoes that I did not hear given how many times that particular psalm has been set to music. Later, however, when I read Enns's comments on the composition in program notes, they confirmed my intuition that I was hearing the traces of a Mennonite legacy: "Psalm 121 is typically read, and often set musically, as a text of assurance and comfort. My setting is similar in that regard. What I find compelling, though, is the second phrase of the psalm: 'from whence commeth [*sic*] my help (?).' Many musical settings treat the phrase simply as a modifier (no question mark) … (take, for example, Mendelssohn's 'Lift thine eyes'). Most current translations, however, treat it as a question."

I have barely touched on what looks to me like a Mennonite musical renaissance that is still occurring. If it were not for the fact that the more visible literary renaissance draws attention to it, this musical phenomenon might well have remained invisible. I do not see that as any cause for concern. It is surely one lesson to be learned from the stories that I have told that reducing music to a verbal message destroys the music, whether that message is a theology or a collective identity. My own experience, however, and that of Mennonites whose stories I have heard, do not make it possible for me to opt for a formalist aesthetic. Music does not transcend the material out of which it is made. It just uses that material to communicate in languages that are beyond words.

Sola Gratia: "What Shadows We Are and What Shadows We Pursue"

Confronted with the riddling complexities that bedevil any critic who attempts to compare different ways of making art, Michael Fried concludes that "I am tempted far beyond my knowledge to suggest that . . . it is, above all, to the condition of . . . a continuous and perpetual *present*—that the . . . contemporary modernist arts, most notably poetry and music, aspire" (1998, 167). In the famous last two sentences of that essay, Fried concludes that "we are all literalists most or all of our lives. Presentness is grace" (168). Grace is a concept that has come up frequently in my conversations with musicians. It was violinist Bill Derksen who first alerted me to how it can be seen as a response to the problem of "music with a message." Derksen told me that he agreed with Sandra Birdsell that Mennonites are engaged in a "joyless search for meaning" (1982, 98), adding that "what we are missing is grace." After listening to all my interviews with musicians, it seemed to me that he gave voice to what is a widely shared aesthetic. Many musicians, unknown to each other, echoed Derksen. Doreen Helen Klassen, for example, told me that she is drawn to the Anglican Church, "where there is an emphasis on grace. That's something that I really missed in the Mennonite context." Randolph Peters expressed the view that there are "various problems with Mennonite theology" and that the main one is "a kind of behaviourism." Mennonites, he said, are intent on "the idea that we are out there creating the Kingdom of God" when in fact "we are much more in need of grace." When I interviewed Stephanie Martin, the concept of grace was implicit in her account of how she is drawn to "the ritual and the sacramental effect" of the High Anglican liturgy. Many of the musicians whom I interviewed were educated in Mennonite institutions, drawn there by the excellence of the music programs. Having studied Anabaptist history, they might well see how the principle of *sola scriptura* has been distorted by print-based literalism. Music, then, becomes a way of countering with an insistence on *sola gratia*.

What I take away from the stories and songs that have swirled around me during the writing of this chapter is a lesson of respect—respect for the integrity of particular kinds of music and for the history of that music but also respect for difference, for other people's varieties of nostalgia and ways of making do. There has never been a time when I have felt this at a deeper level than on the day when I listened to Rennie Regehr play his viola in Mount Pleasant cemetery at the graveside of my husband, Clarence Redekop. I had requested that he play just before the burial, during the time when a single dove was to be released. When that ritual was suggested to me by the undertaker, at first I said no because it sounded like a gimmick. Then I said yes. At such times, you reach for any comfort, however small the shred. With the first notes that came from Regehr's viola, I recognized a familiar *Kernlied*. As he played, the undertaker slowly removed the cover of the wicker cage that contained the dove. I expected the bird to fly away instantly, but it sat, turning its head toward the music, as if mesmerized. The friends gathered around laughed a little, but the dove just listened along with us while Regehr made the viola sing. He played with what Ben Horch once described as that "'utter simplicity' of expression [that] requires the utmost in musical training" (quoted in Letkemann 2007, 262). After a few bars, the dove lifted itself gracefully into the air, soared up, and gradually vanished. I looked at the grief-stricken face of my mother-in-law and was deeply grateful that Regehr had chosen to play a *Kernlied*. This was a song of my husband's people, who were therefore also my people. I could not recall the words of that particular *Kernlied*, but I could tell from the face of my mother-in-law that the song comforted her. If she had been asked, she probably would have talked of heaven, but to me it seemed as if the song told her where she had come from and where she was going. Sometimes a tune is more than just a tune.

CLOWNING WITH MASKS*

Shputt nich. Dei uel haft uck en zoejel.

Mock not. The owl also has a tail.

In January, 2008, I decided to take a course in Pochinko clowning that I had seen advertised on a billboard during a visit to Spain. The poster caught my attention because the method was described as "Canadian Clowning." I had never heard of such a thing but was intrigued by the information that Sue Morrison, the woman who was offering the course, had trained some of the clowns that perform with Cirque du Soleil. Later I learned that "Canadian Clowning" was a method developed by Richard Pochinko using a mixture of European and Indigenous traditions, and that it involved the making of masks. All this appealed to me at that time in part because I was ready to move past the linguistic clowning that I had done as Sush Funk. I had the vague idea

---

* With gratitude to Sue Morrison and all the other baby clowns in my class.

that this course would be a good way to test the Latin aphorism coined
by Giambattista Vico, an eighteenth-century professor of rhetoric:
Verum esse ipsum factum. James Groetsch translates this as "the truth
is the same as the made" and notes that in Vico's "metaphysics of the
body" metaphor "is not an abstraction or an observation but a true act
of original *poiesis*" (29–30; 32).

I quote these high sounding words because they are applicable to
the argument of this book. At the time, however, I had no idea how
challenging this would be in practice. Early every cold morning for six
weeks I took public transit to an address on Gerrard Street, in the east
end of Toronto. It was an echoing warehouse called Centre of Gravity,
which struck me as an odd misnomer. There I subjected myself to the
discipline dictated by Sue Morrison, a remarkable clown teacher. The
goal was for the "baby clowns" in the class to earn a red plastic nose,
but the course was rewarding in ways that I cannot begin to describe
here. Suffice it to say that I gained a hands-on experience of playing on
a boundary where making and making believe are hard to tell apart.

The course required each of us, a group of about twenty clowns
from around the world, to make six masks out of clay and papier
mâché. The making of each mask was followed by a series of exercises
designed to explore both the innocence side and the experience side of
that mask. Although some of these exercises involved storytelling, this
kind of clowning was not really about words. Each mask was worn only
once. On that day, a costume trunk was opened, and we were allowed
to construct our own costumes, like children playing dress-up. This was
followed by anarchic dance. After that event, the mask was not worn
at all. The assumption was that the qualities of that mask had been
internalized by this process. Every clown then designed and performed
for the others a solo act based on that mask. We were allowed to
choose our own costumes but required to wear that ridiculous plastic
red nose. After every such performance, Sue would ask the rest of the
clowns "Did you believe?" It is a daunting challenge to be told not that
you must make people laugh and cry (they are supposed to happen as
side effects) but that you must make them believe so that they will feel
transformed afterward.

The making of my first mask was wrenching beyond anything that I had anticipated. Blindfolded and with our hands resting over a cold wet lump of clay, we were instructed to make an image that we would later make into a mask. Instantly I imagined my fingers as the spreading branches of a tree and pressed down hard to make them. Overcome with an unaccountable urgency, I hastily turned the lump around and did the same at the other end—imagining the spreading roots. There remained only the job of connecting the two halves with a trunk, and this was easily done, even blindfolded. I scored a rectangle of clay with my thumbnail to make bark, thinking at the same time how ridiculous a thing is a nose. At that stage, I was inordinately pleased with myself. Sue Morrison expressed surprise when I signalled that I was finished so soon, but she agreed to remove my blindfold. The shock was intense. There was plenty of time to contemplate the mess that I had made and weep all over it since the other clowns in the class took their time to make more meticulous images. Afterward I remembered the shock of looking at the misshapen clay and thought of Victor Frankenstein's failed efforts. That experience has led me to refer in this book to a Frankenstein effect when talking about responses to the making of art. We were not allowed to cheat by reshaping the clay, so my first papier mâché mask would be made, layer by layer, on this ridiculous object. It looked more like a tree after we had gone through the mask-painting ritual. I call my first mask *Boum*/Tree.

My favourite mask is the one I call *Fesh*/Fish. Depending on which is up and which is down—it could also be some kind of owl. Do owls have tails? As a child, not having heard of Till Eulenspiegel, I wondered about the maxim that was used to repress those of us who had a tendency to *shputt* or mock. I assumed then that it meant something like this: You think you see everything with those big eyes but you have an earthy body just like the rest of us.

Four of the masks that I made were creatures of some kind. Each time I finished and then saw what other clowns had made, I was surprised by their inventive abstractions. All that I could ever think of was being different kinds of creatures. Only later did I notice how many of my creatures had noses that might be something else—fins or wings or handles. I came to realize that a big part of clowning is dealing with

self-pity. It took me quite a while to come to the humbling realization
that wearing an uncomfortable and silly plastic nose while people
laughed at me was stirring up a childhood memory of having had my
nose bloodied by a bully during recess.

I did make one abstract mask, but only because I told myself in
advance not to make yet another creature. I could not break completely
free of representation and found myself imagining a volcano.
Something about not being able to project my self-pity into one of
those pathetic creatures may have put me in touch with some deep
rage. I remember painting one of the volcanic craters orange and then
thinking that it looked too angry. So I added blue at the top to hint at
sky, green at the bottom on a shape that might be a leaf, and purple on a
blob that could be some kind of beetle. I called it "Loch/Hole."

We were instructed to choose one mask for a final performance,
to which family and friends were invited. I chose the mask that I call
Kjniepa/Bug and decided to perform the experience side of it. For
inspiration, I reached back, as I mostly do when I create anything, to
memories of my mother. She would often exclaim about the beauty of
roses. Art cannot compete, she would say, with God's creation. When
it was my turn that night, *Kjniepa* appeared on the stage wearing her
hard-earned red clown nose and a floor-length blue velvet cape. She
carried a vase with a single beautiful pink rose. A real one, not a fake.
She produced a container of pink playdough and set out to show
off to the audience how well she could make a flower. To help in the
goal of realistic representation, she peeled a petal off the real rose so
that she could copy it. Then another. And another. The result was
predictable. The playdough rose was revealed as hideous at just the
moment when the real rose had been completely destroyed. Overcome
with frustration, *Kjniepa* knocked over the vase, spilling water over
everything. She tore off her velvet cape, revealing that she was dressed
underneath in Stanfield combination underwear. Hastily she wrapped
up the entire mess with the cape and then, clutching her bundle, made
her ignominious exit to the sound of laughter.

6.

ICONOCLASH
REDECORATING THE SPIELRAUM

Väh daut kjleene nich eht
Ess daut groute nich veht.

Who the small does not honour
Is not worthy of the great.

"The Stage Is Set": Dialogue with Tear

The first time that I saw Wanda Koop's *Tear* I was mesmerized. As I stood
still in front of it, tears came to my eyes, followed by self-conscious laughter at my aping of the image. The hook that drew me in was recognition.
I saw it *as* a teardrop (Plate 4). At the same time, something made me
question that assumption. Koop herself has commented that the painting
"has a strange effect on people when they see it." She reports that her ten-
year-old niece, "with a quivering voice," pronounced "'It's God's teardrop.'"
Her somewhat older nephew said "'It's a globular mass'" (Koop 1996, 21).
Tear has been exhibited with a series called *Native Fires*. Mary Reid reports
that the lights along the waterfront in that series look to her like "stylized
elongated fluorescent orange tear drops" (2010, 70) (Plate 5). A similar
yellow shape is stretched in another painting to the point where it could

be mistaken for another kind of tear—a slash or rip in the canvas. In *Art and Illusion*, his influential book on the psychology of representation, E.H. Gombrich argued that the beholder's response to this kind of "visual ambiguity" involves matching up the image with pre-existing categories or "mental sets" (1960, 60). He emphasized that this rational process comes after the act of making, which unleashes "the secret hopes and fears that accompany [any] act of creation" (1960, 94). Ovid captured these feelings in *Metamorphoses* with the story of a sculptor called Pygmalion whose statue, Galatea, comes to life.

The term "Pygmalion effect" refers to what happens when the maker of art beholds his own work (Gombrich 1960, 94). Where does this leave the beholder of *Tear* who is not the maker but also not content to simply match up the shape with some pre-existing category? Here, in this place of uncertainty, "the beholder's share," to use the term made famous by Gombrich, is to join the maker in the dialogical process of making believe that is the subject of this book. My own experience of an actual making with clay happened while I was part of a group of clowns, all making masks and then beholding each other's creations. I think of what I experienced as a "Frankenstein effect" because I imagine the *Spielraum* of art as a contact zone inhabited by tricksters or clowns. This zone is made visible by the reception of Mary Shelley's *Frankenstein: A Modern Prometheus* (1818) which, as the subtitle shows, dramatizes a turn to modernity. Far from being thrilled, like Pygmalion, by a sculpture that exceeds his wildest expectations, Frankenstein is horrified. Significantly, the "being" is never called a monster in the novel. A blind man provides hospitality to him and listens to the story transcribed in the novel. The reception of the novel, however, has consisted of cinematic efforts to visualize the creature, and during this process of perpetual translation he has been given the name of the man who made him.

Koop's *Tear* is no monster, but any work of visual art that leaves the viewer in a state of uncertainty can be experienced as threatening. This is related to how we respond to icons, as poet Sarah Klassen suggests with the wordplay in the title of her book *Monstrance* (2012). In Chapter 4, I described Rudy Wiebe's fiction as a rewriting of *Frankenstein* in order to show how it deals with anxieties about representation. As I turn my attention now to the place of the visual arts in Mennonite culture, I feel myself approaching the hot centre of these anxieties. To counter these I will make an appeal to hospitality, as Wiebe does in his fiction and as do all the artists I will write about in this chapter. I keep in mind, however, that collective Mennonite anxieties are a tiny part of a larger global crisis of representation. All artists now have to survive in what I have heard Koop describe as a "killer culture." Ours, in the words of W.J.T. Mitchell, is a "culture dominated by pictures, visual simulations, stereotypes, illusions, copies, reproductions, imitations, and fantasies." Mitchell defines the danger as "secular idolatry" and notes that it is "a commonplace of modern cultural criticism that images have a power in our world undreamed of by the ancient idolaters." He adds that "the real miracle has been the successful resistance of pictorial artists to this idolatry" (1994, 2). When images multiply exponentially, it is often impossible to determine agency. It is indeed a "real miracle" when artists are able to respond with an act of making that carves out a space, however small, for freedom. My task in this chapter is to consider the part played in this miracle by Canadian artists whose Mennonite ancestry requires them to perform it while dealing with the legacy of Anabaptist hostility to images.

In my Introduction, I suggested that a painting in Koop's *Hybrid Human* series could be seen as staging the crisis of representation (Plate 2). In *Tear*, Koop restages it again, working what Deborah Koenker has called "the blurred boundaries between landscape, portraiture, the figure and abstraction" (n.d., 52). In Canada, the modernist paintings of the Group of Seven still act as a template when we look at quasi-abstract landscapes. If you try to look at *Tear* the way that you might look at a Lawren Harris, the slanted horizon almost makes you tilt your head as you deal with the back-and-forth pull between outer space and magnified close-up. The painting brings to mind the Latin phrase *sunt lacrimae rerum*. Seamus Heaney translated it as "there are tears at the heart of things" (2008). I am aware, however, that the painting that makes me cry might leave others unmoved.

In *Pictures and Tears: A History of People Who Have Cried in Front of Paintings*, James Elkins (2001) puzzles over the reasons why people now tend to look at paintings with dry eyes. No less a person than Gombrich himself confessed to Elkins that he had never wept in front of a painting. With his account of viewers' responses to paintings in the Rothko

Chapel, Elkins shows that strong emotions remain part of our responses to paintings. Who's afraid of abstract art? That question is deflected by an online visual joke called "Amish Christmas Lights," which consists of a black square in a white frame. How is that different from a painting by Mark Rothko? One explanation that people gave Elkins for why they found themselves crying in the Rothko Chapel is also a good description of why I cried in front of *Tear*: "Sudden, unexpected, out-of-control *presence*." Elkins defines this feeling of "sudden plenitude" as "a religious feeling" (174) and notes that it might be accompanied by a paradoxical sense of "painful absence" (195). The virtually unanimous opinion of the art historians consulted by Elkins, however, was that tears are "unprofessional, embarrassing, 'feminine'" (96). The same goes for giggling. Why did I do both in front of Koop's *Tear* in spite of being a scholar, and what, if anything, does this have to do with the fact that I am a Mennonite? Elkins blames his inability to cry on the fact that he knows too much art history (85–87). Did I cry simply because I do not know enough? So I find myself drawn into a territory where a scholar, especially one named Magdalene, risks being dismissed as maudlin.

I stage my small personal crisis for reasons similar to those that I put forward when I dramatized my own nostalgia in an earlier chapter. In the absence of a written social history that deals with Mennonites and art, doing so might provide an entry into questions that are seldom addressed by Mennonite scholars. This is not because my response is typically Mennonite but because the ways in which it is atypical might provoke a much-needed dialogue about a range of different responses. Since my argument is that only dialogue brings art to life, it would defeat my purpose to simply offer static descriptions of an object. The lesson of *Frankenstein* is that questions about reception must be addressed if we are to make some space for free play and genuine dialogue within this "killer culture." This being the case, I am always on the lookout for indications of how Mennonite viewers interact with art. The awkward truth is that I have only anecdotal evidence on which to base any generalization. My conversations with Mennonites of my generation suggest to me that among them there is no love lost for abstract expressionism, but I know younger Mennonites who are informed art collectors. These are only impressions. In an earlier essay, I dealt with the lack of evidence by imagining myself as wearing the mask of a "'Mennonite' spectator" (Redekop 1999). In her thoughtful response to that essay, artist Susan Shantz rightly questioned this strategy and wrote that "in my experience Mennonites are more likely to *not* see art than to see it" (1999, 106–7).

At the risk of sounding obstinate, I think it worth pointing out the obvious—that refusing to *see* art is in itself a response and that doing so does not, in any case, make the art go away. No matter what you say or do in front of *Tear*, it is still hanging there after you walk away from it. Unlike music, which invites us to associate the spiritual with the ephemeral, the art of painting or sculpture is more like an incarnated presence. Koop has said that "the spiritual aspect of being Mennonite is very intense" and that this "has had a profound effect" on her work (1986, 96). The trouble for many viewers begins when the artist claims to have somehow embodied this spiritual experience, not in some song that vanishes but in a tangible object. In an essay entitled "Mennonites and the Artistic Imagination," Margaret Loewen Reimer offers a dramatic account of her response to the illustrations in a book on liturgical fabric art. "For a Mennonite reader like me," she writes, "the book should have contained a warning: 'Beware the shock of encountering the spirit made visible'" (1998, 18). And that was only the illustrations. If Reimer was right to assume that her "shock" was part of a broader Mennonite experience, then it is surely astonishing that conversations on this subject happen so seldom among Mennonites.

Although I abandoned my effort to define a "Mennonite spectator," I remain interested in how Mennonite responses to images (or failures to respond to them) might be inflected by our history. In "Mennonites and the Arts: An Unsettled Past," for example, Eleanor Martens confesses, with disarming candour, that art galleries make her feel that she is "on alien ground." She suspects "that there are other Mennonites, perfectly at ease in a concert hall," who share her "discomfort in an art gallery" (1994, 9–10). The apparent assumption behind this contrast is telling—that art is there to provide comfort and make us feel that we belong. My approach, like that of Margaret Loewen Reimer, is based on a contrary presupposition: that good visual art involves deliberate alienation from fixed ways of seeing—what Gombrich termed "mental sets." The playwright Bertolt Brecht coined the word *Verfremdung* to describe the distancing that is part of the performance arts, and Viktor Shklovsky (1965) took it further,

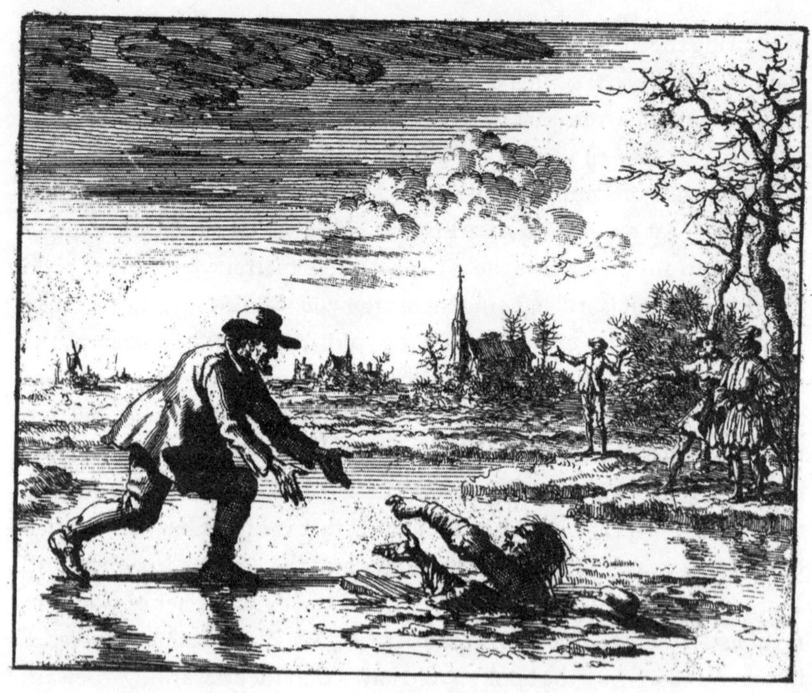

Figure 9. Jan Luyken, *The Martyrdom of Dirk Willems* (1569). Etching (*Martyrs Mirror*, 1685 ed., vol. 2, 741). Courtesy of Mennonite Archives of Ontario, Conrad Grebel University College.

arguing that the experience of estrangement or defamiliarization is central to the power of all art.

How is this estrangement related to the sense of awe that is part of religious experience? Like many viewers, I see *Tear* as among the signs that made up Wanda Koop's breakthrough 1983 exhibition *Nine Signs: Hayroll, Heap, Container, Stump, Raven, Transformer, Incinerator, Antenna, Rock.* Each of these "signs" is estranged. Robin Laurence writes that each of them takes on "an iconic or 'primal' presence" (2010, 20). When does a sign or an image become an icon? Is *Tear* an icon? The Greek word *eikōn* means image or likeness and is used by Orthodox Christians to indicate that Jesus is a visible image of the invisible God. Confusion about what an icon is sometimes surrounds Mennonite responses to the illustrations by Jan Luyken in the *Martyrs Mirror.* Most popular among these is Luyken's illustration of the 1569 martyrdom of Dirk Willems. The pursuer of Willems fell through the ice in a pond and Willems turned back to rescue him (Figure 9). This Good Samaritan act did not save him from being burned at the stake (Van Bright 1950, 741). Nancy Heisey, a professor of Biblical Studies at Eastern Mennonite University, refers to this as the "quintessential Anbaptist image" (Heisey 2012, 356). In 2007, when she was president of the Mennonite World Conference, Heisey presented Pope Benedict XVI with "an icon of Dirk Willems, written by iconographer Jivko Donkov, based on the copper etching [*sic*] by Jan Luyken" (Heisey 2012, 355). She observes that afterwards historian James Juhnke "engaged [her] in a lively debate about the appropriateness (or lack thereof) of our gift" (355), but it is not clear from her report whether either of them questioned the decision to refer to it as an icon. Certainly the story about Willems is flattering to Mennonites,* which may be why it has provoked self-mocking responses such as a series of pen and ink drawings by Ian Huebert. These include, for example, a cartoon entitled: "Views from a Pond: Dirk—Cat and Mouse" (Beachy ed. 2010, 215). If you assume that the original is an icon, then Huebert's playful revisions could be called iconoclastic. If my intuition is right about the resonance of stories about the sixteenth-century Low

---

* Sculptor Peter Sawatzky was commissioned to create a life-size statue of it as part of a peace exhibit at the Mennonite Heritage Village in Steinbach, Manitoba (Warkentin 2018).

German trickster Till Eulenspiegel, then this kind of iconoclasm has been a part of Mennonite sensibility for centuries.

At the level of popular culture, all you need to do now to be iconoclastic is to admit that you do not like Celine Dion. Often the word *iconic* appears to be a synonym for *nostalgic* or *archetypal* or even just *popular*. At the same time, however, the word *icon* is routinely used in an older, narrower sense as referring, for example, to the tiny picture of a printer on a computer screen. Reduce the size of *Tear*, and it could serve as an emoticon. Laurence describes *Nine Signs* as "portentous, almost hieratic, signs" and writes that the paintings reflect Koop's "ferocious need to speak to people" (20). Just what is it, then, that Koop is trying to say? Nancy Tousley translates by reaching for a literary analogy when she describes *Nine Signs* as having "the directness and simplicity of Biblical parables or cautionary tales" (quoted in Reid 2010, 58). It is a good choice since parables, like *Nine Signs*, communicate mystery or enigma. The insight offered feels a lot like blindness. Indeed, you might already be protesting that you see nothing much in *Tear*. The validity of that response is reflected in many of Koop's titles. *In Your Eyes*, for example, was the title of the exhibition by Koop that resulted from a trip to Ukraine with her mother to visit the sites of family traumas. As far as I can tell, there is nothing that a viewer could point to in the abstract paintings that are part of that exhibition to prove that they represent the fall of the Mennonite Commonwealth.

The anonymous viewer who scrawled "Wanda Koop should be hanged" in the visitors' book of a gallery might or might not have been a Mennonite. Perhaps he or she was a curator with a taste for ironic puns. Reflecting calmly on the comment as a death threat, Koop speculated that people become angry because they don't know "the language of art" and conclude that artists are "trying to make them look stupid" (1986, 96). Awareness of this problem, she explained, sometimes leads her to use familiar images and then transform them, as she did in *Tear*. Surely all viewers, not only Mennonites, must feel a degree of relief when the artist admits that she started by intending a particular "globular mass" to look like a familiar teardrop. However, as Northrop Frye pointed out, "the function of the recognizable in the arts is not aesthetic but anaesthetic. A painter of cows in a field is bound to be addressing some people who want to be reminded of cows more than they want to see pictures" (1980, 9). There is an undeniable pleasure in such recognition, but in Koop's art it becomes part of a process inseparable from what we talk about together while looking at pictures.

I begin my entry into this process by assuming that pictures talk to each other. I am not referring to literal conversations among artists, although those do happen on occasion. I have no idea, for example, whether or not Wanda Koop ever converses with Gathie Falk about art. What fascinate me are the resonances that happen in between works of art when two artists share a collective history, as do Falk and Koop. What, then, does *Tear* have to say to the art made by Gathie Falk? Consider the conversation going on between *Tear* and Falk's *Development of the Plot III: #1 The Stage Is Set* (1992) (Plate 8). Both paintings stage a crisis of representation, but Falk's surrealism invites questions about narrative. What is the plot? What play is being staged? Who is the audience? What is that grey object at the top of the canvas? What *deus ex machina* is responsible for that bunch of flowers? I imagine myself entering Falk's picture and sitting down on one of those inviting chairs. If others were to join me, then I might observe that the grey shape hanging over us bears some resemblance to the "globular mass" in Koop's *Tear.*

Does Falk's painting represent some kind of church where people are waiting for enlightenment from above? Is that stage in fact an altar? My discomfort makes me conscious of having arrived once again at the place that I have come to think of as the vanishing point of this book. Is it worth labelling any of this as Mennonite? Or will doing so make others feel excluded? There is some evidence that Falk herself has pondered such questions. I have never met her, but I wrote to her in 1992 requesting slides for a lecture that I was preparing. She wrote back that "I have no axes to grind. . . . I therefore think my work has very little to do with my being a Mennonite."* In the same letter, however, she responded to an essay that I had sent to her: "There was a lively discussion about it in this household and there were disagreements with some of the ideas in it. Of course, that is the Mennonite way. It's a good way." Robin Laurence reports, however, that, when Falk was asked to paint a mural on the dome of the little Anglican church in Vancouver where she now worships, at first she refused,

---

* Gathie Falk, letter to the author, 1992.

"not so much out of Anabaptist iconoclasm as out of a practical apprehension of the 'discord such work usually breeds'" (2000, 131). Eventually, however, she made *Heavenly Bodies, Stars and Moon* and *Heavenly Bodies, Suns*. Like all her art, it is charged with ambivalence about icons.

Although it is gratifying to have graphic proof that Falk would agree with my emphasis on dialogue, even going so far as to call it "the Mennonite way," it is important to note that she is an influential artist in Canada because the dialogue that she generates is *not* peculiar to Mennonites. It is also the Jewish way and the Muslim way and the Indigenous way. That circle of chairs in the painting is *not* a representation of a Mennonite church. As Laurence (2000) has pointed out, however, Falk's play with iconography is so persistent and complex that it does invite viewers to ponder how it might be related to her Anabaptist ancestry. The questions raised by *Development of the Plot III*, like the ones stirred up by *Tear*, are left hanging. Mystery is what draws me in to engage with the picture, but I am aware that some viewers will conclude that the whole thing is a pointless postmodern exercise in futility. I would direct such viewers to note that this is a painting in a series that has an ending: *Development of the Plot III: #8 Conclusion* (Plate 9). Here the grey shape has split and resolved itself into two figures, a man and a dog. The stage is still there, but the upper half of the painting is filled with light bulbs, a recurring image in Falk's work, suggesting the possibility of moments of epiphany or grace.

When I pay attention to the conversation between *Tear* and *Development of the Plot*, I come away with the sense that both artists are interested in exploring varieties of religious experience. The beholder who wishes to join that discussion would be advised to follow the advice of Gombrich and abandon the assumption that progress wiped out "a primitive stage of man when all was magic" (1960, 112–13). The historical development of that view is laid out by Keith Thomas in *Religion and the Decline of Magic* (1971). W.J.T. Mitchell argues that "magical attitudes towards images are just as powerful in the modern world as they were in so-called ages of faith" (2005, 8), but the default critical position now assumes that all art is secular. Yasmina Reza's celebrated play *Art* (1996), for example, is assumed to present a secular dilemma. The "dialogical object" around which the drama swirls is a painting that is entirely white. Does it matter at all that Yasmina Reza and Mark Rothko are Jewish? How could it not? Yet our "distinctly modern condition," in the words of Joseph Koerner, is one in which "the private experience of art … replaces organized religion as [the] site of spiritual transcendence" (2004, 9). Many abstract expressionist artists, indeed, have promoted their art as part of a "spiritual revolution" (Besançon 2000, 341). Dominant in all such models are the interiority and alienated individualism assumed to come with modernity. These conflict with the high value attached to community in Mennonite culture, a value that I see as a powerful idealization in *Development of the Plot III.*

Idolatry: An Intimate History

Whenever questions about Mennonites and art multiply, as they did during my dialogue with *Tear,* I try to follow the advice of Fredric Jameson: "Always historicize!" (2002, ix). When I do this I come up against the enormous gap in scholarship to which I have already drawn attention (Stoltzfus 1998, 77; Visser 1994, ix). Church historians and theologians mostly ignore art history. This is a conspicuous blind spot since the Protestant Reformation is a crucial context for conflicts about art. Joseph Koerner describes that period of European history as a time when "images were broken, burned, toppled, beheaded and hanged. They were spat, pissed, and shat on, tossed into toilets, sewers" (2004, 12). In *The Stripping of the Altars: Traditional Religion in England, 1400–1580,* Eamon Duffy (1992) argues that the destruction of centuries of popular visual traditions constitutes a collective trauma from which we have not yet recovered. When I try to discern the historical roots of Mennonite conflicts about art, my intuition tells me that they lead back to the same struggle against the dominance of the Word that was my focus with relation to music. *Sola scriptura.* I imagine the gigantic finger in that well-known portrait of Menno Simons pointing to a specific text: "Thou shalt not make unto thee any graven image, or any likeness of anything that is in heaven above, or that is in the earth beneath" (Deuteronomy 5:8) (Figure 5). Centuries of Mennonite repression are based on this text, and it has been used to reinforce the "myth of aniconism" that underlies plain style. David Freedberg describes this as the myth "that there can be a culture that has no images of the deity at all" (1989, 54). This is an educated guess on my part but I cannot point to a body of scholarship that provides evidence for it.

The most glaring gap in Mennonite study of the visual arts exists with relation to the Dutch Golden Age. There has been speculation for centuries, to be sure, about Rembrandt's Mennonite connections. Reflecting on this fact, art historian Stephanie Dickey concludes that whether or not Rembrandt was Mennonite, he painted scenes of martyrdom as if he were (1996, 93; see also Covington 2011). In a lavishly illustrated book focusing on Rembrandt's Mennonite dealer, Hendrick Uylenburgh, Friso Lammertse and Jaap Van Der Veen show how thoroughly Mennonites were enmeshed in the cultural and economic life of the time (2006). Perhaps the most egregious example of a scholarly blind spot is the life of Karel van Mander, the poet and painter who is sometimes referred to as the Dutch Vasari. Piet Visser calls him a "striking example of orthodox Mennonitism [who] embraced the Dutch Renaissance cult of classical Antiquity" (Visser 1994, 71). Van Mander's *Schilder-Boeck* (Book on Picturing) was published in 1604 and remains influential, as Walter S. Melion shows in *Shaping the Netherlandish Canon: Karel van Mander's* Schilder-Boeck (1991). Melion describes van Mander's approach to a painting of the golden calf as an optical dilemma that "poses the problem of what and how we see, calling into question the kind of pleasure we take in the image" (5). It apparently did not occur to him to wonder whether this question might have anything to do with Mennonite views on idolatry. Indeed, as far as I can tell, there is not a single mention in the book of Van Mander's Mennonite beliefs. In a two-page conclusion, Melion uses Bruegel's *Parable of the Sower* as a case study to sum up his argument about van Mander's influence on our way of thinking about picturing (183–84). The possibility that this way of reading the Bible might have something to do with being Mennonite, once again, does not come up.

In the absence of scholarly frameworks, I am often at a loss when dealing with my personal responses to art. I am all too aware that some readers will consider me to be the central case study. This is not a comfortable realization for a Mennonite conditioned to think that the ego must be repressed at all costs. I am often reminded of lines from a sonnet by Gerard Manley Hopkins: "I am gall, I am heartburn. God's most deep decree / Bitter would have me taste: my taste was me" (Hopkins 62). Unlike Hopkins, I do not blame God for this situation and unlike him I have no choice but to deal with this "decree" as a woman. Saint Augustine defined idolatry as the "subordination of the true spiritual image to the false material one" (quoted in Mitchell 1986, 32). The fact is that centuries of male efforts to eliminate idolatry have been inseparable from the relentless efforts to control the unruly bodies of women. W.B. Yeats wrote about a deep longing to find a space for creation where "the body is not bruised to pleasure soul" (1963, 244). I believe a Mennonite renaissance has happened because so many artists have acted on that longing and I consider it no coincidence that many of them are women. The objectification of women by a male gaze is a well-known constant in art history. In *Ways of Seeing,* John Berger describes how a woman is "split into two. A woman must continually watch herself. She is almost continually accompanied by her own image of herself" (1972, 46). This passage echoes the words of W.E.B. DuBois, who described the "double consciousness" of being black as "this sense of always looking at one's self through the eyes of others" (1961, 17). Although the otherness of being racially different and of being a woman should not be conflated, dissociation may be intensified for a person who is other not only because of gender but also because of ethnicity or race. Such questions are explored eloquently by Pamela Klassen with relation to Mennonites in an essay entitled "What's Bre(a)d in the Bone: The Bodily Heritage of Mennonite Women" (1994).

The adolescent Nomi in *A Complicated Kindness* clearly has her female body in mind when she lists all the things that are forbidden to Mennonites: "dancing, smoking, . . . movies, drinking, rock 'n' roll, having sex for fun, swimming, make-up, jewellery" (Toews 2004, 5). Nomi's list matches my experience closely. Even as I laughed the first time that I read it, however, I was thinking about things that she left out. For example: Christmas trees. Toews grew up in a liberal home and is younger than I am, but even by the standards of our community my father was unusually strict when I was an adolescent in the 1950s. It was never entirely clear to me why we were forbidden to have a Christmas tree. The only reason that I remember being given was that my father thought it an idolatrous practice. All the children in the one-room school that I attended were Kanadier Mennonites, and all claimed they had Christmas trees in their homes. Despite his considerable power in the community as an Ältester, my father did not protest when a tree was displayed in Roseville School for the most thrilling event of the year, the annual Christmas program. When that tree was lit up on

Christmas Eve, it was a glory to behold and to smell. Once, while singing along with "O Tannenbaum," I snuck a look at my father sitting on a plank along with all the other parents. It looked very much as if Ältester Wilhelm Falk enjoyed looking at that tree too. After which the preacher and his family went home to an undecorated house.

It was my mother who taught me, by example, the many creative forms that resistance can take. She followed the rules carefully and made no effort to challenge her husband's edict on matters such as Christmas trees and jewellery. She even taught her daughters that it was a sin for a woman to cut her hair, a sin for which you could go to hell. Even bangs were forbidden. It was the Apostle Paul who was to blame for this rule (1 Corinthians 11:15). What compromises she made inwardly I do not know, but scissors never touched my mother's hair, and she always kept her head covered with a small kerchief. She showed by example, however, how irrepressible the imagination is. Nothing could stop my mother from painting flowers on the cement floor of the basement if that was what she set her mind to do. Her love of colour was so intense as to be like intoxication. She indulged it with a large collection of gloxinia—a flowering house plant with velvety petals. The cobalt blue of Noxzema jars so delighted her that she could not throw them out. Instead, she took off the labels and painted flower patterns on them with "liquid embroidery" that she had ordered from some catalogue. One of them is on my desk, a container for paper clips. Propped up against it is a postcard I picked up in some gallery shop, an exquisite "illumination" by Pacino di Bonaguida entitled *The Communion of Mary Magdalene* (c. 1340). This Magdalene, dressed in her own hair like a wild beast, has fallen on her knees but at the same time hovers in mid-air as she receives the host.

My parents called me Magdalene simply because they had used up all the more popular biblical names for my six older sisters. At home, I was Maglena, easy to say, but school was another story. When I abandoned braids and opted for a ponytail in grade eight, bullies called me Mag the Horse, Meg being a common name for horses at the time. Since I wore glasses, the maxim about owls also having tails must have seemed apt. By coincidence, I have a name that I am required to spell out repeatedly for people. Each time I do so it implicitly leads back to the figure of a woman who resides on a precarious borderline between madonna and whore. Mary

Magdalene is the object of the male gaze, the woman who wept on the feet of Jesus and then dried them with her hair (Luke 7:38). After visiting numerous art galleries in various countries, I have come to the conclusion that there is not a single gallery that does not feature somewhere, in some room, an image of this woman waiting to ambush me. The fact that she is called *the* Magdalene surely says it all. My inner clown sometimes mutters that she hopes the sex was good since the poor woman has endured centuries of penitence for it. The many ways in which the Magdalene gets her hair styled are celebrated by art critics in the language of abstruse iconography. Once, while in a small gallery in Bruges, I was absorbed in the art of the Flemish Primitives for which I have a particular fondness. Stepping up close to a small painting, I was ambushed once again. There she was, cowering abjectly and totally covered with her own hair, like some animal or some metal musicians I know.

In *Reading in Detail: Aesthetics and the Feminine*, Naomi Schor observes that every scholar has an idiosyncrasy, and if you "catch it in the act" you behold the scholar's family (1987, 7). Her father was a goldsmith, "a master of the ornamental detail." Schor acknowledges her double motivation to valorize details as part of a "feminist hermeneutics" and to give "value" to her father's craft (7). A similar family motivation lies behind my approach. I seek to give value to the lives of my parents while challenging the ideologies that restricted their freedom to create. With the epigraph to this chapter, often spoken by my mother, I honour her example. As I learned while writing my book on Alice Munro, Virginia Woolf was right that, when a woman insists on having her subjectivity (or that of her mother) acknowledged, it has the potential to turn basic assumptions about art inside out. My heightened sensitivity to iconoclash is almost certainly the result of the peculiarities of my upbringing. I cannot look at Gathie Falk's streamers and fir trees, for example, without remembering my father's rule against Christmas trees.

Who knows where the feelings any of us bring to art really come from. Awareness of the multiple unknowns is reflected in the title of the National Film Board film about Wanda Koop's journey to Ukraine: *In Her Eyes* (2000). There is a dreamlike sequence in that film following the fate of a severed braid of hair which the camera eye discovers in the drawer of a dresser. Decades after seeing that film, I watched Amalie Atkins's

"Requiem for Wind and Water" on my computer screen. During a series of ominous overlapping scenes with witch-like figures and young girls in braids, a pair of scissors appears suddenly and a braid is cut off. I gasped.

Talking About Art: "Ekphrastic Fascination" and Iconoclash

The more intense my response to art, the greater is my need to find ways of entering into dialogue with others about it. As Margaret Loewen Reimer has observed, such dialogue cannot begin until we question our assumptions about what is "real." She follows up with a radical idea. "Inferior art (or would-be art)," she writes, "is the real violation of the commandment against images, for it circumscribes and limits the possibilities of the human spirit. It confuses 'real life' with what comes naturally. . . . True art, sometimes through abhorrent means, strives to expand our experience of reality, to reveal more angles of the truth. But that may mean less certainty" (1998, 17). Uncertainties about what art means often reflect anxieties about status, and dialogue ends in a stalemate when it turns into a quarrel between snobs and philistines. The same uncertainties, however, can stimulate useful dialogue when tastes are acknowledged to be interactive and intersubjective.

This everyday experience is captured by Charles Schultz in a *Peanuts* cartoon. The children play a game that I remember from my own childhood on the prairie. Lying flat on their backs, Charlie Brown and Linus are ordered by Lucy to use their imaginations and describe what they see in the clouds. Linus waxes eloquent, describing a series of scenes that ends with an "impression of the stoning of Stephen." He announces that "I can see the Apostle Paul standing there to one side." When Lucy calls on Charlie, he says, "Well, I was going to say a Ducky and a Horsie, but I changed my mind!" I can't help seeing Linus as the Menno in the picture, quickly matching up an ambiguous image with scripture and then speaking with authority. Most viewers will identify with Charlie, the lovable loser, and recoil from Linus's reductive reading. This cartoon is one example of ekphrasis, a rhetorical device that has become central to all my thinking about art. At a basic level, the word refers simply to a verbal description of a visual work of art. The study of ekphrasis on a broader level enriches our understanding of how cultural translation works. This simple cartoon dramatizes the crisis of representation, complicated here by the fact that there is more than one person responding.

When people perform ekphrasis together, the person with the most power sometimes tries to dictate meaning for the whole group. Within a dialogical aesthetic, the perpetual imbalance of power is compounded by an ambivalence about images that many art critics now also see as perpetual. W.J.T. Mitchell usefully describes this in relation to ekphrasis. He identifies a moment of "ekphrastic hope" when we want to overcome the "otherness of visual representation" but argues that this moment coexists with a state of "ekphrastic fear" in which the hope "that the mute image be endowed with a voice" begins to look "idolatrous and fetishistic." The result of this ongoing tension is that we hover in a state of "ekphrastic fascination" (1994, 152–56). There is a constant vacillation "between magical beliefs and sceptical doubts" that Mitchell sees as "a deep and abiding feature of human responses to representation" (2005, 7–8). Bruno Latour, with reference to the same perpetual ambivalence, coined the term "iconoclash," which Joseph Koerner glosses as a "mix of having images and having done with images" (2004, 12).

I have invoked this rather elaborate terminology because it has helped me to understand what I am seeing in art that I define as part of a Mennonite sensibility. It is most often when I attempt to historicize art by Mennonites that I become conscious of iconoclash. Jan Luyken, for example, is well known to Mennonites for his illustrations in the *Martyrs Mirror* but these are talked about as if they were an isolated phenomenon. Sarah Covington has shown that Luyken's ways of seeing were belated and influenced not only by earlier martyrologies but also by the artists working around him during the Dutch Golden Age (Covington 2011). Simon Schama comments particularly on how Rembrandt influenced Luyken (1997, 491–93). It was after reading this that I noticed how many of Luyken's engravings manage to have an icon and have done with it at the same time. Often there is a cross, yet there is not a cross. Luyken's engraving of the martyrdom of Anneken Hendriks, for example, represents her bound to a ladder that is about to be thrust into the flames (Figure 10). Knowing of Rembrandt's influence on Luyken, I browsed through a collection of Rembrandt drawings and found a sketch made in preparation for his 1633 painting *The Raising of the Cross* (Benesch 1947, #30).

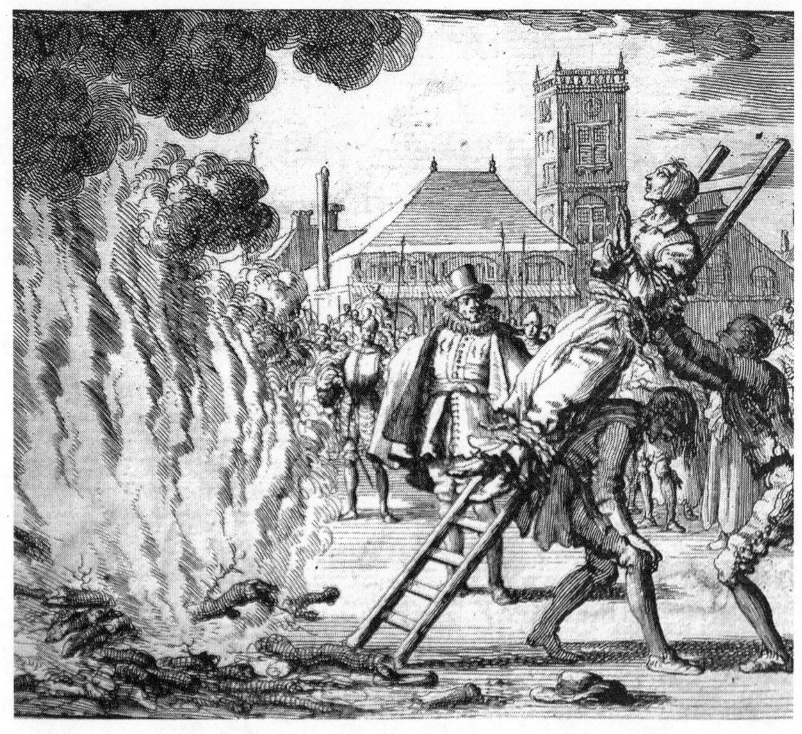

Figure 10. Jan Luyken, *The Martyrdom of Anneken Hendriks* (*Martyrs Mirror*, 1685 ed., vol. 2, 539). Courtesy of Mennonite Archives of Ontario, Conrad Grebel University College.

The composition bears an uncanny resemblance to the engraving of Anneken Hendriks.

Perhaps iconoclash is more noticeable in art by Mennonites because the struggle is conscious, sometimes even theatrical. In any case, I experience much art made by Mennonites as similar to what Mitchell sees in the writings of John Milton. He describes them as "the scene of a struggle between iconoclastic distrust of the outward image and iconophiliac fascination with its power" (1986, 36). I think of both iconoclash and "ekphrastic fascination" as roughly analogous to the Frankenstein effect that I experienced after making my first Pochinko mask. I prefer the word *iconoclash* because I like how the *clash* in it conveys how sparks can fly in a contact zone when people talk about images together. As I engage with works of art in this chapter, I will be on the lookout for instances of iconoclash, relating them to what Michel de Certeau calls "the practice of everyday life" (1988). This level playing field includes famous people who are making art and ordinary people like Charlie Brown who are just "making do." Art, however, does have a special status because it is a form of making believe that "'authorizes' a playing-space (*Spielraum*) to be produced" (de Certeau 1985, 141).

Such an authorized space becomes a theatrical scene of ekphrasis in Miriam Toews's *Irma Voth* (2011), a novel that has become a touchstone for my thinking about the relationship between art and life. In that novel, three sisters run away from their home in a Mexican Mennonite colony and arrive in Mexico City. The youngest sister is a baby, and the oldest, Irma, is an adolescent. The middle sister, Aggie, is a child artist whose name echoes that of two well-known Mennonite artists—Gathie Falk and Aganetha Dyck. Irma is a translator, a significant part of Toews's aesthetic, but she is also a surrogate mother to her sisters. After their arrival in the city, Aggie runs away repeatedly, and each time Irma is frantic. After one such vanishing, Irma finds her sister in the National Palace "staring at a massive mural" by Diego Rivera. Aggie's "face was covered in snot and she spoke in the spaces between her sobs. . . . It is making you sad? I said. No, she said" (173). Toews is casting children here to restage the famous scene of ekphrasis found in Virgil's *Aeneid* summed up with the same Latin tag that I have already attached to Koop's *Tear*: *lacrimae rerum*. Aeneas (his face wet with tears) looks at a painting of the Trojan War and speaks these words: "*sunt lacrimae rerum et mentem mortalia tangunt*" (*Aeneid* 1.462).

Loosely translated this says that there are tears for things, and we are moved by mortality. Even as Aggie cries, the reader laughs, and together these responses convey a sense of how much is lost in translation while we take in any work of art. I read the simultaneity of tears and laughter as a reminder of the iconoclash that is present in varying degrees in all our responses to art. This ekphrastic scene is emblematic of the argument of this chapter, and indeed of this book, that art provides a space where we can deal with the crisis of representation by making believe together and by participating in dialogue.

Although I have found the concept of iconoclash to be a helpful framework, it can become counterproductive when it is applied in static ways. If you look *for* something in any work of art, you are almost certain to find it. If, for example, I look at the geometry in the signature paintings of Piet Mondrian and think about his strict religious upbringing, then it is hard not to see crosses that are not crosses. There is nothing much to be gained from identifying iconoclash in that way and the art of Gathie Falk often anticipates the tendency of viewers to look for that kind of certainty. There are numerous paintings by Falk that invite iconographic interpretations while simultaneously erasing them. *Chair with Fish and Maple Leaves* (1985), for example, combines a fish and nails in such a way as to make it nearly impossible not to visualize a crucifix or to think of the fishermen who followed Jesus. The power of Falk's art, however, is in how the viewer cannot walk away from it clutching some reductive meaning. You have to go look at it again.

This is easiest to do when you own a work of art, which is at least one reason why people collect art and hang it on the walls of their homes. There is a painting by Wanda Koop that I have seen often because it hangs in the home of my nephew Jeff Neufeld and his wife Katrina Lee Kwen (Plate 6). Not far from it hangs a Gathie Falk silkscreen print from a well-known series called *Crossed Ankles* (1998). I am intrigued by how the crossings in these two works, both done in signature styles, seem to speak to each other. My nephew and I have always referred to his Koop as *Green Cross*. In May of 2019, however, when I requested permission to reproduce it here, he checked the back of the painting and confirmed with Wanda Koop that it is entitled: *Sightline – Green Crosshair.* While I am intrigued by title changes, as are many art critics, there is in my view nothing to be gained by aiming for precision about what an artist intended to represent. Everything that matters happens in between the painting and the people looking at it.

Curating as Hospitality: How to Redecorate a Spielraum

In his study of traditional Kanadier house designs in Manitoba, archaeologist Roland Sawatzky notes that calendars were sanctioned decorations because they were useful. He reports that in many homes calendars were "the main source of decoration." Some people, however, hung them above eye level so as to minimize temptation, and "some families removed the pictures from calendars because they were considered worldly" (2005, 180). I remember doing the opposite in my room on the farm. I detached the pictures and thumbtacked them to my wall in a row at eye level. Many decades later I found myself lining up paintings on a wall at the University of Toronto. It did not occur to me then to call myself by so grand a title as curator. I was simply doing my share of administrative work at Victoria College. Although the shows I organized during that time had nothing to do with Mennonites, I have a vivid memory of the thrilling moment in 1975 when I first saw a work of art by Gathie Falk. I was strolling through the National Gallery of Canada in Ottawa when I turned a corner and came upon *Herd Two* (Figure 11). Created with pencil on white enamel paint, these carousel horses made out of plywood were exhibited in a separate alcove all to themselves. They nearly took my breath away. When I looked to see who had made them, I was startled to see my own "maiden" name: Falk. Although I wondered whether we might be related (we are not), I was only mildly interested in what these flying horses might have to do with Mennonite culture or history. I remember having trouble pulling myself away from *Herd Two*, but I had no context at all for the intensity of my response.

In the spring of 1990, I puzzled over Falk's *Hedge and Cloud Series* at the Isaacs Gallery in Toronto and could make little sense of it. In July of that year, however, I was in Winnipeg and saw an exhibition of art curated by Priscilla Reimer and hosted by the Manitoba Mennonite Historical Society. It opened my eyes to the fact that a flowering of visual art by Mennonites was happening alongside the explosion of literature by Mennonites that had happened during the 1980s. In the essay that Reimer wrote for the exhibition catalogue, she observed that "there is no identifiable tradition of Mennonite art" unless one includes "fraktur,

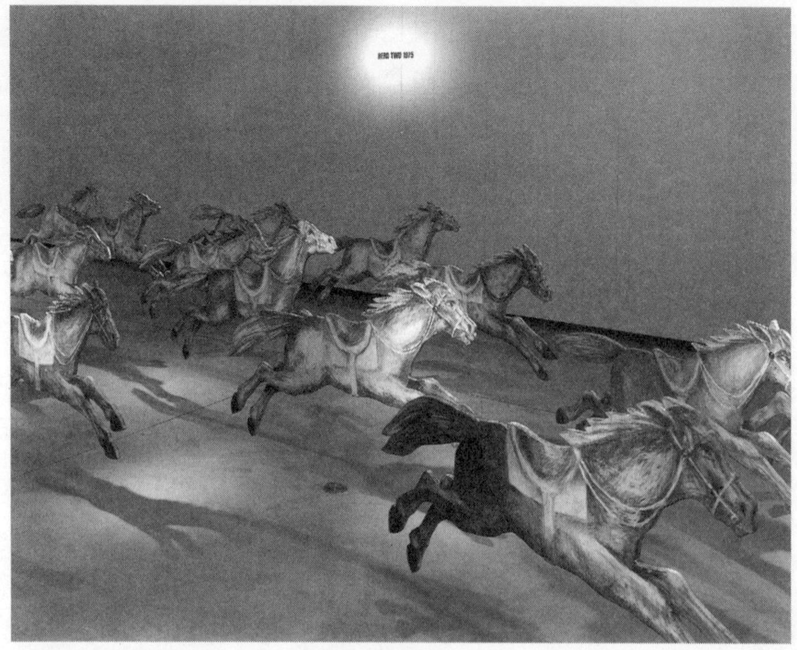

Figure 11. Gathie Falk, *Herd Two*, 1975, plywood with pencil over white enamel paint. Photo of installation view, Vancouver Art Gallery 1975. Collection National Gallery of Canada, Ottawa. Courtesy of the artist.

quilting, and other forms of decorative design" (1990, 5). The logical next step caught my attention immediately, though Reimer did not spell it out. If we do include the decorative arts, then we do have an identifiable tradition of Mennonite art. As early as 1988, Hildi Froese Tiessen noted the "impulse of so many Mennonite artists: to foreground the pragmatically familiar deprived of its function," noting how "Gathie Falk preserves shoes in cabinets" and Aganetha Dyck "preserves (mock) fruit in jars" (1988b, 22). When deprived of their functions, then, are these shoes and fruits "merely" decorative? The question touches a charged line that separates interior design from high art. As Gombrich notes, it was "a sensitive, not to say a neurotic point in twentieth-century criticism" to make certain that abstract art must be "far removed from the humble craft of decorative design" (1984, 62). Gathie Falk echoed this collective concern when she told Robin Laurence that she was "leery of the marginalizing connotations of craft and domesticity" (Laurence 2000, 73).

Falk's art does not aim to make a viewer feel comfortable. On the contrary, she often estranges familiar furnishings and ornaments in bizarre ways. My purpose here, however, is to begin by increasing the level of comfort for beholders. I hope to counter the dominant view that an art gallery is like a church, a place where the images are sacrosanct and where meaning is controlled by some art critic who speaks an abstruse language. To focus on interior decorating is to begin on a level playing field and on common ground. E.H. Gombrich provides evidence that the decorative arts are "rooted in man's biological heritage" (1984, xii) and that the "urge to expend vast amounts of energy on covering things with dots and scrolls, chequerboard or floral patterns" is universal and necessary to our very survival (1984, xii). If this is true, then it is not surprising that decorative art has flourished among Mennonites, as it has among Jews and Muslims, even when representational art is forbidden. Gathie Falk has always resisted having her art associated with feminine crafts. Her recent memoir, *Apples, etc.* (2018), however, includes stories that show how decoration and hospitality are intertwined for Falk at deep levels when she shares her art. In conversation with Robin Laurence she describes, for example, how she supervised the construction of the kitchen floor in her new house. "I wondered if I was crazy," she writes, "demanding painted checkerboard floors—not linoleum tiles or painted concrete but painted wood, which is so much warmer" (162). When Falk's friend Elizabeth Klassen has hung the curtains she made, Falk marvels at the beauty of "the shiny grey-and-white checkerboard floors" and throws "a small housewarming party for family and a few close friends" (163). The spirit of hospitality is so powerful in *Apples, etc.,* that when I finished reading it I found myself thinking that if Frankenstein's creature were to appear on the threshold of their home, Gathie Falk and Elizabeth Klassen would welcome him with open arms and listen to his story.

Since 1990, when Priscilla Reimer put together her exhibition, there has been an astonishing proliferation of visual art by Mennonites in Canada. In response to this embarrassment of riches, I found it helpful to begin by imagining myself as a curator responsible for putting on an exhibition. I went so far as to sketch an outline for a gallery with rooms that helped me map out the historical contexts. As it turned out, however, this was no ordinary art gallery because I could not stop myself from thinking of myself as needing to offer hospitality. In fact it was a lot like a house. The *groute shtove* (big room) contained benches where visitors could sit down to take time with pictures. There was a flower room dedicated to my mother, a children's play room and a quilting room. As my exploration uncovered ever increasing numbers of artists, however, I eventually had to admit that the diagram could not accommodate my ways of responding to the art. Although I abandoned it, the room divisions remained useful to some extent. All the walls are porous, however, and my primary goal here is to extend hospitality to readers interested in questions about Mennonites and art. I invite readers to look at selected pictures with me and join me in testing my hypothesis, which is that Mennonites who make art often call on the resources of decorative traditions as a means of dealing with our "killer culture." Because my focus is on the Canadian renaissance, the artists are primarily from the Dutch/North German ethnic stream now known as Russian Mennonite, and many of them grew up on the prairie. I picture myself in the early stages of preparation in which pictures are still lined up on the floor awaiting decisions.

Gathie Falk and Iconoclash

Near the entrance to my gallery, I would provide an opportunity for visitors to view *Red Angel*, designed and performed by Gathie Falk on 1 May

1972 at the Vancouver Art Gallery. This would be a way of honouring her pioneering role in Canada. Her performance art during the 1960s was part of West Coast Funk. It cracked open old rigidities and anticipated the more recent trend toward interactive and collaborative art. I see it, at the same time, as part of the larger Mennonite counter-awakening that challenged the rigidities of fundamentalist thinking. Daring and bizarre as they often were, the performances offered dramatic evidence of the need to explore multiple languages across mediums. *Red Angel* was not recorded on that day in 1972, but a restaging of it can now be seen online.* The piece begins with Falk sitting on a red sideboard wearing a white dress and huge white wings constructed from foam rubber and chicken feathers. In front of Falk are five tables, each holding a turntable on which is a red apple on which is a red parrot. In a 1990 review of *Red Angel,* John Bentley Mays describes it as one of the "quietly joyful works" produced with "members of Falk's Mennonite community in Vancouver." In them, "if only for a moment, there was peace on earth and freedom from the hungry games of power. There was the loveliness of cherishing ordinary things—from cabbages and eggs to old songs and old friends—as an act of religious gratitude and blessing, and the beauty of dwelling on the earth in the bonds of kindness." The title of this review labelled Falk a "Mennonite Artangel," but Falk herself made no grandiose claims for her performance art. Her aim, she said, was to contrast ordinary actions—such as eating an egg or washing clothes—with "slightly exotic events such as shining someone's shoes while he is walking backwards singing an operatic aria . . . sawing popsicles in half and using them as weapons of assault and defence" (1987, 310). These images do not suggest either Mennonite pacifism or the exotic so much as a children's world of make believe in which tiny things become epic.

When Robin Laurence questioned Falk about Scott Watson's published view (1985) that her "entire oeuvre" can be interpreted "in the light of her difficult life and her strong Mennonite faith," Falk responded that she "disagreed with Watson's reading, feeling he wasn't informed enough about Mennonitism to make analogies between its beliefs, rites and sacraments and her own imagery" (Laurence 2000, 99). Her wariness

---

* See https://front.bc.ca/events/red-angel/.

should be considered in relation to the political events happening during the early stages of her career. Following the 1967 centennial celebrations, Joyce Wieland was showing how feminine crafts could be practised in a way that could shake up colonialist rigidities. Her 1971 show *True Patriot Love* invited viewers to see Canada as a woman who was the victim of a double rape by the United States and Great Britain. There is no denying the liberating impact of Wieland's bold iconoclasm. I think, for example, of *Arctic Passion Cake*, an installation made of styrofoam and sugar that allowed you to have your icon and eat it too. *Reason over Passion* is made out of quilted cotton and constructs an ironic folk art frame around words from a speech by Prime Minister Pierre Elliott Trudeau. Word and image are in tension but saturated with the politics of 1968.

The iconoclasm of Gathie Falk is of a more subtle variety. She creates iconoclash in ways that resist reductive interpretations. My gallery includes some of the quilts that Falk created. The first of them, *Beautiful British Columbia Multiple Purpose Thermal Blanket*, came about when she was asked by a committee to "warm up" a space in the British Columbia Credit Union building in Vancouver. Made up of large canvas squares of painted flowers, it was a gargantuan task, completed with the help of her friends (Lind 1989, 11). Falk went on to make an obsessive series of more gigantic quilts as gifts for friends, but she insisted to Robin Laurence that the series "was not alluding to quiltmaking traditions." She preferred to think of the work as "a 'sculpted painting' or a highly painted relief-sculpture rather than a quilt" (2000, 73). I would be tempted to put up a sign in front of this exhibit with the words *This Is Not a Quilt*—echoing a surrealist painting by Rene Magritte known as *This Is Not a Pipe*.

Word and Image

The most visible thread of argument that I carry forward from the previous chapter is a movement from the tension between song and word to the related tension between word and image. In my gallery, I would look for ways to involve viewers in an exploration of this tension and to suggest historical contexts for it. One way to do so might be to consider what hangs on the walls in Mennonite homes, but this would need to be done with an awareness of differences that depend on time and place. The walls of Mennonite homes in Amsterdam during the time of Rembrandt, for example, would have been graced by art. The economic developments during the Dutch Golden Age produced a middle-class group of *liefhebbers*—passionate art collectors, many of them Mennonite, who amassed large collections. The descendants of those Mennonites moved first to Prussia and then to Russia, where they eventually once again became both makers and collectors of art. This pattern is now being repeated in Canada, but my own earliest experience with art was as part of the pioneering Kanadier group.

When I was growing up, Christian "plaques" were often the only decoration on the walls of Mennonite homes. These wall mottoes served to enforce the fundamentalism that took root in southern Manitoba after the revival movement. The earlier art of *fraktur*, however, was free of the need to communicate an evangelical message and it helped to moderate the impact of wall mottoes. I have noticed how artists often seem to reflect on the tension between word and image, using folk art motifs to inject new life into old words. In 1995, for example, my sister Elizabeth Falk decorated six dinner plates "using, among other recycled materials, a Bible, a hymnal, and white plates with a gold rim from a local MCC store" (Falk 2007, 19, 25). In each, an arrangement of thin strips of text cut from the Bible forms a pattern with various found objects: bits of knotted thread, strips of music notation, a lock of hair, a sprinkling of mustard seeds, and so on. When I first saw these plates, I was reminded of Judy Chicago's *The Dinner Party*, an installation now seen as an icon of the 1970s. My sister's dinner plates are not on that monumental scale. True to the epigraph of this chapter, they honour the small detail. The courage that it took to dismantle a Bible and cut up the pages now strikes me as the necessary first step to redecorating a *Spielraum* so that the dead words of the past can come alive again.

A similar tension can be felt in the "typoems" that Norman Schmidt has been making since the 1970s. As he writes, "I took to designing typoems as an experiment into exploring a word and image conundrum, in which one (the image) is seen instantaneously in its entirety (a gestalt), and the other (the written word) is understood sequentially through time, yet both are textural."[*] In a typoem about the Manitoba maple, Schmidt's insertion

---

[*] Norman Schmidt, email to the author, 22 March 2019; quoted with permission.

of the Low German word for "sugar tree" jars the viewer into participation: "i once hid in a ssockaboom" (Plate 7). Going back and forth from textile to text in this kind of art makes the viewer conscious of enacting dialogue as a form of translation.

Talking Back to the Camera: Translation as Dialogue

Susan Sontag's (1973) claim that there is something inherently predatory about the camera comes to mind not only when I see pictures of naked women but also when I see voyeuristic photographs of the Amish. John Berger (1972, 17) has argued that the invention of the camera exposed perspective as a convention and changed our ways of seeing. How are Mennonites who are part of the Canadian renaissance responding to the challenges resulting from the invention of the camera? Which creative ways have they found to talk back to the camera—to simultaneously resist the stereotypes and the illusion of realism that fuels "secular idolatry"? My imaginary gallery contains a room devoted to exploring such questions. Several installations created early in her career by Susan Shantz suggest that learning how to talk back to the camera might be an important first step for Mennonite makers of art. One of these installations, entitled *Ancestral Spirits: Bed* (1988), was part of the 1990 Winnipeg exhibition curated by Priscilla Reimer. In a style that suggests both collage and quilting, Shantz alters a photograph in such a way that conventions are made visible and open to change and questioning (see Redekop 1998, 39–40). Shantz creates with technology rather than retreating from it.

As camera technology has developed, so have the challenges for artists, and Shantz's art has deepened over time. Digital technology has intensified an inherent conflict between the human control that we associated with cybernetics and the life forces inherent in biology that elude our control. The challenges faced by artists now were not even dreamt of in 1935 when Walter Benjamin wrote an influential essay called "The Work of Art in the Age of Mechanical Reproduction." W.J.T. Mitchell defines some of these in an essay entitled "The Work of Art in the Age of Biocybernetic Reproduction" (2003). In a recent series called *Creatures in Translation*, Shantz takes on this challenge, using digitally sculpted animal shapes to explore how visual languages change as a result of technology. Adapting shapes that recycle the conventions of ancient decorative traditions, in this case Japanese Banko Ware teapots, Shantz works with a visual rhetoric that lures the beholder into a dialogical process (Plate 10). As Bruce Russell notes, "This is not nostalgia for a lost authenticity" (in Russell 2013, 53). Artifacts can now be "readily replicated, cloned as it were," but in Shantz's art "this is not necessarily something to be feared, as originality is no longer invested in the original" (49), offering "limitless possibilities for playful exploration" (53).

Perhaps no artist in Canada has talked with and back to the camera in more complex ways than Wanda Koop, who often refers to the video camera as an extension of her eyes. Her *Spielraum* is no quiet retreat. She carries it with her, and she carries a camera, her way of sketching. It is an ongoing process brilliantly captured by Katherine Knight in her film *Koop* (2011), which has Koop in a freighter floating down the St. Lawrence River while framing what she sees. Knight's film shows what Robin Laurence has observed, that Koop refuses to conform to the conventions based on "the assumption that photography has displaced painting from its mimetic function" (1998, 4). Koop takes countless photographs, but like Shantz she also adapts various decorative traditions. On one trip to Toronto, she discovered Chinese paper cutouts in a shop on Spadina Avenue. Her excitement at the possibilities that they opened up eventually led her to travel to China and to the creation of a series called *Flying to the Moon*, made up of sixty large paintings, done with acrylic on plywood. In *Three Fractured Heads* (1985), she translates the colours and shapes of Chinese opera masks. The density of visual allusions in these paintings is reminiscent of Picasso. At the same time, there is in them a decorative quality that valorizes small details, which might explain why I hear an echo of the word *fraktur* in the title.

Translation and dialogue are also at the heart of the art made by Aganetha Dyck. Chris Dafoe describes Dyck's "modus operandi" as "the transformation of everyday objects into otherworldly ones using techniques derived from housework." Shrunken sweaters form the basis of one installation, in which "tiny wool figures seem to be on a pilgrimage to some unknown destination" (Dafoe 1996, C1). Something experimental, a childlike curiosity, seems to motivate Dyck's art. Putting buttons in jars and seeing what happens when you pickle them, for example, is a little like a science fair project. Dyck is best known now for the art that she has created in collaboration with bees. In *The Extended Wedding Party*, she experimented by putting assorted objects into a beehive to see how the designs varied depending on the object. The centrepiece is a wedding dress now entitled *The Glass Dress: Lady in Waiting* (Plate 11). I saw it at the Winnipeg Art Gallery when it was still inside a glass cage, and the bees were busily embroidering it with honeycomb. After completion, it was eventually purchased by the National Gallery of Canada. Evidence of the power of Dyck's playfully dialogical art exists in the form of a series of ekphrastic poems by Sarah Klassen entitled "A Partial Guide to *The Extended Wedding Party*" (1998, 26). The poet embroiders the empty wedding dress with metaphors and gives the bride a voice. In a rare back-and-forth ekphrastic process, Aganetha Dyck had Di Brandt's poetic responses to her art translated into Braille and then mounted them on panels and inserted them into a beehive, there to be "interpreted" by the bees. When this collaborative art was exhibited at the Burnaby Art Gallery in April 2009, Gathie Falk was there for the opening. A reviewer noted that Falk and Dyck chatted and that "there is something distinctly Falk-like about the exhibition, which Dyck describes as celebrating 'the power of the small'" (Dyck 2009).

I am not suggesting that a valorizing of small details is unique to Mennonite women. Women from many cultures in Canada are embarked on similar projects. Tazeen Qayyum, for example, transforms the decorative art that she learned when she mastered the Indian art of miniature painting. In a 2015 piece called *Infiltration*, magnified images of cutouts of cockroaches multiply across a wall, creating a powerful "ekphrastic fascination." As is the case in literature, queer artists are now transforming our ways of seeing at a deep level that includes a challenge to how decoration has been diminished by association with the feminine. In the paintings of Kent Monkman, a queer artist of Cree and Irish ancestry, an Indigenous presence looks back at the beholder from painted classical scenes in the form of a shape-shifting trickster named Miss Chief Share Eagle Testickle. The technique of *Verfremdung* or estrangement resembles Falk's strategy in *Red Angel*, but Monkman takes it forward into the troubled political landscape of our time. Art does not transcend the conflicts now surrounding the politics of identity. As beholders, we should respect differences and keep in mind that power is never distributed equally. There is virtual unanimity among artists, however, that they do not want their art to be locked inside the walls of some ethnic or racial ghetto. Carl Beam, for example, is considered one of Canada's most important Indigenous artists but objects to being called a "Native artist." Beam is of Anishinaabe ancestry, but his art has made use of Anasazi traditions of pottery, just as Koop makes use of Chinese conventions and Shantz of Japanese ones.

The Differing Arts of Russländer and Kanadier Mennonites

Some Mennonite visitors to my imaginary gallery might have noticed already that there is an elephant in the *Spielraum*. The major artists, those who have achieved the highest levels of recognition, are women whose ancestry is Russländer—Gathie Falk, Wanda Koop, and Aganetha Dyck being the best known. The reasons for this are of a complexity beyond my study, but one central factor is surely the collective Russländer memory of the rich culture of the Mennonite Commonwealth created and then destroyed in Russia. Numerous critics have commented on how the belatedness of trauma has shaped the art of Koop and Falk. But why are so many of the artists women? The title of a history written by Marlene Epp offers a clue: *Women without Men: Mennonite Refugees of the Second World War* (2000). For some of the Mennonite refugee groups, there was a period when men had been killed or exiled. Women were left in charge of the families and forced to take up leadership roles. Since women have also traditionally been the ones to keep a decorative tradition alive in the home, this might explain why women who are descendants of Russländer survivors have taken up leadership roles in the arts.

In my imaginary gallery is a room devoted to the lost art of the Mennonite Commonwealth. Research on that culture was difficult before the fall of the Soviet Union and is still fragmentary. Enough information is available, however, that it would be possible to exhibit some of the art that has been salvaged as well as the work of a few artists who escaped.

Among the latter was Henry Pauls, who recorded his memories of his childhood in Russia by painting in a style that art critics call naive. In *Watermelon Syrup Cooking*, Pauls lingers over a community scene, paying attention to "the details of a people's material and ritual culture, . . . both what things looked like and how things were done" (Tiessen and Tiessen 1991, n.p.) (Plate 12).

Among the artists who did not survive is the painter Jakob Sudermann. An exhibition of a few of his salvaged paintings, entitled *Sketches from Siberia*, took place in 2003 at the Mennonite Heritage Centre in Winnipeg. After viewing this show, Sarah Klassen wrote a series of poems entitled "Letters from Siberia" in which she combined ekphrasis (a technique that she has honed) with a spare epistolary form (2006, 69–70). Sudermann's poignant story has been told in *Sketches from Siberia: The Life of Jacob D. Sudermann* by his nephew Werner Toews (2018).

In my gallery I would hang an empty frame as a memorial to the many whose art died along with them. It would serve as a reminder of how profoundly the art of contemporary Russländer Mennonites has been influenced by that loss. The same is not true for artists from the Kanadier group. During the early years in Canada, those Mennonites were preoccupied with pioneering labours, but by the time the Russländer arrived many were already urbanized and assimilating. After years of intermarriage and assimilation, such group distinctions might seem irrelevant, but these historical differences remain important to our different ways of making and seeing art.

Even during the earliest days of settlement in southern Manitoba during the 1870s, Mennonite women continued to quilt and to embroider pillowcases, and men continued to make furniture. During the fifty years before the Russländer arrived in Manitoba, the Kanadier also lived close to Indigenous people. In my family, at least, we were conscious of the fact that Indigenous people practised their different crafts. There were colourful braided rag rugs on our floor that we bought from them when they came to our farm. My imaginary gallery contains a room devoted to the art of the pioneers, my ancestors, but it remains mostly empty because of my ignorance about that history. I do not remember anybody in my family creating *fraktur*, but I learned from archivist Conrad Stoesz that his great-grandfather, David B. Penner (1882–1954), a farmer in the Rudnerweide area of the Mennonite West Reserve, practised what he says they called *Schönschreiben*. I would include in my gallery Penner's 1896 New Year's wish for his parents (Plate 14).

My impression is that artists from the earlier generations of the Kanadier group make "outsider art," a term coined by Roger Cardinal in 1972 and used as a marketing tool to refer to art made by self-taught artists.

The term comes to mind when I consider the art of Marta Goertzen, born in Manitoba in 1923, when Gathie Falk was five years old and my mother eleven. Goertzen grew up in the village of Chortitz in Manitoba but spent most of her life in Toronto, where I first met her. She was married to Jay Armin, a legendary Rußländer violin teacher, originally from Winkler, Manitoba. I enjoyed hearing Marta tell their love story because she and I had in common that we had both married up. Indeed, her husband was my late husband's violin teacher back in the Winkler days. The four Armin children, taught by their father, performed widely as the Armin String Quartet in the 1970s before disbanding and pursuing separate careers. As the mother in that musical family, Marta lived a life of constant translation. I remember seeing one collage in which an abandoned violin string became a kite string.

Marta studied for two years in New York at the Brooklyn Museum Art School, and she told me once that she saw all the art that she had made before that as "garbage." Like all the other artists in this gallery, however, Goertzen always balanced the competing claims of abstraction and representation and did so by adapting various decorative traditions, not only Mennonite ones. She made a series of "quipus," abstracts in which she adapted an Inca counting tradition and arranged knotted strings in circles using various colours and textures. I own two of her quipus, one of which she made for me as a gift after reading my story "The Little Dipper" (Redekop 1990a). The story ends with an image of a field of flax and my inability to find a word for my mother's favourite shade of blue. Marta never met my mother, but she made a quipu in what she imagined was that shade of blue. All artists are both insiders and outsiders, but perhaps some are more outside than others. The violence of war is not the only way for art to be lost. Goertzen, however, did not see herself as deprived or a victim. She did a series of sketches as a way of expressing gratitude for her rich heritage. Each sketch was glossed in three languages and then photocopied to distribute as gifts to her friends (Figure 12).

I would invite Manitoba artist Margruite Krahn to decorate the floor of this room in my imaginary gallery with one of the floral designs that she uncovered while restoring Mennonite housebarns. I would also want to exhibit some of the paintings from her series on community life in rural Manitoba next to the ones by Henry Pauls of community life in Russia.

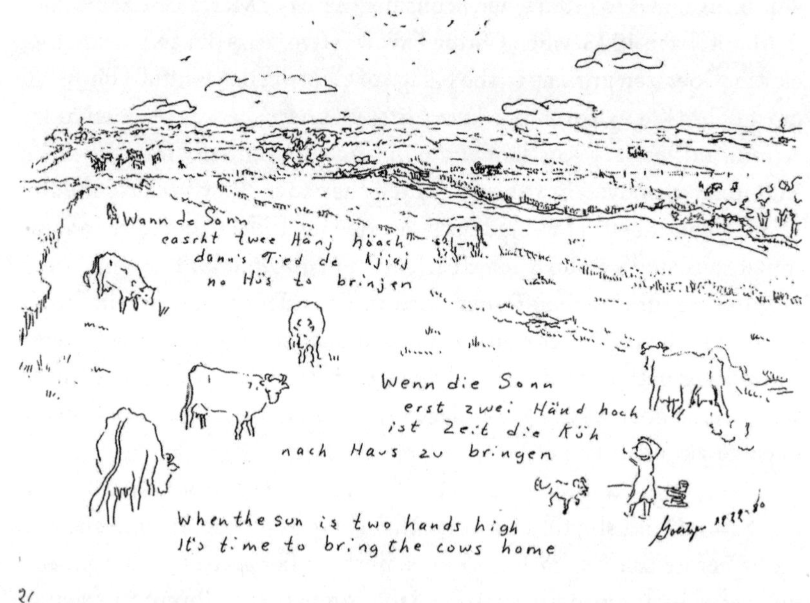

Figure 12. Marta Goertzen (Armin), *When the sun is two hands high*. Pencil sketch. Courtesy of Adele Armin.

Svetlana Boym (2011) might call all of these paintings examples of creative nostalgia, but style changes with time and place. Krahn is a fifth-generation Kanadier reflecting on community life in Manitoba. Unlike the paintings of Pauls, her paintings are self-consciously naïve. The flat table-tops in Pauls's *Watermelon Syrup Cooking* seem to be lifted up by some undercurrent of prairie wind in MCC *Quilters* (Plate 13). Krahn consciously deploys decorative conventions in a way that resonates with the playful art of modernists such as Paul Klee. *Sposz mutt zenne.*

I would exhibit in this room a collaborative series made by Margruite Krahn and my sister Elizabeth Falk. Krahn photographed three pieces of fabric art by my sister, entitled *Well, Wall, Water.* These images were then transferred onto large printer plates at Friesens in Altona. Krahn then interacted with these reproduced designs by superimposing linocut images on them with printers ink. The collaborative pieces were exhibited alongside the original fabric art pieces at Gallery in the Park in Altona. I was there for the opening of that exhibition on 7 June 2018 and had the pleasure of watching and listening as the argument of this book came to life and translations across media led to lively conversations.

Fabricated Ghosts: Mennonite Gothic Translations

The exhibition that I saw in Winnipeg in 1990 contained one installation that I found particularly compelling: Lois Klassen's *Household Lamps* (Figure 13). Empty hospital uniforms are displayed in a way that mimics decorative household objects that can be filled with artificial light. With one flick of the switch, the artist locates an aesthetic experience in the technological place where we all live. I remember thinking instantly of Florence Nightingale, the Lady with the Lamp. Klassen's fabricated ghosts continued to haunt me, and they alerted me to other works of art in which the implied presence of the female body is felt as a presence even when the body is *not* represented (see Redekop 1998). Over time, I have become interested in how the violence against women that is entrenched in the history of art might be illuminated with relation to Mennonite plain style and anxieties about ornamentation. The notorious rants of Adolf Loos, a nineteenth-century architect who deemed ornament a crime, remind me a little of a Mennonite preacher exhorting the women and girls in his congregation not to cut or curl their hair or wear jewellery. Indeed, Mennonite plain

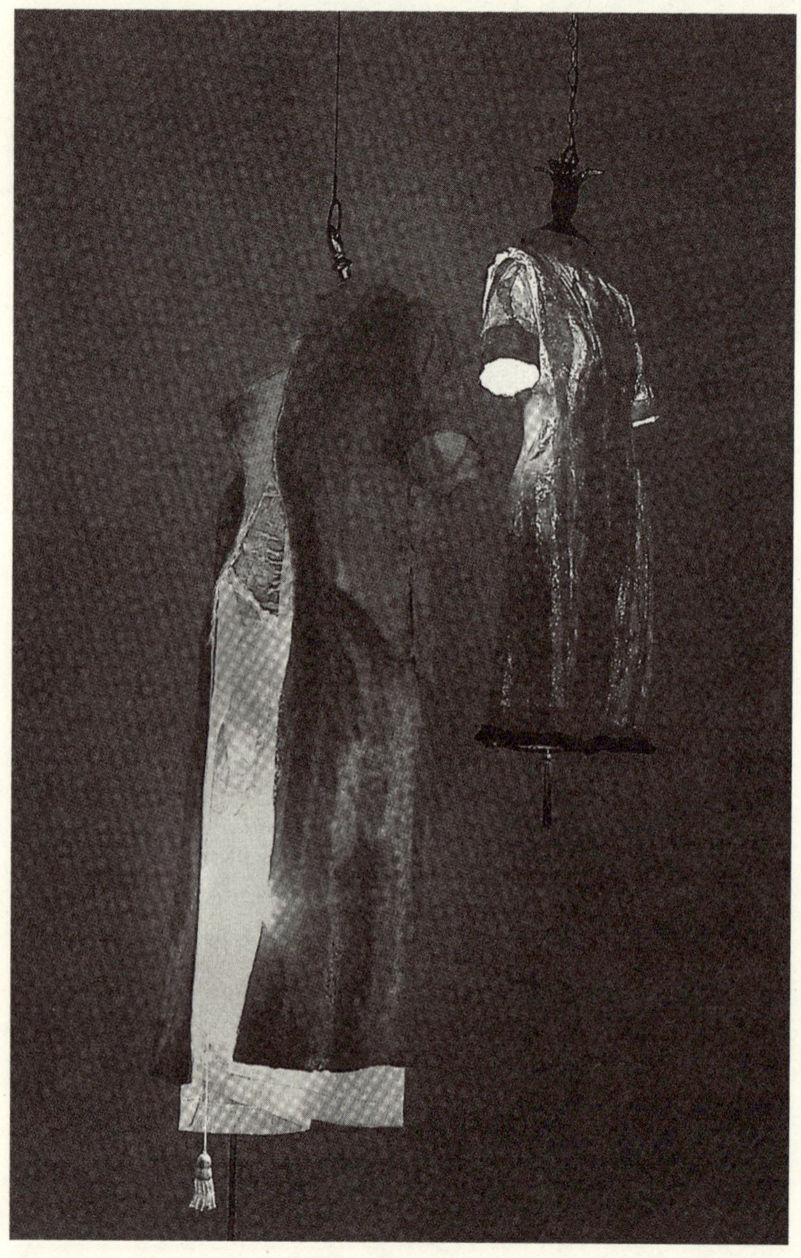

Figure 13. Lois Klassen, *Household Lamps,* Plug In Institute of Contemporary Art, Winnipeg, 1988. Photograph by C. Wiebe. Courtesy of the artist.

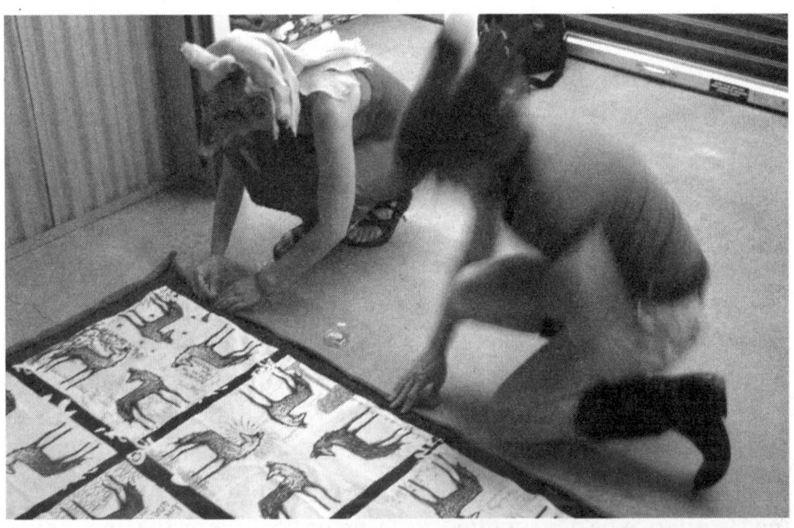

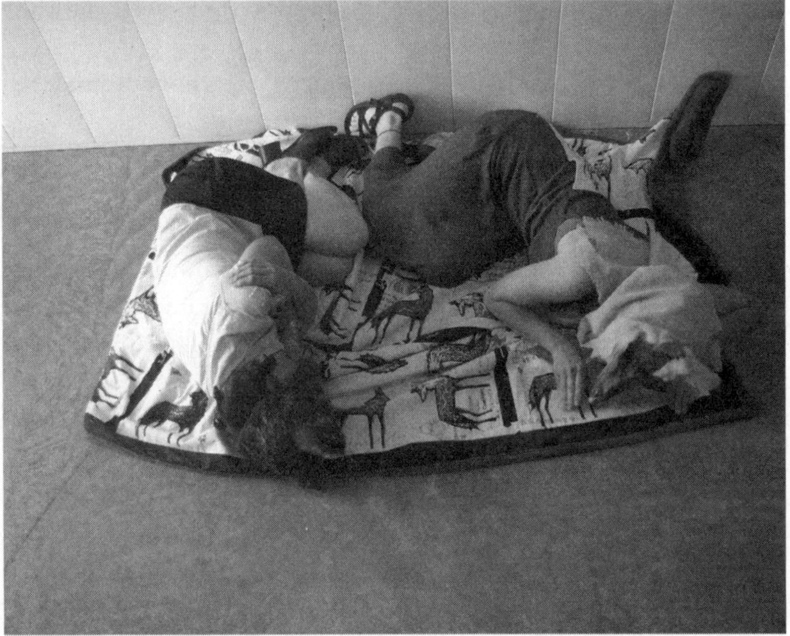

Figures 14 and 15. Lois Klassen and Maggie Winston, *Coyote Comforts*, performance and blankets, with coyote print on fabric by Pat Beaton, as seen in the series "3084: Short-term storage for materialized ideas/ideated materials" (Jem Nobel, artist-curator), Maple Leaf Storage, Vancouver, 2009. Photo by J. Nobel. Courtesy of the artists.

style resonates oddly with the "two cardinal principles" of the influential "international style" that informs modernist art: utility and simplicity. After reflecting on the writing of Loos, Gombrich comments, it is instructive to see "how closely aesthetic condemnation remains linked with moral qualms" (1984, 18).

One room in my imaginary gallery is devoted to empty dresses. There I would exhibit Lois Klassen's *Household Lamps* as well as Aganetha Dyck's *Wedding Dress*. An alcove of this room would contain a series of papier mâché dresses by Gathie Falk entitled *Reclining Figure (after Henry Moore)*. As Robin Laurence notes, they are "replete with cheerful ironies and inverted homages: where Moore's reclining figures are large-scale nudes—bodies without clothes—Falk's are life-size clothes without bodies" (2000, 134–35). Some of these dresses stand up on their own and are accompanied by altars. The one subtitled *Stella* lies on her back on the floor, skirts blown up by some invisible wind. It seems an obvious allusion to the white dress worn by Marilyn Monroe while standing on a subway grate in a scene now considered "iconic." In this case, however, there is no body inside the icon, and the iconoclash is intense.

In this room, I would exhibit an installation made by my sister Elizabeth Falk. Entitled *I'll Fly Away*, it translates into visual language the feelings associated with a popular gospel song. My sister first created this piece using a piece of wood from the old pump organ that always stood in our dining room on the farm (Plate 16). In 2016, she was invited to exhibit with Buffalo Creek Artists at the Eden Mental Health Centre in Winkler. Having moved and downsized, she created a new version of *I'll Fly Away*, a black crepe gown absorbing objects from her past: a wedding band, a rosary from a friend, three or four worn keys from the organ. The braided legs were gone, but the music rack was still there, still pressed down on the woman's garment (Plate 17).

The act of sewing is primarily a female activity among Mennonites as it is in most Western cultures. During the decades since making *Household Lamps*, Lois Klassen has moved on to various projects, many of them requiring the use of a sewing machine. These include a collaboration called *Coyote Comforts* in which sewing becomes part of a performance. Working alongside Maggie Winston, Klassen used textile squares from a previous social project, each square bearing a coyote print. The two women, after sewing together, describe themselves as "cohabiting" this comforter (Figures 14 and 15). I see them as tricksters making believe together.

Quilting projects of all kinds recur in the art made by Mennonites, often setting up a tension between aesthetic freedom and ethical urgency. Gathie Falk's fierce commitment to the freedom of play is echoed in the work of Amalie Atkins, an artist originally from southern Manitoba. Atkins describes herself as "a multidisciplinary artist whose work hopscotches from filmmaking to fabric-based sculpture to performance" (quoted in Legris 2015, 42). Her main tools are her camera and her Singer sewing machine. Like Falk, she often works on a boundary between magic realism and surrealism, as she does in *We Live on the Edge of Disaster and Imagine We're in a Musical*. Poet Sylvia Legris writes about this series that "Atkins' formidable attention to the miniscule, albeit wondrous details we often overlook[,] instills her films with a magical disorientation, with moments of déjà vu-like disjunction" (48). Atkins's installations often feature the kind of staging that happens as part of carnival, but as Grace Kehler observes, "there's a gravitas even in the most playful films" (2015, 35) (Plate 18). Kehler describes Atkins as "positioning the contemporary western world on the *edge of disaster*—by offering visions of other worlds in which identity is emphatically relational, never singular or private" (35). Her theme is "the connectedness of all organisms . . . and of the primacy of responding to and taking responsibility for all manner of life" (35). An indefinable menace seems to me to hover over scenes such as the one of a mother and daughter hanging braids on a line (Plate 19), but perhaps that is only "in my eye."

In many ways, the exuberant art of Amalie Atkins, summoning the viewer to a process of "listening, embracing, caretaking, and gift-giving" (Kehler 2015, 35), exemplifies what I see as a Mennonite sensibility. At the same time it does the exact opposite, making me think how absurd it is to label any art in my imaginary gallery as Mennonite. All of it is created at that vanishing point into which my book keeps disappearing. It brings me back, once again, to Robert Kroetsch's question: "what remains of what does not remain?" and to Hildi Froese Tiessen's conclusion that we are left with a "trace" (Kroetsch 2001, 8, quoted in Tiessen 2012, 14). Where I see and hear these traces of Mennonite aesthetic accents, I often feel myself to be in the presence of something deeply spiritual. This is not as something that can be embodied in an artifact—that would be idolatry—but rather something that happens in between the work of art and those who take it in with all their senses.

Let me try to show what I mean by sharing my experience of two separate times that I took in Gathie Falk's *Herd Two*. Earlier I told the story of how thrilling it was to see it for the first time in 1975 in the National Gallery in Ottawa. I have looked at reproductions of it many times since then, of course, but never with the shock of reframing that happened to me in the spring of 2019 after I read Falk's just published memoir, *Apples, etc.* I was startled when I read that *Herd Two* was made by Falk during what Robin Laurence has described as her "brief and disastrous marriage to an ex convict" (2000, 65). Falk's account of how she ended up taking care of him and the pet rhesus monkey he brought into the house is hilarious and horrifying. What is almost impossible to believe is that she created the twenty-four galloping carousel horses during that same time. Each one was unique, "each mane, bridle, rein, and saddle carefully rendered," she writes, "I was working as fast as I could, with a small dog draped around my neck like a fur collar, a screaming monkey in the other room ... A big, bad smell invaded the house" (Falk 2019, 129). Falk observes: "Art critics often read a state of panic in my herd of stampeding horses. Perhaps they are right" (129).

After reading that, I looked again at a reproduction of *Herd Two*. The sensation reminded me of a moment in John Berger's *Ways of Seeing,* in which a reproduction of Van Gogh's *Wheatfield with Crows* appears twice. On top of the first image are the words: "This is a landscape of a cornfield with birds flying out of it. Look at it for a moment. Then turn the page" (Berger 1972, 27). When you turn the page you find the exact same picture. Under it are the words: "This is the last picture that Van Gogh painted before he killed himself." Berger notes: "The image now illustrates the sentence" (28). This intriguing exercise demonstrates the interactive and fluid search for meaning that has been my subject throughout this book. In some ways Gathie Falk's *Herd Two* illustrates the search for *Spielraum* that informs the argument of this book, but that is not because it is a static representation. It is because of how powerfully it evokes a dynamic process. No matter who you are, you can make believe that these animals are breaking out of the circle game when you stop looking. "Now faith is the substance of things hoped for, the evidence of things not seen" (Hebrews 11:1). To adapt the words of Hildi Froese Tiessen once more, these are *everyone's* horses (Tiessen 2012, 14).

The Sculpture Garden

My original sketch for a gallery included a sculpture garden. When I look at the diagram now, I notice that I installed a wine bar near the door leading out from the *groute shtove* into the garden. I imagine my visitors helping themselves to a glass of wine before stepping over the threshold. This act, all by itself, has the effect of raising questions about how gender shapes an artist's choice of raw material. Of course men are free to work with textiles and women are free to work with marble. The reality is that the choice of medium is often gender-specific. I think, for example, of the powerful sculptures done by artist Todd Braun with stone and those done with wood by Victor Klassen. Both of them are often commissioned to make furniture, so I would invite them to construct some benches and chairs for people in my garden. Since assumptions about gender and about what belongs inside or outside often inspire artists to make mischief, I would include an installation that Gathie Falk created after her marriage ended. When the man returned to prison, Falk was left with a 1936 Ford coupe that had flame-painted doors. "She decided to fill it with ceramic watermelons" and it ended up parked on "a bed of Astro-turf at the Vancouver Art Gallery," the centrepiece for an installation called *Picnics* (Laurence 2000, 65). I would park it right in the middle of my sculpture garden and let the children play in it. Since I can't seem to stop myself from imagining this gallery as being on the prairie near where I grew up, I would exhibit sculptures made by Ken Loewen from old farm machinery. Another Manitoba artist, Barbara Wiebe, was once known primarily as a potter but now makes whimsical ceramic sculptures. Her chicken coop filled with ceramic red hens was part of a group exhibition by the Buffalo Creek Artists that I saw at Gallery in the Park in Altona in 2018. They looked just like the Bantams we used to have on our farm. I would find room for them in among Loewen's machinery.

Back to the Shtahp: Representing Fields

Oddly enough, it is often when I am looking at abstract art that I return to the question: Where do you come from? Geography is a powerful presence in the room of my gallery where I invite questions about the relationship between plain style and abstraction. The subject is of a complexity that has long intrigued but baffled me. I am convinced that it is an area where a Mennonite sensibility is often most palpable yet most difficult to define. I feel this as something inarticulate, for example, when I look at one of my favourite paintings, Gathie Falk's *Cement with Black Shadow*. As a way of raising questions about the influence of Mennonite plain style on landscape painting, I would invite a few American artists as guests in this part of the gallery. The Great Plains extend up and down the middle of the continent, but just as the words for land change with dislocation—*prairie, steppe, shtahp*—so too do the visual languages used by artists.

The most important painter to consider in this regard is Warren Rohrer, a major Philadelphia painter. Susan Rosenberg describes Rohrer as a ninth-generation American and the son of "austerely religious Lancaster Mennonite farmers." She offers an illuminating account of his progress through stages that led him to develop a signature style (2002, 10). He eventually came to view the field of the canvas as analogous to an actual farmer's field. An announcement of an exhibition of his work in 1971 contained a photograph of Rohrer holding a painting while standing in a field (Figure 16). In a series called *Field: Language*, the textures and lines represent rows in a field while at the same time exploring languages that escape the literalism of plain style. The simple geometry of his paintings might seem to support "the myth of aniconism," the illusion that there is a society that can do without images of the deity. The fragments of his life that emerge from Rosenberg's account, however, undermine that myth.

I might be wrong, but it is my impression, based on the art that I have seen, that American Swiss Mennonite women make art that is more exuberant than that of their male counterparts. In my imaginary gallery, I would invite questions about gender and medium by hanging, next to Rohrer's work, a piece by Erma Martin Yost from a series called *Felted Fields*. These fields are hand-felted and -stitched.

In a series called *School Papers*, created by Philadelphia artist Douglas Witmer, plain style is taken in a direction that invokes the decorative

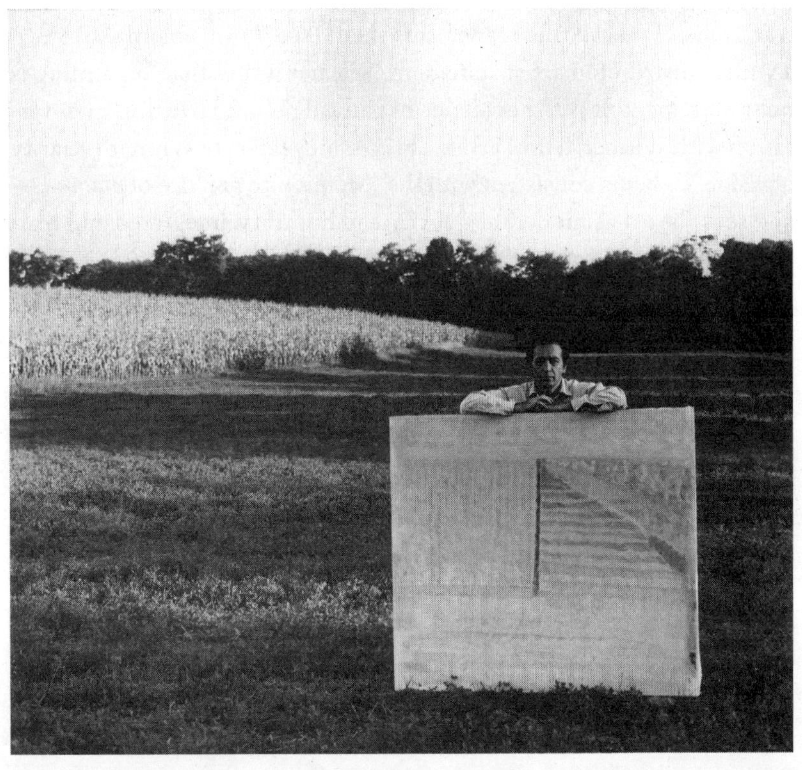

Figure 16. Warren Rohrer with his painting *Farm: August 1971*. Photograph by David Chapman. Courtesy of Locks Gallery.

traditions of *fraktur* and transforms them (see Tannenbaum 2015). In a widely distributed artist statement, Witmer writes that "a painting is not a statement. It is the evidence of painting" (n.d.). During a conversation with Witmer, fellow artist Chris Ashley refers to Witmer's "clarity of vision" as being consistent with the "Mennonite practice of *plain-ness*" and sees the art as modelling "purity and humility, integrated and realized as thought and action" (Witmer 2005). Judith Tannenbaum similarly describes Witmer as "a painter of abstraction that is 'pure'—it does not reference the perceived world" (2015, 64). These uses of the adjective *pure* are infected by stereotypes about Mennonites. I find it more useful to think of Witmer as getting carried away with the decorative fun of *fraktur* in the *School Papers*. The series comes across as an indirect tribute to Warren Rohrer but moves beyond the limits of his more earnest vision and beyond the artists who pioneered colour field abstraction. The lines of colour on a yellow field are meant to be written on, but the artist is like a child or a trickster who refuses to do a test and instead absconds with the paper, using it for play and improvisation. Over 200 "school papers" have now been completed. Each one is unique, but they all have as a background the fixed lines on yellow school paper intended for words (Plate 15).

Since I have been envisioning cultural translation as an unpacking of gifts, it seems apt that, as I was working to bring my discussion of fields to a conclusion, I received a gift from my sister Elizabeth Falk: a representation of the *shtahp* that we both come from, entitled *Met Pahpe opp'e Shtahp* (With Papa on the Field). Made in her signature style, this is a moonlit landscape that literally sparkles because of the fabrics that my sister chose for the base (Plate 20). On 12 October 2018, she sent me a brief account of the making:

> Woven throughout the piece is a recollection of our father draining
> water from a cold, black field of Manitoba gumbo in early spring,
> accompanied by an unexplained sense of danger, a loss of control
> over the forces of nature. . . . Drawn in by the text of Matthew 13:44
> in Low German, fabric and objects from my workspace began
> to stir and ask to be chosen. Nearing completion, although I had
> consciously focussed mainly on balancing colours, textures, and

shapes in relation to each other, I experienced an opening, sudden bursts of recognition: ahh, *that* is what this is[*]

The view is looking west from our house on the farm to a field bounded by the railway track. When I saw the poppies, I remembered that this is the same track that leads to Newton Siding, to the crossing where my sister's son was killed in a car-train crash in 1984. When I mentioned this to her on the phone, she said that she was not making a conscious association with his death when she was embroidering the poppies. She said that after she had made it she realized that the strip of decorative white lace looked like a row of crosses, and then she thought of "In Flanders Fields." If you imagine water being guided by gravity, then the blue braid at the bottom looks like an underground stream made visible. It also resembles the braided rag rugs that Indigenous people made and sold when we were children. Indigenous presence is there also in the beadwork of an earring that hangs from the figure on the *shtahp* in defiance of our father's rule against earrings.

The Low German word for field, *shtahp*, appears in the title and in a passage from the parable of the buried treasure. *Met daut Himmelrikj es daut soo aus met een Scha(h)tz, dee opp de Schtahp vegroft es*, "The kingdom of heaven is like unto treasure hid in a field." Every detail in this field is alive and changeable depending on your angle of vision. It means something different to me each time I look at it depending on the time of day and how the light falls on it. Is that the figure of Father in the field? If so, then is he like one of those Anabaptist "field preachers" who urged people centuries ago to destroy images? Or is that a cross? Or maybe a scarecrow? I especially like the crooked smile on the face of the one-eyed woman in the moon. The clock in the pocket reminds me of my father's pocket watch, but the minute hand is actually moving. If time is the buried treasure, then it is only now that matters.

I see how this realization brings me back, full circle, to the conclusion that I came to at the end of my chapter on music. To quote Michael Fried once again, "we are all literalists most or all of our lives. Presentness is grace" (1998, 168). The word *grace* makes me think there would need to be a chapel somewhere in my gallery. As the insistent questions multiply,

---

[*] Elizabeth Falk, email to the author, 12 October 2018; quoted with permission.

they can lead to a "joyless search for meaning" (Birdsell 1982, 98) that blinds us to moments of grace. I imagine this chapel as "plain and simple," to echo the words of the weepy song, "Crying in the Chapel," made famous by Elvis Presley. I would not look, however, for a place "where people are of one accord," but rather for the kind of *Spielraum* where differences are so fully embraced that people can be quiet together in their shared unknowingness. I would not want the interior of this chapel to be a stark reminder of what was lost as a result of "the stripping of the altars" (Duffy 1992), but instead a place where sheer beauty would create peace. To this end I would invite Gathie Falk to decorate the walls of the chapel with her *Heavenly Bodies*.

Rips and Tears: There Is a Fracture in Everything

As I come to the end of this chapter, I am acutely aware of the limits placed on my efforts to be a hospitable curator. My imaginary gallery is full to overflowing and yet I have been at all times aware of how many artists will be left out in the cold. Just how large this number might be was brought home to me forcefully during the process of negotiating permissions for reproductions. Almost every curator I consulted came up with additional names of artists with Mennonite backgrounds who, in their opinion, ought to have been included. Although I found this disconcerting, I was gratified to note how many of the suggestions resonated with the questions I have been asking. I was also surprised to find how many non-Mennonite curators, at least in western Canada, were aware of the Mennonite phenomenon. One curator urged me to consider an installation by Doris Wall Larson entitled *An Uneasy Sleep* and sent me an image of it. It was too late to include it, but I noticed how it plays with decorative traditions in ways that echo the art that I do include. Another curator referred me to the art of Marian Penner Bancroft, a photographer who talks back to the camera, and still another drew my attention to Diana Hiebert's engrossing "story bones."

Overcome by the magnitude of my own ignorance, I found that I could not exit from my imaginary gallery without thinking of the curator as a teacher. I am comfortable in that role because my teaching style has always been Socratic and grounded in my awareness of how little I know. In my diagram, near the exit and just before you get to the gift shop, there is a discussion room. On the farm we used to refer to any organized discussion as a *shnetje konferenz*. I imagine myself offering *shnetje* (biscuits) and wine to people wishing to talk about what they have seen. On one wall of the room I would hang Gathie Falk's *Theatre in B/W and Colour: Bouquets in Colour* (1983), which would be on loan from the Glenbow Museum in Calgary. It is one in a series of paintings which feature bunches of flowers fastened to wooden stakes. The painting always reminds me a little of a military cemetery with rows of crosses. It would be an excellent "dialogic object" for a teacher who aims to bring questions about iconoclash into focus. I would put a circle of chairs in front of it and hope for a lively discussion. As Gathie Falk wrote to me so long ago: "Of course, that is the Mennonite way. It's a good way."

By contrast with that scene of an imagined community, the task of the critic who writes is absurdly solitary. I think about the invisible multitude of artists that I have not included because I did not know about them and I add to that my awareness that the ones I have collected have already done their vanishing act. When I do this I see how foolish it is to make any concluding generalizations. What I have done is the job of a reporter—reporting on what I see with my partial vision. Foolish though it be, however, I will conclude by reporting on my own efforts to generalize—to relate the local and the personal to the larger historical contexts.

The timing of this Mennonite renaissance, like the literary one, shows that it began as part of a broader ferment in Canada during the 1970s and 1980s. Mindful of that fact, and on the lookout for ways to historicize the Mennonite forms of iconoclash, I sat down to reread *Remembering Postmodernism: Trends in Canadian Art, 1970–1990*, co-authored by Mark Cheetham and Linda Hutcheon (2012). I was intrigued to find, among the case studies in that book, the name Robert Wiens, whose 1986 work *The Rip* is described as "redolent of [the artist's] childhood trips to the Vogue Theatre in Leamington, Ontario" (87). Most Mennonite readers would recognize the name Wiens as Mennonite and know that Leamington is a place where Mennonites settled in large numbers. Cheetham describes *The Rip* as a result of "Wiens's recollections of a movie theatre in Whitehorse" where a screen was ripped—a "knife wound" made as "a gesture of anger and frustration at the stereotyped representation of Aboriginal people" (87). Although his comments on it did not include anything about Wiens's

Mennonite history or culture, *The Rip* resonated for me with Koop's *Tear* and her *Native Fires* series. The absence of any mention of Mennonite history seemed to me significant since the argument of the book is that we ought to historicize questions about representation. In her afterword to *Remembering Postmodernism*, Hutcheon observes that "we cannot avoid representation. We *can* try to avoid fixing our notions of it and assuming it to be transhistorical and transcultural" (133). Why did Cheetham's comments on *The Rip* not include anything about the artist's ethnicity? Was that because Wiens did not wish to be identified as Mennonite? Curiosity got the better of my fear of being intrusive. When I finally tracked him down, Wiens confirmed that his Mennonite grandparents (with whom he was "very close") had come to Canada from Russia as refugees in the 1920s.* What to make of this information?

During a conversation with Hutcheon about my dilemma, she made the intriguing suggestion that it might be more useful to speak of degrees of "Mennoniteness" in all the artists in *Remembering Postmodernism* than to identify one of them as a "Mennonite artist." Her suggestion is happily in tune with my approach to resonance, but it does not change how media coverage works in Canada. If the artist does not identify as Mennonite, and art critics are nervous about touching on topics related to religion and ethnicity, the logic of a celebrity culture takes over. This often leaves me alone with what I hear and see as Mennonite accents. Let me offer just one example to illustrate my dilemma. I was startled one morning at breakfast when I opened the *Globe and Mail* and found an article about artist Karel Funk (Lederman 2016). As most Mennonite readers would do, I registered the fact that Funk is a common Mennonite name and that the artist is from Winnipeg, where Mennonites live in large numbers. The article associated Funk's hyperrealist portraits of hooded figures with Dutch and Flemish art. The director of the Winnipeg Art Gallery, Stephen Borys, was quoted as saying that the show "connects people with centuries of art making and to a particular genre, the portrait, that has never left us." I thought back to Rembrandt's self-portraits and to the conflicts about portrait painting that divided the Mennonite churches in Amsterdam

---

* Robert Wiens, email to the author, July 2016; quoted with permission.

during the Dutch Golden Age. An ominous figure wearing a hoodie is now a cliché in the visual rhetoric of cinema as well as a possible target for racial profiling in cities, and the female version of a veiled figure now often evokes Islamophobia. Something about Funk's art takes up all these social forces in a way that rides the time warp while connecting with "centuries of art making." I recognized this as characteristic of the Mennonite contributions to the anachronic renaissance that I have been witnessing. But what should I do with this recognition?

My response to this dilemma is a repetition of what I have been emphasizing throughout this book. It is to remind myself that each one of us is only one small part of a larger cultural dialogue. All I can do is contribute what I see from where I sit at my breakfast table, as I have done now by sharing it with you, my reader. The safest response to the intractable complexity of questions about ethnicity and art is to be honest about where we come from and to admit how little we all really know about our own and other people's histories. My focus on the art made by my own people has led me repeatedly to a sense of the urgent need for comparative study. In January 1996, motivated by this urgency, I attended a conference on Jewish women's art in Toronto, From Memory to Transformation. I was curious in particular about the different strategies used by contemporary women artists from Mennonite and Jewish backgrounds as they adapted their decorative traditions to a culture in which image is dominated by word. I might have been the only non-Jewish woman at the conference, but I was warmly welcomed. I remember arriving early at one session and sitting next to a woman busy with needlework. I explained to her why I was there and asked her what she was making. She said that she was making a holder for a Torah pointer and explained that women were not allowed to make the pointer itself but could make the container for it. When I asked what the pointer looked like, she reached down into her craft bag and pulled out an exquisitely carved wooden long-stemmed rose. I was at a loss for words.

On the closing night of the conference, there was a reception to launch a group art exhibition. It happened that on that day I had, for the first time, been fitted with bifocals. The exhibition was mounted on the second floor of a house on Spadina Avenue, and as I climbed the stairs I was conscious of having to take extra care to place my feet. All such concerns went out of my mind when I entered a room that contained, on the floor in the middle, an installation by Sylvia Safdie. It was a sculpture made of stone and glass that made me think of stone gardens that I had seen in Japan. It transported me to a place neither outside nor inside. After pulling myself away from it, I began to circle the small room, looking at the art hanging on the walls, much of it fascinating and decorative combinations of word and image. As I stepped back to get a better perspective on one of them, I stumbled and fell backward into the Safdie sculpture. I heard the distinct crack of glass on stone as I fell. In an instant, I was surrounded by concerned women, including Safdie herself. Not one of them so much as glanced at the work of art. My embarrassed apology was met with reassuring comments about how broken glass means good luck when you are among Jews. I was guided to a room down the hall, given a glass of water, and allowed time to compose myself. After a while, I became aware that I was sitting on the wooden floor of a room with pretty wallpaper. The room was entirely empty, which puzzled me since the other small rooms were jammed with art, and space was clearly at a premium. When I looked at the wall against which I was leaning, I was startled to realize that the pattern on the wallpaper consisted of innumerable tiny swastikas. Recoiling from them, I got up and walked back down the hall toward the sound of women laughing and talking. As I did so, an aphorism created by James Baldwin came to me: "Life is more important than art. That's why art is so important" (Baldwin 2014, 31).[*] When I went into the room, I slipped in among the chattering bodies to check on the Safdie sculpture. I was reassured to see that it had been reassembled and seemed intact. But when I looked more closely I saw, at the bottom of the glass near the stones, a very small crack.

---

[*] These are not Baldwin's precise words. The aphorism developed during years when the 1961 radio interview cited was not available in print and people were quoting from memory. I have used my own version of it before, most recently in an article on Alice Munro. There, as the result of a trick of ventriloquism, the words are spoken by a thrush (Redekop 2017, 303).

ON ENDINGS

Runde runde rouze kraunz,
Butta shtaunz,
Chlingt dole,
Noch ein mole,
Aule chinga faule dole

Round and round the rosy crown,
Butter dance,
Clink down,
Another time,
All the children fall down

Making Schluss

When he came to the end of a sermon, my father often seemed visibly overwhelmed, both by what he had said and by what he had not been able to say. As a teenager, I was always relieved when he gave up, wiped his tears, and concluded by reading a poem. After that, it was time for *schluss möke*, end making. He would announce the closing hymn, in the singing of which he would join lustily from behind the pulpit. One of his favourites was "Grosser Gott, wir loben dich," a German version of the Latin Te Deum that dates back to the eighteenth century. "Great God, We Praise Thee." He did not always remember to step away from the microphone, and this created an imbalance in the four-part harmony since he was not singing the melody. The amplification of his deep bass voice evoked in me an adolescent mixture of pride and embarrassment even as I added my alto to the congregational mix. Matters were made worse by the fact that my mother, from her place on the women's side of the church, sang soprano with the same loud abandon in a high vibrato for which the Low German word is *flautrich* or fluttering. In "Through the Mennonite Looking Glass," I described how my father made use of his large handkerchief when the tears flowed and how my mother's role was to keep those handkerchiefs dazzlingly white (Redekop 1988, 241). When my feminist rant was done, however, I reminded myself that she performed that task lovingly and with pride.

After both my parents died, I began the process familiar to us all of continuing my relationship with them on a level that combines memory and imagination. I now reimagine those Sunday mornings in ways not available to me then. Yes, my parents were joining their voices in praise to "Grosser Gott," but I also hear them singing to each other, their voices like camouflaged love birds hidden somewhere in among the pews of the Altona Rudnerweider Church. We are all trapped in what Fredric Jameson called "the prison-house of language" (1974), but in that sanctuary there was plenty of room for *Spiel* as the Word of God splintered into many words and as those words dissolved into music. High German was mixed with some English during the service, and afterward, outside the church, conversations continued in Low German, to be dropped and then picked up again in different homes in different ways.

Why did my father weep? Answers would not be hard to find in his life story. Consider that his first wife died in childbirth, count the number of his brothers who took their own lives, add the four children who died in infancy and the twin brother who died of alcoholism (Neufeld 2008). The question changes, however, if you move from the private to the public realm and consider weeping as part of his performance as an orator. Was he being manipulative? In the previous chapter, I reflected on Wanda

Koop's painting *Tear* and considered how gender influences our responses to such questions. I did not meet Di Brandt until many years after I left Manitoba, but she once told me that after coming home from church her mother sometimes mimicked my father's weeping. I was reminded that my mother also sometimes mocked a preacher who cried. She believed that her husband's tears were sincere, whereas the man whom she made fun of was crying *kruckedell's trone* or crocodile tears.

In hindsight, it is not hard to see why the preachers in my father's church might have made some people laugh. Even without the addition of unmasculine tears, they must have been easy targets for satire. They were uneducated farmers, and since they preached in High German, a language that most of them did not know well, there was plenty of material for burlesques such as Jack Thiessen's *Predicht fier Haite* (Sermons for Today, 1984). Educated preachers in supposedly "liberal" Mennonite churches, however, were sometimes mocked in my home for their smarmy English "messages." Whether real or not, the tears of preachers, if studied in the context of social history, might help to shed light on how Mennonites use gestures and rhetorical conventions to convey intense religious experiences.

Why did my father weep? In my hazy memory, I hear him performing in an incantatory style that was the residual influence of his experience in the Sommerfelder Church. As a preacher in that church, he read from handwritten sermons written by earlier generations of preachers and was required to do so in a rising and falling chant designed to prevent personal expression of feeling. How must it have felt to set aside the prewritten scripts and suddenly be required to speak spontaneously? One account of the early days of the Rudnerweider Church contains this description: "When William Falk preached and stood behind the pulpit—hanky in one hand—he wept almost all the time.... I remember one day when William Falk looked up this way like he was free—looking into the congregation. He was able to talk to the people" (Neufeld 2008, 84). I do not remember that "he wept almost all the time" in later years, but at least once during every sermon he would be momentarily overcome. Why did my father weep? The question is a riddle to which the only answer might be *lacrimae rerum*—"tears are at the heart of things" (Heaney 2008).

The fact that my father reached for poetry after wiping his tears was a gesture that makes a bridge from his life work to mine. The link between preaching and teaching, however, is an anxious one, as is the one between poetry and pedagogy. "Who breaks a butterfly upon a wheel?" Alexander Pope framed this oft-quoted question in "Epistle to Dr. Arbuthnot" (Pope 1966, 336). My entire career has gone against the grain of such mockery. I count it among the greatest joys of my life to have had the privilege of teaching a course called "Reading Poetry" to undergraduates. Unlike my father, I did not have to be content with tacking on a poem at the end of a lecture. It was my practice to read an assigned poem once at the beginning of a class and again at the end, after discussion had deepened understanding of it. There were doubtless students who made themselves scarce for fear of killing butterflies. For those of us who stayed with the process, there was the shared pleasure of circling around words on a page and feeling them come to life. The practice of doing that, over and over again during my years of teaching, is the basis for the dialogical aesthetic that I have applied in this book.

As I approach the end of this book, it seems logical to reflect on what we are doing when we *make* endings together. How do you bring to an end a book that has been an open-ended exploration? Since I have no final answers to any of the questions that I have raised, I am ending with a metagesture—reflecting on what we do when we make *schluss*. This self-reflexive turn has made me aware that this book is written with a Mennonite accent of the kind that Jesse Nathan has defined in relation to poetic closure. He writes about certain Mennonite poets that "they keep asking questions. There is no closure, and there is the embrace of this lack of closure" (2015, 190). In this regard, however, Mennonite accents might have changed. It was my impression that, when he ended his sermons with a poem, my father did so because he thought that the poem summed up his message. The kind of lyric poetry that I have in mind is very different from the didactic poems that he favoured.

Ben Lerner argues in *The Hatred of Poetry* (2016) that lyric poetry communicates the failure of representation. Every actual poem, he writes, is a "false representation" and implicitly set off against an idea of the perfect poem. In Chapter 4, I argued, in relation to the rise of poetry by Mennonites during the 1980s, that this conscious failure makes lyric poetry uniquely suited to undermine the mastering goals of master narratives. The aesthetic of failure has deep roots, going back to Plato, who expelled poets from his Republic because of this perceived failure. Lerner spells it out in a way that resonates with what is sometimes called "romantic irony": "You're moved to write a poem, you feel called upon to sing, because of [a transcendent or divine] impulse. But as soon as you move from that impulse to the actual poem, the song of the infinite is compromised by the finitude of its terms" (8). As my father's concluding gesture shows, the failure of representation is felt most forcefully when you are trying to make an end. For this reason, I will focus primarily on lyric poetry in this chapter, but I will part company with my father when this failure leads me to an affirmation of the power of dance.

"End-Feeling"

The children's singing game in the epigraph to this conclusion echoes the one with which I began my first chapter, a gesture which resonates with the words of Sandra Birdsell: "Start again? Was it all a circle?" (1989, 64). As T.S. Eliot shows in *Four Quartets* (1944), the borderline where endings and beginnings merge can be a place of religious ecstasy but can also lead to a sense of futility. Children's circle games also reflect on the circularity of time, while taking a conscious delight in play. Iona and Peter Opie repudiate the persistent myth that "Ring a Ring o' Roses" refers to a symptom of the plague and insist that the game should not be contaminated by adult concerns (Opie 1988, 221). Sometimes a rosy wreath is just a rosy wreath, to be sure, but William Blake was closer to the truth of play when he posed the worlds of adults and children as contraries reflecting each other. Many children did die during the Black Death, just as many chimney sweeps died of cancer of the scrotum in Blake's day. The joyful dancing of the boys in "Songs of Innocence" finds a dark reflection in "Songs of Experience," where the "little black thing among the snow" cries "weep, weep, in notes of woe" (1979, 25–26; 6). The Low German version of "Ring a Ring o' Roses" resonates for me on both the levels of innocence and experience. I have transcribed the rhyme as I remember it, but I notice that where I have *Butta shtaunz* Victor Friesen remembers "Weppestauns," which he translates as "Pedal-stance" (1987, 74). The Low German word for dance is in fact *taunz* not *shtaunz* and it would be more accurate to translate *krauntz* as wreath. Sadly this is not one of the rhymes Jay Macpherson translated for me, but I have attempted to emulate her way of putting sound before sense.

I begin by imagining children's games as a way of grounding myself in an earthy *Spielraum* before I turn my attention to questions about *eschatology*, the word used to denote religious doctrines about the end of the world. Children's circle games often end with a tumbling down that is quickly followed by a new start of the same game, but the delights of play cannot eliminate the fear of that moment when the play will have to end and the night will fall. In *The Sense of an Ending*, Frank Kermode notes that Christianity has been described as the most anxious of the world's great religions and that "Reformation theology strengthened this emphasis" (1966, 27). This is particularly so in relation to eschatology. It would be hard to exaggerate how important the Bible is to Mennonite ways of dealing with this fear. The model of history in it, beginning with an ideal garden and ending with an ideal city, is comforting to those who see it as divinely ordained and themselves as among the "saved." Less so if you find yourself wondering whether you are a sheep or a goat. Heaven and hell might seem like quaint concepts in an age that fancies itself secular, but as Kermode notes "these old paradigms continue in some way to affect the way we make sense of the world" in an age of "perpetual crisis in morals and politics" (14).

Anabaptist approaches to eschatology were "firmly rooted in the soil of medieval apocalypticism," and they were shared in varying forms by other religions during the Reformation, as they are to this day (Klaassen 1985, 13). These deep roots came to the surface in Canada during the revival meetings of 1957 that I put forward as one of the root causes of the Mennonite literary renaissance that peaked in the 1980s. Fear of the Second Coming was a collective obsession in southern Manitoba at that time. The biblical prediction about "wars and rumours of wars" (Matthew 24:6) matched up with news about the Cold War and the looming threat of nuclear disaster. Was that Sputnik in the night sky, or was it Jesus coming back to Earth? Before you laugh, take note of how our own ignorance—about climate change and about religious terrorism—now fuels fears that the world might end.

An "abhorrence of the 'excesses' of apocalyptic expectations," according to Walter Klaassen, has led Mennonite historians to downplay the subject (1985, 13). It has not done so for artists. Having confronted the "end-feeling" in Koop's *Tear*, I was not surprised when I read that Koop told Robert Enright "I'm always afraid the world is ending, so what some of these paintings represent is that cold, isolating fear in my mind" (Enright 1984, 41). How this "end-feeling" is experienced or communicated varies widely. For those of us who grew up being inundated with fundamentalist rhetoric, those fears were attached to the Bible during the 1950s. We were warned that the Last Judgement could happen without a moment's notice: "Then shall two be in the field; the one shall be taken, and the other left" (Matthew 24:40). Rudy Wiebe dramatizes the resulting terror in *The Blue Mountains of China* (1970). Released after six weeks in a cell, Jakob returns to his home in Chortitza. It has been destroyed by the anarchists, and his family is gone. Briefly he imagines that "*jesus has come again and taken them and I am left for hell and the devil and his angels and the place prepared*" (14).

David Bergen was born in 1957, the year of the revival movement. In his fiction, as in Koop's paintings, the cultural repercussions of that time are evident but distanced in ways that refract all the questions. Bergen's *The Time in Between* (2005) takes place in Viet Nam, but it is charged with an intensity that comes across to me as a Mennonite sensibility. Bergen's signature plain style is performed in a time of perpetual crisis. Kermode refers to this "end-feeling" as a "'time-between' . . . one's moment and one's death" (1966, 25). In a scene that involves a brother and sister trying to make sense of the notes that their father wrote about a novel that he carried with him, Bergen's dialogue carries the narrative like a delicate steel thread moving back and forth from "Jon said" to "Ada said" and back to "Jon said." The word *said* creates the illusion of improvisation, leaving gaps in the dialogue into which readers project their own longings. "He said that he couldn't think beyond the moment" (Bergen 2005, 183). Bergen's plain style here conveys, in secularized form, an urgency central to the theology of Rudolf Bultmann: "In every moment slumbers the possibility of being the eschatological moment. You must awaken it" (Bultmann 1957, 155; quoted in Kermode 1966, 25).

Every novelist and poet, every musician and painter, faces the problem of how to bring things to an end. Wiebe opts for an open ending to *The Blue Mountains of China* (1970) with a section entitled "On the Way." "To be a pilgrim," to quote the words that Robin Laurence (2000) found on the wall in the home of Gathie Falk, is by definition to hope for progress of some sort, even if not the kind that John Bunyan envisioned. We all want to be "on the way" to something, even if we are not all walking across Canada lugging a big cross, as Wiebe imagines his pilgrim doing, for all the world like a Mennonite boldly embracing iconoclash. I feel this hope myself as I wend my way to the end of my own book. The eschatological context might seem to cast a lurid light on the conflicts about art that I have explored. As Kermode shows, however, thinking about eschatology helps to shed light on everyday events that appear to us as crises related to belief.

This kind of crisis is captured by Wallace Stevens in a poem entitled "Asides on the Oboe":

> The prologues are over. It is a question, now,
> Of final belief. So, say that final belief
> Must be in a fiction. It is time to choose. (1990, 250)

"So, say that . . . ": this improvisational style is not the "you must decide" moment of an altar call at a revival meeting. Bergen's (2005) speaker is forever suspended in the "now," the crisis time of having to choose. Being in this time in between might account for the intensity that often characterizes Mennonite ways of making believe. "Already in St. Paul and St. John," writes Kermode, "there is a tendency to conceive of the End as happening at every moment; this is the moment when the modern concept of crisis was born" (1966, 25).

"Asides on the Oboe" is a poem that came to mind the first time that I read a poem by G.C. Waldrep, entitled "Mennonite Poem," published in an "American Issue" of *Rhubarb* in 2009 (24–25). This prose poem concerns the plight of an oboe player on his way to rehearsal. It begins: "Every Mennonite poet has to write a Mennonite poem. But I am not a Mennonite, and so instead this is a poem about a frieze portraying a small band of oboe players." Waldrep plays mischievously with the ekphrastic effects central to my argument in the previous chapter. The oboe players are "playing their all-oboe orchestration of Song of the Shoes, only of course there is no way of telling this in the frieze, because a frieze is silent. It is a visual representation of an action, which is to say a longing, and in this way is a lot like being Mennonite. Which I am not." This ironically laboured explanation goes on while the oboe player gets lost in the frieze, "completely blocked by a line of larches" that begins to hum along with him the "melody line from the second movement of the Song of the Shoes." This encouraging development is quickly thwarted: "They are musical larches; they sing in four-part harmony, as they most certainly would if they were Mennonites, or at least the sort of Mennonites most likely to appear in a Mennonite poem." The oboe player fantasizes that the larches, "being musical," will let him through, but this does not happen. Instead, the poem ends with the following tour de force sentence that plays seemingly impossible tricks with grammar:

> Perhaps, standing atop one of the taller dunes, one of them will make out the forest, blinking away, or even the missing oboe player's automobile, and this, the missing oboe player thinks, is probably a lot like being Mennonite, though whether by this he means himself, or his colleague on the dune, or the act of seeing, or being seen, or possibly his other colleagues who are by now driving home, having meals with their families, shopping, etc., things Mennonites do, or even the automobile, perfectly serviceable, perfectly stationary, engine idling, inside of which his body comfortably rests, neither the forest nor the music is sure.

Reading this poem for the first time in 2019, I was both delighted and disturbed. I was delighted by the playful staging of exactly that crisis on the borderline between identities that informs the argument of this book. I was disturbed by the ominous enacting of the foundational Mennonite gesture of shunning and by the fact that the musician is stuck. As a lover of American poetry, I enjoyed the many echoes that I was hearing from familiar poems. That last sentence, for example, resonates with Wallace Stevens's "Connoisseur of Chaos." Stevens posits A and B in that poem as the kind of order not like statuary in a museum. "They are things chalked / On the sidewalk so that the pensive man may see." In the brief final section of that poem, "the pensive man" is like the beholder in Waldrep's last sentence: "He sees that eagle float / For which the intricate Alps are a single nest" (Stevens 1990, 216). Waldrep's inflation of this famous instance of poetic closure into an absurdly extended sentence seemed to me to be almost satirical in tone. When I reread the poem, I saw how the clichéd self-congratulatory marker of identity—four-part singing— becomes an instrument of shunning and how the bourgeois stasis of that resting automobile makes a mockery of that kind of Mennonite identity.

I had assumed that Waldrep must be a Swiss Mennonite name, but when I checked online I discovered that he was at one time an "intentional Mennonite." He joined a Mennonite congregation in 1992, then an Amish community in 1995. When that community disbanded, he affiliated, in 2005, with the Old Order River Brethren. When a poem so clearly invites dialogue, it is surely impossible for a critic not to respond. When I emailed Waldrep about "Mennonite Poem," he said that it began as "a response to the commodification of Mennonite heritage" that he observed in a group of poems published in an American journal called *Mennonite World Review*. Those poems, he said, "dramatized the distance I felt from the 'heritage' thrust of Menno-lit." As a convert, he explained, he found "arguments of 'heritage' and culture divorced from faith . . . not only problematic, but also exclusive: indeed, they perform an erasure."*

This place that Waldrep experienced and protested as the site of his erasure is an old conflict for Russian Mennonites in Canada—an ongoing tension between ethnic and religious identity charged by issues surrounding Germanic identity. I am not familiar with the American Swiss Mennonite contexts that precipitated the writing of this poem. I share my response to it, however, because Waldrep's retelling of the parable of the lost sheep stages the crisis that I am concerned with here. In the moment of that poem "slumbers the possibility" of something that "you must wake." The ekphrastic terms made so explicit in "Mennonite Poem," moreover, make it clear that the oboe player is locked into a work of art. This is making believe. While we enter into play on the ground of the poem, there is a reassuring childlike awareness that we are playing and that it is a joy to play. And, oddly enough, there is a moral in the story, as there is in all the parables. There is still hope. We can aim at being better people. The pun on the word *frieze/freeze* says it all. Art can become fixed and life denying. The flying sparks and the dialogue are what make it come alive.

"Ending with Music": Beyond the Mennonite Martyr Myth

When first I seized on the idea of emulating my father by ending with a poem, I settled on Maurice Mierau's "Ending with Music." The title drew me because ending with a poem is at the same time a way of ending with

---

* G.C. Waldrep, email to the author, 11 August 2015; quoted with permission.

music. This is most apparent if you focus on *praxis*, on the act of composition. Poet Roo Borson writes that "poetry is made of words, yet it is exactly as articulate as music, and as distinct from ordinary speech. Spoken in a near monotone, the motion of thought is its real melody" (2008, 12). "Ending with Music," a poem about a murder that looks like a suicide, is the title poem in a collection also called *Ending with Music* (2002). A section of that book includes a series of poems under the heading "Murders," a significant designation since several of those poems were previously published by Mierau under the title "The Martyrdom Method: A Cycle of Poems" (1985, 111–16). The earlier cycle was prefaced by a note stating that the poems are "based on oral and written accounts of sixteenth-century Anabaptists and twentieth-century Hutterites and Mennonites" (111). Writing beyond the Mennonite martyr myth in 2002, Mierau transmutes the longings and fears in such a way that "Ending with Music" becomes "simply, utterly *everyone's* text" (Tiessen 2012, 14). It is a poem about music, but it also *makes* music of the kind described by Borson.

The reference in the poem is to guitarist Lenny Breau, whose body was found in his swimming pool in 1984. This literal fact is crucial to the impact of the poem. Unlike Sarah Binks, this man is no mythical martyr poet. The poem locates the fact of Breau's death in a centuries-old elegiac tradition of drowned poets such as Milton's "Lycidas" and Shelley's "Adonais," but the poet drowned in this poem is Maurice Mierau. The word *I* is absent in the poem except for a parenthetical passage in which a strange voice is heard, as if in conversation with an unseen other:

> *(I need to get composed. I can't*
> *talk about Lenny. He was a genius but*
> *that's all. He was like a son.)* (2002, 83)

From where is this voice coming? The prose is divided up into lines as if to help with the composing, but just who is it that needs to "get composed"? What is clear is that the person who says he "can't / talk about Lenny" is the one doing just that—talking about Lenny.

In the last lines of the poem, the dissolution of the lyric *I* pays off. With a few lines, Mierau performs his part in "the unending Orphic task" of luring the shadowy figure of the other into relation with the self (Stewart 2002). Just as the speaker in "Asides on the Oboe" does not play an oboe, so too this poet who plays the part of Orpheus has no musical instrument. As Borson writes, "poor poetry, I want to say—fluteless, impoverished. But it is still beautifully cantabile" (2008, 12). Mierau draws the reader into participating in the act of composition:

> You float in the swimming pool,
> still
> like the framing shot in a film noir.
> You think a line
> with a stutter-rest, jump into a 13 chord. You have
> an ending with music,
> but silent. (2002, 84)

The first lines collapse beginnings and endings into a single frame with an allusion to the famous opening sequences of Billy Wilder's *Sunset Boulevard*, which ends with an image of a dead body floating in a pool. The visual arts and music are there as analogies, but all there is in fact are printed words on a page. Dialogue flows as you read because there is a constant shift in the meaning of *you*. The word appears three times, first as an apostrophe to *you*, the dead body of the musician. The second *you* is self-reflexive, referring to the poet composing a line. The last *you* is colloquial, combining the poet and the *you* reading the poem. You could translate it into colloquial speech and say there you have it—an ending with music. The last two words of the poem—"but silent"—undercut that neat solution. They take the reader back to the beginning, to the commitment to wrestle with words, to talk even when you are convinced you cannot talk—which, of course, is exactly what most of us do after someone we love has died.

"Ending with Music" is not a container chock full of Mennonite meanings. It is an excellent illustration, however, of what Ben Lerner (2016) calls the "bitter logic" of poetry. Lerner meditates at length on the poem by Marianne Moore from which, in Chapter 2, I took my organizing tropes: "imaginary gardens with real toads in them." That poem, entitled "Poetry," begins with a flat statement: "I, too, dislike it." The "it" appears to refer back to the title, "Poetry," but Moore moves with swift logic to a strange reversal: "Reading *it*, however, with a perfect contempt for *it*, one discovers in / *it* after all, a place for the genuine" (1935, 36; emphasis added).

Mierau embraces this "bitter logic" in "Ending with Music." Adopting a pose of humility that is now a prerequisite for the writing of poetry, such poems constitute a gesture, not claiming to do anything more than point to that place. The real toad in Mierau's imaginary garden points to real places. The poem is not happening in some vaguely metaphysical realm but with reference to an actual musician. It matters that Lenny Breau made music in Winnipeg for many years. It matters that he died in Los Angeles. It matters that his death was not a suicide but an unsolved murder. Mierau's way of dealing with "end-feeling," of negotiating among suicide, martyrdom, and murder, comes across to me as the expression of a Mennonite sensibility. I hear it as an elegy for the loss of community. At the heart of the ironically alienated "I" of the lyric is a deep longing for connection.

The figure of the poet in "Ending with Music" does not fit with romantic ideas about where poetry should originate. Paul Hiebert mocks those ideas in the introductory poem to *Sarah Binks*, in which the poet is pictured as "Poeming" as his "mouth is foaming" (1995, 13). This absurd but still powerful figure has left a trace of his presence in Marianne Moore's "Poetry":

> Hands that can grasp, eyes
> that can dilate, hair that can rise
> if it must (1935, 36).

Moore tags on to these romantic tropes, however, an important qualifier:

> these things are important not because a
> high sounding interpretation can be put upon them but
> because they are
> useful. (36).

Useful. The word sits on a line all by itself, demanding our attention. Deliberately bad poems, like earnest doggerel, expose the simple fact that all poetry, like music, is useful and acquires meaning within particular social contexts. "Whatever we think of particular poems," writes Lerner, "'poetry' is a word for the meeting place of the private and the public, the internal and the external" (2016, 12). Our strong feelings about poetry derive, he argues, from "this sense of poetry's tremendous social stakes (combined with a sense of its tremendous social marginalization)" (13). Poetry tends to overlap with music in just those places where the stakes are high for marginalized people. In such cases, you can feel the truth contained in the title of an essay by Audre Lorde: "Poetry Is Not a Luxury" (1984), echoed by Toronto dub poet Afua Cooper in a poem recorded in 1990. The lowly Low German rhymes that I have included in this book are a repeated reminder that all poetry, good or bad, is embedded in the social textures of our daily lives. We need it in order to live. It is not a luxury.

Freiwilliges: *Sharing Poetry in Public*

Public recitations and readings of poems happen in a shared space, a place where performance makes cultural *poiesis* visible with all the imperfections. During the symposium of Mennonite writers convened by Robert Enright for the magazine *Border Crossings* in 1986, discussion turned to the place of public poetry readings in Mennonite communities. Sandra Birdsell described a "tradition of old men who would always write poems for an occasion" (23), and Rudy Wiebe commented that sentimental poems "with nice turns at the end" were a common feature at gatherings of all kinds (23). The four people who participated in the discussion were unanimous when it came to the question of evaluation. Nobody challenged Birdsell when she said that the poems "always rhymed and were clearly doggerel" (23). Patrick Friesen responded to Wiebe's memory by observing that in his experience it was the women who read poetry in public. Di Brandt related this to church practices: "In my church, if you were a man you could preach and pray, but if you were a woman you could only sing and play the piano, and if you were unfortunate enough not to be able to do those things, then you could read very bad poetry in church. . . . The only people who were remotely connected with poetry were the failed musicians" (Enright 1986, 22). None of the participants thought to wonder how these Mennonite customs might be related to Hiebert's habit of pulling poems by Binks out of his pocket at various gatherings.

Questions about public readings of poetry in Mennonite communities would reward closer consideration than I can give them here. I note, for example, that Friesen compared the "Missing Mennonite Cabaret" to the Mennonite practice of *Freiwilliges*—a term that literally means "freewillingness" and applies to the time after a wedding when people volunteer contributions of various sorts—singing, speaking, or reading poetry. Many of these poems, like the ones that my father found useful, would now be labelled useless doggerel by learned readers and earn the added damning label of being didactic. Hiebert's satire in *Sarah Binks*, however, shows that our denigration of what we call doggerel might say as much about us as about those who create or sing it. It is worth noting that composers have been drawn to Hiebert's "very bad poetry" by the very features that make contemporary readers anxious—regular rhyme and meter. These qualities are also making a return in performance poetry of all kinds. Contempt for poetry is now less likely to be directed at supposed doggerel than at the kind of free verse easily dismissed as so much self-pitying drivel.

Enormous quantities of poetry are being published in Canada and it sometimes appears as if poets write and perform primarily for each other. My teaching experience tells me otherwise. It tells me that poetry is "useful" in the sense conveyed by Moore. As always, however, the question that I have left over is whether or not it is useful to separate out poets who are Mennonites for special study. Comparative discussion with poets in other minority groups is helpful. When poet George Elliott Clarke came to speak to my class and read his poetry, we were all moved by how the individual and often oratorical voice was interwoven in his poems with powerful choric sounds. Often this involved complex ways of alluding to the Bible, and all of this is part of what Clarke calls "Africadian" culture. There is no body of scholarly work, however, that has identified a Mennonite tradition of poetry, let alone begun the task of comparing it with other traditions such as the "Africadian" and the Jewish. Still needed is a response to the invitation in the title of Leonard Cohen's first book of poetry: *Let Us Compare Mythologies*.

Recent writing about poetry suggests that such a study would confront the fierce tensions between song and word and image and word that I have been exploring. Polyphony is a useful musical analogy for verbal art, but it remains an analogy. As my study of Glenn Gould's *The Quiet in the Land* (1977) has shown, it tends to turn a blind eye to those "real frogs." Katherine McLeod pushes the idea of polyphony in a fascinating dissertation on poetry and performance in Canada. She articulates "the interdisciplinary question of whether one art form can employ the tools of another. In other words, what is at stake, critically, in positing a writing that is singing? A music that is dancing? A dancing that is writing?" (2010, 4). What is at stake for ordinary readers, however, might not be the same as what is at stake for critics. Scholars have written, in glowing terms, about public readings. McLeod claims that "the Q&A session [that follows a public reading] exemplifies a call-and-response exchange between performer and audience" (3). She wisely adds a qualifier: "Whether or not both interlocutors are listening to each other is another matter altogether" (3). Indeed.

The critical tendency to celebrate public participatory readings might be a reaction in part to the reality that poets are alone while they write their poems and that for the most part we are alone when we read them. Furthermore, we do need to read poems one at a time. This is the case even for the poetry of Robert Bringhurst, who has done more than any other poet in Canada to nurture cultural polyphony and to create bridges among poetry, music, and dance. As I see it, the critics now doing comparative studies of cultural poiesis are moving in the right direction (see Sherbert, Gérin, and Petty 2006; Vautour et al. 2015). Increasingly scholars are concerned with how specific traditions, that of prairie poetry, for example, need to be situated "within a broader performative framework of textual and acoustic experimentation" (McLeod 2010, 7). A study of public readings of poetry, because it necessarily must be located within material contexts, can shed light on questions confronted by scholars who attempt to map out the literary territory of a particular minority group.

Shall We Dance? Beyond the Mennonite Joke

I remember the pleasure of being the first person to tell Rudy Wiebe the joke about why Mennonites don't believe in having intercourse standing up, the answer being that it might lead to dancing. By the time Wiebe inserted it into *My Lovely Enemy* (1983), the joke was already stale for me. There is no way of telling how many of his readers had heard the joke before or how many associated it with a different religious group. Jokes of that kind are easily transferable from one group to another. As I learned from my study of jokes in the stories of Alice Munro, it is worth paying attention to how jokes expose unequal distributions of power (see Redekop 1992a, 25–34, 107–14). I smiled when I read Wanda Koop's account of her recurring dream: "In this dream I would have a choice of becoming a dancer or a painter and then I would wake up with a start and realize that I would be a painter because, being a Mennonite, you couldn't dance" (Enright 1986,

95–96). I think that I smiled because I was fairly certain that prohibitions against dancing had not constituted much of a barrier for Koop's fierce talent. Indeed, I think it possible that Mennonite jokes about dancing can be seen as one of those trickster ploys made famous by Menno Simons, in this case designed to protect the artist looking for *Spielraum*. The artist who wants to be left alone to paint or to compose new music or to perform some literary trick or even to dance could be saying something like this: "Don't mind me. I'm a Mennonite. I don't dance." In support of this possibility, I note that Koop (1993, n.p.) told Claire Gravel that painting, for her, is "like a meditation or like dancing, . . . 'an act of intimacy' in which the body is involved with the painting."

Dance, both as a metaphor and as actual performance, provides the most powerful example of a point made by Judith Hamera in relation to cultural poiesis. Hamera notes that "the social work of aesthetics is especially central to performance, where the labors of creation and the dynamics of consumption are explicitly communal and corporeal" (2006, 47). The challenge of "ethnic dialogism" takes different forms with changes in medium and genre, but actual dance form makes it possible to observe the "social work of aesthetics," as Hamera points out. My engagement with Emmanuel Gat's choreography in *The Goldlandbergs* has shown one way that this could work.

In Di Brandt's *questions i asked my mother*, a Mennonite questioning accent is pushed to a place where poetry itself is performed as a dance of rebellion: "i will dance mighty ones i will dance / on your brittle bones" (1987, 48). Brandt dances with words, but rhetorical subtleties are lost when stereotypes take over, as they regularly do when a writer is branded as Mennonite. Jokes about Mennonites and dancing are part of what Homi Bhabha calls "fetishism, as the disavowal of difference" (2004, 67). If you are a Mennonite, then by definition you are always somebody who does not dance, and this stereotype is made visible when the titles of books are used as marketing tools. The titles of two books by Brandt reflect both the central place of dance in her poetic strategies and the existence of market forces: *Wild Mother Dancing: Maternal Narrative in Canadian Literature* (1993) and *Dancing Naked: Narrative Strategies for Writing across Centuries* (1996). Titles point not only inward to the book but also outward to the larger social contexts and to issues of reception. Darcie Friesen

Hossack's *Mennonites Don't Dance* is a collection of short stories of evenly high quality. By the time it was published in 2010, the word *Mennonite* had acquired some cash value, but is the target audience us or them? Is the question why don't they dance? Or is it why don't we dance? It is against the backdrop of this social context that Mennonite writers and dancers and musicians make their art. My impatience with hackneyed jokes about dancing coexists with a sense that our ways of responding to dance are part of cultural poiesis. Failure to realize this results in failure to do justice to the achievements of the artists.

The dance of *poiesis* can be seen as a metaphor for the "performative nature of cultural communication" (Bhabha 2004, 224). Political philosopher Charles Blattberg makes an eloquent case, in *Shall We Dance? A Patriotic Politics for Canada* (2003), for thinking of dance as an interactive performance applicable to pluralistic cultures. One of the most sustained developments of this idea in relation to Mennonite culture is Michael A. King's *Fractured Dance: Gadamer and a Mennonite Conflict over Homosexuality*. King sees dance, gesture, and performance as antidotes to the print fundamentalism that is an undertow in Mennonite culture and bases his study on the writing of Hans-Georg Gadamer. This is an approach to hermeneutics shaped by the view that conversation is a form of play. According to Gadamer, "*spiel*, the German word for play, originally meant 'dance'" (1994, 103; quoted in King 2001, 103). King goes so far as to suggest that "one important analogue of prayer is play" and that prayer is a kind of dance (103). He follows Gadamer in seeing "a play of conversation [as] unfolding in and through God's presence." The "sacred seriousness" of this kind of play is "an explicit interaction with God, who is viewed as a kind of playing field in which the entire game unfolds" (105). Gadamer's ideas also resonate with those put forward by American Mennonite theologian Philip Stoltzfus in *Theology as Performance: Music, Aesthetics, and God in Western Thought* (2006). These playing fields invite comparison with de Certeau's *Spielraum*. Poets and dancers, however, do not wait for permission from theologians. As Patrick Friesen put it in "The Dance Floor (Apparitions)," "I came by dance naturally. . . . All movement, leaf, animal or human is interesting. . . . Dance is what we begin with. One foot in front of the other. A leap in the dark" (1992, 111).

Of all the dance and music forms, jazz might be the best analogy for Friesen's poetic style, in part the result of his frequent collaboration with improvisational jazz pianist Marilyn Lerner. The composition of a poem entitled "Loose in the House of Fundamentalism" invites comparison with jazz, but the poem is about rock and grounded in a flashback to adolescent rebellion. Like the fiction of Miriam Toews, the first stanza plugs into that source of electricity:

> you go dancing around your room banging off red walls
>   pictures swinging wildly on their hooks
> shivers down your backbone tailfeathers ruffling and you
>   playing piano with a ball peen hammer (Friesen 2011, 58)

"Loose in the House of Fundamentalism" dramatizes the swerve away from fundamentalism that I have identified as a primary moving force of the Mennonite cultural renaissance. In an email to me, Friesen provided an autobiographical context for the poem. As a teenager, he bought a cheap portable record player: "I'd put my duvet over it, and me, and listen quietly to the one or two albums I bought. I'd lock my bedroom door.... When [my parents] were out of the house I'd crank up my record player or the radio (CKY and CKRC) and dance like a wild man."*

In this densely allusive poem, the allusions circle around a small number of powerful images, a central one being the wall. In the first stanza alone, there are echoes from "Ballpeen Hammer" (Joe Bonamassa), "Shiver down My Spine" (King Khan and The Shrines), and "Shakin' All Over" (Johnny Kidd and the Pirates and The Guess Who). The poem illustrates Wai Chee Dimock's (1997) notion of a text as an "echo chamber." All the allusions are grounded in the figure of an adolescent who is simultaneously the poet and *you*, "kicking / your way through the room's furniture" (Friesen 2011, 58). This is much more than a nostalgic reflection on adolescence. It is an entry into a place where creation and destruction dance together, a place where you accept and live with contradiction.

The carefully crafted jazz momentum carries the reader forward into the poem. There are bones that shiver and tail feathers that shake, and

---

* Patrick Friesen, email to the author, 24 April 2015; quoted with permission.

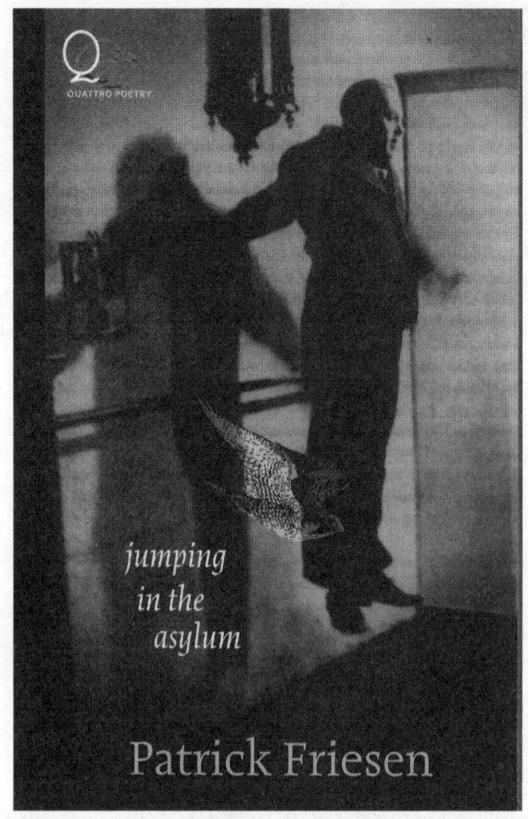

Figure 17. Cover of Patrick Friesen's *jumping in the asylum* (2011), depicting Vaslav Nijinsky. Cover design by Marijke Friesen. Courtesy of Quattro Books.

there is the adolescent with his boner. Then there are the birds, the beating of their wings, and the dark flowers. Always there are the claustrophobic walls of "the house of fundamentalism." The rhythm builds from "skid scuffing linoleum all feathers and mischief" to "just holy ghost and a slippery foot," and the crescendo effect catapults the reader into the last stanza and finally out of the poem. The last lines create a fade-out effect. The "Cockeyed Optimist" (from South Pacific) sings along with both Cole Porter and Guns N' Roses, who chime in with "Anything Goes." There is a final sense of exhausted abandonment in the last words of the poem: "and always it does." When the poem is finished, there is a feeling similar to what happens at the end of a party or at the end of a jazz performance when you don't want the music to stop.

"Loose in the House of Fundamentalism" is contained in a book entitled *jumping in the asylum* (Friesen 2011). The cover of that book contains imagery suggestive of a displacement or translation of the wildly jumping adolescent. Designed by Friesen's daughter, Marijke Friesen, the cover features a famous photograph of Vaslav Nijinsky, the legendary Russian ballet dancer whose gravity-defying leaps are often described as enrapturing the world (Figure 17). Nijinsky went mad and lived his last years in an asylum. The picture was taken by a visitor who witnessed something that happened as the result of a strategy developed by Nijinsky's wife to try to bring the dancer back to dancing. She invited a dancer, dressed as Nijinsky himself had once been dressed, to perform for him a particular dance for which he was famous. Nijinsky sat in a chair, dressed in a buttoned-up suit. For a while, he stared intently at the dancer. Then he stood up and leaped into the air. The image illustrates a point made by Robert Bringhurst: "What poetry knows, or what it strives to know, is the dancing at the heart of being" (2007, 52).

In the title poem, "Jumping in the Asylum," all the questions are literally up in the air. They act like a refrain, circling around the words *raptured, ravished,* and *ravaged.* There is an "end-feeling" in every line, yet the singing in the poem echoes beyond its own boundaries and beyond the life of the singer. There are no other punctuation marks in the poem, giving the question marks an extra weight. They act like open windows, pointing out of the poem:

"are you ravaged fire licking along your arms?"
"what flinches at the corner of your eye are you raptured?"
"arms flayed are you ravished?"
"are you seared in the conflagration are you?"
"high in the trees there where it begins are you ravaged?"
"do you whistle where you loiter are you raptured?"
(Friesen 2011, 23)

Jetzt: *"Quick now, here, now, always—"*

Being part of a dissenting tradition has been useful to me as an educator. Indeed, I have spent my life enjoying what Johan Huizinga (1970) refers to as the agonistic aspect of play—the push and pull of the exchange of ideas. Much more difficult for me are those aspects of being Mennonite that require *Gelassenheit*—the acceptance of things that cannot be changed. This might explain why, in my fascination with my father's closing poem, I almost forgot about his long closing prayer and then the relief of the pre-scribed benediction. "Der Herr segne dich und behüte dich":

> The Lord bless you and keep you;
> The Lord make His face shine upon you,
> And be gracious unto you;
> The Lord lift up His countenance upon you,
> And give you peace. (Numbers 6:24–26)

The words are still as comforting to me as they are ancient, no less so be-cause I do not believe in a personal God. Even more pleasurable, because more communal, are the times when a benediction is sung at Mennonite social gatherings, a cappella and in four-part harmony. Some but not all of this comfort derives from nostalgia. I remember my father announcing "O Gott sei gelobt" (O God be praised) and, after a few notes of melody, plunging instantly downward into the bass part, confident that my mother would carry the soprano line and that the other voices would chime in, moving along in harmony:

> *Hallelujah! Sei gepriesen!*
> *Hallelujah, Amen!*
> *Hallelujah! Sei gepriesen!*

Herr segne uns jetzt.
Hallelujah! Be praised!
Hallelujah! Amen!
Hallelujah! Be praised!
Lord bless us now!

I took pleasure then and still do now in the fact that the last word is *jetzt*—now. In *Four Quartets*, T.S. Eliot offers a redemptive vision based on that word: "Quick now, here, now, always" (1959, 20). His profoundly Christian vision echoes the benediction of Julian of Norwich: "And all shall be well and / All manner of thing shall be well" (1959, 57). Such powerful idealized visions of future harmony are necessary to keep a pilgrim moving forward.

Ted Chamberlin has written eloquently about the covenants that we make as human beings when we make believe. It is something that we learn to do "early in our lives, with the nursery rhymes and bedtime stories that are a staple of childhood in all cultures; and they constitute our first covenant in wonder with the world" (2012, 18–19). The goal, as Chamberlin defines it, is to embrace contradiction, to believe and not believe at the same time. This is a way of making do by letting go and abandoning ourselves to the possibility of grace. I felt this happening when I was sitting in the audience at Koerner Hall in Toronto on the evening of 1 June 2016 to hear readings by the poets who had been shortlisted for the Griffin Poetry Prize. The hall was filled to capacity, which filled me with wonder. What did it mean that so many people bought tickets for a public reading of poetry when the evidence shows that very few people buy and read books of poetry? I was sceptical, perhaps unfairly so. I am aware that my farm girl bias can lead to reverse snobbishness. Part of me could not believe that people who get into fancy dress to hear poetry read in public could really be there for the poetry. Another part of me did believe and found the sight heartening. This is what Chamberlin would call a "ceremony of belief" (2012, 29). The sheer number of people embodied the contradiction pointed out by Ben Lerner between the "sense of poetry's tremendous social stakes (combined with a sense of its tremendous social marginalization)" (2016, 13).

I was in attendance because my friend Patrick Friesen had been co-nominated for *Frayed Opus for Strings and Wind Instruments*. The book is a collection of poetry by Ulrikka S. Gernes (2015), a celebrated Danish poet, and the back-cover blurb describes it as "elegantly translated by Canadian collaborators Per Brask and Patrick Friesen." Although I concede my bias, I am not alone in considering Friesen to be one of our most underrecognized poets. I could not help wondering if it was in some way significant that, when he finally got nominated for a major award, it was not for his own poetry but for translation—and a collaborative one at that. One reason that I conclude by gesturing toward this event is that it shows both how important and how irrelevant geography can be at the same time. I do not live, after all, on the *shtahp* of Manitoba. This event happened in Toronto, my home. But something about this event felt dislocating. For reasons that I cannot quite define (something to do with jeans), both Brask and Friesen looked like displaced Manitobans up on that platform in Koerner Hall, and Gernes was obviously the visitor from Denmark (something to do with warmth and blonde hair). These are stereotypes, I hasten to concede, but they show that this public reading happened in the messy place where this entire book has been located. Homi Bhabha calls this "the space of the translation of cultural difference," which demonstrates "the performative nature of cultural communication" (2004, 225). This is not only "the location of culture" but also the place where community happens.

No mention was made in any of the advertising related to the Griffin Poetry Prize competition of the fact that Friesen is a Mennonite. That is as it should be. Neither was there any mention of the ethnic origins of others who participated in this collaboration. Indeed, it was such an anomaly in the history of the prize that if it had won people could have claimed that it had broken the rules. The original poet, after all, is not Canadian. The book did not win that night, and Friesen's nomination, as part of this group, was not the vindication of his "solo" music for which his fans might wish. On the contrary, it felt like a sideways and "frayed" celebration of shared music. The fact that the committee chose to nominate a translation almost bound to lose spoke eloquently about the dispersal of poetry as a conversational dance not walled in by any single culture. This book was the result of three poets working together in a contact zone, and it spoke to what is best in Canadian poetic culture. Friesen himself, unfazed by the loss, told me that the high point of the evening for him was meeting Adam Zagajewski, the Polish poet there to receive the Griffin Lifetime Achievement Award.

For me, the high point was the joint reading done by Ulrikka Gernes, Per Brask, and Patrick Friesen. It was clear from the beginning that they had carefully planned their presentation to fit into the allotted time. When they took up their positions at the lectern, I thought of a trio about to sing. Brask spoke first, describing how their collaboration works. Gernes then expressed her gratitude to the translators and read a single poem in Danish. Friesen was standing to the back, slightly behind them, and had not yet spoken a single word. The musical sound of the Danish language, foreign to me, was still echoing in my ears when Gernes and Brask moved aside and Friesen moved forward to the microphone. It seemed as if he was taking choreographed dance steps. There was a hushed silence in the auditorium. Then he read the English translation of the same poem:

> I have to find F. I don't know why and I don't know
> where, but if I find F I'll get the answer to an important
> question. I don't know the question, but at some
> point I'll be told. It's something to do with an
> envelope. (Gernes 2015, 19)

None of us can tell what the envelopes of the future will contain, but this book has been written out of a deep conviction that art is not a frivolous pursuit in the midst of the crisis of our time. Talking *about* art is another matter altogether. When I think of the disasters, political and environmental, that threaten the planet now, I am struck by how the evident desire of theorists to save the world contrasts with how ineffectual theory has been in the real world. Despite how much I have learned from theorists, the various positions that they espouse could be seen as a rearranging of the deck chairs on the *Titanic*. To echo the familiar folk song, it will be sad if the great ship of our species goes down to the bottom of the sea. The question of what to do to prevent the disaster is too big for any one person. What we all do together is what matters most, and it is this doing that I have been describing as a collective act of making believe. If our ship does go down, and you find me singing along with "Nearer, My God, to Thee," then it will be because I am making believe.

ACKNOWLEDGEMENTS

When a book has been as long in the making as this one, the list of people who need to be thanked is very long and many on the list have died. Foremost among these is Clarence Redekop, my late husband, who believed in me more than I have ever believed in myself. His love sustained me after his death and made it possible to go on living and eventually to write this book.

Numerous colleagues have offered support along the way. I am particularly indebted to W.J. Keith, who got me to take the reluctant first step when he persuaded me to write an essay on Rudy Wiebe. Many years later, when I found myself lured into a border between music and poetry, it was Jay Macpherson who responded with fiercely loyal encouragement. Linda Hutcheon read an early draft of my introduction and responded with generous and useful insights about representation. Ted Chamberlin read portions of the book and encouraged me to pursue questions about belief. Paul Stevens took time to meet with me and talk about secularized versions of grace.

I am indebted to scholars who have supported this venture with invitations to write or present papers on Mennonite topics. Harry Loewen was the first to do so when he asked me to contribute to the book *Why I Am a Mennonite*. Some years later he followed through with an invitation to give a series of talks at the University of Winnipeg. The generous response of Al Reimer to those talks encouraged me to keep returning to the questions I first asked there.

Like all who write about Mennonites and literature, I am indebted to Hildi Froese Tiessen, whose example gave me the courage to take risks. I will always be grateful to Ervin Beck for uncovering the stories about Menno Simons as a trickster that helped me to deal with questions about martyrdom. I owe a lot to Robert Zacharias, whose lucid arguments and commitment to dialogue give me hope for the future of this field.

I am grateful for the encouragement of Carol Ann Weaver, whose generous collaborations are a model for how scholarship should work. Doreen Klassen inspires me constantly with her mischievous intelligence and her wisdom about oral cultures. My Low German conversations with her helped give me the courage to make our mother tongue visible in this book.

I am grateful to all the musicians who agreed to be interviewed and then to be quoted in this book. They gave generously of their time, thought deeply about the questions I asked, and trusted me by responding with honest answers and fascinating stories. My nephew Jeff Neufeld and his wife Katrina Lee Kwen offered their home in Winnipeg as a place to do those interviews and I thank them for their gracious hospitality.

My intention had been to publish a collection of interviews with musicians but I abandoned that plan (and stopped doing interviews) when I discovered how labour intensive the job of transcription would be. Many years later, when I began to write this book, my sister Mary Neufeld generously offered to listen to the tapes and transcribe selective passages. Her labour of love made it possible for me to quote from those stories. Although I had room only for fragments from them, *all* the stories I was told have helped to shape my thinking. The names of the musicians are listed in the bibliography so I will not single out any here, but I am especially grateful to those who read and responded to drafts of the music chapter. Lee Bartel and Howard Dyck agreed to belated interviews, long after I had abandoned the project. Howard took the time to read not only a draft of the music chapter but also a draft of the chapter in which I quote from his interviews with Glenn Gould. His thoughtful responses were invaluable.

A single telephone conversation with Priscilla Reimer provided helpful perspectives during the time that I was constructing an imaginary art gallery. Roland Sawatzky and Ray Dirks were rich sources of information about the arts in Manitoba and archivist Conrad Stoesz supplied me with copies of Glenn Gould's interviews with Mennonite musicians.

Joe Springer, curator at Mennonite Historical Library, Goshen College, provided copies of the Dutch playing cards that contain images of Menno as trickster. Antje van Dijk, president of Landelijke Federation von Doopsgezinde Zusterkringen, sent me information about the cards and gave permission to reproduce them.

Throughout the years of writing this book I have had the support of my friends at the Mennonite Heritage Centre at St. Clair-O'Connor in Toronto. They are too many to list here but I am especially indebted to Harvey Dyck, whose vision created that centre and whose enthusiasm kept it going.

Since much of this book was written in solitude after my retirement from teaching, I have relied on email support. James Urry often provided crucial information that led me to reframe ideas. As the years passed I came increasingly to depend on my email exchanges with Patrick Friesen. I would write him with some question that was baffling me and his quick response would instantly light up the territory around that question. My email conversations with my cousin John Schellenberg, a philosopher, helped me to clarify my ideas about religious belief in ways that resonated with our shared family history.

John Warkentin was a kind companion during a time when I was struggling to be clear about the connections between nostalgia and geography. I thank him for sharing his memories of Paul Hiebert as well as their unpublished correspondence and, most of all, for the constancy of his encouragement. I lost track of how many drafts of that chapter I ran by him. Each time I marvelled, as have countless others, at the extraordinary generosity of John Warkentin.

Clowning, both as theory and practice, are central to this book. My friend Mary Lowery helped me to create the character of Sush Funk and her friendship has helped to shape my way of looking at the world. My clown teacher, Sue Morrison, pushed me to places where I could laugh and grieve at the same time.

I am blessed to have a network of loving family support, at the heart of which is my husband, Dennis Duffy. My debt to him is too deep and private to acknowledge adequately but he has enriched this book in countless ways. The most pleasurable of these for me is how our shared repertoire of remembered poetry created threads of allusion. These often helped me to stitch together the different parts of my argument. I am grateful to Dennis for his patience during the long years of revising. When I finally arrived at a draft that I was willing to release, it was my husband who was my first and most important reader.

It is impossible for me to give adequate thanks to all the members of my very large family—the Falks, the Schellenbergs, the Redekops, and the Duffys. I have room here to name only a few. My sisters Mary Neufeld and Elizabeth Falk are my rock solid support as are my two children. My conversations with my son Jonathan helped to shape the chapter on music and my daughter Susanna's work with the cooperative movement in Toronto influenced my thinking about collective ideals. The early drafts of my chapter on the visual arts included a diagram of an imaginary art gallery for which I relied on my daughter's computer skills. The love of my children and grandchildren brings me deep joy and hope for the future, without which I would not have bothered writing this book.

I am grateful to the many people who helped me to package my ideas in book form. Kailin Wright helped in the compiling of an initial bibliography. When I was still trying to decide what shape this material would take, I relied on the editorial skills of Maureen Epp. Her critical eye and her seemingly infallible ear come with an openness to new ideas and this helped me to see my way forward.

At the University of Manitoba Press it was David Carr whose belief in this book when it did not exist accounts, in large part, for why it eventually came into existence. I am grateful to him for his excellent choice of readers, one Mennonite and one non-Mennonite. Julia Kasdorf chose to break with the academic convention of anonymity and identified herself at the outset. Her writing has influenced my thinking for decades and her responses pushed me to clarify ideas and situate them more clearly within various Mennonite contexts. The non-Mennonite reader maintained anonymity and his/her help was a model for how academic publishing should work. For the scholar who has spent years writing a book, it is deeply gratifying when another scholar reads that book very carefully and with an open mind. This reader responded with generosity but also by putting his/her finger unerringly on the weaknesses that needed to be addressed.

My response to the reader reports led me to rearrange chapters and this strengthened the book. Even so, that draft of the manuscript benefited greatly from the editorial eye of Jill McConkey. Her gentle nudges were both encouraging and critical and they made it possible to finally wrap up the book in a form that was ready for publication, after which Glenn Bergen shepherded me through the final stages of this process.

Needless to say, these readers and editors have caught many mistakes and spared me embarrassment. I take full responsibility for the errors that will inevitably remain.

I am grateful to the artists who have given me permission to reproduce their art. Their names are listed with the illustrations. I am also grateful, however, for the invisible help of the curators who supplied me with images and helped me in the process of acquiring permissions. These include: Danielle Currie, Ava Hassinger, Timothy Long, Marie Olinik, Amiro Raven, and Bruce Spielman. I thank Peter Legris for photographing my Pochinko masks with such a brilliant use of light and shadow that he brought them back to life for me. It was his support that gave me the courage to share them in this book.

There is perhaps no greater thrill for a writer than the moment when you can hold your own book in your hands. I anticipate that moment with gratitude to David Drummond, who surprised me by coming up with a cover design that seemed to me to capture everything that I have been trying to say. I am hopeful that people will judge this book by its cover.

Whenever I think about the thousands of students that I have taught during the course of my career I am overwhelmed with gratitude. My style of teaching was interactive and I have therefore learned from all my students. Since it is impossible to thank them individually, I have dedicated this book to them.

BIBLIOGRAPHY

Interviews

Armin, Marta and Jay, Toronto, 19 March 2000.

Buhr, Glenn, Winnipeg, 20 February 1998.

Derksen, Bill, Winnipeg, 19 February 1998.

Dyck, Howard, Toronto, 15 November 2010.

Engbrecht, Henry, Winnipeg, 17 February 1998.

Enns, Leonard, Toronto, 27 May 2016.

Klassen [now Geddert], Heidi, Winnipeg, 17 February 1998.

Klassen, Doreen Helen, Toronto, Fall 1998.

Klassen, John and Bertha, Winnipeg, 18 February 1998.

Letkemann, Peter, Winnipeg, 16 February 1998.

Martens, John, Winnipeg, 17 February 1998.

Martin, Stephanie, Toronto, 18 January 2000.

Peters, Randolph, Winnipeg, 16 February 1998.

Redekop Fink, Joyce, Toronto, 2 September 1999.

Schellenberg, Henry, Winnipeg, 19 February 1998.

Schwartz-Trivett, Linda, Winnipeg, 20 February 1998.

Weaver, Carol Ann, Toronto, 18 May 1999.

Wiebe, Willie, Winnipeg, 18 February 1998.

Works Cited

And When They Shall Ask: A Docu-Drama of the Russian Mennonite Experience.
1984. Mennonite Media Society.

Appiah, Kwame Anthony. 2000. "Thick Translation." In *The Translation Studies
Reader,* edited by Lawrence Venuti, 417–29. London: Routledge.

———. 2017. *As If: Idealization and Ideals.* Cambridge, MA: Harvard
University Press.

———. 2018. *The Lies that Bind: Rethinking Identity, Creed, Country, Color, Class,
Culture.* New York: Liveright Publishing Corporation.

Aristotle. 1991. *The Art of Rhetoric.* Translated by H.C. Lawson-Tancred.
London: Penguin.

———. 2013. *Poetics.* Translated by Anthony Kenny. Oxford: Oxford
University Press.

Armstrong, Karen. 2005. *A Short History of Myth.* Edinburgh: Canongate.

Arnason, David. 1992. "A History of Turnstone Press." In *Acts of Concealment:
Mennonite/s Writing in Canada,* edited by Hildi Froese Tiessen and Peter
Hinchcliffe, 212–22. Waterloo: University of Waterloo Press.

Atwood, Margaret. 1982. "What's So Funny? Notes on Canadian Humour."
In *Second Words: Selected Critical Prose,* by Margaret Atwood, 175–89.
Toronto: Anansi.

Augustine, Saint. [c. 397–400] 1992. *Confessions.* Trans. Henry Chadwick.
Oxford: Oxford University Press.

Badt, Karin Luisa. 2007. "*Silent Light* or Absolute Miracle: An Interview with
Carlos Reygadas at Cannes 2007." *Bright Lights Film Journal,* 1 August.
http://brightlightsfilm.com/silent-light-absolute-miracle-interview-carlos-
reygadas-cannes-2007/#.WSnjS-vyuHQ.

Bakhtin, M.M. 1968. *Rabelais and His World.* Translated by H. Iswolsky.
Bloomington: Indiana University Press.

———. 1981. *The Dialogic Imagination: Four Essays by M.M. Bakhtin.* Edited
by Michael Holquist. Translated by Caryl Emerson and Michael Holquist.
Austin: University of Texas Press.

Baldwin, James. 2014. "An Interview with James Baldwin" [Interview by Studs
Terkel originally conducted in 1961]. In *James Baldwin: The Last Interview
and Other Conversations,* 3–34. Brooklyn and London: Melville House.

Balzer, Geraldine. 2015. "Singing New Stories: Provoking the Decolonization of
Mennonite Hymnals." *Sound in the Land: Music and the Environment,* edited

by Carol Ann Weaver, Doreen Klassen, and Judith Klassen, special issue of *Conrad Grebel Review* 33, no. 2: 282–90.

Barber, John. 2011. "Miriam Toews: It's a Mennonite Thing." *Globe and Mail*, 8 April. Updated 2 May 2018. https://www.theglobeandmail.com/arts/books-and-media/miriam-toews-its-a-mennonite-thing/article4267807/ (accessed 7 July 2019).

Barnes, Julian. 2015. *Keeping an Eye Open: Essays on Art*. London: Jonathan Cape.

Barthes, Roland. 1985. *The Responsibility of Forms: Critical Essays on Music, Art, and Representation*. Translated by Richard Howard. New York: Hill and Wang.

Baym, Nina. 1981. "Melodramas of Beset Manhood: How Theories of American Fiction Exclude Women Authors." *American Quarterly* 33, no. 2: 123–39.

Beachy, Kirsten, ed. 2010. *Tongue Screws and Testimonies: Poems, Stories, and Essays Inspired by the Martyrs Mirror*. Scottdale, PA: Herald Press.

Beck, Ervin. 1987. "Mennonite Trickster Tales: True to Be Good." *Mennonite Quarterly Review* 61, no. 1: 58–74.

———. 2015. "Mennonite Transgressive Literature." In *After Identity: Mennonite Writing in North America*, edited by Robert Zacharias, 52–69. Winnipeg: University of Manitoba Press; University Park: Pennsylvania State University Press.

Bender, Harold S. (1936) 1944. *The Anabaptist Vision*. Scottdale, PA: Herald Press.

Benesch, Otto. 1947. *Rembrandt: Selected Drawings*. Oxford and London: Phaidon Press.

Benjamin, Walter. (1955) 1969. "The Storyteller: Reflections on the Works of Nikolai Leskov." In *Illuminations*, edited by Hannah Arendt and translated by Harry Zohn, 83–110. New York: Schocken Books.

———. (1955) 1969b. "The Work of Art in the Age of Mechanical Reproduction." In *Illuminations*, 217–52.

Berg, Wesley. 1985. *From Russia with Music: A Study of the Mennonite Choral Singing Tradition in Canada*. Winnipeg: Hyperion.

Bergen, David. 1993. *Sitting Opposite My Brother*. Winnipeg: Turnstone Press.

———. 2005. *The Time in Between*. Toronto: McClelland and Stewart.

Berger, John. 1972. *Ways of Seeing*. London: British Broadcasting Company.

Besançon, Alain. 2000. *The Forbidden Image: An Intellectual History of Iconoclasm*. Translated by Jane Marie Todd. Chicago: University of Chicago Press.

Bhabha, Homi K. 1994. *The Location of Culture*. London: Routledge.

———. 1998. "On the Irremovable Strangeness of Being Different." *PMLA* 113, no. 1: 34–39.

Birdsell, Sandra. 1982. *Night Travellers*. Winnipeg: Turnstone Press.

———. 1989. *The Missing Child: A Novel*. Toronto: Lester and Orpen Dennys.

Blake, William. 1979. *Blake's Poetry and Designs*. Edited by Mary Lynn Johnson and John E. Grant. New York: Norton.

Blattberg, Charles. 2003. *Shall We Dance? A Patriotic Politics for Canada*. Montreal and Kingston: McGill-Queen's University Press.

Bloom, Harold. 1973. *The Anxiety of Influence: A Theory of Poetry*. 2nd ed. New York: Oxford University Press.

Boccadoro, Patricia. 2014. "Emmanuel Gat Dance: *The Goldlandbergs*." *Culturekiosque*, 15 May. http:www.culturekiosque.com/dance/reviews/ gat_goldlandbergs877.html.

Bogel, Fredric V. 2001. *The Difference Satire Makes: Rhetoric and Reading from Jonson to Byron*. Ithaca, NY: Cornell University Press.

Borson, Roo. 2008. *Personal History*. Toronto: Pedlar Press.

Boym, Svetlana. 2011. *The Future of Nostalgia*. New York: Basic Books/ Perseus Books Group.

Brand, Dionne. 2014. *Love Enough*. Toronto: Vintage.

Brandt, Di. 1987. *questions i asked my mother*. Winnipeg: Turnstone Press.

———. 1993. *Wild Mother Dancing: Maternal Narrative in Canadian Literature*. Winnipeg: University of Manitoba Press.

———. 1996. *Dancing Naked: Narrative Strategies for Writing across Centuries*. Stratford, ON: Mercury Press.

———. 1999. "Remembering Paul Hiebert." *Rhubarb* 1, no. 3: 43–44.

———. 2007. *So this is the world & here I am in it*. Edmonton: NeWest Press.

———. 2010. *Walking to Mojácar*. Winnipeg: Turnstone Press.

Brandt, Di, and Barbara Godard, eds. 2005. *Re:Generations: Canadian Women Poets in Conversation*. Windsor, ON: Black Moss Press.

Braun, Connie. 2008. *The Steppes Are the Colour of Sepia*. Vancouver: Ronsdale Press.

Braun, Lois. 1986. *A Stone Watermelon*. Winnipeg: Turnstone Press.

Breitsameter, Sabine. 2015. "Ordering of Sounds: The Homogenization of Listening in the Age of Globalized Soundscapes." *Sound in the Land: Music and the Environment*, edited by Carol Ann Weaver, Doreen Klassen, and Judith Klassen, special issue of *Conrad Grebel Review* 33, no. 2: 142–50.

Bringhurst, Robert. 2007. *Everywhere Being Is Dancing: Twenty Pieces of Thinking*. Kentville, NS: Gasperau.

Bultmann, Rudolf. 1957. *The Presence of Eternity: History and Eschatology*. [The Gifford Lectures]. New York: Harper.

Carroll, Lewis. 1960. *The Annotated Alice: Alice's Adventures in Wonderland and Through the Looking Glass*. Illustrated by John Tenniel. Introduction and notes by Martin Gardner. New York: Bramhall House.

Caruth, Cathy, ed. 1996. *Unclaimed Experience: Trauma, Narrative, and History*. Baltimore: Johns Hopkins University Press.

Cave, Terence. 1988. *Recognitions: A Study in Poetics*. Oxford: Oxford University Press.

Chamberlin, J. Edward (Ted). 2003. *If This Is Your Land, Where Are Your Stories? Finding Common Ground*. Toronto: Alfred A. Knopf.

———. 2012. *A Covenant in Wonder with the World: The Power of Stories and Songs*. The 2010 Grand River Forum Lecture, Wilfrid Laurier University. Vancouver: Ronsdale Press.

Chatwin, Bruce. 1987. *The Songlines*. New York: Penguin Books.

Cheetham, Mark, and Linda Hutcheon. 2012. *Remembering Postmodernism: Trends in Canadian Art, 1970–1990*. 2nd ed. With an afterword by Linda Hutcheon. Don Mills, ON: Oxford University Press.

Chislett, Anne. 1983. *Quiet in the Land*. Toronto: Coach House Press.

Churchill, Caryl. 2016. *Escaped Alone*. Toronto: Playwrights Canada Press [Nick Hern Books].

Clarke, George Elliott. 2002. *Odysseys Home: Mapping African-Canadian Literature*. Toronto: University of Toronto Press.

Clifford, James. 1988. *The Predicament of Culture: Twentieth-Century Ethnography, Literature, and Art*. Cambridge, MA: Harvard University Press.

Coleman, Daniel, and Donald Goellnicht. 2002. "Introduction: Race into the Twenty-First Century." *Race*, edited by Daniel Coleman and Donald Goellnicht, special issue of *Essays on Canadian Writing* 75: 1–29.

Coleridge, Samuel Taylor. 1994. *Samuel Taylor Coleridge: A Selection of his Finest Poems*. Ed. H.J. Jackson. Oxford and New York: Oxford University Press.

Cook, Eleanor. 1998. "Melos versus Logos, or, Why Doesn't God Sing? Some Thoughts on Milton's Wisdom." In *Against Coercion: Games Poets Play*, by Eleanor Cook, 159–71. Stanford, CA: Stanford University Press.

Cooper, Afua. 1990. *Poetry Is Not a Luxury*. CD recording.

Couser, G. Thomas. 2012. *Memoir: An Introduction*. Oxford: Oxford University Press.

Covington, Sarah. 2011. "Jan Luyken, the *Martyrs Mirror*, and the Iconography of Suffering." *Mennonite Quarterly Review* 85, no. 3: 441–76.

Cruz, Daniel Shank. 2019. *Queering Mennonite Literature: Archives, Activism, and the Search for Community*. University Park: Pennsylvania State University Press.

Dafoe, Chris. 1996. "Minding her beeswax" (article on Aganetha Dyck). *The Globe and Mail*, 28 February, C1.

Dante. (c. 1302–5) 1996. *De vulgari eloquentia*. Edited and translated by Steven Botterill. Cambridge: Cambridge University Press.

Dargis, Manohla. 2008. "Into the Mennonite World to Explore One Man's Test of Faith" (review of *Stellet Licht*). *New York Times*, 23 September. http://www.nytimes.com/2008/09/24/movies/24sile.html.

Davies, Alan. 2010. *The Crucified Nation: A Motif in Modern Nationalism*. Brighton, UK: Sussex Academic Press.

Davies, Victor. 2005. "A Non-Mennonite Writes a Mennonite Piano Concerto." In *Sound in the Land: Essays on Mennonites and Music*, edited by Maureen Epp and Carol Ann Weaver, 95–99. Kitchener, ON: Pandora Press.

Davis, D. Diane. 2000. *Breaking Up [at] Totality: A Rhetoric of Laughter*. Carbondale and Edwardsville: Southern Illinois University Press.

de Certeau, Michel. 1985. "Practices of Space." In *On Signs*, edited by Marshall Blonsky, 122–45. Baltimore: Johns Hopkins University Press.

———. 1988. *The Practice of Everyday Life*. Translated by Steven Rendall. Berkeley: University of California Press.

de Coster, Charles. (1867) 1918. *The Legend of the Glorious Adventures of Tyl Ulenspiegel in the Land of Flanders and Elsewhere*. Translated by Geoffrey

Whitworth and illustrated by Albert Delstanche. New York: Robert M. McBride and Company.

De Fehr, William, et al., eds. 1974. *Harvest Anthology of Mennonite Writing in Canada*. Altona, MB: Centennial Committee of the Mennonite Historical Society of Manitoba.

Deleuze, Gilles. 1998. "He Stuttered." In *Gilles Deleuze: Essays Critical and Clinical*. Trans. Daniel W. Smith and Michael A. Greco, 107–14. London and New York: Verso.

de Luca, Tiago. 2014. *Realism of the Senses in World Cinema: The Experience of Physical Reality*. New York: I.B. Tauris.

De Vries, Peter. 1967. *The Vale of Laughter*. Boston: Little, Brown and Company.

Dickey, Stephanie S. 1996. "Mennonite Martyrdom in Amsterdam and the Art of Rembrandt and His Contemporaries." In *Contemporary Explorations in the Culture of the Low Countries*, edited by William Z. Shetter and Inge Van der Cruysse, 81–104. Lanham, MD: University Press of America.

Dimock, Wai Chee. 1997. "A Theory of Resonance." *PMLA* 112, no. 5: 1060–71.

Doerr, Anthony. 2014. *All the Light We Cannot See: A Novel*. New York: Scribner.

Doyle, John. 2017. "CBC's *Pure* is about more than Mennonites – it's about morals." *The Globe and Mail*. Published 6 January. Updated 13 April 2017. https://www.theglobeandmail.com/arts/television/john-doyle-cbcs-pure-is-about-more-than-mennonites-its-about-morals/article33532031/.

Du Bois, W.E.B. (1953) 1961. *The Souls of Black Folk: Essays and Sketches*. Greenwich, Conn.: Fawcett Publications.

Dueck, Dora. 1989. *Under the Still Standing Sun*. Winnipeg: Kindred.

Dueck, Jonathan. 2005. "Encountering (Mennonite) Singer-Songwriters: J.D. Martin and Cate Friesen." In *Sound in the Land: Essays on Mennonites and Music*, edited by Maureen Epp and Carol Ann Weaver, 159–75. Kitchener, ON: Pandora Press.

Dueck, Lynnette. 1992. *Sing Me No More*. Vancouver: Press Gang Publishers.

Dueck, Nathan. 2014. *he'll*. St. John's: Pedlar Press.

Duerksen, Rosella Reimer. 1956. "Anabaptist Hymnody of the 16th Century." PhD diss., Union Theological Seminary, New York.

Duffy, Eamon. 1992. *The Stripping of the Altars: Traditional Religion in England, 1400–1580*. New Haven, CT: Yale University Press.

Dunham, Bertha Mabel. 1924. *The Trail of the Conestoga*. Preface by William Lyon Mackenzie. Toronto: Macmillan.

Dyck, Arnold. 1974. *Lost in the Steppe*. Translated by Henry D. Dyck. Steinbach, MB: Derksen Printers. Originally self-published 1944–48 as *Verloren in der Steppe*.

Dyck, E.F. 1982. *The Mossbank Canon*. Winnipeg: Turnstone Press.

———. 1990. "The Rhetoric of the Plain Style in Mennonite Writing." *Mennonite/s Writing in Canada*, edited by Hildi Froese Tiessen, special issue of *The New Quarterly* 10, nos. 1–2: 36–52.

Dykk, Lloyd. March 25, 2009. "Aganetha Dyck's Collaborations at the Burnaby Art Gallery." *The Georgia Straight*. https://www.straight.com/ article-209435/aganetha-dyck-collaborations (accessed 26 August 2019).

Eagleton, Terry. 1988. "The Critic as Clown." In *Marxism and the Interpretation of Culture*, edited by Cary Nelson and Lawrence Grossberg, 619–31. Urbana: University of Illinois Press.

Ebert, Roger. 2009. Review of *Silent Light*. 18 March. http://www.rogerebert. com/reviews/silent-light-2009 (accessed 27 October 2015).

Ebert, Teresa L. 1986. "The Crisis of Representation in Cultural Studies: Reading Postmodern Texts." *American Quarterly* 38, no. 5: 894–902.

Edwards, Brian T. 2013. "The World, the Text, and the Americanist." *American Literary History* 25, no. 1: 231–46.

Eire, Carlos M.N. 2016. *Reformations: The Early Modern World, 1450–1650*. New Haven and London: Yale University Press.

Eldridge, Richard. 1996. "Introduction: From Representation to *Poiesis*." In *Beyond Representation: Philosophy and Poetic Imagination*, edited by Richard Eldridge, 1–13. Cambridge, UK: Cambridge University Press.

Elias, David H. 2004. *Sunday Afternoon*. Regina: Coteau Books.

———. 2012. "If I Am a Mennonite Writer: One Anabaptist Author's Literary Neurosis." *Manitoba Mennonite Writing*, special issue of *Rhubarb* 30: 7–9.

Eliot, T.S. (1944) 1959. *Four Quartets*. New York: Faber and Faber.

Elkins, James. 2001. *Pictures and Tears: A History of People Who Have Cried in Front of Paintings*. New York: Routledge.

———. 2003. *What Happened to Art Criticism?* Chicago: Prickly Paradigm Press.

Ellis, Carolyn. 2004. *The Ethnographic I: A Methodological Novel About Autoethnography*. Walnut Creek, CA: AltaMira Press.

Emerson, Ralph Waldo. 1959. *Selections from Ralph Waldo Emerson: An Organic Anthology,* edited by Stephen E. Whicher. Boston: Houghton Mifflin Company.

Empson, William. 1935. *Some Versions of Pastoral.* London: Chatto and Windus.

Enns, Mary M. 1984. "Paul Hiebert Looks Back on a Satisfying Life and a Contented Retirement." *Mennonite Mirror* 13, no. 8: 5–6.

Enns, Victor Jerrett. 1979. *Jimmy Bang Poems.* Winnipeg: Turnstone Press.

———. 1985. *Correct in This Culture.* Saskatoon: Fifth House.

———. 1992. "The Missing Mennonite Cabaret: Excerpts from the Correspondence of Patrick Friesen." *Patrick Friesen,* edited by Hildi Froese Tiessen and G.N. Louise Jonasson, special issue of *Prairie Fire* 13, no. 1: 45–52.

Enright, Robert. 1984. "Thinking Big" (on Wanda Koop). *Canadian Art* 1, no. 1: 36–41.

Enright, Robert, moderator. 1986. "Write Speaking Mennonites: A Border Crossing Forum." *Border Crossings* 5, no. 4: 21–28.

Epp, Frank H, ed. 1957. *Revival Fires in Manitoba.* [A report on the work of Brunk Revivals, Inc., in the Manitoba communities of Steinbach, Winkler, Altona and Winnipeg, June to September, 1957; Printed by D. W. Friesen & Sons Ltd., Altona, Manitoba, Canada]. Denbigh, Va.: Brunk Revivals, Inc.

Epp, Joanne. 2015. *Eigenheim.* Winnipeg: Turnstone Press.

Epp, Marlene. 2000. *Women without Men: Mennonite Refugees of the Second World War.* Toronto: University of Toronto Press.

Epp, Maureen. 2005. "New Readings of Text and Music in the *Ausbund.*" In *Sound in the Land: Essays on Mennonites and Music,* edited by Maureen Epp and Carol Ann Weaver, 34–49. Kitchener, ON: Pandora Press.

Epp, Maureen, and Carol Ann Weaver, eds. 2005. *Sound in the Land: Essays on Mennonites and Music.* Kitchener, ON: Pandora Press.

Epp, Maureen, Carol Ann Weaver, Doreen Klassen, and Anna Janecek, eds. 2011. *Sound in the Lands: Mennonite Music Across Borders.* Kitchener, ON: Pandora Press.

Epp-Tiessen, Esther. 1982. *Altona: The Story of a Prairie Town.* Altona, MB: D.W. Friesen.

Falk, Elizabeth. 1990a. "The House." *Prairie Fire* 11, no. 2: 28–50. Interactive memoir published jointly with "The Little Dipper," by Magdalene Redekop.

———. 1990b. "No Stone." *Canadian Literature* 127: 10–28. Interactive memoir published jointly with "Still Life with Menno," by Magdalene Redekop.

———. 2007. "Plates." *Rhubarb* 13: 19, 25, 28, 37, 40.

Falk, Gathie. 1987. "A Short History of Performance Art as It Influenced or Failed to Influence My Work (1981)." In *Documents in Canadian Art*, edited by Douglas Fetherling, 310–12. Peterborough, ON: Broadview Press.

Falk, Gathie, with Robin Laurence. 2018. *Apples, etc.: An Artist's Memoir.* Vancouver/Berkeley: Figure 1 Publishing.

Finnigan, Harry. 2015. "Lives Lived: Erika Adelheit Koop." *Globe and Mail*, 3 April.

Francis, E.K. 1955. *In Search of Utopia: The Mennonites in Manitoba.* Altona, MB: D.W. Friesen.

Fraser, Caroline. 2017. *Prairie Fires: The American Dreams of Laura Ingalls Wilder.* New York: Henry Holt and Company.

Freedberg, David. 1989. *The Power of Images: Studies in the History and Theory of Response.* Chicago: University of Chicago Press.

Fried, Michael. 1998. *Art and Objecthood: Essays and Reviews.* Chicago: University of Chicago Press.

Friedrich, Otto. 1990. *Glenn Gould: A Life and Variations.* Toronto: Lester and Orpen Dennys.

Friesen, Eric. 2010. "Johnny, Wild Willy, and Me." *Queen's Quarterly* 117, no. 1: 115–23.

Friesen, Patrick. 1974. "Patriarchal Light." In *Harvest: Anthology of Mennonite Writing in Canada*, edited by William De Fehr et al., 85. Altona, MB: Centennial Committee of the Mennonite Historical Society of Manitoba.

———. 1976. *The Lands I Am: Poems.* Winnipeg: Turnstone Press.

———. 1980. *The Shunning.* Winnipeg: Turnstone Press.

———. 1984. *Unearthly Horses.* Winnipeg: Turnstone Press.

———. 1987. *Flicker and Hawk.* Winnipeg: Turnstone Press.

———. 1988. "I Could Have Been Born in Spain." In *Why I Am a Mennonite*, edited by Harry Loewen, 98–105. Scottdale, PA: Herald Press.

———. 1992. "The Dance Floor (Apparitions)." *Patrick Friesen*, edited by Hildi Froese Tiessen and G.N. Louise Jonasson, special issue of *Prairie Fire* 13, no. 1: 110–11.

———. 1994. *Blasphemer's Wheel: Selected and New Poems*. Winnipeg: Turnstone Press.

———. 2011. *jumping in the asylum*. Toronto: Quattro Books.

———. 2015. *A Short History of Crazy Bone: Long Poem*. Salt Spring Island, BC: Mother Tongue Publishing.

———. 2018. *Songen*. Salt Spring Island, BC: Mother Tongue Publishing.

Friesen, Victor Carl. 1987. *The Windmill Turning: Nursery Rhymes, Maxims, and Other Expressions of Western Canadian Mennonites*. Edmonton: University of Alberta Press.

Frost, Robert. 1963. *Selected Poems of Robert Frost*. New York: Holt, Rinehart, and Winston.

Frye, Northrop. 1963. *The Educated Imagination*. Toronto: Canadian Broadcasting Corporation.

———. 1971. "Preface to an Uncollected Anthology." In *The Bush Garden: Essays on the Canadian Imagination*, by Northrop Frye, 163–80. Toronto: Anansi.

———. 1976. "Charms and Riddles." In *Spiritus Mundi: Essays on Literature, Myth, and Society*, by Northrop Frye, 123–47. Bloomington: Indiana University Press.

———. 1980. *Creation and Recreation*. The Larkin-Stuart Lectures. Toronto: University of Toronto Press.

———. 1981. *The Great Code: The Bible and Literature*. Toronto: Academic Press Canada.

Gadamer, Hans-Georg. 1994. *Truth and Method*. 2nd ed., revised. Translated by Joel Weinsheimer and Donald G. Marshall. New York: Continuum.

Gernes, Ulrikka S. 2015. *Frayed Opus for Strings and Wind Instruments*. Translated by Per Brask and Patrick Friesen. London, ON: Brick Books.

Gerson, Carole. 1992. "Sarah Binks and Edna Jaques: Parody, Gender, and the Construction of Literary Value." *Canadian Literature* 134: 62–73.

Gerson, Carole, and Jacques Michon, eds. 2007. *History of the Book in Canada*. Vol. 3, *1918–1980*. Toronto: University of Toronto Press.

Gilman, Sander. 1985. *Difference and Pathology: Stereotypes of Sexuality, Race, and Madness*. Ithaca, NY: Cornell University Press.

Gilroy, Paul. 1991. "Sounds Authentic: Black Music, Ethnicity, and the Challenge of the Changing Same." *Black Music Research Journal* 11, no. 2: 111–36.

Goertz, Hans-Jürgen. 1988. "The Confessional Heritage in Its New Mold: What Is Mennonite Self-Understanding Today?" In *Mennonite Identity: Historical and Contemporary Perspectives*, edited by Calvin Wall Redekop and Samuel J. Steiner, 1–12. Lanham, MD: University Press of America.

Goethe, J.W. 1954. *Selected Poems*. London: William Heinemann.

Goetsch, James Robert, Jr. 1995. *Vico's Axioms: The Geometry of the Human World*. New Haven and London: Yale University Press.

Goffman, Erving. 1959. *The Presentation of Self in Everyday Life*. New York: Random House.

Gold, Joseph. 2002. *The Story Species: Our Life-Literature Connection*. Markham, ON: Fitzhenry and Whiteside.

Gombrich, E.H. 1960. *Art and Illusion: A Study in the Psychology of Pictorial Representation*. A.W. Mellon Lectures in the Fine Arts, 1956, National Gallery of Art, Washington, DC. Bollingen Series 35, 5. Princeton, NJ: Princeton University Press.

———. (1979) 1984. *The Sense of Order: A Study in the Psychology of Decorative Art*. London: Phaidon Press.

Gonzalez, Ed. 2007. Review of *Silent Light*. *Slant Magazine*. 5 September. https://www.slantmagazine.com/film/silent-light/ (accessed 7 July 2019).

Goossen, Benjamin W. 2017. *The Chosen Nation: Mennonites and Germany in a Global Era*. Princeton: Princeton University Press.

Gordon, Charles. 1995. Afterword to *Sarah Binks*, by Paul Hiebert, 170–80. New Canadian Library. Toronto: McClelland and Stewart.

Gould, Glenn. 1977. *The Quiet in the Land*. Solitude Trilogy: Three Sound Documentaries (1967–77). Canadian Broadcasting Corporation.

———. 1992. *Glenn Gould: Selected Letters*. Compiled and edited by John P.L. Roberts and Ghyslaine Guertin. Toronto: Oxford University Press.

———. Recorded interviews. Ben Horch fonds at the Mennonite Brethren Archives in Winnipeg.

Graber, Katie J. 2005. "Identity and the Hymnal: Can Music Make a Person Mennonite?" In *Sound in the Land: Essays on Mennonites and Music*, edited by Maureen Epp and Carol Ann Weaver, 64–77. Kitchener, ON: Pandora Press.

Greenblatt, Stephen, ed. 1981. *Allegory and Representation*. Baltimore: Johns Hopkins University Press.

Grey, Tobias. 2008. "Nonprofessional Actors Give European Films a New
    Realism." *The Wall Street Journal*. https://www.wsj.com/articles/
    SB122600891243306167.

Gundy, Jeffrey Gene. 2005. *Walker in the Fog: On Mennonite Writing*. Scottdale,
    PA: Herald Press.

Gzowski, Peter. 1974. *Peter Gzowski's Book about* This Country in the Morning.
    Edmonton: Hurtig Publishers.

Hamera, Judith. 2006. "Performance, Performativity, and Cultural *Poiesis* in
    Practices of Everyday Life." In *The Sage Handbook of Performance Studies*,
    edited by D. Soyini Madison and Judith Hamera, 46–64. Thousand Oaks,
    CA: Sage Publications.

Hamilton, Alistair, Sjouke Voolstra, Piet Visser, eds. 1994. *From Martyr to
    Muppy (Mennonite Urban Professional): A Historical Introduction to Cultural
    Assimilation Processes of a Religious Minority in the Netherlands: The
    Mennonites*. Amsterdam: Amsterdam University Press.

Harari, Yuval Noah. 2014. [First published in Hebrew in 2011]. *Sapiens: A Brief
    History of Humankind*. New York, NY: Harper.

Harrison, Robert Pogue. 2003. *The Dominion of the Dead*. Chicago: University of
    Chicago Press.

Harron, Don. 2012. *My Double Life: Sexty Yeers of Farquharson Around with Don
    Harron*. Toronto: Dundurn Press.

Hawthorne, Nathaniel. (1850) 1978. *The Scarlet Letter: An Authoritative
    Text, Backgrounds and Sources: Criticism*. Edited by Sculley Bradley,
    Richmond Croom Beatty, E. Hudson Long, and Seymour Gross. New
    York: W.W. Norton.

Heaney, Seamus. 2008. "Virgil's Poetic Influence." An essay broadcast on BBC
    Radio 3 as part of the *Greek and Latin Voices* series, 15 July.

Heisey, Nancy R. 2012. "Remembering Dirk Willems: Memory and History
    in the Future of Ecumenical Relationships. *Journal of Ecumenical Studies*
    47, no 3: 355–75.

Heller-Roazen, Daniel. 2008. *Echolalias: On the Forgetting of Language*. New
    York: Zone Books.

Herder, Johann Gottfried (author), and Philip V. Bohlman (author and
    translator). 2017. *Song Loves the Masses: Herder on Music and Nationalism*.
    Oakland, CA: University of California Press.

Hershberger, Guy F., ed. 2001. *The Recovery of the Anabaptist Vision: A Sixtieth Anniversary Tribute to Harold S. Bender.* Paris, Arkansas: The Baptist Standard Bearer.

Hiebert, Paul. 1966. *Tower in Siloam.* Toronto: McClelland and Stewart.

———. 1967. *Willows Revisited.* Toronto: McClelland and Stewart.

———. 1976. *Doubting Castle.* Winnipeg: Queenston House.

———. 1984. *Not As the Scribes.* Winnipeg: Queenston House.

———. (1947) 1995. *Sarah Binks.* Afterword by Charles Gordon. New Canadian Library. Toronto: McClelland and Stewart. The first McClelland and Stewart edition was published in 1964.

Hoad, Phil. 2007. "The Carlos Reygadas Guide to Cinema." *The Guardian,* 7 December. https://www.theguardian.com/film/filmblog/2007/dec/07/carlosreygadasmycinema.

Hoberman, J. 2008. "The Miraculous Is Sublime in Director Carlos Reygadas's *Stellet Licht.*" *Village Voice,* 23 September. https://www.villagevoice.com/2008/09/23/the-miraculous-is-sublime-in-director-carlos-reygadass-stellet-licht/.

Hoffer, Eric. 1951. *The True Believer: Thoughts on the Nature of Mass Movements.* New York: Harper and Brothers.

Hogg, James. (1824) 2001. *The Private Memoirs and Confessions of a Justified Sinner: Written by Himself; with a Detail of Curious Traditionary Facts and other Evidence by the Editor.* Edited by P.D. Garside, with an afterword by Ian Campbell. Edinburgh: Edinburgh University Press.

Homer. 1932. *The Odyssey.* Translated by J.W. Mackail. Oxford: The Clarendon Press.

Hopkins, Gerard Manley. 1953. *Poems and Prose of Gerard Manley Hopkins.* Selected and with an introduction by W.H. Gardner. London: Penguin Books.

Hossack, Darcie Friesen. 2010. *Mennonites Don't Dance.* Saskatoon: Thistledown Press.

Houpt, Simon. 2007. "The Accidental Film Star." *Globe and Mail,* 12 May, R10.

Housman, A. E. 1965. *Collected Poems.* New York: Holt, Rinehart, and Winston.

Huizinga, Johan. (1949) 1970. *Homo Ludens: A Study of the Play Element in Culture.* London: Paladin.

Hutcheon, Linda. 1985. *A Theory of Parody: The Teachings of Twentieth-Century Art Forms*. New York: Methuen.

———. 1988. *The Canadian Postmodern: A Study of Contemporary English-Canadian Fiction*. Toronto: Oxford University Press.

———. 1994. *Irony's Edge: The Theory and Politics of Irony*. London: Routledge.

———. 2006. *A Theory of Adaptation*. New York: Routledge.

———. 2012. "Postmodernism's Ironic Paradoxes: Politics and Art." Afterword to *Remembering Postmodernism: Trends in Recent Canadian Art, 1970–1990*, 2nd ed., by Mark Cheetham, 113–36. Don Mills, ON: Oxford University Press.

Hyde, Lewis. 1998. *Trickster Makes This World: Mischief, Myth, and Art*. New York: Farrar, Straus and Giroux.

James, Henry. 1975. Preface to the New York edition of *Portrait of a Lady*, by Henry James, 3–15. New York: W.W. Norton.

James, William. (1902) 1916. *The Varieties of Religious Experience: A Study in Human Nature* (The Gifford Lectures Delivered in Edinburgh 1901–1902). New York: Longmans, Green, and Company.

Jameson, Fredric. 1974. *The Prison-House of Language: A Critical Account of Structuralism and Russian Formalism*. Princeton, NJ: Princeton University Press.

———. 1981. *The Political Unconscious: Narrative as a Socially Symbolic Act*. Ithaca, NY: Cornell University Press.

Janacek, Anna. 2005. "(On) Being Mennonite, Being a Composer, and Composing 'Mennonite Music.'" In *Sound in the Land: Essays on Mennonites and Music*, edited by Maureen Epp and Carol Ann Weaver, 143–58. Kitchener, ON: Pandora Press.

Janzen, Rebecca. 2015a. *The National Body in Mexican Literature: Collective Challenges to Biopolitical Control*. New York: Palgrave Macmillan.

———. 2015b. "Still Life/Mexican Death: Mennonites in Visual Culture." *Arizona Journal of Hispanic Cultural Studies* 19: 75–90.

Janzen, Rhoda. 2009. *Mennonite in a Little Black Dress: A Memoir of Going Home*. New York: Henry Holt.

Jaques, Edna. (1966) 1974. *The Best of Edna Jaques*. Saskatoon: Western Producer Book Service.

Judt, Tony, with Timothy Snyder. 2012. *Thinking the Twentieth Century*. London: Penguin Books.

Kasdorf, Julia Spicher. 2001. *The Body and the Book: Writing from a Mennonite Life*. Baltimore: Johns Hopkins University Press.

———. 2013. "Sunday Morning Confession." *Mennonite Quarterly Review*. Vol. 87, No. 1: 7–10.

———. 2015. "The Autoethnographic Announcement and the Story." In *After Identity: Mennonite Writing in North America*, edited by Robert Zacharias, 21–36. Winnipeg: University of Manitoba Press; University Park: Pennsylvania State University Press.

Keats, John. 1959. *Selected Poems and Letters*. Edited by Douglas Bush. Boston: Houghton Mifflin.

Kehler, Grace. 2011. "Representations of Melancholic Martyrdom in Canadian Mennonite Literature." *Journal of Mennonite Studies* 29: 167–85.

———. 2015. "Reimagining Eden." In *Amalie Atkins: We Live on the Edge of Disaster and Imagine We Are in a Musical*, edited by Timothy Long and Ryan Doherty, 35–40. Published in conjunction with an exhibition co-organized by the Mackenzie Art Gallery (Regina) and the Southern Alberta Art Gallery (Lethbridge). Versions of the exhibition presented at Open Space (Victoria) and Kenderdine Art Gallery (Saskatoon).

Keith, W.J. 1981. *A Voice in the Land: Essays by and about Rudy Wiebe*. Edmonton: NeWest Press.

Kermode, Frank. 1966. *The Sense of an Ending: Studies in the Theory of Fiction*. London: Oxford University Press.

King, Michael A. 2001. *Fractured Dance: Gadamer and a Mennonite Conflict over Homosexuality*. Telford, PA: Pandora Press US; Scottdale, PA: Herald Press.

King, Thomas. 1999. *One Good Story, That One*. Toronto: HarperPerennial.

Klaassen, Walter. 1985. "Visions of the End in Reformation Europe." In *Visions and Realities: Essays, Poems, and Fiction Dealing with Mennonite Issues*, 13–57. Winnipeg: Hyperion Press.

Klassen, Bertha. 1993. *Da Capo: "Start Once from the Front": A History of the Mennonite Community Orchestra*. Winnipeg: Centre for Mennonite Brethren Studies.

Klassen, Doreen Helen. 1989. *Singing Mennonite: Low German Songs among the Mennonites*. Winnipeg: University of Manitoba Press.

———. 2005. "Benjamin Horch as an Insider-Outsider Musical-Theological Visionary." In *Sound in the Land: Essays on Mennonites and Music*, edited by Maureen Epp and Carol Ann Weaver, 83–94. Kitchener, ON: Pandora Press.

———. 2015. "'What You Intended to Say?' Howard Dyck Reflects on Glenn Gould's *The Quiet in the Land*." *Sound in the Land: Music and the Environment*, edited by Carol Ann Weaver, Doreen Klassen, and Judith Klassen, special issue of *Conrad Grebel Review* 33, no. 2: 176–85.

Klassen, Pamela E. 1994a. *Going By the Moon and the Stars: Stories of Two Russian Mennonite Women*. Waterloo, ON: Wilfrid Laurier University Press.

———. April 1994b. "What's Bre(a)d in the Bone: The Bodily Heritage of Mennonite Women." *Mennonite Quarterly Review* 68, no. 2 (April): 229–47.

Klassen, Sarah. 1988. *Journey to Yalta*. Winnipeg: Turnstone Press.

———. 1998. *Dangerous Elements*. Kingston, ON: Quarry Women's Books.

———. 2006. *A Curious Beatitude*. Winnipeg: J. Gordon Shillingford.

———. 2012. *Monstrance*. Winnipeg: Turnstone Press.

Klassen, Sherri. 2017. "O, what fresh hell is this?" (Series of blog posts on the CBC series called *Pure*). 2 March. https://slklassen.com/tag/cbc-pure/.

Knight, Katherine, dir. 2011. *KOOP: The Art of Wanda Koop*. Cinematography by Marcia Connolly. Produced by David Craig, Katherine Knight, and Site Media.

Koenker, Deborah. N.d. "Face to Face with Wanda Koop." In exhibition catalogue published in conjunction with the exhibit *Face to Face*, 51–60. Richmond, BC: Richmond Art Gallery.

Koerner, Joseph Leo. 2004. *The Reformation of the Image*. London: Reaktion Books.

Konrad, Anne. 1985. *The Blue Jar*. Winnipeg: Queenston House.

———. 2012. *Red Quarter Moon: A Search for Family in the Shadow of Stalin*. Toronto: University of Toronto Press.

Koop, Wanda. 1986. "The Transformative Art of Wanda Koop." Interview with Robert Enright. *Border Crossings* 5, no. 4: 94–104.

———. 1996. "The Beauty of Longing: A Conversation with Wanda Koop." Interview with Robert Enright. *Border Crossings* 15, no. 4: 12–23.

Kroeker, Travis. 2018. "Scandalous Displacements: 'Word' and 'Silent Light' in *Irma Voth*." *Journal of Mennonite Studies* 36: 89–100.

Kroetsch, Robert. 1977. *Seed Catalogue*. Winnipeg: Turnstone Press.

———. 2001. *The Hornbooks of Rita K*. Edmonton: University of Alberta Press.

Kuerti, Anton. 1994. "Glenn Gould's Manipulations" (review article). *Literary Review of Canada*, March. http://reviewcanada.ca/magazine/1994/03/glenn-goulds-manipulations/.

LaCapra, Dominick. 2001. *Writing History, Writing Trauma*. Baltimore: Johns Hopkins University Press.

Lambek, Michael. 1996. "The Past Imperfect: Remembering as Moral Practice." In *Tense Past: Cultural Essays in Trauma and Memory*, edited by Paul Antze and Michael Lambek, 235–54. New York: Routledge.

Lammertse, Friso, and Jaap Van der Veen. 2006. *Uylenburgh & Son: Art and Commerce from Rembrandt to De Lairesse 1625–1675*. Amsterdam: The Rembrandthouse Museum; Zwolle: Waanders Publishers. Published on the occasion of the exhibition *Rembrandt & Co: Dealing in Masterpieces*, Dulwich Picture Gallery, London, 7 June–3 September 2006; and *Rembrandt en Uylenburgh, handel in meesterwerken*, The Rembrandt House Museum, Amsterdam, 16 September–10 December 2006.

Laurence, Robin. 1998. "Wanda Koop: See Everything/See Nothing." In *Wanda Koop: See Everything/See Nothing* (exhibition catalogue), 1–15. Published in conjunction with the exhibition *See Everything/See Nothing*, Contemporary Art Gallery, Vancouver, 14 February to 21 March.

———. 2000. "To Be a Pilgrim." In *Gathie Falk*, edited by Robin Laurence et al., 17–50, 62–65, 69–73, 76–77, 80, 83, 88–89, 96, 98–100, 102–03, 109–11, 115–20, 126, 130–31, 134, 136–38. Vancouver: Vancouver Art Gallery; Toronto: Douglas and McIntyre. Published in conjunction with an exhibition at the Vancouver Art Gallery and the National Gallery.

———. 2010. "Wanda Koop: Beginnings." In *Wanda Koop: On the Edge of Experience*, edited by Mary Reid, 13–27. Winnipeg: Winnipeg Art Gallery.

Leacock, Stephen. (1912) 1996. *Sunshine Sketches of a Little Town*. Edited by Gerald Lynch. Ottawa: Tecumseh Press.

———. (1914) 2002. *Arcadian Adventures with the Idle Rich*. Edited by D.M.R. Bentley. Nepean, ON: Borealis Press.

Lederman, Marsha. 2016. "Hyperrealist Artist Karel Funk's Paintings to Be Shown in Winnipeg." *Globe and Mail*, 5 June.

———. 2017. "Eden Robinson is laughing all the way to the dark side." *The Globe and Mail*. 10 February. Updated 14 April 2017. https://www.theglobeandmail.com/arts/books-and-media/eden-robinson-is-laughing-all-the-way-to-the-dark-side/article33979533/ (accessed 6 July 2019).

Legris, Sylvia. 2015. "Mobile Home: The Transportable Worlds of Amalie Atkins" and "Single Car Garage: Where Atkins Parks Her Art." In *Amalie Atkins: We Live on the Edge of Disaster and Imagine We Are in a Musical*, edited by Timothy Long and Ryan Doherty, 41–66. Published in conjunction with an exhibition co-organized by the Mackenzie Art Gallery (Regina) and the Southern Alberta Art Gallery (Lethbridge). Versions of exhibition presented at Open Space (Victoria) and Kenderdine Art Gallery (Saskatoon).

Leonardson, Eric. Spring 2015. "Acoustic Ecology and Ethical Listening." In *Sound in the Land: Music and the Environment,* edited by Carol Ann Weaver, Doreen Helen Klassen, and Judith Klassen, Special issue of *Conrad Grebel Review* 33, no. 2: 151–57.

Lerner, Ben. 2016. *The Hatred of Poetry*. Toronto: McClelland and Stewart.

Letkemann, Peter. 2007. *The Ben Horch Story*. Winnipeg: Old Oak Publishing.

Lind, Jane. 1989. *Gathie Falk*. Vancouver: Douglas and McIntyre.

Lionnet, Françoise. 2005. "Translating Grief." In *Nation, Language, and the Ethics of Translation*, edited by Sandra Bermann and Michael Wood, 315–25. Princeton, NJ: Princeton University Press.

Loewen, Harry, ed. 1980. *Mennonite Images: Historical, Cultural, and Literary Essays Dealing with Mennonite Issues*. Winnipeg: Hyperion Press.

———. 1988. *Why I Am a Mennonite: Essays on Mennonite Identity.* Kitchener, ON: Scottdale, PA: Herald Press.

Loewen, Royden. 1999. "Making Menno: The Historical Images of a Religious Leader." *Conrad Grebel Review* 17, no. 3: 18–31.

———. 2015. "A Mennonite *Fin de Siècle*." In *After Identity: Mennonite Writing in North America*, edited by Robert Zacharias, 37–51. Winnipeg: University of Manitoba Press; University Park: Pennsylvania State University Press.

Lorde, Audre. 1984. "Poetry Is Not a Luxury." In *Sister Outsider: Essays and Speeches*, 36–39. Berkeley: Crossing Press.

Luxon, Thomas H. 1995. *Literal Figures: Puritan Allegory and the Reformation Crisis in Representation*. Chicago: University of Chicago Press.

MacDonald, Tanis. 2015. "Thirty Years of Questions: An Afterword to Di Brandt's *questions i asked my mother*." In *questions i asked my mother*, revised edition, by Di Brandt, 71–88. Winnipeg: Turnstone Press.

Macmillan, Margaret. 2008. *The Uses and Abuses of History*. Based on the Joanne Goodman Lecture Series. London, ON: Viking.

Macpherson, Jay. 1981. *Poems Twice Told: The Boatman and Welcoming Disaster.* Toronto: Oxford University Press.

Manickam, Samuel. 2013. "The Other Mexico through the Cinematic Eyes of Carlos Reygadas." *Journal of Mennonite Wrtiting* 5, no. 1. http://www. mennonitewriting.org/journal/5/1/other-mexico-through-cinematic-eyes-carlos-reygada/.

Martens, Eleanor. 1994. "Mennonites and the Arts: An Unsettled Past." *Sophia* 4, no. 3: 9–10.

Mays, John Bentley. 1990. "Christian Faith Permeates Work of Artangel Falk." *Globe and Mail*, 24 March.

McFarlane, Matthew. 2002. "Common Visionaries: Glenn Gould, Jean Le Moyne, and Pierre Teilhard de Chardin." *Glenn Gould Magazine* 8, no. 2. Republished in *eContact!* 7, no. 3. http://econtact.ca/7_3/mcfarlane_visionaries.html.

McKenzie, Stephanie. 2007. *Before the Country: Native Renaissance, Canadian Mythology.* Toronto: University of Toronto Press.

McLeod, Katherine. 2010. "Poetry and Performance: Listening to a Multi-Vocal Canada." PhD diss., University of Toronto.

McLuhan, Marshall. 1964. *Understanding Media: The Extensions of Man.* New York: McGraw-Hill.

Mehlman, Jeffrey. 1972. "The 'Floating Signifier': From Lévi-Strauss to Lacan." *Yale French Studies* 48: 10–37.

Melion, Walter S. 1991. *Shaping the Netherlandish Canon: Karel van Mander's Schilder-Boeck.* Chicago and London: University of Chicago Press.

Mierau, Maurice. 1985. "The Martyrdom Method: A Cycle of Poems." In *Visions and Realities: Essays, Poems, and Fiction Dealing with Mennonite Issues*, edited by Harry Loewen and Al Reimer, 111–16. Winnipeg: Hyperion Press.

———. 1987–88. "Rebel Mennos Move into the Arts." *Midcontinental* 19: 18–23.

———. 1992. "Friesen and Akhmatova, or Silence as a Career." *Prairie Fire* 13, no. 1: 178–80.

———. 2002. *Ending with Music.* London, ON: Brick Books.

———. 2004. "Why Rudy Wiebe Is Not the Last Mennonite Writer." *Conrad Grebel Review* 22, no. 2: 69–82.

———. 2012. "The Voice Is Coming (Faintly) from the Grave, and It Says Mennonites Are Dead, and So Is Mennonite Writing. . . ." *Rhubarb* 30: 27–29.

———. 2018. *How Mind and Body Move: The Poetry of Patrick Friesen*. Victoria: Frog Hollow Press.

Miles, Jack. 2015. "Introduction." *The Norton Anthology of World Religions*. Vol. 2. Edited by Jack Miles, 1–51. New York and London: W.W. Norton.

Mitchell, Margaret. (1936) 1961. *Gone With the Wind*. New York: Macmillan.

Mitchell, W.J.T. 1986. *Iconology: Image, Text, Ideology*. Chicago: University of Chicago Press.

———. 1990. "Representation." In *Critical Terms for Literary Study*, edited by Frank Lentricchia and Thomas McLaughlin, 11–22. Chicago: University of Chicago Press.

———. 1994. *Picture Theory: Essays on Verbal and Visual Representation*. Chicago: University of Chicago Press.

———. 2003. "The Work of Art in the Age of Biocybernetic Reproduction." *Modernism/Modernity* 10, no. 3: 481–500.

———. 2005. *What Do Pictures Want? The Lives and Loves of Images*. Chicago: University of Chicago Press.

Moctezuma, Jose-Luis. 2009. "Silent Light: Miracles and Mennonites." *Hydra Magazine*, 18 November. http://www.hydramag.com/2009/11/18/silent-light-miracles-and-mennonites/.

Moore, Marianne. 1935. *Selected Poems*. With an introduction by T.S. Eliot. New York: Macmillan.

Morgan, David, ed. 2009. *Religion and Material Culture: The Matter of Belief*. London: Routledge.

Morris, Rosalind C., ed. 2010. *Can the Subaltern Speak?: Reflections on the History of an Idea*. New York: Columbia University Press.

Morton, W.L. 1957. *Manitoba: A History*. Toronto: University of Toronto Press.

Mount, Nick. 2017. *Arrival: The Story of CanLit*. Toronto: Anansi.

Mukherjee, Siddhartha. 2016. *The Gene: An Intimate History*. New York: Scribner.

Munro, Alice. 1978. *Who Do You Think You Are?* Toronto: Macmillan of Canada.

———. 1986. *The Progress of Love*. Toronto: McClelland and Stewart.

———. 1990. *Friend of My Youth*. Toronto: McClelland and Stewart.

———. 1996. *Selected Stories*. With a new introduction by the author. Toronto: Penguin.

Nagel, Alexander, and Christopher Wood. 2010. *Anachronic Renaissance*. New York: Zone Books.

Nashe, Thomas. 1594 (1972). *The Unfortunate Traveller and Other Works*. Penguin.

Nathan, Jesse. 2015. "Question, Answer." In *After Identity: Mennonite Writing in North America*, edited by Robert Zacharias, 159–93. Winnipeg: University of Manitoba Press; University Park: Pennsylvania State University Press.

Neary, Lynn. 2009. "From Kingsolver, the Fiction of a Split Psyche." Review of *The Lacuna: A Novel*, by Barbara Kingsolver. North Country Public Radio, Morning Edition, 8 November. https://www.northcountrypublicradio.org/news/npr/120182303/from-kingsolver-the-fiction-of-a-split-psyche.

Nestruck, J. Kelly. 2013. "Choreographer puts Gould's Radio Documentary into Motion." *Globe and Mail*, 30 August, updated 11 May 2018, https://www.theglobeandmail.com/arts/theatre-and-performance/goulds-radio-documentary-is-set-in-motion/article14045114/ (accessed 6 July 2019).

Neufeld, Elsie K. *"Ort und Vertreibung:* My Mother of the 1920s." *Journal of Mennonite Studies* 36: 171–79.

Neufeld, Mary. 2008. *A Prairie Pilgrim: Wilhelm H. Falk*. Altona, MB: Friesens.

———. 2016. *Prairie Pioneers: Schönthal Revisited*. Winnipeg: Manitoba Mennonite Historical Society.

New, W.H. 1997. *Land Sliding: Imagining Space, Presence, and Power in Canadian Writing*. Toronto: University of Toronto Press.

Nicolson, Adam. 2014. *The Mighty Dead: Why Homer Matters*. New York: Henry Holt.

Nixon, Rosemary Deckert. 1991. *Mostly Country: Stories*. Edmonton: NeWest Press.

Noble, Allen G. 2007. *Traditional Buildings: A Global Survey of Structural Forms and Cultural Functions*. London: I.B. Tauris.

Noonan, Gerald. 1978. "Incongruity and Nostalgia in *Sarah Binks*." *Studies in Canadian Literature* 3, 2: 264–73.

Nurse, Donna Bailey. 2004. "Author Profiles: Di Brandt." *Quill and Quire*, 13 May. http://www.quillandquire.com/authors/di-brandt/.

Opie, Iona, and Peter Opie. 1988. *The Singing Game*. Oxford: Oxford University Press.

Oppenheimer, Paul, ed. 2001. "Introduction." *Till Eulenspiegel: His Adventures*. Author unknown, translated by Paul Oppenheimer. New York: Routledge.

Osborne, Troy. 2014. "The Development of a Transnational 'Mennonite' Identity among Swiss Brethren and Dutch Doopsgezinden in the Sixteenth and Seventeenth Centuries." *Mennonite Quarterly Review* 88, no. 2: 195–218.

Oyer, Mary. 2005. "The Sound in the Land." In *Sound in the Land: Essays on Mennonites and Music,* edited by Maureen Epp and Carol Ann Weaver, 21–33. Kitchener, ON: Pandora Press.

Panofsky, Ruth. 2004. "'Literary Swan' or 'Village Goose': Paul Hiebert's *Sarah Binks.*" *Publishing History* 56: 71–88.

Park, Noon. 2010. "Rebirth through Derision: Satire and the Anabaptist Discourse of Martyrdom in Miriam Toews' *A Complicated Kindness.*" *Journal of Mennonite Studies* 28: 55–68.

Payzant, Geoffrey. (1978) 1984. *Glenn Gould: Music and Mind.* Toronto: Key Porter Books.

Peacock, Kenneth. 1962. "Notes to Recording of Mennonite *Kernlieder,* Sung by Mennonite Brethren Choir, North Kildonan, Winnipeg, MB." Recorded by Kenneth Peacock. In Documents of the Canadian Centre for Folk Culture Studies, National Museum of Man, National Museums of Canada, Ottawa, 116–21. Unpublished document.

Penner, Christina. 2008. *Widows of Hamilton House: A Novel.* Winnipeg: Enfield and Wizenty.

Penner, Jessica. 2013. *Shaken in the Water.* Lorain, OH: Foxhead Books.

Perkins, David. 1992. *Is Literary History Possible?* Baltimore: Johns Hopkins University Press.

Pivato, Joseph. 2003. *Echo: Essays on Other Literatures.* Toronto: Guernica.

Plett, Casey. 2018. *Little Fish.* Vancouver: Arsenal Pulp Press.

Poetker [Poetker-Thiessen], Audrey. 1986. *I Sing for My Dead in German.* Winnipeg: Turnstone Press.

Poirier, Richard. 1992. *The Performing Self: Compositions and Decompositions in the Languages of Contemporary Life.* New Brunswick, NJ: Rutgers University Press.

Pope, Alexander. 1966. *Pope: Poetical Works,* ed. Herbert Davis. London: Oxford University Press.

Porter, Elizabeth. 1982. "Sarah Binks: Another Look at Saskatchewan's Sweet Songstress." *World Literature Written in English* 21, no. 1: 95–108.

Power, Peter. 2011. "Hockey's Real Winter Classic" (photo essay). *Globe and Mail*, 14 January. http://www.theglobeandmail.com/multimedia/camera-club/hockeys-real-winter-classic/article631129/.

Pratt, Mary Louise. 1991. "Arts of the Contact Zone." *Profession* (MLA) 91: 33–40.

Prokosh, Kevin. 2011a. "Escape Artist: Like Her Characters, Author Miriam Toews Has a Bit of the Desperado in Her." *Winnipeg Free Press*, 16 April. https://www.winnipegfreepress.com/arts-and-life/entertainment/books/escape-artist.html.

———. 2011b. "Inside Out: Patrick Friesen's Play about Ostracism Opened the Door for Other Mennonite Writers." *Winnipeg Free Press*, 10 February. https://www.winnipegfreepress.com/arts-and-life/entertainment/arts/inside-out-115705949.html.

Pruden, Eileen. 1988. "Paul Hiebert—Humorist." *Canadian Author and Bookman* 63, no. 2: 5–6.

Quayson, Ato. 2007. *Aesthetic Nervousness: Disability and the Crisis of Representation*. New York: Columbia University Press.

Rak, Julie. 2013. *Boom: Manufacturing Memoir for the Popular Market*. Waterloo, ON: Wilfrid Laurier University Press.

Redekop, Corey. 2012. *Husk: A Novel*. Toronto: ECW Press.

Redekop, Magdalene. 1981. "Translated into the Past: Language in *The Blue Mountains of China*." In *A Voice in the Land: Essays by and about Rudy Wiebe*, edited by W.J. Keith, 97–123. Edmonton: NeWest Press.

———. 1983. Review of *My Lovely Enemy*, by Rudy Wiebe. *Conrad Grebel Review* 1, no. 3: 57–62.

———. 1985. "Authority and the Margins of Escape in *Brébeuf and His Brethren*." *The Proceedings of the Long-Liners Conference on the Canadian Long Poem, York University, Toronto, May 29–June 1, 1984*. Edited by Frank Davey and Ann Munton, special issue of *Open Letter*, Sixth Series, nos. 2–3: 45–60.

———. 1988. "Through the Mennonite Looking Glass." In *Why I Am a Mennonite*, edited by Harry Loewen, 226–53. Scottdale, PA: Herald Press.

———. 1990a. "The Little Dipper." Interactive memoir published jointly with "The House," by Elizabeth Falk. *Prairie Fire* 11, no. 2: 28–50.

———. 1990b. "Still Life with Menno." Interactive memoir published jointly with "No Stone," by Elizabeth Falk. *Canadian Literature* 127: 10–20.

———. 1992a. *Mothers and Other Clowns: The Stories of Alice Munro.* London: Routledge.

———. 1992b. "The Pickling of the Mennonite Madonna." In *Acts of Concealment: Mennonite/s Writing in Canada*, edited by Hildi Froese-Tiessen and Peter Hinchcliffe, 100–28. Waterloo, ON: University of Waterloo Press.

———. 1993a. "Charms and Riddles in the Mennonite Barnyard." *English Studies in Canada* 19, no. 2: 209–27.

———. 1993b. "Escape from the Bloody Theatre: The Making of Mennonite Stories." *Journal of Mennonite Studies* 11: 9–22.

———. 1998. "The Painted Body Stares Back: Five Female Artists and the 'Mennonite' Spectator." *Conrad Grebel Review* 16, no. 3: 6–49.

———. 1999. "Alice Munro and the Scottish Nostalgic Grotesque." In *The Rest of the Story: Critical Essays on Alice Munro*, edited by Robert Thacker, 21–43. Toronto: ECW Press.

———. 2000. "Alice Munro's Tilting Fields." In *New Worlds: Discovering and Constructing the Unknown in Anglophone Literature: Festschrift for Walter Pache*, edited by Martin Kuester, Gabriele Christ, and Rudolf Beck, 343–62. Munich: Verlag Ernst Vögl.

———. 2004. "The Importance of Being Mennonite." Review of *A Complicated Kindness*, by Miriam Toews. *Literary Review of Canada* 12, no. 8: 19–20.

———. 2009. "The Mother Tongue in Cyberspace." *Journal of Mennonite Studies.* 1 January. http://www.mennonitewriting.org/journal/1/1/mother-tongue-cyberspace/.

———. 2011. "Haunted by Hymns: The Fate of Melody in 'Mennonite' Poetry." In *Sound in the Lands: Mennonite Music across Borders*, edited by Maureen Epp et al., 243–70. Kitchener, ON: Pandora Press.

———. 2013a. "Farm Animals' Desertion: In Which Puss in Boots Learns that the Kota Is Full." *Journal of Mennonite Writing*, 14 October. http://mennonitewriting.org/journal/5/4/farm-animals-desertion/.

———. 2013b. "Fixing a Spoiled Biography: Mennonite Identity and the Second World War." Review of *The Constructed Mennonite: History, Memory, and the Second World War*, by Hans Werner. *Literary Review of Canada* 21, no. 7: 9–10.

———. 2015. "'Is Menno in There?' The Case of 'The Man Who Invented Himself.'" In *After Identity: Mennonite Writing in North America*, edited by Robert Zacharias, 194–209. Winnipeg: University of Manitoba Press; University Park: Pennsylvania State University Press.

———. 2017. "On Sitting Down to Read 'Lichen' Once Again." In *Alice Munro's Miraculous Art: Critical Essays,* edited by Janice Fiamengo and Gerald Lynch, 289–306. Ottawa: University of Ottawa Press.

———. 2019. "Seven Times with My Father." In *Finding Father: Stories from Mennonite Daughters,* edited by Mary Ann Loewen, 57–68. Regina: University of Regina Press.

Regehr, Ted D. 1996. *Mennonites in Canada, 1939–1970: A People Transformed.* Vol. 3 of *Mennonites in Canada.* Toronto: University of Toronto Press.

Reid, Mary, ed. 2010. *Wanda Koop: On the Edge of Experience.* With essays by Josée Drouin-Brisbois and Robin Laurence. Winnipeg: Winnipeg Art Gallery. Published in conjunction with the exhibition *Wanda Koop: On the Edge of Experience,* organized by the Winnipeg Art Gallery in collaboration with the National Gallery of Canada, Winnipeg Art Gallery, 11 September to 22 November 2010, National Gallery of Canada, 18 February to 15 May 2011.

Reimer, Al. 1985. *My Harp Is Turned to Mourning: A Novel.* Winnipeg: Hyperion Press.

———. 1988. "Coming In out of the Cold." In *Why I Am a Mennonite,* edited by Harry Loewen, 254–67. Scottdale, PA: Herald Press.

———. 1993. *Mennonite Literary Voices: Past and Present.* North Newton, KS: Bethel College.

Reimer, Douglas. 1989. *Older than Ravens.* Winnipeg: Turnstone Press.

Reimer, Margaret Loewen. 1998. "Mennonites and the Artistic Imagination." *Conrad Grebel Review* 16, no. 3: 6–24.

Reimer, Margaret Loewen, and Paul Tiessen. 1985. "The Poetry and Distemper of Patrick Friesen and David Waltner-Toews." In *Visions and Realities,* edited by Harry Loewen and Al Reimer, 243–53. Winnipeg: Hyperion Press.

Reimer, Mavis. 1997. "'Literary and Artistic Voices' in T.D. Regehr's *Mennonites in Canada, 1939–1970*: A Response, Two Observations, and Some Questions." *Journal of Mennonite Studies* 15: 116–23.

Reimer, Priscilla B. 1990. "Introduction." In *Mennonite Artist: The Insider as Outsider: An Exhibition of Visual Art by Artists of Mennonite Heritage* (Catalogue published on the occasion of an exhibition at Main/Access Gallery, Winnipeg, Manitoba, 6–29 July 1990), 7–27. Winnipeg: Manitoba Mennonite Historical Society.

Rempel, Byron. 2005. *Truth Is Naked, All Others Pay Cash: An Autobiographical Exaggeration.* Winnipeg: Great Plains.

Rempel, Gwen. 1994. "The Manitoba Mound Builders: The Making of an Archaeological Myth, 1857–1900." *Manitoba History* 28. http://www.mhs. mb.ca/docs/mb_history/28/moundbuilders.shtml.

Rempel, Herman. 1995. *Kjenn Jie Noch Plautdietsch? A Mennonite Low German Dictionary.* 2nd rev. ed. Rosenort, MB: PrairieView Press.

Rempel, Peter Gerhard, John D. Rempel, and Paul Tiessen, eds. 1981. *Forever Summer, Forever Sunday: Peter Gerhard Rempel's Photographs of Mennonites in Russia, 1890–1917.* Translated by Hildegard E. Tiessen. St. Jacobs, ON: Sand Hill Books.

Reygadas, Carlos. 2007. *Stellet Licht* [Silent Light]. Film.

Reza, Yasmina. 1996. *Art.* Translated by Christopher Hampton. London: Faber.

Rich, Adrienne. 1975. *Adrienne Rich's Poetry.* Selected and edited by Barbara Charlesworth Gelpi and Albert Gelpi. New York: W. W. Norton.

Rifkind, Candida. 2005. "Too Close to Home: Middlebrow Anti-Modernism and the Sentimental Poetry of Edna Jaques." *Journal of Canadian Studies* 39, no. 1: 90–114.

Rimstead, Roxanne. 2000. *Remnants of Nation: On Poverty Narratives by Women.* Toronto: University of Toronto Press.

Roberts, John P.L., and Ghyslaine Guertin, eds. 1992. *Glenn Gould: Selected Letters.* Toronto: Oxford University Press.

Robertson, Roland. 1990. "After Nostalgia? Wilful Nostalgia and the Phases of Globalization." In *Theories of Modernity and Postmodernity,* edited by Bryan S. Turner, 45–61. London: Sage Publications.

Robertson, R.T. 1973. "Another Preface to an Uncollected Anthology: Canadian Criticism in a Commonwealth Context." *Ariel* 4, no. 3: 70–81.

Rosen, Charles. 2012. *Freedom and the Arts: Essays on Music and Literature.* Cambridge, MA: Harvard University Press.

Rosenberg, Susan. 2002. *Warren Rohrer: Paintings 1972–93.* Philadelphia: Philadelphia Museum of Art.

Russell, Bruce. 2013. "Susan Shantz: Polytypes." In *Creatures in Translation* [Exhibition catalogue], 49–53. Published on the occasion of the travelling exhibition *Susan Shantz: Creatures in Translation.* Co-published by Kenderdine Art Gallery, University of Saskatchewan, Saskatoon, Saskatchewan; Alberta College of Art & Design (ACAD), Calgary, Alberta; and Esplanade Arts & Heritage Centre, Medicine Hat, Alberta.

Ruth, John. 1978. *Mennonite Identity and Literary Art*. Scottdale, PA: Herald Press.

Sacks, Oliver. (2007) 2008. *Musicophilia: Tales of Music and the Brain*. Toronto: Vintage.

Safarik, Allan. 1992. "Good Night Louis." *Prairie Fire* (special issue on Patrick Friesen), 13, no. 1: 53–58.

Said, Edward W. 1975. *Beginnings: Intention and Method*. Baltimore: Johns Hopkins University Press.

———. 1991. *Musical Elaborations*. The Wellek Library Lectures at the University of California Irvine. New York: Columbia University Press.

Samatar, Sofia. 2017. "The Scope of This Project." *Canadian Mennonite Writing Journal* 9, no. 2. https://mennonitewriting.org/journal/9/2/scope-project/#all.

Santesso, Aaron. 2006. *A Careful Longing: The Poetics and Problems of Nostalgia*. Newark: University of Delaware Press.

Sawatzky, Roland. 2005. "The Control of Social Spaces in Mennonite Housebarns of Manitoba, 1874–1940." PhD diss., Simon Fraser University.

Schama, Simon. (1987) 1997. *The Embarrassment of Riches: An Interpretation of Dutch Culture in the Golden Age*. New York: Knopf, Vintage Books.

Scheffer, J.G. de Hoop. 1868. "Mennisten-Streken." In *Doopsgezinde Bijdragen*, 23–48. Leeuwarden, Netherlands.

Schellenberg, John. 1993. *Divine Hiddenness and Human Reason*. Ithaca, NY: Cornell University Press.

———. 2009. *The Will to Imagine: A Justification of Skeptical Religion*. Ithaca, NY: Cornell University Press.

Schor, Naomi. 1987. *Reading in Detail: Aesthetics and the Feminine*. New York: Methuen.

Schroeder, Andreas. 1984. *Toccata in "D": A Micro Novel*. Lantzville, BC: Oolichan Books.

———. 1986. *Dustship Glory*. Toronto: Doubleday Canada.

———. 2008. *Renovating Heaven: A Novel in Triptych*. Lantzville, BC: Oolichan Books.

Schwartz, Hillel. 1996. *The Culture of the Copy*. New York: Zone Books.

Scott, Duncan Campbell. (1898) 1926. *Poems of Duncan Campbell Scott*. Toronto: McClelland and Stewart.

Sellar, W.C., and R.J. Yeatman. (1930) 1993. *1066 and All That: A Memorable History of England*. New York: Barnes and Noble.

Shantz, Susan. 1999. "Responses to Previous Issue" (response to Margaret Loewen Reimer, "Mennonites and the Artistic Imagination," and Magdalene Redekop, "The Painted Body Stares Back: Five Female Artists and the 'Mennonite' Spectator," *Conrad Grebel Review* 16, no. 3 [1998]). *Conrad Grebel Review* 17, no. 1: 104–08.

———. 2013. *Creatures in Translation* (Exhibition catalogue). Published on the occasion of the travelling exhibition *Susan Shantz: Creatures in Translation*. Co-published by Kenderdine Art Gallery, University of Saskatchewan, Saskatoon, Saskatchewan; Alberta College of Art & Design (ACAD), Calgary, Alberta; and Esplanade Arts & Heritage Centre, Medicine Hat, Alberta.

Shelley, Mary. (1818) 1969. *Frankenstein or The Modern Prometheus*. Edited by M.K. Joseph. London: Oxford University Press.

Sherbert, Garry, Annie Gérin, and Sheila Petty, eds. 2006. *Canadian Cultural Poesis: Essays on Canadian Culture*. Waterloo, ON: Wilfrid Laurier University Press.

Shklovsky, Victor. 1965. "Art as Technique." *Russian Formalist Criticism: Four Essays*. Translated and with an introduction by Lee T. Lemon and Marion J. Reis, 3–24. Lincoln and London: University of Nebraska Press.

Siemens, Reynold. 1974. "Recollections of the Last Days of Bruno Schmidt." In *Harvest: Anthology of Mennonite Writing in Canada*, edited by William De Fehr et al., 41–52. Altona, MB: Centennial Committee of the Mennonite Historical Society of Manitoba.

———. 1977. "Sarah Binks in Retrospect: A Conversation with Paul Hiebert." *Journal of Canadian Fiction* 19: 65–76.

Simons, Menno. 1956. *The Complete Writings of Menno Simons, 1496–1561*. Translated by Leonard Verduin. Edited by J.C. Wenger, with a biography by Harold Bender. Scottdale, PA; Kitchener, ON: Herald Press.

Škvorecký, Josef. 1984 (1977). *The Engineer of Human Souls*. Translated by Paul Wilson. Toronto: Lester and Orpen Dennys.

Smucker, Barbara Claassen. 1981. *Days of Terror*. London: Puffin.

Sontag, Susan. 1966. *Against Interpretation*. New York: Farrar, Straus, and Giroux.

———. 1973. *On Photography*. New York: Delta.

Spies, Marijke. 1994. "Mennonites and Literature in the Seventeenth Century." In *From Martyr to Muppy (Mennonite Urban Professional): A Historical Introduction to Cultural Assimilation Processes of a Religious Minority in the Netherlands: The Mennonites*, edited by Alastair Hamilton, Sjouke Voolstra, and Piet Visser, 83–98. Amsterdam: Amsterdam University Press.

Staebler, Edna. 1968 (2006). *Food that Really Schmecks*. With an introduction by Wayson Choy. Waterloo: Wilfrid Laurier University Press.

Stam, Robert. 1991. "Bakhtin, Polyphony, and Ethnic/Racial Representation." In *Unspeakable Images: Ethnicity and the American Cinema*, edited by Lester D. Friedman, 251–76. Urbana: University of Illinois Press.

Stambaugh, Sara. 1984. *I Hear the Reaper's Song*. Intercourse, PA: Good Books.

Steffler, Margaret. 2017. "The Noise of Identity: Turning to Attentiveness and the Receptive Ear." Review of *After Identity: Mennonite Writing in North America. Journal of Mennonite Writing* 9 no.1, https://mennonitewriting.org/journal/9/1/noise-identity-turning-attentiveness-and-receptive/#all.

Steinbach Committee. 1961. *The Mennonite Treasury of Recipes*. Edited by Mrs. Peter Rosenfeld, Mrs. D. D. Warkentin, and Mrs. Jac. H. Peters. Steinbach: Derksen Printers.

Steiner, George. (1971) 1974. *In Bluebeard's Castle: Some Notes towards the Re-Definition of Culture*. London: Faber and Faber.

Steiner, Samuel J. 2015. *In Search of Promised Lands: A Religious History of Mennonites in Ontario*. Kitchener, ON; Harrisonburg, VA: Herald Press.

Stevens, Wallace. 1990. *The Collected Poems of Wallace Stevens*. New York: Vintage.

Stewart, Susan. 1984. *On Longing: Narratives of the Miniature, the Gigantic, the Souvenir, the Collection*. Baltimore: Johns Hopkins University Press.

———. 2002. *Poetry and the Fate of the Senses*. Chicago: University of Chicago Press.

Stierle, Karlheinz. 1996. "Translatio Studii and Renaissance: From Vertical to Horizontal Translation." In *The Translatability of Cultures: Figurations of the Space Between*, edited by Sanford Budick and Wolfgang Iser, 55–67. Stanford, CA: Stanford University Press.

Stoltzfus, Philip. 1998. "Performative Envisioning: An Aesthetic Critique of Contemporary Mennonite Theology." *Conrad Grebel Review* 16, no. 3: 75–91.

———. 2006. *Theology as Performance: Music, Aesthetics, and God in Western Thought*. New York: T and T Clark International.

Strout, Elizabeth. 2016. *My Name Is Lucy Barton*. New York: Random House.

Swift, Jonathan. 1920. *A Tale of a Tub to Which Is Added the Battle of the Books, and the Mechanical Operation of the Spirit*. Oxford: Clarendon Press.

Tannenbaum, Judith. 2015. "Connecting Present to Past: Contemporary Artists with Links to Fraktur." In *Framing Fraktur: Pennsylvania German Material Culture and Contemporary Art*, edited by Judith Tannenbaum, 69–94. Philadelphia: University of Pennsylvania Press.

Taylor, Charles. 1991. *The Malaise of Modernity*. 1991 Massey Lectures. Concord, ON: Anansi.

———. 1994. "The Politics of Recognition." In *Multiculturalism: Examining the Politics of Recognition*, edited by Amy Gutmann, 25–73. Princeton, NJ: Princeton University Press.

Tennyson, Alfred Lord. 1965. *Poems and Plays*. London: Oxford University Press.

Teodoro, Jose. 2009. "On Heaven As It Is in Earth." Review of *Silent Light*. Film Society of Lincoln Centre. https://www.filmcomment.com/article/silent-light-review/ (accessed 7 July 2019).

Thiessen, Jack. 1972. "Canadian Mennonite Literature." *Canadian Literature* 51: 65–72.

———. 1984. *Predicht fier Haite*. Hamburg: Buske-Verlag.

———. 2003. *Mennonite Low German Dictionary/Mennonitisch-Plattdeutsches Wörterbuch*. Madison: University of Wisconsin.

Thiessen, Vern. 2005. *Shakespeare's Will*. Toronto: Playwrights Canada Press.

———. 2006. *Back to Berlin*. In *The Courier and Other* Plays, by Vern Thiessen, 33–52. Toronto: Playwrights Canada Press.

Thomas, Keith. 1971. *Religion and the Decline of Magic*. New York: Charles Scribner's Sons.

Tiessen, Hildi Froese. 1988a. "Mother Tongue as Shibboleth in the Literature of Canadian Mennonites." *Studies in Canadian Literature* 13, no. 2: 175–83.

———. 1988b. "The Role of Art and Literature in Mennonite Self-Understanding." In *Mennonite Identity: Historical and Contemporary Perspectives*, edited by Calvin Redekop and Sam Steiner, 235–52. New York: University Press of America.

———. 1990. "Introduction." *Prairie Fire* (A Special Issue on New Mennonite Writing), 11, no. 2.

———. 2000. "Mennonite Literature and Postmodernism: Writing the 'In-Between' Space." In *Mennonites and Postmodernism*, edited by Susan Biesecker-Mast and Gerald Biesecker-Mast, 160–74. Telford, PA: Pandora Press.

———. 2004. "Critical Thought and Mennonite Literature: Mennonite Studies Engages the Mennonite Literary Voice." *Journal of Mennonite Studies* 22: 237–46.

———. 2010. "Foreword: Guest Editor." *Journal of Mennonite Studies* 28: 9–12.

———. 2012. "What Remains of What Does Not Remain? A Mennonite Reader Reflects on Mennonites Leaving Home." *Rhubarb* 30: 12–15.

———. 2015. "After Identity: Liberating the Mennonite Literary Text." In *After Identity: Mennonite Writing in North America*, edited by Robert Zacharias, 210–25. Winnipeg: University of Manitoba Press; University Park: Pennsylvania State University Press.

———. 2019. "Our Lives Together, My Father and Me." *Finding Father: Stories from Mennonite Daughters,* edited by Mary Ann Loewen, 89–101. Regina: University of Regina Press.

Tiessen, Hildi Froese, ed. 2002. *Rudy Wiebe: A Tribute.* (Materials compiled for Wiebe on his birthday). Kitchener, ON and Goshen, IN: Sand Hills Books and Pinchpenny Press.

Tiessen, Hildi Froese, and Peter Hinchcliffe, eds. 1992. *Acts of Concealment: Mennonite/s Writing in Canada.* Waterloo, ON: University of Waterloo Press.

Tiessen, Hildi Froese, and Paul Tiessen, eds. 1991. *A Sunday Afternoon: Paintings by Henry Pauls.* St. Jacobs, ON: Sand Hills Books.

Toews, Miriam. 2000. *Swing Low: A Life.* Toronto: Stoddart Publishing.

———. 2004. *A Complicated Kindness.* Toronto: Alfred A. Knopf Canada.

———. 2011. *Irma Voth.* Toronto: Alfred A. Knopf Canada.

———. 2014. *All My Puny Sorrows.* Toronto: Knopf Canada.

———. 2016. "How Pacifism Can Lead to Violence and Conflict." *Literary Hub*, 28 November. http://lithub.com/how-pacifism-can-lead-to-violence-and-conflict/.

———. 2018. *Women Talking.* Toronto: Penguin Random House Canada.

Toews, Werner. 2018. *Sketches from Siberia: The Life of Jacob Sudermann.* Self-published.

Twain, Mark. (1884) 1977. *Adventures of Huckleberry Finn*. Edited by Sculley Bradley. New York: W. W. Norton and Company Inc.

Urry, James. 1991. "From Speech to Literature: Low German and Mennonite Identity in Two Worlds." *History and Anthropology* 5, no. 2: 233–58.

Van Braght, Thieleman J. (1660) 1972. *The Bloody Theatre or Martyrs Mirror of the Defenseless Christians Who Baptized Only upon Confession of Faith and Who Suffered and Died for the Testimony of Jesus, Their Saviour, from the Time of Christ to the Year A.D. 1600*. Translated by Joseph F. Sohm. Scottdale, PA: Herald Press.

Van der Lem, Anton. 1994. "Men of Principles and Men of Learning: The Mennonite Backgrounds of Some Dutch Historians, with Special Reference to Johan Huizinga and Jan Romein." In *From Martyr to Muppy (Mennonite Urban Professional): A Historical Introduction to Cultural Assimilation Processes of a Religious Minority in the Netherlands: The Mennonites*, edited by Alastair Hamilton, Sjouke Voolstra, and Piet Visser, 203–15. Amsterdam: Amsterdam University Press.

Van Toorn, Penny. 1995. *Rudy Wiebe and the Historicity of the Word*. Edmonton: University of Alberta Press.

Vassanji, M.G. 1989. *The Gunny Sack*. Oxford: Heinemann International.

Vautour, Bart, Erin Wunker, Travis V. Mason, and Christl Verduyn, eds. 2015. *Public Poetics: Critical Issues in Canadian Poetry and Poetics*. Waterloo, ON: Wilfrid Laurier University Press.

Verduyn, Christl, ed. 2005. *Must Write: Edna Staebler's Diaries*. Waterloo, ON: Wilfrid Laurier University Press.

Vernon, Karina, ed. 2019. *The Black Prairie Archives: An Anthology*. Waterloo, ON: Wilfrid Laurier University Press.

Veyne, Paul. 1988. *Did the Greeks Believe in Their Myths? An Essay on the Constitutive Imagination*. Translated by Paula Wissing. Chicago: University of Chicago Press.

Virgil. 1930. *The Aeneid*. Edited by J.W. Mackall. Oxford: Clarendon Press.

Visser, Piet. 1994. "Aspects of Social Criticism and Cultural Assimilation: The Mennonite Image in Literature and Self-Criticism of Literary Mennonites." In *From Martyr to Muppy (Mennonite Urban Professional): A Historical Introduction to Cultural Assimilation Processes of a Religious Minority in the Netherlands: The Mennonites*, edited by Alastair Hamilton, Sjouke Voolstra, and Piet Visser, 67–81. Amsterdam: Amsterdam University Press.

Visser, Piet, and Mary Sprunger. 1996. *Menno Simons: Places, Portraits and Progeny.* With assistance from Adriann Plak, translated by Gary K. Waite, photography by Iman Heystek and Esther van Weelden. English edition: Altona, MB: Friesens.

Waldrep, G.C. 2009. "Mennonite Poem." *Rhubarb* 24: 24–25.

Walker, Morley. 2005. "David Bergen: In Country" (author profile). *Quill and Quire*, 11 May. http://www.quillandquire.com/authors/profile. cfm?article_id=6741.

Waltner-Toews, David. 1983. *Good Housekeeping.* Winnipeg: Turnstone Press.

———. 2004. *The Complete Tante Tina: Mennonite Blues and Recipes.* Kitchener, ON: Pandora Press.

Wardhaugh, Robert. 2010. "W.L. Morton, Margaret Laurence, and the Writing of Manitoba." In *The West and Beyond: New Perspectives on an Imagined Region,* edited by Sarah Carter, Alvin Finkel, and Peter Fortman, 329–48. Edmonton: Athabasca University Press.

Warkentin, Abe. 2018. "Willems statue commissioned for Manitoba museum." *Canadian Mennonite,* 26 June, https://canadianmennonite.org/stories/ willems-statue-commissioned-manitoba-museum.

Warkentin, John. 2000. *The Mennonite Settlements of Southern Manitoba.* Steinbach, MB: Hanover Steinbach Historical Society.

Watson, Scott. 1985. "Gathie Falk's Rituals and Sources." In *Gathie Falk Retrospective,* edited by Jo-Anne Birnie Danzker et al., 58–62. Vancouver: Vancouver Art Gallery.

Weaver, Carol Ann, Doreen Helen Klassen, Judith Klassen. 2015. *Sound in the Land: Music and the Environment.* Special issue of *The Conrad Grebel Review* 33, no. 2 (Spring).

Weier, John. 1986. *After the Revolution.* Winnipeg: Turnstone Press.

———. 1995. *Steppe: A Novel.* Saskatoon: Thistledown Press.

———. 2004. *Stand the Sacred Tree: Journeys in Place and Memory.* Winnipeg: Turnstone Press.

Weimann, Robert. 1996. *Authority and Representation in Early Modern Discourse.* Edited by David Hillman. Baltimore: Johns Hopkins University Press.

Werner, Hans. 2013. *The Constructed Mennonite: History, Memory, and the Second World War.* Winnipeg: University of Manitoba Press.

———. 2016. Editorial. *Preservings* 36: 3.

Wiebe, Armin. 1984. *The Salvation of Yasch Siemens.* Winnipeg: Turnstone Press.

———. 1991. *Murder in Gutenthal: A Schneppa Kjnals Mystery.* Winnipeg: Turnstone Press.

———. 2011. *The Moonlight Sonata of Beethoven Blatz.* Winnipeg: Scirocco Drama, an imprint of J. Gordon Shillingford Publishing.

Wiebe, Rudy Henry. 1970. *The Blue Mountains of China.* New Canadian Library. Toronto: McClelland and Stewart.

———. (1962) 1972. *Peace Shall Destroy Many.* Toronto: McClelland and Stewart.

———. 1973a. *The Temptations of Big Bear.* Toronto: McClelland and Stewart.

———. 1973b. "Passage by Land." In *Writers of the Prairies,* edited by Donald G. Stephens, 129–31. Vancouver: UBC Press.

———. 1974. *Where Is the Voice Coming From?* Toronto: McClelland and Stewart.

———. 1977. *The Scorched-Wood People: A Novel.* Toronto: McClelland and Stewart.

———. 1980. *The Mad Trapper.* Toronto: McClelland and Stewart.

———. 1983. *My Lovely Enemy: A Novel.* Toronto: McClelland and Stewart.

———. 1989. *Playing Dead: A Contemplation Concerning the Arctic.* Edmonton: NeWest Press.

———. 1994. *The Discovery of Strangers.* Toronto: A.A. Knopf Canada.

———. 1995. *River of Stone: Fictions and Memories.* Toronto: Vintage.

———. 2001. *Sweeter Than All the World.* Toronto: A.A. Knopf Canada.

———. 2014. *Come Back.* Toronto: Random House.

Wilde, Oscar. 1950. "The Decay of Lying." In *Essays by Oscar Wilde,* edited by Hesketh Pearson, 33–72. London: Methuen.

Williams, Zoe. 2004. "The One that Got Away." *The Guardian,* 24 July. https://www.theguardian.com/books/2004/jul/24/fiction.features.

Witmer, Douglas. n.d. "A Painting Is Not a Statement." http:/douglaswitmer.com/not-a-statement/.

———. 2005. Interview with Chris Ashley, Minus Space (gallery website), 1 December, http://douglaswitmer.com/2005/12/interview-with-chris-ashley/.

———. 2016. "The School Papers." http://douglaswitmer.com/work/paper/.

Woolf, Virginia. (1929) 1957. *A Room of One's Own*. New York: Harcourt Brace Jovanovich.

Yankovic, Alfred Matthew ("Weird Al"). 1996. "Amish Paradise (Official Parody of 'Gangsta's Paradise')."

https://www.youtube.com/watch?v=lOfZLb33uCg (accessed 6 July 2019).

Yeats, William Butler. 1963. *Collected Poems of W.B. Yeats*. London: Macmillan.

Zacharias, Robert. 2013. *Rewriting the Break Event: Mennonites and Migration in Canadian Literature*. Winnipeg: University of Manitoba Press.

———, ed. 2015a. *After Identity: Mennonite Writing in North America*. Winnipeg: University of Manitoba Press; University Park: Pennsylvania State University Press.

———. 2015b. "The Mennonite Thing: Identity for a Post-Identity Age." In *After Identity: Mennonite Writing in North America*, edited by Robert Zacharias, 106–24. Winnipeg: University of Manitoba Press; University Park: Pennsylvania State University Press.

Zimmerman, Eric. 2013. "Manifesto for a Ludic Century." *Kotaku* (online design journal), 9 September. http://kotaku.com/manifesto-the-21st-century-will-be-defined-by-games-1275355204.

INDEX